Between Logic and Reality

LOGIC, EPISTEMOLOGY, AND THE UNITY OF SCIENCE

VOLUME 25

Editors
Shahid Rahman, *University of Lille III, France*
John Symons, *University of Texas at El Paso, U.S.A.*

Editorial Board
Jean Paul van Bendegem, *Free University of Brussels, Belgium*
Johan van Benthem, *University of Amsterdam, The Netherlands*
Jacques Dubucs, *University of Paris I-Sorbonne, France*
Anne Fagot-Largeault, *Collège de France, France*
Bas van Fraassen, *Princeton University, U.S.A.*
Dov Gabbay, *King's College London, U.K.*
Jaakko Hintikka, *Boston University, U.S.A.*
Karel Lambert, *University of California, Irvine, U.S.A.*
Graham Priest, *University of Melbourne, Australia*
Gabriel Sandu, *University of Helsinki, Finland*
Göran Sundholm, *Universiteit Leiden, The Netherlands*
Heinrich Wansing, *Technical University Dresden, Germany*
Timothy Williamson, *Oxford University, U.K.*

Logic, Epistemology, and the Unity of Science aims to reconsider the question of the unity of science in light of recent developments in logic. At present, no single logical, semantical or methodological framework dominates the philosophy of science. However, the editors of this series believe that formal techniques like, for example, independence friendly logic, dialogical logics, multimodal logics, game theoretic semantics and linear logics, have the potential to cast new light on basic issues in the discussion of the unity of science.

This series provides a venue where philosophers and logicians can apply specific technical insights to fundamental philosophical problems. While the series is open to a wide variety of perspectives, including the study and analysis of argumentation and the critical discussion of the relationship between logic and the philosophy of science, the aim is to provide an integrated picture of the scientific enterprise in all its diversity.

For further volumes:
http://www.springer.com/series/6936

Majda Trobok · Nenad Miščević · Berislav Žarnić
Editors

Between Logic and Reality

Modeling Inference, Action
and Understanding

Editors
Majda Trobok
University of Rijeka
Rijeka
Croatia
trobok@ffri.hr

Nenad Miščević
University of Maribor
Maribor
Slovenia
vismiscevic@ceu.hu

Berislav Žarnić
University of Split
Split
Croatia
berislav@ffst.hr

ISBN 978-94-007-2389-4   e-ISBN 978-94-007-2390-0
DOI 10.1007/978-94-007-2390-0
Springer Dordrecht Heidelberg London New York

Library of Congress Control Number: 2011941577

© Springer Science+Business Media B.V. 2012
No part of this work may be reproduced, stored in a retrieval system, or transmitted in any form or by any means, electronic, mechanical, photocopying, microfilming, recording or otherwise, without written permission from the Publisher, with the exception of any material supplied specifically for the purpose of being entered and executed on a computer system, for exclusive use by the purchaser of the work.

Printed on acid-free paper

Springer is part of Springer Science+Business Media (www.springer.com)

Preface

The papers collected in this book analyse the logic-mathematics-reality relationship from different approaches and perspectives. It connects logical theory with more concrete issues of rationality, normativity and understanding, thus pointing to a wide range of potential applications.

Let us say a few words about the context in which the book was created. Continuing a longer tradition that started in the 1980s by the members of the *Rijeka Analytic Philosophy Circle* (V. Muškardin, N. Smokrović, B. Berčić, S. Prijić-Samaržja, the editors of the present volume, and others), the *Department of Philosophy* at the *University of Rijeka* has been active in organizing international philosophical conferences and other philosophical events in Croatia establishing thus global and vital connections between the philosophers from all sides of the world with those from the local region, in particular those coming from academic communities in Bulgaria, Croatia, Hungary, Italy, Serbia and Slovenia. Thanks to its cosmopolitan atmosphere and a regard for logic, the *Department of Philosophy* at *University of Rijeka*, the only analytic department of philosophy in Croatia, has provided a supporting environment for promoting logico-philosophical research. The book originated from two recent conferences that took place in Rijeka.[1]

We were also lucky to have on our side the hospitality of the *Inter-University Center Dubrovnik*, where we organized or helped organizing a series of conferences, most notably the yearly courses/conferences *Analytic Philosophy: Epistemology and Metaphysics*, in particular the 2010 conference *The Philosophy of Logical Consequence* organized by Stewart Shapiro, and the *Mind, World and Action* course. Also, two larger scientific projects funded by the Ministry of Science, Education and Sports of Republic of Croatia have offered further institutional framework for the initiatives that have led to the assembling of the book: *Logic and Reality*, and *Logical Structures and Intentionality*.

---

[1] In 2006, *Analytic Philosophy—Logical Investigations*, and in 2009, *Contemporary Philosophical Issues—Logic and Reality*.

Acknowledgments We would like to thank those who helped in making this book possible. The two mentioned projects *Logic and Reality* (project number: 009-0091328-0941) and *Logical Structures and Intentionality* (project number: 191-1911111-2730) have been financed by the Ministry of Education of Science, Education and Sport of the Republic of Croatia—we are most grateful to the Ministry for its generous support.

We are indebted to *Kruzak*, the publisher of the *Croatian Journal of Philosophy*, for granting permission to republish the articles written by Stewart Shapiro, Dale Jacquette, and Imre Rusza.

Special thanks go to Stewart Shapiro, Dale Jacquette, Zsófia Zvolenszky and Ferenc Rusza for their generous support, and to Lovre Grisogono for technical assistance. And finally, last but not the least, to Lucy Fleet and Hendrikje Tuerlings of Springer for their unrelenting help and patience.

Rijeka, Croatia	Majda Trobok
Maribor, Slovenia	Nenad Miščević
Split, Croatia	Berislav Žarnić
April 2011	

Contents

1 **Introduction** 1
   Majda Trobok, Nenad Miščević, and Berislav Žarnić

Part I Logical and Mathematical Structures

2 **Life on the Ship of Neurath: Mathematics in the Philosophy of Mathematics** 11
   Stewart Shapiro

3 **Applied Mathematics in the Sciences** 29
   Dale Jacquette

4 **The Philosophical Impact of the Löwenheim-Skolem Theorem** 59
   Miloš Arsenijević

5 **Debating (Neo)logicism: Frege and the Neo-Fregeans** 83
   Majda Trobok

Part II Epistemology and Logic

6 **Informal Logic and Informal Consequence** 101
   Danilo Šuster

7 **Logical Consequence and Rationality** 121
   Nenad Smokrović

8 **Logic, Indispensability and Aposteriority** 135
   Nenad Miščević

Part III Dynamic Logical Models of Meaning

9 **Extended Game-Theoretical Semantics** 161
   Manuel Rebuschi

10 **Dynamic Logic of Propositional Commitments** 183
   Tomoyuki Yamada

11	**Is Unsaying Polite?**	201
	Berislav Žarnić	

Part IV Logical Methods in Ontological and Linguistic Analyses

12	**Towards a Formal Account of Identity Criteria**	227
	Massimiliano Carrara and Silvia Gaio	
13	**A Mereology for the Change of Parts**	243
	Pierdaniele Giaretta and Giuseppe Spolaore	
14	**Russell Versus Frege**	261
	Imre Rusza	
15	**Goodman's Only World**	269
	Vladan Djordjević	

Index 281

Contributors

Miloš Arsenijević Department of Philosophy, University of Belgrade, Čika Ljubina 18–20, 11000 Belgrade, Serbia, marsenij@f.bg.ac.rs

Massimiliano Carrara Department of Philosophy, University of Padua, Piazza Capitaniato 3, 35139 Padua, Italy, massimiliano.carrara@unipd.it

Vladan Djordjević Department of Philosophy, University of Belgrade, Čika Ljubina 18–20, 11000 Belgrade, Serbia, vladan@ualberta.ca

Silvia Gaio Department of Philosophy, University of Padua, Piazza Capitaniato 3, 35139 Padua, Italy, silvia.gaio@unipd.it

Pierdaniele Giaretta Department of Philosophy, University of Padua, Piazza Capitaniato 3, 35139 Padua, Italy, pierdaniele.giaretta@unipd.it

Dale Jacquette Universität Bern, Insitut für Philosophie, Abteilung Logik und theoretische Philosophie, Unitobler, Länggassstrasse 49a, Bern 9, CH-3000, Switzerland, dale.jacquette@philo.unibe.ch

Nenad Miščević Department of Philosophy, University of Maribor, Koroška 160, 2000 Maribor, Slovenia, vismiscevic@ceu.hu

Manuel Rebuschi L.H.S.P. – Archives H. Poincaré, Nancy University, France, manuel.rebuschi@univ-nancy2.fr

Imre Rusza (1921–2008) Department of Logic, Eötvös University, Budapest, Hungary

Stewart Shapiro Department of Philosophy, The Ohio State University, 350 University Hall, 230 North Oval Mall, Columbus, OH 43210, USA, shapiro.4@osu.edu

Nenad Smokrović Department of Philosophy, University of Rijeka, Slavka Krautzeka bb, 51000 Rijeka, Croatia, nenad@ffri.hr

Giuseppe Spolaore Department of Philosophy, University of Verona, Lungadige Porta Vittoria, 17 37129 Verona, Italy, giuseppe.spolaore@univr.it

Danilo Šuster Department of Philosophy, University of Maribor, Koroška 160, 2000 Maribor, Slovenia, danilo.suster@uni-mb.si

Majda Trobok Department of Philosophy, University of Rijeka, Slavka Krautzeka bb, 51000 Rijeka, Croatia, trobok@ffri.hr

Tomoyuki Yamada Graduate School of Letters, Hokkaido University, N10 W7, Kita-ku, Sapporo 060–0810, Japan, yamada@LET.hokudai.ac.jp

Berislav Žarnić Faculty of Philosophy, University of Split, Teslina 12, 21000 Split, Croatia, berislav@ffst.hr

Chapter 1
Introduction

Majda Trobok, Nenad Miščević, and Berislav Žarnić

Is reality logical and is logic real? Hegel has famously raised this question exactly two centuries ago although his notion of logic was significantly different from the predominant contemporary one at work in the present book. The ancestor of this logic-reality couple, namely the thematic duo mathematics-reality has opened the history of philosophy, as we know it, with Plato and his critics. The next generation has added logic to it. Logic, reality, mathematics—this trio of concepts (and the corresponding items) has also been in the center of discussion on contemporary scene, in epistemology, philosophy of science and metaphysics.

The papers in the book rely on different theoretical backgrounds and focus on diverse philosophical issues. The point of convergence lies in the exploration of the connections between the reality, be it social, natural or ideal one, and logical structures employed in describing or discovering it. The interface between logical structure and reality is discussed from various perspectives. What is the origin of logical intuitions? What is the role of logical structures in the operations of an intelligent mind? Is there any common pattern in all of the structures? Is the role of logical structures in concept formation regulative or constitutive or both? The questions are addressed with the help of cutting-edge logical techniques, but formulated in an accessible and readable style.

The present book tries to cover a lot of this ground, offering interesting contributions to each of the big topics that contemporary debate centre around. It begins with the riddles of mathematics, proceeds to the epistemology of logic, then to contributions of logic to semantics, and concludes with "logic and reality", the contribution of logic to general ontology.

Beside the variety of topics and approaches, the book offers a hopefully attractive combination of contributions of varied origin, it brings together papers by logicians and philosophers from South-Eastern Europe and papers of their colleagues from the USA, Western Europe and Japan, dedicated to the disentangling of complex logical issues from different and interdisciplinary perspectives. Indirectly, it also offers a unique view on the state of development of logic and its theory in the South Eastern

---

M. Trobok (✉)
Department of Philosophy, University of Rijeka, Rijeka, Croatia
e-mail: trobok@ffri.hr

Europe, in the dialogue with prominent or promising logicians and philosophers from Western Europe, USA and Japan.

Back to the issues of content. The issues of logic are nowadays seen as inseparable from the foundational issues in the philosophy of mathematics and the present book endorses the same view, treating them together whenever possible. The domain of mathematical and logical knowledge is among the most difficult ones in philosophy, and there is practically no agreement between experts on any crucial issue. There is no minimal agreement on what mathematics is about, in other words the ontology of mathematical entities offers an embarrassment of richness. Much worse for the present purposes, there is no agreement even about the superficial features of logical insights and arithmetical intuition: the classics in the field, Frege, Hilbert, Brouwer and Wittgenstein disagree on almost everything, and the recent developments have added new branches to an already richly branching tree of mathematical epistemology and ontology.

Part I addresses fundamental issues in these two domains. Many philosophers following the lead of Frege, believe that mathematical properties do not belong to concrete items and their collections, but to abstract ones. To mention the most relevant property, cardinality, Frege ascribed it to concepts, others ascribe it to sets. Here arises a problem that "a complete philosophy of mathematics must address" as Dale Jacquette argues is his contribution to this volume. As he puts it, "(T)he requirements of a general semantics for the truth of mathematical theorems that coheres also with the meaning and truth conditions for non-mathematical sentences, according to Benacerraf, should ideally be coupled with an adequate epistemology for the discovery of mathematical knowledge." Also, as Jacquette argues in his contribution, the applicability of mathematics (and, we would add, of logic) contributes to their claim to seriousness and truth; this fact has been enshrined in various "indispensability arguments", most famously formulated by Quine and Putnam. Papers in this part address such foundational issues having to do with logical and mathematical structures.

Stewart Shapiro has famously argued in favor of epistemic pluralism in their regard. For instance, small, finite structures are apprehended through abstraction via simple pattern recognition. A subject views or hears one or more structured systems and comes to grasp the structure of those systems. Of course, we do not have direct causal contact with structures, because they are abstract. The idea is that we grasp some structures through their systems, just as we grasp character types through their tokens. Next, we have Fregean abstraction. The most powerful tool, however, is implicit definition. One way to understand and communicate a particular structure is through a direct description of it. Shapiro's paper in this volume *Chapter 2: Life on the Ship of Neurath: Mathematics in the Philosophy of Mathematics* provides an interesting survey of the use of mathematical results to provide support or counter-support to various philosophical programs concerning the foundations of mathematics.

We have already mentioned **Dale Jacquette**'s *Chapter 3: Applied Mathematics in the Sciences* which criticizes standard approaches to the philosophy of mathematics against the background of Benacerraf's dilemma, particularly with respect to the problem of understanding the distinction between pure and applied mathematics. He argues for a kind of Aristotelian inherence concept of mathematical entities.

In *Chapter 4: The Philosophical Impact of the Löwenheim-Skolem Theorem* **Miloš Arsenijević** gives an insightful reconstruction of the Theorem. The author goes beyond the standard approach according to which it is the expressive weakness of the language that is revealed by the theorem, and proposes reinvestigation of the key notions instead. An original and novel thesis is put forward: Löwenheim-Skolem's theorem reveals both the limits of the language and the distinctive character of mathematical structures. The cardinality of an underlying set of a mathematical structure is a non-absolute property of the set since the elements in it can be individuated only by their position in the structure. Using the infinitary $L_{\omega_1 \omega_1}$ extension of first-order language Arsenijević shows how non-standard models can be eliminated (e.g. from the theory of real numbers) while retaining "the basic assumption that the 'world substance' is a set of an infinite number of elements whose cardinal number is $\aleph_0$."

Majda Trobok in her *Chapter 5: Debating (Neo)logicism: Frege and the Neo-Fregeans* come up with a novel reading of Frege, contrasting it with the neo-Fregean orthodoxy and drawing some interesting morals for the historian and philosophers of logic and mathematics. The central item in Trobok's understanding is the notion of justification within the original Fregan program. She reads it as an objective mind-independent relation obtaining between equally mind-independent abstract propositional items. Placed within such an objectivist framework, Frege appears purified from his neo-Kantian associations but also quite distant from contemporary thinker-based mainstream epistemology. Trobok endorses the view that Hume's Principle is not an epistemic (in the mainstream sense) route to number, but a cornerstone in the edifice of objective justification that Frege took himself to be reconstructing.

Papers in Part II are dedicated to the epistemology of logic. The first paper shows how informal logic becomes reconciled with formal logic as the latter encompasses the vast ground of different reasoning styles and processes of belief formation. The next points out to cognitive faculty and linguistic ability as real-life counterparts for theoretical notion of logical consequence. Some authors see logic as an indispensable tool for our wide cognitive projects where the justification of the tool depends on the meaningfulness of the product. Thus, logic becomes part of a much larger picture, getting its meaning from the global processes whose destiny it shares.

Danilo Šuster in his *Chapter 6: Informal Logic and Informal Consequence* asks what informal logic is and whether it is logic at all, and proceeds to answer the latter question in the affirmative. The rationale is that according to the prevalent criteria of informal logic an argument is cogent if and only if its premises are rationally Acceptable, its premises are Relevant to its conclusion and its premises constitute Grounds adequate for accepting the conclusion (the "ARG" conditions according to Govier). Now, the ARG criteria characterize a certain broad kind of consequence relation. We do not (in general) have truth preservation in cogent arguments but if the premises are acceptable and other criteria are met, then so is the conclusion. We can speak about argument form in a loose sense and finally, there is rational necessity of the grounding or support relation. So, a certain broad notion of logical consequence emerges from this comparison.

Nenad Smokrović's paper *Chapter 7: Logical Consequence and Rationality* offers a long awaited detailed analysis of what is in the literature often lumped together under the umbrella term "pre-theoretical notion of logical consequence". The author wisely points out that the term is used for extremely different concepts and conceptions, sometimes for a hypothesized purely ordinary and every-day notion of logical consequence (if such is available at all), sometimes for pioneering proposals like Aristotles', and sometimes for extremely sophisticated professional contemporary proposals. He distinguishes two sub-species, the sophisticated and the ordinary one, bringing a lot of clarity, and pointing to important connections in the work of classics like Tarski and distinguished contemporaries like Shapiro.

Nenad Miščević in his *Chapter 8: Logic, Indispensability and Aposteriority* argues in favor of deploying some a posteriori considerations in justifying logic: it is justified immediately and in this weak sense a priori, but only in a relatively prima facie and unreflective way. The logic-external consideration of indispensability leads directly to empirical considerations having to do with success, actual or potential, of the cognitive enterprise(s) for which logic is so badly needed. And success is an indicator of reliability. In short, staying within the narrow conceptualist circle amounts to placing of a "veil of conception" between us and the logic-in-the world, blocking the understanding of what makes logic objectively valid. Thus, the very dialectics of the conceptualist program points to a less apriorist view of logical knowledge. This is the view to be defended indirectly in the paper, by offering an overview of conceptualist program and a budget of problems for it.

Papers in Part III argue that logic does not live in isolation, neither from the open cognitive project nor from the social reality (re)constituted by communicative acts of intelligent agents. Cognition comes out of communication and logic is indispensable and unavoidable for the flourishing of society of minds, too. The social aspect of logic figures prominently in Hintikka's game semantics, whose scope is in this part being extended to non-logical vocabulary thus providing an account of social construction of language interpretation. Speech acts create commitments, a social obligation pattern. On the side of theoretical philosophy, cognition must have a critical dimension, and contraction of a theory by a refuted element represents a vital, if not crucial part in our global cognition projects. This reminds us again of the wide compass of logic. For instance, in spite of their ontological disagreement, both realism and anti-realism about abstract objects share the same assumption that logical and mathematical knowledge is knowledge about certain objects and their relations. However, the later Wittgenstein's replacement of picture by game metaphor has opened up a broader perspective for understanding of logical knowledge in procedural terms. Knowledge how to fairly win a argumentation game, how to properly respond to commitments brought by speech acts, or how to cooperatively change the mind of the other is constitutive for understanding meaning relations at least to the same extent as is knowledge how to preserve truth in valid proof steps. The logical knowledge encompasses procedural knowledge and propositional knowledge. The distinction reminds us of the one drawn in medieval times between *logica utens* as logical practice and *logica docens* as theoretical construction, the distinction which survived up to the present times as the difference between inferential and non-inferential logical knowledge. The last half of twentieth century has witnessed an emergence of multitude of new logical theories showing that the discipline has achieved a new understanding of procedural logical knowledge. Nowadays it is commonly held that the scope of logic encompasses much more than transformational syntax of a particular language and that inferential practice is just one among other logical activities. Instead of narrowly construing propositional logical knowledge as being about truth-preserving inferential steps that are constitutive of inferential knowledge in virtue of the logical terminology employed, the recent trends in logic take propositional logical knowledge as being about rich plurality of both solitary activities and sociable interactive procedures of cognizing minds in communication. For example, the purported validity of an exercise of procedural knowledge may be conceptualized using a "zero agent" notions like truth or harmony of rules, but it may also be conceived of in social terms, as possession of winning strategy in a game, as fulfilment of commitments, or as preservation of cooperativeness in communication. In this broad perspective of logical procedures in reasoning and communication the art of logic ceases to be pure handmaiden of science, an *ancilla scientiae*, but establishes itself as philosophical reflection on human being as a cognitive social one with a potential of actively taking part in improvement of one's cognitive abilities and social practices.

Manuel Rebuschi in his *Chapter 9: Extended Game-Theoretical Semantics* develops an extension of Hintikka's game theoretical semantics by devising the rules of the semantic game for the non-logical part of vocabulary. The rules for extended game theoretical semantics are introduced both informally and formally. The semantic game does not terminate at the level of atomic sentences, but it continues as the atomic game. In the non-extended semantic game, the game ends if a true sentence is to be verified or a false sentence is to be falsified by the "initial verifier," but not so in the extended game. In the continuation of the game-theoretic semantic decomposition at the "subatomic level" the initial verifier must prove her competence over non-logical part of the language. The proposed extension of game theoretical semantics gives a natural supplement to the original theory, pushing it beyond meaning constitution towards linguistic interpretation. The author shows various ways in which the extended game theoretical semantics might shed light on the theories of meaning and interpretation, as well in addressing the longstanding philosophical puzzles.

Tomoyuki Yamada in his *Chapter 10: Dynamic Logic of Propositional Commitments* develops an original dynamic semantics framework for the analysis of propositional commitments change brought about by speech acts of assertion and concession. The proposed theoretical framework is also applied in the analysis of the speech acts of assertion withdrawal and concession withdrawal. The author uses D.N. Walton's and E.C. Krabbe's philosophical theory of commitments and a variant of Van Benthem's et al. "dynamic epistemic logic." The paper gives an important contribution to the development of formal semantics of speech acts. In particular, by addressing difficult problem of "undoing a speech act" (withdrawing) within a concrete setting the paper opens up new perspectives for the application of dynamic semantics, in which the problem of "downdating" has been so far addressed only at the higher levels of theoretical abstraction. The paper provides the reflection on the methodology employed and in that way makes the text accessible to the reader with no previous knowledge of dynamic semantics.

In *Chapter 11: Is Unsaying Polite?* **Berislav Žarnić** gives a sketch of the history of the distinction between speech act with negative content and negated speech act, and proposes a general dynamic interpretation for negated speech act. The expressive completeness for the formal variants of natural imperative and declarative language utterances, none of which is a retraction, has been proved. Withdrawal of one's speech act is a common practice in language use, a specific type of speech act for which Yamada in the preceding paper has provided theoretical explication using dynamic epistemic logic, while this paper provides another approach relaying on an extension of Veltman's update semantics and developed in accordance with the postulates of AGM theory of belief revision. Žarnić defines the problem of expressive adequacy of a repertoire of speech acts and proves that negative speech acts (withdrawals) are avoidable.

In Part IV logical methods are applied in philosophical analyses of problems of concept revision, temporal mereology, metalinguistic denotata, and counterfactuals.

Massimiliano Carrara and **Silvia Gaio** in their *Chapter 12: Towards a Formal Account of Identity Criteria* deal with an instance of the problem of concept revision when there is discrepancy between concept's extension and intension. The paper presents in a systematic way the approaches to the revision of binary predicates that occur on the right-hand side of a biconditional which defines the sameness of value of a one-place function. Such predicates ought to denote an equivalence relation in order to define identity, but in some cases of language use these predicates fail to be transitive. Carrara and Gaio give a survey of the current state of the problem and propose a further development of De Clercq and Horsten's formal framework for revising the extension of these predicates by taking into account contextual differences and granularity levels, and by introducing a number of concepts useful for formal approach to the problem of identity criteria.

Pierdaniele Giaretta and **Giuseppe Spolaore** in the paper *Chapter 13: A Mereology for the Change of Parts* propose a theory of temporal mereology in which both the principles of Existence and of Uniqueness of Composition hold. The theory is consistent both with a three-dimensionalist ontology and with the change of parts, that is, with the view that at least one object has distinct parts at distinct times. Some interesting consequences of the theory are proven. It is usually held that certain well known ontological puzzles must be solved either by adopting a four-dimensionalist ontology or by restricting some mereological principles. Here a solution to those puzzles is stated, that consists in denying the persistence of some of the entities involved, along the "Chrysippean" lines. The comments on Tibbles-problem show that the authors are concerned with the application of mereology to natural wholes, that exist through time. They are right to note that it is the organization of the components that is responsible for their relative longevity.

The posthumous publication of **Imre Rusza**'s paper *Chapter 14: Russell Versus Frege* is a homage to the logician who had introduced the issues of intentional logic into the Central European intellectual scene several decades ago. His former students are now among the best known philosophical logicians and historians of logic, like Gyula Klima, Anna Szabolcsi, Zoltán Gendler Szabó, and many others. The paper discusses Russell's Gray's Elegy argument according to which Frege's distinction between *Sinn* und *Bedeutung* is problematic when applied to a denoting phrase like "the first line of Gray's Elegy," which denotes a linguistic expression: "The curfew tolls the knell of parting day." The author shows that Russell's Gray's Elegy argument involves imprecision in the use of quotation marks as well as the unwarranted identification of an expression's meaning with the expression itself.

The aim of **Vladan Djordjević**'s paper *Chapter 15: Goodman's Only World*, in the author's words, "is to investigate how ...the highly unlikely situation" of interpretations of Goodman's account of the counterfactual conditional being "imprecise, incorrect, or wrong, in a strange way—the incorrectness is obvious, or at least can be shown very easily." The strategy the author adopts is to show that different interpretations of Goodman imply the CEM sentence, namely the "law of (counterfactual) conditional excluded middle," which Goodman rejects (by stating that counterfactuals with contradictory consequents are not contradictories but contraries). The author shows that the "usual interpretation (of today)" of Goodman implies the problematic law of (counterfactual) conditional excluded middle.

To conclude, the book is connecting logical theory with more concrete issues of speech acts, norms of rationality and issues of understanding, thus pointing to a wide range of potential applications. The treated topics offer a wide spectrum of approaches to the logic-reality relationship hopefully making the book interesting for a broad readership.

Part I
Logical and Mathematical Structures

Chapter 2
Life on the Ship of Neurath: Mathematics in the Philosophy of Mathematics

Stewart Shapiro

2.1 Mathematics, Its Philosophy, and Revisionism

Some central philosophical issues concern the use of mathematics in putatively non-mathematical, or at least not purely mathematical, endeavors. One such endeavor, of course, is philosophy, and the philosophy of mathematics is a key instance of that. The present survey is not meant to provide broad coverage; the topics are somewhat idiosyncratic.

A related matter concerns the relationship—if there is one—between mathematics and the philosophy of mathematics. In general, for any field of study X, there are interesting questions concerning the relationship between the philosophy of X and X itself. Let me begin with a brief overview of this terrain, at least as I see things.

For a long time, many held that philosophical matters determine the proper practice of mathematics. Some still do. The idea is that philosophy sets the agenda, and, thus, in some sense, precedes practice. One first describes or discovers the metaphysical nature of whatever it is that mathematics is about—whether, for example, there are mathematical entities and, if so, whether said entities are objective or mind dependent. This fixes the way mathematics is to be done. Of course, the presumed order here is not historical, nor is it administrative. The mathematician does not typically consult with the philosopher either before or during working hours, although many of them engage philosophy, sometimes as a sort of hobby. The order is conceptual, or metaphysical, aimed at the proper foundational hierarchy. Call this the *philosophy-first* perspective.

If the first philosopher finds that mathematics is not done according to the prescribed canons, then she insists that the practice be changed. This is *revisionism*. An early instance of this comes from Plato, who, of course, held that mathematics is about an eternal, unchanging, objective realm, independent of any activity done by humans here in the paltry world of Becoming. In Book VII of *The Republic*,

---

S. Shapiro (✉)
Department of Philosophy, The Ohio State University, Columbus, OH, USA
e-mail: shapiro.4@osu.edu

he chided mathematicians for not knowing what they are talking about and, consequently, doing mathematics incorrectly:

> [The] science [of geometry] is in direct contradiction with the language employed by its adepts... Their language is most ludicrous,... for they speak as if they were doing something and as if all their words were directed toward action... [They talk] of squaring and applying and adding and the like... whereas in fact the real object of the entire subject is ... knowledge... of what eternally exists, not of anything that comes to be this or that at some time and ceases to be.

The geometers of antiquity did not take Plato's advice, continuing to employ constructive, dynamic language. According to Proclus [485], the *problem* of such language occupied those in the Academy for some time.

Closer to our time, intuitionism is another revisionist program, or group of programs, inspired by putative philosophical insight. L.E.J. Brouwer and Arend Heyting held that mathematics and mathematical objects are mind-dependent, in some sense, founded on something in the neighborhood of Kantian intuition. This supposedly leads to the rejection of the law of excluded middle, and other inferences based on it. A bit later, Michael Dummett argued against classical logic, and thus classical mathematics, on the basis of philosophical doctrines concerning the meaning and deployment of mathematical language. Put one way, his conclusion is that the strictly classical parts of mathematics do not enjoy a certain type of justification. To be more contentious, his conclusion is that mathematics ought to have the level of justification that is attributable only to intuitionistic mathematics.

Some of the disputes over principles like impredicative definition and the axiom of choice were also fought on philosophical grounds. Typically, realists favor the items in question, while various irrealists demur from them.

Of course, not every instance of philosophy-first is revisionist. Some philosophers take themselves to be providing the proper first-philosophy for mathematics as practiced. Kant is probably an example of this, with his view that arithmetic and geometry are synthetic a priori, founded on pure intuition, the forms of possible perceptions. Nevertheless, any first-philosophy is potentially *revisionist*. If the mathematical community should stray from the proposed philosophical foundation, then, according to the first-philosopher, they have erred, and need to correct their ways. A Kantian may find herself in this situation, when confronted with the advent and success of non-Euclidean geometry.

When faced with such a discrepancy, the first-philosopher is free to admit that she was mistaken about the proper philosophical basis for mathematics. A later-day Kantian might concede that it was rash to conclude, on a priori, philosophical grounds, that geometry is and always will be Euclidean. Perhaps she might claim that, on reflection, pure intuition demands some non-Euclidean geometry or, more likely, she might claim that pure intuition is neutral between a number of geometries. Of course, a philosopher is *always* prepared to modify his views in light of unexpected developments in mathematics is not really practicing philosophy-first.

For what it is worth, philosophy-first is not true to the history of mathematics. The discipline tends to have a life of its own, going in various directions for various reasons, typically independently of the musings of us philosophers. Moreover, philosophy-first is not particularly prominent among contemporary philosophers of mathematics. One might go to the opposite extreme, and hold that philosophy is irrelevant to mathematics. On this view, a position in the philosophy of mathematics is at best an epiphenomenon which has nothing to contribute to mathematics, and at worst a meaningless sophistry, the rambling and meddling of outsiders. We might call this the *philosophy-last-if-at-all* perspective.

For present purposes, we need not go much further in articulating this distinction. As I see things, the job of the philosopher is to give an account of mathematics and its place in our intellectual lives. Our goal is to *interpret* mathematics, and thereby answer philosophical questions concerning the place of mathematics in the world view. Since much interpretation is linguistic, a prima facie focus is the language of mathematics. What do mathematical assertions mean? What is their logical form? What is the best semantics for mathematical language? How is mathematical language to be understood? This sets the stage for answering philosophical questions about mathematics. What is its subject matter—if it has one? What is the relationship between mathematics and the subject matter of science which allows such extensive application and cross-fertilization? How do we manage to do and know mathematics? How can mathematics be taught? In short, the philosopher must say something about mathematics, something about the applications of mathematics, something about mathematical language, and something about human mathematicians. This is enough to keep us occupied with interesting questions and issues, without also setting the agenda for mathematics.

This perspective runs against the revisionism that sometimes goes with philosophy-first. It is *mathematics* that is to be interpreted, and not what a prior (or a priori) philosophical theory says that mathematics should be, or what the philosopher says that mathematics should be. To be sure, the anti-revisionism is only a trend of the orientation. In general, interpretation can and should involve criticism. But here at least, criticism does not come from outside—from pre-conceived first principles.

Our question here is the extent to which the philosopher of mathematics is to engage in mathematics along the way. So let us turn to that.

2.2 The Big Three

I propose to begin the survey with the three main programs that dominated the foundations and philosophy of mathematics for much of the twentieth century: intuitionism, logicism, and formalism. I'll include Errett Albert Bishop's [3] constructivism in with intuitionism.

2.2.1 Intuitionism

As noted, intuitionism and constructivism are revisionist programs. Their advocates concede that mathematicians generally accept and invoke the law of excluded middle, along with impredicative definitions and the like, but they argue that these inferences and principles are unjustified, often on grounds of philosophy-first. As such, intuitionism and constructivism do not need any mathematics to bolster or even support themselves. If the philosophical arguments against excluded middle, impredicative definition, and the like, are sound, then excluded middle, impredicative definition and the like are invalid, and the mathematician has to do without them. End of story.

Of course, many of the intuitionists and constructivists were mathematicians, and pursued mathematics accordingly. As a result, the rest of the mathematical community got a good look at what the differences are, and a philosopher who rejects philosophy-first can see what some of the *costs* of intuitionism and constructivism are. In particular, she sees which theorems must be given up, and which can be maintained. Quite often, the same theorem can be proved both constructively and classically. Typically, the constructive proof provides more information—better bounds for example. So there may be some mathematical grounds for at least exploring the weakened mathematics. It should be noted, however, that sometimes classical proofs are more perspicuous, at least for a mathematician who accepts such proofs.

Heyting's formalization of intuitionistic logic lead to an explosion of meta-mathematical results. A number of modeltheoretic systems were developed, which led to sharp results concerning what can and what cannot be proven constructively. We have deep results concerning the role of excluded middle, the axiom of choice, and impredicative definition in mathematics. That is, the classical mathematician has sharp results about what can and what cannot be proved in various constructive systems. Like any other branch of mathematics, some of this meta-theory is, or can be, done constructively, and some of it cannot.

Work like this illustrates a theme one encounters again and again in pursuit of our present topic. The mathematics that is done through, via, or in support of, a philosophical program typically has lasting value independent of the success or failure of the program in question. Even those who reject the intuitionistic revisions to practice see the value and importance of the deep and penetrating logical and mathematical studies. We learn a lot about the logical connections in our own world view.

One area of growing interest in philosophy is the use of mathematics in science—although a pure mathematician and perhaps an advocate of philosophy-first might scoff at this enterprise. Philosophical argument aside, if an intuitionist or constructivist is to sell his wares, he should show that this queen of the sciences is not crippled beyond usefulness, at least for science. There is an ongoing research program of exploring the extent to which the mathematics used in science is, or can be, acceptable to an intuitionist or constructivist. There are some commonly cited theorems that are not available, but in many cases, an acceptable, if awkward, substitute is. To take a crude example, the intermediate value theorem is not constructively provable, but the following is: if f is a continuous function on the real numbers, $fa < 0$ and $fb > 0$, then for every $\varepsilon > 0$, there is a real number c between a and b such that $|fc| < \varepsilon$. For practical applications, this is good enough.

Unlike Bishop's constructivism, some intuitionistic mathematics is inconsistent with classical mathematics. Brouwer's theory of real analysis contains results which, when coupled with excluded middle, lead to contradiction. Another, related example is smooth infinitesimal analysis, although it is not particularly in line with intuitionistic philosophy. Nevertheless, this most interesting theory provides an illuminating account of smooth functions. Yet it is inconsistent with excluded middle.

The existence of such theories raises some interesting philosophical issues, at least for those of us who are not believing intuitionists. If one thinks that the law of excluded middle is a logical truth, then it holds of *all* subject matters. This is what we mean by saying that logic is topic neutral. But if excluded middle is universally valid, then both Brouwer's analysis and smooth infinitesimal analysis are inconsistent, and thus incoherent. They are thus not legitimate branches of mathematics, nor are they legitimate branches of anything else for that matter. But these theories, considered on their own terms, at least appear to be not only coherent, but interesting and illuminating. The very presence of these theories challenges widely held views concerning logic.

The dilemma, in short, is this. It seems eminently plausible to accept intuitionistic analysis and/or smooth infinitesimal analysis as legitimate branches of mathematics, perhaps alongside other, more classical disciplines. After all, works in these subjects appear in mainstream mathematical journals and books, subject to the highest standards of refereeing. If we are not going in for philosophy-first, one would think that the mathematical community is at least a very good judge of what counts as mathematics, and it seems that intuitionistic analysis and smooth infinitesimal analysis pass whatever tests they impose on themselves. But then one must concede that the law of excluded middle is not universally valid, after all. There are legitimate branches of mathematics in which it fails. In other words, one who accepts these theories as legitimate mathematics must concede to the main thesis of intuitionism, that excluded middle is not universally valid.

2.2.2 Logicism

The slogan is that mathematics is, in some sense, logic. Gottlob Frege [17, 18] held that arithmetic and analysis are analytic, and thus not founded on either Kantian intuition or observation. To demonstrate this, he tried to show how the basic propositions of these disciplines can be founded on logic and definitions alone. That, of course, required considerable mathematical work. The most obvious item was the development of mathematical logic [16]. Frege realized that it would not suffice to provide an informal derivation of the basic principles of arithmetic from what look like logical laws and definitions. It may be that intuition is needed to fill in the steps in or otherwise tighten the informal derivation. He thus saw the need to develop the notion of a valid, gap-free deduction for a language rich enough to capture arithmetic and analysis. This was provided with the first presentation of what would later be recognized as a second-order deductive system. And Frege made brilliant mathematical use of the new language, introducing the ancestral and, with that, the notion of minimal closure, the concept that underlies induction. George Boolos [4, p. 336] makes the observation:

> The fact that the *Begriffschrift* contains a subtle and ingenious double induction ... used to prove a significant result in the general theory is not, I think, well-known, and the distinctively mathematical talent he displayed is discussing and proving the result is not adequately appreciated. Frege's accomplishment may be likened to a feat the Wright brothers did not perform: inventing the airplane *and* ending its first flight with one loop-the-loop inside another.

That and much more straight mathematical work permeated Frege's program. And, of course, much remains of value, quite independent of the fate of the underlying philosophy, and despite the underlying contradiction in Frege's mature system.

The other major logicist program, that of Alfred North Whitehead and Bertrand Russell [42], also required a considerable amount of mathematical work, much of which was logical. The ramified type theory required meticulous attention to detail, and substantial studies were needed to see what pre-formal results could be recaptured—and which could not be captured.

In Russell's thinking, or at least in his practice, mathematical needs were played against philosophical considerations, the latter at least tending toward philosophy-first. For example, the vicious circle principle, in its full generality, was developed and defended on more or less metaphysical grounds concerning the nature of propositions and attributes. But the resulting ramified theory proved unworkable, not only because it was horribly complex, but because certain results needed in mathematics were not obtainable. So the principles of infinity, choice, and reducibility were added, the latter explicitly undoing the effects of the vicious circle principle in extensional, mathematical contexts. Russell, at least, hoped to eventually justify these principles on philosophical grounds, but they were clearly proposed for pragmatic reasons, to allow his system to re-capture the mathematics of his day.

This is a stark instance of another recurring theme in the present study. Suppose that a philosopher declares, for whatever reason, that mathematics is (or is just) X (where X might be logic, mental construction, the science of structure, whatever). To make this at all plausible, the philosopher must then show how standard mathematics, or some standard mathematics, or an acceptable surrogate for standard mathematics, can be captured, or recaptured, in terms of X. At least intuitively, this work is itself mathematical. The issue of philosophy-first, or philosophy last-if-at-all, or something in between, arises when a mismatch is found between mathematics, as practiced, and the proposed philosophical interpretation.

2.2.3 Formalism

To complete our trilogy, *formalism* comes in many varieties, and there is not enough space, nor do I have the inclination, to discuss all of them or even many of them. The most influential instance, of course, was David Hilbert's finitism (e.g., [26]). According to Hilbert, the corpus of mathematics is divided into two categories, finitary arithmetic and the rest, which we may call ideal or infinitary mathematics.

There is some exegetical controversy over the exact contents of finitary arithmetic, but it seems to be restricted to certain simple properties of the natural numbers. Hilbert exploited the structural analogy between natural numbers and strings on a finite alphabet, and thereby gave finitary arithmetic a Kantian foundation, or perhaps the view is that finitary arithmetic is so clear and basic that it needs no foundation at all. Linguistic characters are perceived, and numbers are likened to the forms of such characters. Moreover, the grasp of linguistic characters seems to be necessary for any sort of reasoning at all. It is not that finitary arithmetic is absolutely certain, beyond skeptical challenge, but if one does come to doubt finitary arithmetic, it is not clear that she can go on to do any thinking at all (see Tait [38]).

According to Hilbert, the rest of mathematics—the bulk of it—seems to invoke infinite structures and totalities, structures and totalities that are not intuitive, and are not found in nature. The metaphysical existence of these things is at least problematic, and thinking about the infinite has led to contradiction. The key idea of the Hilbert program is that ideal, infinitary mathematics can be pursued independently of any subject matter it may have. We are to formalize each branch, by rigorously stating the syntax and the rules for manipulating the characters of each language and theory. Ideal mathematics can be likened to a game of manipulating linguistic characters; it need not have content. That, of course, is the formalist element. We are to shore up a given branch of mathematics by proving that it is consistent—that the game is not trivial. Even more, we are to show that the branch is conservative over finitary arithmetic—that no false, finitary statements about natural numbers can be produced. In most cases, this conservativeness is equivalent to consistency. The statements of conservativeness/consistency are, of course, contentful, and their proof should be carried out in finitary arithmetic. Then, as Hilbert [26] put it, "no one shall drive us out of the paradise which Cantor created for us", again exploiting the structural isomorphism between natural numbers and strings of characters.

The Hilbert program thus required a substantial amount of mathematics. The Hilbertian had to formalize branches of mathematics and prove consistency/conservativeness results. Much of this was carried out, or at least attempted, by Hilbert himself and by other members of his school. Proof theory, and a rich field of metamathematics, was thus born.

But, of course, the dream was not realized. Kurt Gödel's [19] second incompleteness theorem is that the straightforward formulation of the consistency of a mathematical theory T cannot be proved in T, provided only that T is consistent and sufficiently rich. If finitary arithmetic is a part of, say, real analysis, then the Hilbert program is unattainable. We cannot prove analysis consistent in analysis, let alone in its finitary fragment. As with logicism and intuitionism, however, the mathematical work, and the branches of mathematics founded in support of the Hilbert program, live on, producing insights into the logical relationships between various branches of mathematics, and increasing our understanding of consistency, relative consistency, mutual interpretability, satisfiability, independence, ordinal analysis, reverse mathematics, and the like. And certain ongoing philosophical programs, including advocates of predicative mathematics, various weakened logics, and scaled down versions of the Hilbert program have emerged.

2.3 The Contemporary Scene

For any field of study X, there is an interesting question concerning how much X should one know before one can effectively engage in the philosophy of X, providing insights and the like. Here, our question concerns how much mathematics one should know in order to pursue the philosophy of mathematics. And, of course, the relevant "mathematics" may go well beyond the branches of mathematical logic: set theory, model theory, proof theory, or the like.

I suggested above that the purpose of the philosophy of mathematics is to interpret mathematics. It is a truism that one should know something about what it is one is interpreting. Notice, however, that at least some mathematics is invoked in everyday discourse. People count, add, balance their checkbooks, and compute batting averages. Perhaps someone who restricts his attention to the natural numbers and a bit more—say basic arithmetic and elementary analysis—can provide interesting and valuable philosophical insights without being en rapport with more advanced branches of mathematics, especially if he keeps focused on everyday uses and applications of this mathematics. There is some danger from the other end as well. A philosopher may be focusing her attention on advanced mathematics, say professional mathematics and the mathematics invoked in science, and ignore the role and use of mathematics in ordinary life. Or a philosopher may focus solely on pure mathematics and ignore its applications.

Some of the current accounts of mathematics do not themselves involve much, or even any, mathematical work. One stark example is the anti-nominalist quietism proposed by some naturalists. The idea is to take mathematical statements at face value, and pretty much leave it at that. Much of the philosophical work from that school comes from criticizing other views. Another example, perhaps, is the defense of ontological realism via the indispensability of mathematics for science. The philosopher simply notes that since contemporary science, which we take to be true or nearly true, invokes considerable mathematics, we are committed to the truth of the mathematics. If we interpret the mathematics literally, we are thus committed to the existence of mathematical objects. The indispensability theorist does not do any mathematics to support this. He just comments on the mathematics done by others—scientists in this case. Arguments from this camp would benefit greatly from an account of exactly how mathematics is applied in science. How application works is an interesting philosophical problem in its own right. It may be that one needs to engage in some mathematics to tackle this problem.

2.3.1 The Home Front

Another example of philosophical work sans mathematics is my own ante rem structuralism (Shapiro [32]), along with the closely related view defended by Michael Resnik [29]. Our books contain considerable metaphysics, ontology, epistemology, and an account of applications, but not much mathematics. At the urging of some colleagues and critics, I did include an axiomatization of structure-theory. Perhaps that counts as mathematics, but it is not very deep. The formal theory is modeled after Zermelo-Fraenkel set theory. Mathematics plays a central role in one variety of structuralism. A dedicated group of philosophers and mathematicians use category theory and topos theory to explicate the notion of mathematical structure. These philosophers attempt to develop an account of a wide range of current mathematical practice, not just foundational theories like arithmetic and set theory. The program has a respectable pedigree in the recent history of mathematics itself (see, for example, Awodey [1] and McLarty [27]).

The pursuit of my other main interest in the philosophy of mathematics does invoke some mathematics. To argue that the languages of mathematics are best (or at least well) interpreted as second-order, I provided reconstructions of common mathematical notions, inferences, etc., and provided careful comparisons of the first- and second-order formulations of various notions and theories. In exploring the expressive resources of second-order languages, one is led to its model theory, presenting standard and Henkin semantics, along with explorations of categoricity, Löwenheim-Skolem properties, compactness, indescribable cardinals, Lindström's theorem, etc. And, of course, second-order logic takes on a life of its own, with its distinctive mathematical properties. There is also an industry of exploring intermediate logics, those that are expressively impoverished as first-order logic while not as intractable as full second-order logic (Shapiro [31]).

Early in my career, I got interested in intensional notions, and the interaction of constructive and non-constructive reasoning in the very same mathematics. That led me to a classical formal system with a modal operator that could interpret the intuitionistic connectives and quantifiers. So one can capture statements in the form: constructively, there exists a number n, such that, classically, … The solution to Post's problem is of this form. I stuck to arithmetic, and was able to establish soundness. The project caught the interest of Nicholas Goodman and John Myhill, who proved completeness and extended the project to set theory (Shapiro [30]).

2.3.2 Abstraction

Another prominent program in the philosophy of mathematics is Scottish neologicism, sometimes called abstractionism. The idea is to develop branches of mathematics from abstraction principles, in the form:

$$\S a = \S b \equiv \Phi(a, b) \tag{ABS}$$

where a and b are variables of a given type, typically first-order or second-order, and Φ is an equivalence relation of items of that type. The program begins life with a principle about cardinal numbers:

$$\#P = \#Q \equiv (P \sim Q) \tag{HP}$$

where $(P \sim Q)$ is the statement that there is a one-to-one relation from the P's onto the Q's. This is now called "Hume's principle". In words, it says that the number of F is identical to the number of G if and only if the F's are equinumerous with the G's. Frege [17] provided what amounts to a derivation of the basic principles of arithmetic, the so-called Dedekind-Peano axioms, from Hume's principle. The result is now known as Frege's theorem. No one doubts that Frege's theorem is an interesting and important piece of mathematics. Who would have thought that so much arithmetic can be derived from this simple and rather obvious principle about counting? The Scottish neo-logicist argues that (HP) can be understood as an implicit definition, the sort of thing that can be true by stipulation. Frege's theorem thus shows how basic arithmetic can be known a priori, not requiring intuition or any holistic elements (Hale and Wright [24]).

Mathematics enters the discussion of the program, pro and contra, from several different angles. The Scottish neo-logicists is not content to leave things with an account of arithmetic. The search is on to develop more advanced branches of mathematics, such as geometry, real analysis, complex analysis, and even set theory, from abstraction principles. This involves mathematical work, akin to Frege's theorem, although some of it, at least, consists of adapting well-known results to the abstractionist framework (Shapiro [33] and Hale [22]).

A second use of mathematics is provided by Kit Fine's [15] study of the logical properties of various abstraction principles, and of the consequences and the models of theories whose axioms are various collections of abstraction principles. Through a detailed logical analysis, Fine shows which principles have certain properties, and what models certain combinations of abstraction principles have.

Mathematics also bears on the abstractionist program through the so-called "bad company" objection, brought by Neil Tennant [39], Dummett [11], Boolos [5], and others. The philosophical argument is that one cannot claim that Hume's principle is basic, known a priori by something akin to stipulation, since it is of the same form as Frege's Basic Law V,

$$\mathrm{E}P = \mathrm{E}Q \equiv \forall x(Px \equiv Qx) \tag{BLV}$$

which, of course, is inconsistent. One might argue that any consistent or perhaps satisfiable abstraction principle can be known a priori. It emerged early on that this will not do, since there are pairs of principles which are individually satisfiable, but not satisfiable together. If either can be true by stipulation, one might think, then so can the other. But they cannot both be true. The main response from the Scottish neo-logicists is to formulate properties, such as various conservativeness constraints, that the good abstraction principles must meet. The claim is that any abstraction principle that meets the conditions can be known a priori, via stipulation, and can be used to found a mathematical theory of the defined abstracts. To date, most of the proposed conditions have some mathematical content, and so there is the job of showing just which abstraction principles meet the conditions. Alan Weir and I [37], for example, pointed out that a proposed abstraction for set theory, Boolos's New V, fails the proper formulation of conservativeness, since it entails that the universe is well-ordered. We also show that it is consistent with ZFC that New V has no uncountable models. The search for other abstraction principles that meet the requirements, and for more refined requirements that the principle in question does meet, is ongoing.

Another batch of results compare the "universes" of various abstraction principles with that of standard Zermelo Fraenkel set theory. Fine, for example, shows that all models of the theory axiomatized by the abstraction principles that meet a certain requirement have a certain structural property—being unsurpassable—which is inconsistent with the universe being inaccessible. Thus, if Fine's abstraction theory describes the (entire) mathematical realm, then ZF does not, and vice versa. Roy Cook [9] shows that ZFC entails that a certain generalization of a proposed abstraction principle (to generate the real numbers) has no set-theoretic models.

The philosophical relevance of much of this mathematics depends on one's perspective toward the abstractionist program, and the relationship between it and previously established mathematics. We are in the neighborhood here of the issues concerning revisionism and philosophy-first. Similar remarks apply to just about every philosophical program that is supported with mathematical results, if the "match" between established mathematics and the philosophical reconstruction is not perfect.

There is, first, the orientation of the established mathematician who is observing the abstractionist project. She is interested in determining which mathematical structures have been captured by the Scottish neo-logicist, and for this reason inquires into the meta-theoretic properties of the abstraction-based systems. This is an *external* perspective, where the enterprise is assessed from the point of view of someone who already has (or claims to have) a rich, functioning mathematics. It is generally held that this background ontology is, or can be modeled as, the iterative hierarchy, as described by Zermelo-Fraenkel set theory.

From the external perspective, the mathematician studies the model-theoretic properties of abstraction principles proposed by the neologicist, just as she might study the model-theoretic properties of any other propositions, mathematical or otherwise. In this study, the mathematician uses every tool at her disposal, whether the neo-logicist is able to reconstruct it or not.

A second, *internal* orientation is that of the neo-logicist. The focus is on mathematical principles that can be stated and derived in a standard (second-order) logical deductive system, augmented with various abstraction principles. Among scholars, the received view is that meta-theory, or at least model theory, is foreign to Frege's logicism (see, for example, van Heijenoort [41] and Goldfarb [21]). In the language that Frege envisioned for logic and mathematics, the various quantifiers are unrestricted, ranging over all the objects and all the concepts that there are. Moreover, the language contains no nonlogical terminology. If the same goes for the Scottish neo-logicist, then it is not clear what relevance the model-theoretic results about abstraction principles may have.

To be sure, set theory and model-theoretic semantics are themselves respectable branches of mathematics, and so our neo-logicist would surely want to recapture them from abstraction principles eventually (see Hale [23] and Shapiro [34]). If there were an abstraction-based theory whose strength is in the neighborhood of

ZFC, then the neo-logicist could appreciate the aforementioned model-theoretic results. But those results need not bear on the abstractionist program in its infancy. Moreover, set theory does not play a foundational role for the neo-logicist. There is no working hypothesis that the iterative hierarchy contains (surrogates for) all mathematical objects, or that ZFC correctly describes the mathematical universe.

Fine describes different attitudes that a neo-logicist can take toward "standard set theory (as embodied in ZF or ZFC)". In effect, the internal perspective splits into two. The uncompromising Scottish neo-logicist simply rejects set theory outright, at least until it can be captured with legitimate abstraction principles. This revisionist, or "imperialist", perspective sees "all abstract objects as arising from abstraction". In contrast, a compromising neo-logicist is prepared to accept mathematical theories that are not based on abstraction. The focus here is on which branches of mathematics have, or can have, abstractionist foundations. If set theory and model theory cannot be reconstructed on the epistemic basis of abstraction principles, then their basic principles cannot become known in the privileged manner claimed for arithmetic. But our compromiser would not conclude from this that those branches of mathematics cannot become known at all. Set theory might be justified on holistic or pragmatic grounds, or perhaps it needs no extra-mathematical justification at all, as argued by contemporary naturalists. The compromiser is out to provide a neo-logicist foundation when one is available. In effect, the compromising neo-logicist combines the internal and external perspectives.

When actually engaged in the abstractionist constructions (or reconstructions), the compromiser must be careful not to smuggle in any substantial set theory—unless that set theory can itself be captured on abstractionist grounds. That would undermine the epistemic goals of the program. However, our compromising neo-logicist can assess the model-theoretic properties of various abstraction principles, and use such results to guide her neo-logicist theorizing, from the outside, so to speak. Set theory can help in the context of discovery, perhaps, but not in the context of Scottish neo-logicist justification.

The opening quantifiers in some of the abstractions, such as Hume's principle and, for that matter, Basic Law V, are unrestricted. Hume's principle, for example, is supposed to express a general truth about cardinal numbers. If we are to speak of objects at all, in any domain, we can count them, and thus apply arithmetic to those objects. The universal applicability of arithmetic supports Frege's claim that arithmetic is part of logic, since it is topic neutral. It also dovetails with Frege's contention, against the likes of Dedekind and Cantor, that the proper foundation of a branch of mathematics should flow from its applications. The Scottish neo-logicist follows suit (see Wright [43]).

A key question for the compromising neo-logicist is whether to accept the commonly accepted hypothesis that the iterative hierarchy describes *the* mathematical universe in toto—in the sense that every legitimate mathematical theory can be modeled in it. If so, there is a potential for conflict if the unrestricted abstraction principles make structural demands on the universe inconsistent with those of standard set theory. The issue is pursued in Fine [15] and Shapiro [35, 36].

2.3.3 No Numbers or Sets at All

On the contemporary scene, there are two varieties of *nominalism*, the view that there are no abstract objects, such as numbers and sets. The fictionalist holds that the propositions of mathematics are to be read a face value. The statement that there is a prime number greater than twenty thus entails that there is at least one natural number—and so it entails that natural numbers exist. So, as a nominalist, the fictionalist applies modus tollens. She holds that most of the assertions of mathematicians are either false or vacuously true. It is false that there is a prime number greater than twenty, and it is true that all numbers are prime. In contrast, the *reconstructive nominalist* holds that the mathematical statements are objectively and non-trivially true or false, but such statements are not to be read at face value. The view is that once the basic principles of mathematics are properly understood, they have the truth values they are commonly thought to have, but the principles do not entail the existence of distinctively mathematical objects. Both kinds of nominalistic programs are supported with formal work, much of which is mathematical.

The two main reconstructive programs are those of Geoffrey Hellman [25] and Charles Chihara [8], although a seed of a similar idea can be found in Hilary Putnam [28]. In all three cases, the key philosophical thesis is that mathematical assertions can be understood in modal terms. A mathematical proposition is a statement about what is possible, or about what holds in all possible systems of a certain kind. Hellman and Chihara each provide a formal language with modal terminology, and then show how to translate formalized versions of mathematical statements into the modal language.

Consider the above theorem that there is a prime number greater than twenty. Let S be a system consisting of some objects, together with two distinguished relations on those objects. Say that S is a natural-number-system if it satisfies the Dedekind-Peano axioms. Hellman shows how to express the notion of natural-number-system, using an ordinary second-order language, avoiding use of semantic terminology such as satisfaction. Our theorem then comes to something like this:

> Every possible natural-number-system S contains an object that is prime (in S) and is greater than 20-object in S.

To keep the framework from being vacuous, Hellman adds a postulate that it is possible for there to be a natural-number-system.

Unlike Hellman's, Chihara's reconstruction invokes semantic terminology, relying on the notion of an object satisfying an open sentence. Our theorem is rendered as a statement that it is possible to construct an open sentence with certain semantic properties.

Hellman provides translations of arithmetic, analysis, and set theory into his modal language, and he shows that, given his assumptions, the translations of the axioms are all true. Thus he shows that the translations of common theorems in mathematics have the truth values they are thought to have. If a mathematician manages to prove a proposition P in a standard mathematical theory, then Hellman manages to prove the modal rendition of P.

Chihara's accomplishment is similar. He provides a way to render the language of simple type theory, or what we may call pure ω-order logic, into his language of constructibility, and he argues that the axioms of type theory, so rendered, are all true. He can thus rely on the standard ways to interpret common mathematical theories—short of set theory and category theory—into simple type theory. Chihara provides an insightful way to render real analysis into his system more directly, which sheds light on at least some aspects of how the real numbers are applied.

As noted, the fictionalist is not out to save mathematics, in the sense of showing that its basic principles are true. On the contrary, she holds that all existential mathematical statements are false. So she has no need to reconstruct mathematics in kosher terms. The main problem facing the fictionalist is to account for the applications of mathematics in the natural and social sciences. Why is it that false and vacuously true statements are so useful in coming to understand the material world? Indeed, even the statements of scientific theories are shot through with mathematical terminology. In short, the nominalist must deal with the aforementioned indispensability argument.

This problem is addressed by Hartry Field [12] in one of the most interesting and important intellectual achievements in contemporary philosophy. Field shows how to render classical gravitation theory in a language that does not have quantifiers ranging over abstract objects, such as numbers or sets. Then he shows that adding standard mathematics to this theory, along with the usual bridge principles, is semantically conservative: any model of the nominalistic physics can be extended to a model of the physics plus set theory and bridge principles. So any consequence of the combined theory that is in the nominalistic language is already a consequence of the original nominalistic theory.

The conservativeness result is a substantial result in mathematical logic, model theory in particular, that is brought in to support a philosophical program. So it fits into the theme of this survey. Whether one is a nominalist or not, Field's results are part of a compelling and illuminating account of how mathematics is applied in science via structural representation theorems. There is an interesting question of whether the nominalist is entitled to use these results, however. After all, she holds that the mathematical meta-theory, the model theory and its underlying theory of sets, is not true. So, conservativeness proof or no conservativeness proof, why is she justified in believing that adding mathematics to a physical theory does not produce new consequences in the nominalistic language? Field, of course, is aware of the potential problem, and his subsequent work provides proposals for getting around it, to either find a nominalistically acceptable conservativeness result or to argue that the nominalist is entitled to certain conclusions (see Field [13, 14]). A literature discussing these issues emerged.

The first part of Field's program is also of interest for the present survey. The ontology of his nominalist physics consists of space-time points, which has most of the structure of the real numbers or, to be precise, most of the structure of $\mathbb{R}^4$. Field also invokes, and has quantifiers ranging over, regions of space-time, construed as mereological sums of points. The regions have most of the structure of the powerset of $\mathbb{R}^4$. Field argues that space-time points and regions are concrete, not abstract, and so they can be invoked in a legitimate nominalistic science. This has been challenged, but the details of the debate need not concern us here.

In the technical development, Field then shows how to characterize surrogates of various mathematical operations, such as functions and their derivatives and integrals, directly on space-time points and regions. This allows him to formulate the standard laws of gravitational theory, and provides a model to extend the theory to other, more up to date physical theories. The relationship between Field's nominalistic physics and the more usual, *platonistic* physics, which invokes real numbers and functions on real numbers, is the same as the relationship between synthetic geometry, as found in Euclid's *Elements*, and analytic geometry (see Burgess [7]).

Euclid's *Elements* is mathematics *par excellence*, and one might think the same for the relevant parts of Field's nominalistic physics. Field maintains, however, that his physics is thoroughly not mathematical, since it is about physical, concrete space-time points and regions. But the relevant parts of Field's book sure resemble mathematics. Indeed, that is the point. If some of Microsoft's attorneys ever go to work for Standard Mathematical Physics, Inc., we can expect them to sue Field on the ground that the relevant parts of his theory have the look and feel of mathematics. Mathematicians have told me that *Science without numbers* is not really a science without mathematics. The mathematics is still there, they might say. And those folks should be able to recognize their subject when they see it.

Of course, the philosophical issue is not where to draw boundaries between disciplines. The concern is over the metaphysical status of numbers, sets, and points, and what lies in the range of quantifiers of theories that are literally true. Still, there is some irony here. The nominalistic physics developed in Field [12] looks like a prime example of the theme of this survey, namely the use of mathematics in support of philosophy of mathematics. And I, for one, think it is such an example. But the advocate of the program in question, Field himself, is committed to claiming that it is not such an example, on pain of undermining the philosophical program itself.

References

1. Awodey, Steve. 2004. "An Answer to Hellman's Question: "Does Category Theory Provide a Framework for Mathematical Structuralism?"." *Philosophia Mathematica* 12:54–64.
2. Benacerraf, Paul, and Hilary Putnam, eds. 1983. *Philosophy of Mathematics*. 2nd edition. Cambridge, MA: Cambridge University Press.
3. Bishop, Errett. 1967. *Foundations of Constructive Analysis*. New York, NY: Mc-Graw-Hill.
4. Boolos, George. 1985. "Reading the Begriffschrift." *Mind* 94:331–44; reprinted in Boolos [6], 155–70.
5. Boolos, George. 1997. "Is Hume's Principle Analytic?." In *Language, Thought, and Logic*, edited by Richard Heck, Jr., 245–61. Oxford: Oxford University Press; reprinted in Boolos [6], 301–14.
6. Boolos, George. 1998. *Logic, Logic, and Logic*. Cambridge, MA: Harvard University Press.
7. Burgess, John. 1984. "Synthetic Mechanics." *Journal of Philosophical Logic* 13:379–95.
8. Chihara, Charles. 1990. *Constructibility and Mathematical Existence*. Oxford: Oxford University Press.

9. Cook, Roy T. 2001. "The State of the Economy: Neo-Logicism and Inflation." *Philosophia Mathematica* 10:43–66.
10. Davis, Martin. 1965. *The Undecidable*. Hewlett, NY: The Raven Press.
11. Dummett, Michael. 1998. "Neo-Fregeans: In Bad Company?" In *The philosophy of Mathematics Today*, edited by Matthias Schirn, 369–87. Oxford: Oxford University Press.
12. Field, Hartry. 1980. *Science Without Numbers*. Princeton, NJ: Princeton University Press.
13. Field, Hartry. 1989. *Realism, Mathematics and Modality*. Oxford: Blackwell.
14. Field, Hartry. 1991. "Metalogic and Modality." *Philosophical Studies* 62:1–22.
15. Fine, Kit. 2002. *The Limits of Abstraction*. Oxford: Oxford University Press.
16. Frege, Gottlob. 1879. *Begriffsschrift, eine der arithmetischen nachgebildete Formelsprache des reinen Denkens*. Halle: Louis Nebert; translated in van Heijenoort [40], 1–82.
17. Frege, Gottlob. 1884. *Die Grundlagen der Arithmetik*. Breslau: Koebner; *The Foundations of Arithmetic*, translated by J. Austin, 2nd edition, New York, NY: Harper. 1960.
18. Frege, Gottlob. 1893. *Grundgesetze der Arithmetik 1*. Hildescheim: Olms.
19. Gödel, Kurt. 1931. "Über formal unentscheidbare Sätze der Principia Mathematica und verwandter Systeme I." *Montatshefte für Mathematik und Physik* 38:173–98; translated as "On Formally Undecidable Propositions of the Principia Mathematica", in Davis [10], 4–35, and in van Heijenoort [40], 596–616; also Gödel [19], 144–95.
20. Gödel, Kurt. 1986. *Collected Works I*. Oxford: Oxford University Press.
21. Goldfarb, Warren. 1979. "Logic in the Twenties: The Nature of the Quantifier." *Journal of Symbolic Logic* 44:351–68.
22. Hale, Bob. 2000. "Reals by Abstraction." *Philosophia Mathematica* 8:100–23; reprinted in Hale and Wright [24], 399–420.
23. Hale, Bob. 2000. "Abstraction and Set Theory." *Notre Dame Journal of Formal Logic* 41:379–98.
24. Hale, Bob, and Crispin Wright. 2001. *The Reason's Proper Study*. Oxford: Oxford University Press.
25. Hellman, Geoffrey. 1989. *Mathematics Without Numbers*. Oxford: Oxford University Press.
26. Hilbert, David. 1925. "Über das Unendliche." *Mathematische Annalen* 95:161–90; translated as "On The Infinite", in van Heijenoort [40], 369–92 and in Benacerraf and Putnam [2], 183–201.
27. McLarty, Colin. 2007. "The Last Mathematician from Hilbert's Göttingen: Saunders Mac Lane as Philosopher of Mathematics." *British Journal for the Philosophy of Science* 58:77–112.
28. Putnam, Hilary. 1967. "Mathematics Without Foundations." *Journal of Philosophy* 64:5–22.
29. Resnik, Michael. 1997. *Mathematics as a Science of Patterns*. Oxford: Oxford University Press.
30. Shapiro, Stewart. 1985. *Intensional Mathematics*. Amsterdam: North Holland Publishing Company.
31. Shapiro, Stewart. 1991. *Foundations Without Foundationalism: A Case for Secondorder Logic*. Oxford: Oxford University Press.
32. Shapiro, Stewart. 1997. *Philosophy of Mathematics: Structure and Ontology*. New York, NY: Oxford University Press.
33. Shapiro, Stewart. 2000. "Frege Meets Dedekind: A Neo-Logicist Treatment of Real Analysis." *Notre Dame Journal of Formal Logic* 41:335–64.
34. Shapiro, Stewart. 2003. "Prolegomenon to Any Future Neo-Logicist Set Theory: Abstraction and Indefinite Extensibility." *British Journal for the Philosophy of Science* 54:59–91.
35. Shapiro, Stewart. 2004. "The Nature and Limits of Abstraction." *Philosophical Quarterly* 54:166–74.
36. Shapiro, Stewart. 2005. "Sets and Abstracts." *Philosophical Studies* 122:315–32.
37. Shapiro, Stewart, and Alan Weir. 1999. "New V, ZF and Abstraction." *Philosophia Mathematica* 7:293–321.
38. Tait, William. 1981. "Finitism." *The Journal of Philosophy* 78:524–46.

39. Tennant, Neil. 1987. *Anti-realism and Logic*. Oxford: Oxford University Press.
40. Van Heijenoort, Jean, ed. 1967. *From Frege to Gödel*. Cambridge, MA: Harvard University Press.
41. Van Heijenoort, Jean. 1967. "Logic as Calculus and Logic as Language." *Synthese* 17:324–30.
42. Whitehead, Alfred North, and Bertrand Russell. 1910. *Principia Mathematica 1*. Cambridge: Cambridge University Press.
43. Wright, Crispin. 2000. "Neo-Fregean Foundations for Real Analysis: Some Reflections on Frege's Constraint." *Notre Dame Journal of Formal Logic* 41:317–34.

Chapter 3
Applied Mathematics in the Sciences

Dale Jacquette

3.1 Pure and Applied Mathematics

The distinction between pure and applied mathematics is widely recognized in the philosophy of mathematics. There is nevertheless scant agreement about how precisely the distinction is to be drawn or what significance it should be understood to have. Among theorists who acknowledge the two categories, applied mathematics is often denigrated as less important, dignified, or valuable than pure mathematics.

Pure mathematics is not merely mathematics that is not applied. Nor, paradoxically is applied mathematics any and every use or application of mathematics. A system of mathematics concerning fluid mechanics is rightly classified as applied rather than pure, even if it is never actually put to use in any practical application; if, for example, it is worked out on paper but is never taken down from the shelf by an engineer. Moreover, using one branch of mathematics, such as set or group theory, to model another branch, such as ring theory or category theory, is in one sense an application of mathematics, but would generally still be considered part and parcel of pure mathematics, because it makes no contact with and is intended to have no reference to anything beyond mathematics.

We shall, accordingly, distinguish between internal and external applications of mathematics, respectively, within or outside of mathematics itself. We can then restrict the phrase "applied mathematics" to external or extra-mathematical applications that fall outside the realm of mathematics, and more positively to its uses to model, modify and control especially physical phenomena in the natural sciences. This is undoubtedly the sense in which the concept of applied mathematics is usually intended. Applied mathematics for present purposes thus means mathematical systems that are supposed to be externally or extra-mathematically applied to describe, predict or control physical phenomena. Applications of mathematics in a more general and nontechnical sense to other branches of mathematics are considered to fall within the category of pure mathematics. Where there is a potential for confusing

---

D. Jacquette (✉)
Universität Bern, Bern, BE, Switzerland
e-mail: dale.jacquette@philo.unibe.ch

M. Trobok et al. (eds.), *Between Logic and Reality*, Logic, Epistemology, and the Unity of Science 25, DOI 10.1007/978-94-007-2390-0_3,
© Springer Science+Business Media B.V. 2012

these two senses of applied mathematics, we shall speak of practical rather than purely formal applications of mathematics, as in theoretical physics and engineering, astronomy, chemistry, hydrology, biometrics, and other mathematicized sciences.

3.2 Plato's Philosophy of Mathematics and the Realm of Forms

Plato is the most venerable champion of pure mathematics who posits a distinct nonspatiotemoral realm of ideal abstract mathematical entities. In his dialogue the *Gorgias*, Plato deprecates applied mathematics as mere engineering or "mechanics", because it is a practice involving "action" (*praxis*) in the world of Becoming, in contrast with "speech" or reason (*logos*). Socrates describes mathematics as *logos*-related, like board games similarly involving formal relations, as relatively independent of those kinds of practical activities in which mathematics might be applied:

> ...there are other arts which achieve their whole effect by speech, and have no need of action—or very little—arithmetic, for example, and calculation and geometry and I would add games like backgammon and so on. In many of them speech and action play almost equal parts, but in many speech is the more important and is entirely responsible for the whole business and its result. (450c–d)

Later, Socrates adds:

> Yet if he chose to use big words about his function, like you and your friends, Callicles, he could make out a strong case and overwhelm you with reasons why everybody ought to be an engineer and no other profession is of the smallest importance. All the same you despise him and his art and use the term 'mechanic' as a term of contempt, and you would not hear of marrying your daughter to his son or taking his daughter to wife yourself. (512b)

Plato's reference to mechanics is significant, particularly if understood in a sufficiently general sense. The concept so construed seems to involve the application of mathematics in any practical or scientific purpose.

By reputation, we expect Plato to take this storied view of the relation between pure and applied mathematics. We know that for Plato it is only the eternal realm of the Ideas or Forms, the world of Being, where all mathematical entities and relations most properly reside, purified of any contamination with the changing world of mere appearance, that constitutes reality with a claim to value as the domain of knowledge. Applied mathematics by definition involves activities in the imperfect world of Becoming, where all is approximation and opinion, subjects at best of correct belief, rather than genuine knowing. The distinction between pure and applied mathematics neatly marks the major partition in Plato's metaphor of the divided line in the *Republic*, representing a progression of topics for the education of the guardian class in the ideal city-state, beginning with objects of perception and

3 Applied Mathematics in the Sciences

proceeding through applied and pure mathematics to the ascending ranks of Forms, and finally at the pinnacle to the Form of the Good.[1]

Thus, in the *Philebus*, Plato distinguishes hierarchically between pure and applied mathematics similarly in such a way as not only to place pure above applied mathematics, but to separate them into entirely different metaphysical categories with entirely different presuppositions of epistemic accessibility. Inquiring into the nature of the good life, Socrates and Protarchus have the following exchange concerning the nature of mathematics:

> SOCRATES: Suppose arithmetic, measurement and weighing were subtracted from all the sciences: the remainder of each science would be pretty trivial.
>
> PROTARCHUS: It would indeed.
>
> SOCRATES: In fact only speculation would be left, and the training of the senses by experience and experiment. We would have to use guesswork, which is commonly thought of as science, if practice succeeds in making it dependable.
>
> PROTARCHUS: Yes, that's bound to be all that's left ...
>
> SOCRATES: Look at ship-building, house-building and many other types of carpentry. As I see it, they use ruler, lathe, callipers, chalk-line and an ingenious tri-square.
>
> PROTARCHUS: Quite, Socrates; you're right ...
>
> SOCRATES: The most precise sciences, however, are those we recently called essential.
>
> PROTARCHUS: I suppose you mean arithmetic and the other sciences you mentioned along with it.
>
> SOCRATES: I do. Here again, however, Protarchus, oughtn't we to speak of two sets of sciences, not one? What do you think?
>
> PROTARCHUS: Which sets do you have in mind?
>
> SOCRATES: Take arithmetic first: shouldn't we distinguish between the common and the philosophical variety?
>
> PROTARCHUS: What's the criterion for distinguishing these two kinds of arithmetic?
>
> SOCRATES: The boundary between them is clearly visible, Protarchus. Some arithmeticians operate with unequal units: for example, they add two armies together, or two cows, or two things one of which might be the smallest and the other the largest thing in the world. Others, however, would never follow their example unless every unit, no matter how many there are, is taken to be identical to every other unit... We may take that statement of yours to be definitive and reliable. With that assurance, our response to cunning word-twisters is ...
>
> PROTARCHUS: What?
>
> SOCRATES: ...that there are two techniques of arithmetic, two techniques of measurement, and so on for many other related sciences, which have this duality despite having been allotted a common name. (55e1–57d10)

---

[1] Plato's myth of the divided line appears in *Republic* 509d–513e.

Plato in Socrates' name distinguishes between kinds of mathematics, different in their relative certainty and "purity". "Philosophical" types of mathematics are more certain and pure than their "common" countertypes, the latter of which are nevertheless useful in house and ship building, among other practical engineering applications. The mere fact that both types are popularly referred to as mathematics disguises the fact, as Plato sees things, that there are really two categories of arithmetic, calculation, and geometry—pure or philosophical and common or applied. Interestingly, Socrates in this context points to the fact that in common or applied mathematics the units involved in arithmetic are unequal, as when a large red apple and a small yellow apple are added together in a practical application of counting to arrive at the sum by which there are two apples. In the case of pure or philosophical arithmetic, by contrast, the units concerned as abstract timeless and changeless eternal entities, are altogether indistinguishable and in every way interchangeable. We see this in caveman stick figure notations for simple arithmetical relations, when we write, for example: $|| + ||| = |||||$.

The relation between pure and applied mathematics remains a difficulty in Plato's metaphysics. The answer, unfortunately, is not found in philosophically satisfactory terms anywhere in Plato's writings. Plato is the archetypal advocate of pure mathematics as a study of purely formal mathematical entities and their properties. When it comes to explaining the metaphysics of the one and the many, the relation between pure and applied mathematics in engineering, however, Plato has nothing more insightful or enlightening to offer than a handful of metaphors according to which spatiotemporal particulars "imitate" or "participate" in their corresponding Forms.[2] Lacking a clear and cogent analysis of imitation or participation, let alone of the "striving" to approximate an ideal of which Plato also speaks, we are left with no guidance as to the connection between pure and applied mathematics generally, or more specifically with respect to engineering and applied mathematics in the sciences. Whether or not we consider mechanics and other practitioners of common or applied mathematics in Plato's extended sense to be suitable prospective sons-in-law or fathers-in-law, we can agree with Plato off the bat that there exists a distinction between pure or philosophical and applied mathematics. There is mathematics as a purely formal discipline that exists in its own right independently of its usefulness or lack thereof, and applications of mathematics in which principles, theorems, and calculation methods are put to use in practical problem solving, in making change at the grocery store, building bridges and moon rockets.

The trouble is to understand how pure and applied mathematics are related. This is precisely where Plato's metaphysics lets us down by substituting myths, metaphors, and poetic analogies for sound theoretical explanation. Plato in a sense is not to be faulted for perversely withholding a straightforward account of the metaphysics linking pure and applied mathematics, or more generally for failing to explain how the Ideas or Forms of the world of Being are related to the

---

[2] The problems of imitation of, participation in, and striving to attain approximation to archetypal Platonic Forms are discussed by Allen [1], Lee [25], Nehamas [31] and Sweeney [44].

spatiotemporal particulars of the world of Becoming. He is not more forthcoming about the relation between pure mathematics and its applications to the particulars in empirical experience because the problem is among the most difficult if not ultimately intractable challenges for a realist metaphysics and philosophy of mathematics; yet there are compelling if not ultimately conclusive reasons for positing mathematical entities along with the Forms as abstract existents subsisting in a timeless realm of things distinct from the phenomenal order.

3.3 Mathematical Realism and Knowledge of the Ideal

The philosophical problems confronting Platonic mathematical realism have nowhere been more clearly identified than in Paul Benacerraf's landmark [6] essay, "Mathematical Truth". There Benacerraf raises in an especially trenchant way the epistemic dilemma of discovering and verifying truths about mathematical entities, given their imperceivability and causal inaccessibility. He maintains:

> It is my contention that two quite distinct kinds of concerns have separately motivated accounts of the nature of mathematical truth: (1) the concern for having a homogeneous semantical theory in which semantics for the propositions of mathematics parallel the semantics for the rest of the language, and (2) the concern that the account of mathematical truth mesh with a reasonable epistemology. It will be my general thesis that almost all accounts of the concept of mathematical truth can be identified with serving one or another of these masters at the expense of the other. Since I believe further that both concerns must be met by any adequate account, I find myself deeply dissatisfied with any package of semantics and epistemology that purports to account for truth and knowledge both within and outside of mathematics. For, as I will suggest, accounts of truth that treat mathematical and nonmathematical discourse in relevantly similar ways do so at the cost of leaving it unintelligible how we can have any mathematical knowledge whatsoever; whereas those which attribute to mathematical propositions the kinds of truth conditions we can clearly know to obtain, do so at the expense of failing to connect these conditions with any analysis of the sentences which shows how the assigned conditions are conditions of their truth. (403–4)

Benacerraf projects a logical dilemma whereby the philosophy of mathematics can meet either one but not both of its semantic and epistemological obligations. He claims that the dilemma arises for virtually any complete philosophy of mathematics, but he devotes most of his attention to Platonic realism as the most widely accepted metaphysics of mathematics.

Statistically speaking, Benacerraf is surely right to identify the default ontology of mathematics for most mathematicians and philosophers of mathematics as some form of Platonic realism. Mathematicians typically consider themselves to be engaged in the task of discovering and elaborating truths about a domain of abstract ideal entities, consisting of the mathematical objects whose properties and interrelations it is their task to articulate and rigorously demonstrate, primarily, though not exclusively, by the methods of formal axiomatic proof. Platonic realism is furthermore a prime target for Benacerraf's assault against standard approaches to the philosophy of mathematics. By positing an ideal abstract mathematical realm, Platonic realism characteristically places mathematical entities outside the reach at least of all the usual epistemic modes of access that standardly involve some sort of causal interaction with objects of knowledge in order both to determine their existence and properties. We can make no direct contact with abstract or ideal mathematical entities in Platonic heaven, because we cannot perceive them as we can in the case of physical objects belonging to the empirical sciences. They are instead, as Plato himself repeatedly insists, objects of reason, discourse, or *logos*.

There are philosophers still today who accept Plato's elitist conclusion that applied mathematics should be disregarded or relegated to secondary status relative to pure or philosophical mathematics, and that only pure mathematics, redundantly so designated, should be considered to be mathematics in the true and proper sense. We might also come to agree that applied mathematics as the application of mathematics is not mathematics itself. In that case there is mathematics, and there are uses of mathematics that are not themselves mathematics, in somewhat the same way, by analogy, that the use of a hammer is not itself a hammer. If we adopt such a stance, moreover, then we might not avoid the problem of understanding how mathematics is applied, but we could thereby minimally circumvent the need to explain the semantics, metaphysics and epistemology of applied mathematics, whatever it finally turns out to be, as a kind or category or branch of mathematics properly conceived.

To fully comprehend the philosophy of mathematics, where such a distinction is observed, it is not necessary to understand the nature, possibility, conditions or limitations of applied mathematics, however independently interesting the requirements of applied mathematics might also be. If the problem of applied mathematics rears its head within the philosophy of mathematics, consequently, as a philosophical problem involving concepts specifically of mathematics, it arises in that case as a set of questions concerning the relation between pure mathematics and its applications as two different things. The same is true regardless of whether a Platonic realist or non-Platonic nonrealist mathematical ontology is adopted. The outlook for a satisfactory philosophy of mathematics is complicated in that event in the following way. We must then know what mathematics is, what applied mathematics is, and how the two are related. Importantly, on the other hand, however, we are spared the need to explicate applied mathematics as itself any part of mathematics.

A muted note of hope for the success of such a project is sounded when Benacerraf qualifies his skepticism to "almost all accounts of the concept of mathematical truth". He thereby leaves open the possibility, however remote, that some philosophy of mathematics might yet be proposed to satisfy the twin goals of providing both an adequate general semantics and epistemology of mathematics. While his conclusion is negative, Benacerraf's highly influential argument has posed a problem for other theorists in the philosophy of mathematics to try to solve. Benacerraf's incisive statement of the complexly interrelated semantic, epistemic, and ultimately metaphysical problems to be addressed by an adequate philosophy of mathematics has invited a wide variety of responses on the part of philosophers attempting to fit together an appropriate sense of the nature of mathematical entities with a theory of knowledge and criteria of discovery and verification for the justification of mathematical truths.

We might mention in this context, among the scores of contemporary philosophers of mathematics who have taken Benacerraf's problem as the explicit point of departure for their semantic-metaphysical-epistemic analyses of the nature of mathematical entities and the relation of mathematical methods to the determination of mathematical truths, and who in the process have collectively ventured very different kinds of solutions, Michael Jubien, Michael Resnik, Penelope Maddy, Hartry Field, Charles S. Chihara, and Stewart Shapiro. We shall briefly consider the advantages and disadvantages of some of these interesting recent efforts, concluding that in one way or another they each fail to provide a fully satisfactory philosophy of mathematics. Then we shall take up Benacerraf's challenge by proposing a very different ontology of mathematical entities that makes it possible to satisfy both of Benacerraf's desiderata by providing both a semantics for the truth of mathematical propositions and theorems that meshes seamlessly with a general semantics and facilitates an epistemology of mathematical discovery, justification by intuition and demonstrative proof, and knowledge.

3.4 Critique of Standard Solutions to the Problems of Applied Mathematics

Among the problems confronting a philosophy of applied mathematics there must prominently be included the following. The adequacy of any such theory depends in large part on its ability to provide satisfactory answers to these questions:

a. How are pure and applied mathematics to be distinguished?
b. How are pure and applied mathematics semantically, ontically or metaphysically, and epistemically related?
c. How is it possible for pure mathematics to describe the world of physical phenomena?
d. How is it possible for applied mathematics to facilitate scientific research, hypothesis and testing of previously unknown and unpredetermined physical phenomena, and to facilitate their explanation, prediction, manipulation and control in practical activities and scientific engineering?

We shall consider the strengths and infirmities of frequently discussed philosophies of mathematics with respect to the above problems concerning the nature of applied mathematics and the relation between pure and applied mathematics. The examination of contemporary approaches to the philosophy of mathematics in explaining applied mathematics is meant to be representative of some of the most important and influential theories rather than exhaustive or complete.

Limitations of space make it necessary to restrict synopses of most of these well-established approaches to the philosophy of mathematics and in particular to the problems of applied mathematics to a mere caricature. So, in any case, they are likely to seem to their defenders. They may nevertheless be of use in highlighting the differences from the alternative concept of mathematical entity to be proposed. Some of the following philosophical theories of mathematics are problematic on their own merits, while others are disadvantaged more particularly with respect to their treatment of the relation between pure and applied mathematics, in responding to the four main problems of applied mathematics.

3.4.1 Platonism or Platonic Mathematical Realism (Plato, Frege, Gödel, Quine)

As we have seen, *Platonism* or *Platonic realism* is the default ontology for mathematics. Historically, it has been the most widely and enthusiastically accepted.[3] The attraction of the theory is that it posits an ideal abstract realm of mathematical entities to which mathematical properties and relations can be truly predicated. When we say, for example, that 3 is a prime number, Platonic realism interprets the pronouncement as implying or presupposing that there exists a timeless unchanging ideal but no less real abstract number 3 that has the mathematical property of being prime, being evenly divisible only by 1 and itself. The analogy of an object possessing a property is thereby extended from physical entities having certain physical properties and standing in physical relations to other physical entities to an imperceivable world of mathematics.

The most obvious pinch in Platonism, as dramatized in Benacerraf's dilemma, is its commitment to a causally epistemically inaccessible realm of ideal abstract mathematical entities. Benacerraf's dilemma is implicitly directed specifically against Plato's philosophy of mathematics. Plato's theory provides us with a semantics that is parallel in every way to the semantics for the reference and predication of properties to ordinary physical objects, but leaves us without a satisfying comparable epistemology by which mathematical entities and their properties can be known. It is unclear how we are supposed to be able to learn about the properties of objects that we cannot see and with which we cannot otherwise empirically interact.

More importantly, the relations between abstract entities and physical phenomena are generally obscure. Plato provides in lieu of explanations only mythic-poetic, analogical, or metaphorical ways of describing the connection between mathematical Ideas or Forms and physical spatiotemporal phenomena. Where we would like to know exactly how abstract mathematical entities are supposed to be related to the objects of experience to which mathematics is applied in counting, measurement, calculation, and engineering, in theory and practice, there all that Plato has to offer

---

[3] See Balaguer [4] and Azzouni [3].

is the conceit of a physical entity imitating or participating in or striving to make itself as like as possible to its corresponding ideal archetypal Form. The two realms of pure abstract mathematics and applied concrete physical entities to which applied mathematics is applied in theory and practice seem to be so separate and distinct that there is no bridge linking them, and no obvious way as a result to understand how the properties of abstract mathematical entities can have anything to do with the properties of concrete physical entities. At best it is unclear how positing a realm of ideal abstract mathematical entities to which of necessity we can have no causal epistemic access can help to explain the success of applied mathematics in the spatiotemporal world. The specific relation between abstract mathematical entities and the concrete physical entities of applied mathematics remains abstruse, and consequently goes no distance toward explaining the possibility of effectively applying mathematics externally to nonmathematical things.

3.4.2 Conceptualism (Ockham)

William of Ockham is well-known as a nominalist in the medieval metaphysical controversy with Platonic realism. *Nominalism* considered only in and itself, however, as the doctrine that there are no universals and that things are only of the same kind in the sense that they have been given the same name for the convenience of thought and language, appears arbitrary unless a nonuniversalist reason for assigning the same name or predicate to different things can be justified.

Ockham as a nominalist is also a *conceptualist*. In the *Summa Logicae I*, he adopts a theory of the common naming of things by which their predicate names do not denote universals but concepts in the mind, which Ockham speaks of as *second intentions of the soul*. When I use the name of a putative mathematical object, such as the number π, according to Ockham, the name is not arbitrary, for example, in speaking of the ratio between the circumference and diameter of more than one circle, nor does it refer to a universal or ideal abstract mathematical entity, but to a certain concept or intention in the mind, which is to say as something psychological. The possibility of explaining applied mathematics is thereby raised. We can then perhaps try to understand the effectiveness of applied mathematics as resulting from the way we think about the structures and relations among physical entities in empirical experience to which we assign the names of mathematical entities and properties, in marked contrast with Plato's theory of Forms, as relations among occupants of the same physical spatiotemporal world.[4]

The difficulty for such a theory, and a potentially devastating one for conceptual nominalism, is what might be called the problem of the subjective disunity of mathematical entities. If the number π is a psychological concept, then there must be a different number π, numerically distinct, if we can even make sense of that concept within a conceptualist framework, from the number π that any other

---

[4] Ockham [32]. See also Boehmer [8].

thinker entertains in thought. Such a conclusion seems absurd, and if anything the implication makes the possibility of applied mathematics by many thinkers equally if not more mysterious than it is for Platonic realism.

3.4.3 Formalism (Hilbert)

The limitations of Platonism, and the fact that so much of mathematics involves the gamelike formal rule-governed manipulation of mathematical symbolism, has suggested the possibility of another kind of nonconceptualistic nominalism that is often associated with David Hilbert's *formalism* in the philosophy of mathematics. The idea is that there is no reality to mathematics beyond the formalism implied by the rules for transforming strings of mathematical syntax into other definite strings. The activity of mathematics is thus compared to that of playing a board game, and with no further significance as to its meaning or referents, whether ideal and abstract, conceptual and psychological, or something else yet again, than that which attaches to the tokens of games like chess or checkers or backgammon or go.[5]

The difficulty with formalism in efforts to understand the nature of applied mathematics is that rule-governed syntax game-playing makes mathematical relations self-contained. Game-playing generally might be productive by virtue of sharpening a mathematician's strategic skills or rule-following discipline, in the way that playing marathon sessions of Monopoly^{TM} might benefit the sales objectives of an ambitious real estate agent. Board games considered in and of themselves by definition nevertheless have no direct applicability to real life, as we would soon discover if we tried to make a downpayment on a hotel on Atlantic Avenue or Boardwalk with the play money included in the game, or use the Get Out of Jail Free card if we happened to be arrested in the process of trying to become millionaires. A game is perhaps an appropriate model or metaphor for pure mathematics, which in turn might have been all that Hilbert was finally concerned with understanding. Using mathematics properly to build a bridge or skyscraper on which the lives of thousands of people depend on the other hand does not seem to be as gamelike an activity. This is especially true in the sense that we cannot simply contrive whatever consistent (or paraconsistent) set of rules we like with the same sort of freedom by which we devise games like chess and go for amusement. There are external constraints imposed on applied mathematics, as we might say, by the world, that make the relation between physical reality and applied mathematics less capricious than game-playing, and that for the same reason make the effectiveness of applied mathematics in predicting and controlling events in the real world even more challenging to understand.

---

[5] Hilbert [19, 20] and Jacquette [23, pp. 85–89].

3.4.4 Conditionalism (If-Thenism) (Putnam)

Hilary Putnam in several sources has endorsed what has come to be known as *conditionalism* or *if-thenism*. The idea of conditionalism is that the necessity of mathematics is to be explained not in terms of an abstract Platonic realm of ideal abstract mathematical entities, but rather by virtue of the logical necessity of deductive inference. The necessity of mathematics is thereby itself made conditional. If certain axioms or principles of mathematics are true, then certain consequences would logically necessarily follow.[6]

Like the other forms of nominalism or anti-Platonism that we have considered, conditionalism has much to recommend it. The theory seizes upon a recognizable feature of mathematical theory and practice by which it proposes more generally to explain the nature of all mathematics. We do have concepts, as Ockham rightly observes, that enter into the construction and use of mathematics; mathematics, as formalists like Hilbert would have it, is rather like formal game-playing; and mathematics, in the way that Putnam emphasizes, involves a conditional commitment to axioms and other first principles which it then relates by logical inference and typically with deductive necessity to theorems and other kinds of mathematical consequences in mathematical reasoning and formal proofs and demonstrations.

The trouble with Putnam's conditionalism from the standpoint of understanding the philosophical connection between pure and applied mathematics is that, while applied mathematics might reasonably be construed as among the extra-pure-mathematical consequences of pure mathematics, its applications, in mathematical physics or biometrics, for example, do not hold with the same sort of deductive logical necessity as do the consequences of assumptions validly derived from axioms within pure mathematics. There is again something arbitrary about the choice of conditions from which any number of different systems of mathematics might conditionally follow if such assumptions were to be made. Applied mathematics, hard at work in the real world of mechanics, engineering, and other practical activities, does not seem to enjoy the same luxury of explaining its effectiveness as the result of the necessity that holds between any arbitrarily considered axioms and their logical consequences. It lacks the freedom that prevails in the case of whatever rules might be chosen by which to play any number of different purely mathematical games in a formalist philosophy of mathematics where the syntax of mathematical languages are likened to otherwise meaningless tokens moved about in rule-governed ways on a gameboard. In this respect, formalism and conditionalism are philosophically not far apart, and might be regarded as two different ways of expressing the same limited insights about the nature of pure mathematics in its relation to applied mathematics.

---

[6] Putnam [35, 36].

3.4.5 Intuitionism (Brouwer, Heyting)

There are many forms of *intuitionism*. Some but not all explicitly acknowledge an intellectual debt to Kant's thesis that arithmetic has its origins in the experience of successions of events in time and geometry in the experience of objects in space, where space and time alike in Kant's transcendental aesthetic are construed as pure forms of intuition. As a rule, intuitionists agree that mathematical propositions are not to be considered as true or false, even hypothetically, unless they have been first respectively rigorously proved or disproved. One of the well-known consequences of an intuitionistic logic and philosophy of mathematics is therefore to deny certain classical principles of deduction, such as the rules of excluded middle and double negation. For the same reasons, by virtue of adhering to a strict canon of protocols for mathematical demonstration, most intuitionists do not accept the truth of propositions implying the existence of infinite or transfinite numbers or sets, nor are they willing to countenance mathematical proofs that could in principle require an infinite or transfinite number of steps.[7]

The main objection to intuitionism in the present context is that it makes no special provision for applied mathematics. Intuitionism is more of a methodological inhibitor of mathematical excess and a principled restriction to proceeding only on the basis of what has actually been rigorously proven or disproven by accepted mathematical techniques of derivation. It in effect curtails the enthusiasms of Platonic realism and encourages more scrupulous epistemic caution in mathematics by not assuming that mathematical entities and their properties and hence mathematical truths exist independently of the bounds of extant demonstrated mathematical knowledge. Restraining the pretensions of Platonistic mathematics, however, does not help to explain how mathematics comes to be so effectively applied in such disciplines as mathematical physics, astronomy, chemistry, and the like.

3.4.6 Manifest Realism or Physicalism (Maddy)

The recent development of a theory that mathematical entities, sets, in particular, are empirically perceivable has been explored by Penelope Maddy in *Realism in Mathematics* and *Naturalism in Mathematics*.[8] This is a bold, but also puzzling and in some ways vague theory, that has undergone significant transformations in these two books, and whose strengths and weaknesses it is beyond the scope of the present inquiry to present in detail or with any real justice. Suffice it to say that the proposal seems to suffer from the counterpart of the subjective disunity with which Ockham's conceptualist nominalism has been charged, and which might therefore be labeled the problem of the objective disunity of mathematical entities. If a set

---

[7] See, inter alia, Brouwer [9] and Heyting [18]. A useful introduction to Brouwer's intuitionism in its formal and philosophical aspects is found in Van Atten [45].

[8] Maddy [26–28].

is perceivable here at this place in the physical world, but also and equally in at least another place, as Maddy's metaphysics would appear to allow, then there is a parallel problem for Maddy as for Ockham. It is the problem of understanding how the same mathematical objects can be supposed to exist simultaneously in several different places and how they are all supposed to be related, whether objectively or physically as in Maddy, or subjectively or psychologically as in Ockham's doctrine that mathematical objects are concepts that can presumably exist simultaneously in the minds of several different thinkers.

3.4.7 Fictionalism (Field)

Hartry Field's *fictionalism* seeks to avoid ontic commitment to mathematical entities, regardless of their metaphysics, by denying that there are any mathematical truths or any true mathematical propositions. Field does not dispute the popular semantic assumption that the truth of a mathematical proposition is to be understood as the existence of a corresponding mathematical fact in which an existent mathematical object possesses the corresponding property attributed to it by the proposition.

By denying the existence of mathematical truths he hopes to cut off questions about the existence of mathematical entities at their semantic root. The innovation in Field's theory is to adopt a Quinean instrumental account of the theories that together with a base mathematics such as Zermelo-Frankl set theory supplemented with Ur-elements (ZFU) entailing a certain useful conclusion φ of mathematicized natural science N can be determined to follow from N alone.[9] Charles S. Chihara, in his recent book, *A Structural Account of Mathematics*, has nevertheless raised a serious difficulty challenging Field's reliance on what he calls the conservation principle. The principle in effect allows mathematics to serve an instrumental role in deriving the propositions of natural science, from which it then drops out as inessential. It follows, as Field has argued in *Science Without Numbers, Realism, Mathematics, and Modality*, and numerous articles, that from the standpoint of the useful applications of mathematics in science we can regard mathematical objects as fictitious in merely facilitating derivations of the truths of science which they serve in no way to constitute:

Field's conservation principle

$$ZF + U \wedge N \models \varphi \to N \models \varphi$$
$$M \wedge N \models \varphi \to N \models \varphi$$
(CP)

The difficulty for Field, according to Chihara among other critics, is in justifying the conservation principle (CP). Field's efforts to establish the principle seem to require that he accept the truth of at least some metalogical theorems needed to derive (CP),

---

[9] Field [14–17].

contrary to the spirit of fictionalism as a general philosophy of mathematics. He proposes to justify it by keeping it at arms length through *reductio* reasoning, but all such attempts to date do not appear to provide a genuinely nominalistic proof of (CP). Thus far, Field has only sketched how the proof might proceed, but has not yet delivered the argument. He nevertheless needs the principle, as the key to upholding the claim that a physical theory can produce all of its salient results without the benefit of a consistent mathematics with which it is otherwise apparently allied and from which its formal implications seem to derive. If Field's fictionalism cannot be consistently reconstructed, and in particular if there is no noncircular genuinely nominalistic proof of (CP), then the theory does not provide an adequate solution to the problem of understanding the relation between pure and applied mathematics.[10]

3.4.8 Structuralism (Resnik, Shapiro)

A variation on fictionalism is propounded by Michael Resnik, Stewart Shapiro, and others, in several forms as *structuralism* or structuralist philosophy of mathematics. Structuralism emphasizes the mathematical preoccupation with formal structures, and offers to explain mathematical truth in terms of the structural features of mathematical syntax and the formalisms of mathematical sentences in mathematical languages. Applied mathematics is then supposed to be understood in terms of the isomorphisms or approximations of the structures of physical phenomena to which applied mathematics is applied to the formal mathematical structures in the theorems of pure mathematics.[11]

The major drawback that invalidates structuralism as an adequate philosophy of mathematics considered on its own terms is that formal syntactical morphologies, at least as they usually appear in standard expressions of mathematical formulas, are not uniquely distinctive or characteristic. Many very different mathematical relations are expressed by syntactically structurally identical mathematical sentences. The Pythagorean theorem, for example, $a^2 + b^2 = c^2$, has precisely the same syntactical structural features as unlimitedly many other mathematical sentences that have nothing whatsoever to do with triangles or geometry. Similarly for such sentences of applied mathematics as $f = ma$ (force = mass × acceleration) or $e = mc^2$ (energy = mass × the square of the (constant) speed of light). These two formulas, in particular, might either be said to be structurally identical or not identical, depending on whether or not "a" expressing the acceleration value in $f = ma$ can be understood as the square of some numerical value; as of course at least trivially it always can. One of the theoretical limitations of structuralism is thus that it does not provide a decisive way of correctly determining whether or not the sentence of applied mathematical physics "$f = ma$" is or is not structurally identical to such another sentence of applied mathematical physics as "$e = mc^2$".

---

[10] See Chihara [12, especially pp. 108–13, 317–48].
[11] Resnik [38–40] and Shapiro [41, 42].

3 Applied Mathematics in the Sciences   43

We are given no guidance by the theory, in this among other ways, as to whether the exponent in $e = mc^2$ is an essential or superficial accidental component of the formula's syntactical structure.

The only way to avoid such exact structural isomorphisms particularly in applied if not also and equally in pure mathematics, and the uninformativeness as to mathematical content and truth they imply, is to suppose that there is a deeper level of formal structural analysis of mathematical sentences in which these equivocations of structural properties do not obtain. Thus far, however, no structuralist has come forward with a deeper analysis of the mathematical structures of mathematical sentences than those that already appear in standard mathematical languages, where the possibility of confusions among superficially identical syntactical structuralisms abound. Nor is it clear precisely how structural isomorphisms between mathematical languages and physical phenomena are supposed to be sufficient to explain the possibility and effectiveness of applied mathematics in the natural sciences. Structuralists collectively seem blithely unaware that there might be any sort of problem here. The mere fact that a sentence of mathematics exhibits a structural isomorphism with a physical phenomenon does not begin to explain how the sentence in question might make it possible to predict or exert engineering control over events within the empirical world. How is structural isomorphism in and of itself supposed to be able to make any of these things possible?

3.4.9 Constructibility Theory (Chihara)

A more sophisticated form of fictionalism and structuralism is developed by Chihara in what he designates as *constructibility theory*. Chihara denies the common assumption that mathematical sentences must be true in order to express useful mathematical information, and that in order to be true or to lend themselves to practical everyday and scientific applications mathematical sentences must refer to existent mathematical entities.

Chihara's constructibility theory construes mathematics as a system of formal principles for syntactically constructing certain kinds of open sentence tokens. Instead of interpreting the mathematical sentence $2 + 3 = 5$ as the true universally quantified sentence, $\forall x[2x + 3x = 5x]$, Chihara substitutes for the universal quantifier a constructibility quantifier "C", as in $Cx[2x + 3x = 5x]$. The meaning of the constructibility quantified formula is then explicated as an open-ended sequence of open sentences, $2x + 3x = 5x$, $2y + 3y = 5y$, $2z + 3z = 5z, \ldots$, none of which, as open sentences, is true (or false). An open sentence S is satisfiable when it is such that it can be completed by the insertion of terms to create a corresponding closed sentence S^*. Closed sentence S^* is true or false, and makes ostensible reference to specific objects with mathematical properties that are ultimately reducible to or constructible from such concepts as equinumerosity. S^*, however, immediately upon completion or satisfaction, is not a sentence of pure mathematics, but is instead what Chihara follows Frege in calling a *mixed sentence*. If Chihara's analysis succeeds, then there is never any need to consider the sentences of pure mathematics as true or consequently as making reference to any mathematical objects.[12]

One source of difficulty in Chihara's constructibility theory is that it seems to require the truth, and not merely the constructibility, of a metatheoretical mathematical sentence that ascribes higher-order cardinalities to the constructible open sentences by which the constructibility quantifier **C** is interpreted. The cardinality of the list of open sentences that are successively constructible even as possibilities in unpacking the meaning of the constructibility quantifier would appear to be no greater than and hence restricted in application to subinfinitary enumerations. We are supposed to have learned from Church's theorem that reducing the universal quantification even to a potentially infinite specification of cases, as in Wittgenstein's account of the quantifiers in the *Tractatus Logico-Philosophicus*, can never succeed in capturing the meaning of "all" in a universalized expression, unless we also circularly add that these are "all" of the possible cases, thereby scotching the reduction.

Thus, the following sentence must be true and not merely constructible in Chihara's constructibility theory Ct. As such, in the extensional semantic framework to which Chihara is committed, but inconsistent with the theory's intent, the sentence must after all make reference to mathematical entities:

$$Ct \models [Ct \rightarrow [Con(x) \wedge Con(y) \wedge Con(z) \wedge \ldots] \wedge Card\{x, y, z, \ldots\} \geq \aleph_0] \quad (P)$$

As it stands, (P) is an open sentence, but in that form it is insufficient for the requisite cardinality of Ct, unless it is not merely constructible in but true of Ct, or at least of Ct's metatheory. Nor does it help to regard the language of Chihara's theory as supporting the mere constructibility of such open sentences as $x \geq y^{\aleph_0}$.

The trouble is that Chihara wants to proceed constructively from minimal syntax combinations through elementary number theory via such relations as one-one-pairing and equinumerosity step by step eventually to the further reaches of higher mathematics. If that is how mathematics is supposed constructively to proceed, how and at what stage of construction do we arrive at an interpretation for the term "$\aleph_0$"? (Whitehead and Russell in *Principia Mathematica* cut the Gordion knot here by helping themselves to at least one denumerably infinite set via the Axiom of Infinity.)

If (P) is made true by an internal rather than external application of Ct, where the open sentence (P) constructible in Ct needs for relevance sake to be satisfied also by Ct itself, then (P*) is not a true mixed sentence closure of (P) for an appropriate choice of open sentences constructible in Ct. Rather, by virtue of being satisfied by a higher level mathematical theory, Ct, (P*) will presumably constitute a purely mathematical truth. If (P*) does not represent such a metatheoretical mathematical truth about Chihara's Ct, then it is hard to see how the theory can possibly be

---

[12] Chihara [12, pp. 107–8, 163–217]. Also Chihara [11].

adequate to guarantee the constructibility of a sufficient supply of open sentences to cover the purely structural properties of all of classical infinitary and transfinitary mathematics.

Ironically, this is the same sort of criticism now leveled against Chihara's constructibility theory that Chihara has raised against Field's fictionalism. Just as Field seems unable adequately to defend the conservation principle without presupposing the truth of certain metamathematical principles, which he is at pains everywhere in his nominalist philosophy of mathematics to deny, so similarly Chihara is apparently committed to the truth rather than the mere constructibility of principle (P) in order to secure the possibility of constructibility theory's extension to infinite and transfinite mathematics. If Chihara's constructibility account of mathematics is supposed to be strictly finitist, or if the cardinality of constructibility theory is something that, as in Wittgenstein's picture theory of meaning, is supposed to be structurally shown rather than said, Chihara has not acknowledged these implications or made provision for them within his analysis of the applications of mathematics. Unsurprisingly, perhaps, Chihara's constructibility theory combining fictionalism with structuralism inherits the limitations of both theories. The constructibility account in particular does not avoid the problem of understanding the plurality of structural isomorphisms within and outside of mathematical syntax, or of how the mere isomorphism holding between the syntax of a given mathematical expression and a physical state of affairs in the spatiotemporal world enables a mathematical theorem or principle to be applied to identically structured empirical phenomena.[13]

3.4.10 Logicism (Frege, Russell) (Honorable Mention)

We shall give logicism only a cursory consideration. The proposal that all of classical mathematics might be reduced to principles of logic, at least in its original forms in Frege and Whitehead and Russell, is generally believed to have been defeated by the limiting metatheorems of Gödel, Church, and Rosser. The early formulations of logicism in any case were never truly logicist in the first place, but made use of such extra-logical principles, among others, as the Axiom of Infinity, together with the axioms of set theory whose status as propositions of logic is problematic if not question-begging in the context of advancing a logicist reduction. Merely using logical notation to formulate mathematical propositions in and of itself is not enough to reduce mathematics to logic. Logicism, finally, with respect to the problems in view, offers no special provision for applied mathematics. In Frege and Whitehead and Russell, especially, logicism is not essentially different from a Platonic realist philosophy of mathematics from which it acquires all the same semantic, ontic and epistemic difficulties and limitations.

---

[13] I offer a more extensive criticism of Chihara's constructibility theory in my Jacquette [24] review of Chihara [12].

3.5 Inherence Philosophy of Mathematics

The failure of standard philosophical theories of mathematics to explain the relation between pure and applied mathematics should naturally incline us to seek elsewhere for adequate solutions to the four problems we have identified. We now propose an Aristotelian *inherence* metaphysics, according to which a universal mathematical property nominalized as a mathematical entity exists if and only if it inheres in an existent physical phenomenon.

The orientation and priorities with which the philosophy of mathematics is approached make an enormous difference in the kinds of theories that are found acceptable or unacceptable. If a theorist is most convinced of and impressed with the universality, aprioricity and logical necessity of mathematical theorems, then it will be reasonable to see Platonic realism as the best mathematical ontology, despite its epistemic liabilities. We have been addressing a different set of problems, making an adequate explanation of the possibility and nature of applied mathematics the first order of business for the philosophy of mathematics, while hopefully not losing sight of the features of mathematics that standard theories have given explanatory precedence over other aspects of mathematics. Beginning as we have with the problems for a satisfactory account of applied mathematics and of how pure mathematics relates to its applications, offers a different and in some ways more pragmatic perspective on the strengths and weaknesses of traditional concepts in the philosophy of mathematics. We have seen the difference that prioritizing an understanding of applied mathematics makes in the criticism of the received theories presented above, and in what follows we observe more positively the rather different kinds of theory such a perspective affords in developing an Aristotelian inherence philosophy of mathematics.

It is disconcerting, in a way, that, whereas Platonism is often counterposed to Aristotelianism in other branches of philosophy, in the theory of universals, metaphysics generally, epistemology, ethics, and theory of the arts, there has been slight attention to the potential for an Aristotelian inherence philosophy of mathematics to stand in sharp opposition to Platonic realism. If overlooking Aristotelianism in philosophy of mathematics is not a mere historical accident, and if reasons are sought for the fact that Aristotelian inherentism is not among the traditional theories frequently discussed along with Platonism, formalism, intuitionism, and the rest, it might be that Aristotle's metaphysics of secondary substances (forms with a small "f") inhering or embodied and embedded in primary substances, has been thought to be inadequate to account for the universality, aprioricity, or necessity of mathematics, or for such classical mathematical implications as its commitment to actual as opposed to merely potential infinity, and to infinite and transfinite cardinals.

We shall later consider and propose answers to such objections. First, we note that Aristotle himself in the *Physics* seems to deny the possibility of an inherence philosophy of mathematics by virtue of arguing that mathematics cannot be the same as mathematical physics. He explains:

> The next point to consider is how the mathematician differs from the student of nature; for natural bodies contain surfaces and volumes, lines and points, and these are the subject-matter of mathematics...Now the mathematician, though he too treats of these things, nevertheless does not treat of them as the limits of a natural body; nor does he consider the attributes indicated as the attributes of such bodies. That is why he separates them; for in thought they are separable from motion, and it makes no difference, nor does any falsity result, if they are separated. The holders of the theory of Forms do the same, though they are not aware of it; for they separate the objects of natural science, which are less separable than those of mathematics. This becomes plain if one tries to state in each of the two cases the definitions of the things and of their attributes. Odd and even, straight and curved, and likewise number, line, and figure, do not involve motion; not so flesh and bone and man—these are defined like snub nose, not like curved. (193b23–194a6)

Aristotle acknowledges a distinction between pure and applied mathematics. He distinguishes between mathematics and mathematical physics on the grounds that as disciplines pure mathematics concerns itself with mathematical concepts abstracted from the world of nature. Mathematicians, unlike physicists or "students of nature", do not speak of round apples or oranges, but of roundness, circularity, and the like. While the theory and language of mathematics are different from those of physics, however, it does not follow that mathematical entities, properties and relations exist independently of the physical world.

This is precisely the view to which Aristotle is committed by virtue of denying the existence of Forms except insofar as definitions or secondary substances inhere in primary substances. In the classical metaphysical dispute between Plato and Aristotle, Plato's theory of Forms implies that an abstract universal Form of Horse exists in the world of Being even if there are no particular horses in the phenomenal world of Becoming. Aristotle in contrast holds that there is no secondary substance or non-Platonic form (with a small "f") of *horse* unless there are at least some actually existent flesh and blood primary substance horses in which the secondary substance *horse* inheres. The same is now said as part of the present proposal with respect to mathematical properties nominalized as mathematical entities insofar as they inhere in the empirical world of physical phenomena.

To consider the implications of an inherence metaphysics of mathematics, we shall distinguish between applicable "pure" mathematics and inapplicable pure mathematics. Applicable "pure" mathematics is the formal theory of that part of mathematics that deals with nominalized mathematical properties inhering or embodied and embedded in the actual world, that are, just as Aristotle says, abstracted theoretically and in the languages of mathematics from the physical things in which they inhere. Inapplicable pure mathematics, by contrast, is that part of standardly recognized mathematics that putatively describes mathematical entities, properties and relations, that do not inhere in the natural world and by definition are therefore extra-mathematically inapplicable. We shall say that inapplicable pure mathematics is akin to what W.V.O. Quine has described as "recreational" mathematics.[14] Inapplicable pure mathematics can be understood formalistically, as mere

---

[14] Quine [37, p. 400] speaks of the higher reaches of set theory as a "mathematical recreation...without ontological rights".

formal games involving the manipulation of symbolic tokens that do not correspond to any existent mathematical entities, properties or relations. They are formal languages that extend the legitimate formulations of mathematical languages beyond those that rightfully describe nominalizations of mathematical properties that inhere in physical reality, and to which such mathematical systems properly apply.

Since inapplicable pure mathematics is inapplicable, there is no need to explain its applicability, and hence no problem of understanding the nature of applied mathematics where such systems are concerned. We accordingly devote most of our attention first and foremost to applicable "pure" mathematics, where, as previously suggested, the scare quotes indicate that mathematical languages describe formal properties that on the present Aristotelian account inhere in the physical world. They are "pure" in an attenuated Aristotelian sense, not in the manner of Platonic realism, but only in that they are considered from a mathematical perspective as abstracted from the physical world of primary substances in which the mathematical entities, properties and relations they describe and about which they theorize, inhere.

3.5.1 Applicable "Pure" Mathematics—Consequences for the Philosophy of Applied Mathematics

A. There is an exact subsumption of that part of "pure" mathematics capable of being applied to physical phenomena in the natural sciences, and what is otherwise designated, even from a Platonic realist perspective, as applied mathematics. All "pure" mathematics capable of being applied to natural phenomena is indistinguishable from applied mathematics in an Aristotelian inherence philosophy of mathematics.

Mathematics in this sense just is applied or applicable mathematics, even if it is "pure" in that its principles are abstracted from language explicitly making reference to the world of nature. The substantial part of mathematics that an inherence theory comprehends includes all of (at least potentially infinitary) arithmetic, geometry, algebra, calculus, set theory, group and category theory, and much else besides. This hefty fragment of applicable "pure" mathematics is coextensive with applied mathematics as traditionally conceived. There is no difference between "pure" and applied mathematics in an Aristotelian inherence philosophy of mathematics, there is only mathematics, concerning the formal properties that inhere in the physical phenomena in which mathematical properties are embodied and embedded and to which mathematical theorems apply in everyday and scientific practice. This is part of the inherence theory answer to problem (a) (B)–(D) below further explicate the solution.

B. The inherence theory answer to problem (b) is divided into three topics.

(i) *Semantic relation*

The semantic connection between applicable "pure" and applied mathematics on the inherentist conception as a result is that the two sets of terms refer identically to the nominalized mathematical properties that inhere or are embodied and embedded in the physical world. There is no semantic problem of reference to mathematical entities as abstract, because they are properties that are exemplified in the actual world. In the same way that we can refer to other properties exemplified in the physical order, colors and tastes, for example, so we can refer in thought and language to the mathematical properties that inhere in physical things, nominalized as mathematical entities for convenient expression in mathematical formulas. It follows, then, that there is no conflict such as Benacerraf envisages for the semantics and epistemology of mathematics, as in Platonic realism and the other more standard and popularly considered philosophies of mathematics; this is the "solution", or, better, the reply, to Benacerraf's dilemma. Benacerraf maintains only that virtually all philosophies of mathematics are subject to the problem of providing an adequate general semantics for mathematical languages on the model of the language of physical objects at the expense of being unable to defend an adequate epistemology of mathematical discovery. In an Aristotelian inherence metaphysics of applicable "pure" mathematics, the problem does not arise.

(ii) *Ontic (metaphysical) relation*

The ontic or metaphysical relation between applicable "pure" and applied mathematics is once again that the two concepts precisely coincide. There is no difference between them on the present theory. Hence there is also no problem, as in Platonic mathematical realism, of trying to understand how distinct abstract and phenomenal orders might be interrelated by reference to physical objects "imitating", "participating in", or "striving to maximize likeness with" abstract ideal mathematical archetypes.

There nevertheless remains an outstanding ontological question as to the metaphysics of inherence. Several kinds of theories might be advanced to fill in this gap in a more complete inherentist philosophy of mathematics. It is in keeping with the Aristotelian and best insights of the later Scholastic tradition as reflected even in Spinoza's concept of substance, as well as common-sense consideration of similar ideas even today, to regard physical (primary) substances as that which most properly exists, while all other existences are understood as ontically dependent on them.

This includes, if the present proposal is right in main outline, all existent applicable "pure" mathematical properties nominalized as mathematical entities that inhere in existent physical phenomena. The ontic dependence of applicable "pure" mathematical properties on the physical entities that embody them or in which they inhere is reminiscent of the metaphysics of supervenience sometimes invoked in contemporary discussions of cognitive psychology, philosophy of mind, and theories of consciousness. It may be appropriate, therefore, to further characterize the inherence of applicable "pure" mathematical entities inhering in physical phenomena as supervening on the physical substances in which they are also said to inhere. For present purposes, in the special case of the ontic dependence of applicable "pure" mathematics on the physical phenomena in which mathematical entities, nominalized mathematical properties and relations, inhere, we can say qualifiedly that the inherence relation is equivalent to Jaegwon Kim's analysis of strong supervenience.

(iii) *Epistemic relation*

As to the epistemology of mathematical inquiry, at least for the considerable domain of applicable "pure" mathematics, there is no philosophical problem such as Benacerraf projects for an Aristotelian inherentist philosophy of mathematics. Unlike the Platonistic mathematical realism commonly accepted by mathematicians and philosophers of mathematics, mathematical knowledge gathering is not rendered impossible by virtue of commitment to an abstract causally inaccessible realm of eternal unchanging Platonic mathematical entities. The world of Aristotelian applicable "pure" mathematics is right before us. It inheres in the empirical world experienced by means of the five physiological senses. We learn mathematical truths when we discover the mathematical properties inherent in the physical phenomena we study in everyday observations and the natural sciences, particularly but not exclusively in mathematical physics.

What, then, of the necessity and aprioricity of mathematics as standardly conceived? Several responses are suggested. We might bite the bullet, as John Stuart Mill does in *A System of Logic*, and maintain that all mathematics is after all and despite appearances and the proclamations of Platonists actually only *a posteriori* and logically contingent. Alternatively, we might argue that mathematical properties despite being empirically discoverable and verifiable are necessary and *a priori* in the same way that other ostensibly nonmathematical metaphysical properties inhering in primary physical substances in an Aristotelian ontology or ousiology are reasonably supposed to be. These include at least such properties as being self-identical, being spatiotemporal, and being conditionally such that if certain properties obtain then certain other properties logically must obtain, as in Putnam's conditionalism or if-thenism. Such interpretations are perfectly compatible with an Aristotelian inherence metaphysics of mathematics, and may arguably account for all that can anyway be legitimately attributed to the necessity or aprioricity of mathematics. The account explains these features of mathematics, moreover, without requiring that we buy into a Platonistic mathematical realism of eternal, unchanging and causally epistemically inaccessible abstract mathematical entities that all forms of nominalism have struggled to resist.

C. The question in (c) of how it is possible for mathematics to describe the world of physical phenomena is answered straightforwardly in an inherence philosophy of mathematics. Mathematics applies to empirical reality because all applicable mathematics inheres as the formal properties of physical phenomena. Mathematics on the inherence theory does not exist in a separate realm of eternal abstract ideal entities to which it must then somehow be related to a changing spatiotemporal order. Rather, applicable "pure" mathematics, according to an inherentist ontology, exists in and only in the physical world of existent spatiotemporal entities in which mathematical properties and relations inhere. When we study the mathematical properties of physical systems we are already engaged in the only (applicable) mathematics about which the inherentist thinks it makes any sense to speak. We note that natural philosophers such as Isaac Newton and generations of physicists before and after him even today would not have sharply distinguished between doing mathematical physics, physics, and mathematics, except in the way that Aristotle explains.

D. Does an Aristotelian inherentist philosophy of mathematics, as question (d) asks, shed light on the problems of applied mathematics that Mark Steiner in *The Applicability of Mathematics as a Philosophical Problem* has emphasized in his exposition of the heuristics of mathematical discovery?[15]

If an inherentist philosophy of mathematics is correct, then it requires all of mathematics to supervene in the appropriate sense or ontically depend on the real inherent mathematical properties of the real physical phenomena to which applied mathematics is applied. The first task of applied mathematics in the sciences is accordingly to identify a correctly positively corresponding mathematical system or language to model the physical phenomena under study. This is not always an easy requirement to fulfill, but one that must often proceed hypothetically and through an adjustment period during the growth of science in which refinements in both choice and all aspects of the development of mathematical methods take place. These tinkerings in turn often interactively affect the scientist's understanding of the physical phenomena themselves as different mathematical formalisms are tried out, invented or adapted for specific needs, corrected, improved, rejected, or finally accepted.

When this process is complete, as we believe has satisfactorily occurred in various branches of applied mathematics in the natural sciences, then it should come as no further surprise and no deep philosophical mystery to be resolved by appeal to conceptual resources beyond those available to an inherentist philosophy of mathematics, that applied mathematics both describes and can be used to predict and control events in the physical world. The requisite mathematics in that case will be literally embodied and embedded in the physical phenomena, so that the system's formal consequences must correspond with the nature, disposition and behavior, including the previously unnoticed and future behavior, of the relevant physical system. If this did not happen, then we could not yet be said to have arrived at the appropriate applied mathematics for the phenomena in question. We should note with reassurance that this process of fitting the right mathematical language to a settled conceptual grasp of the physical phenomena to which an applied mathematics is supposed to be applied is precisely what we find in the history and contemporary practice of applied mathematics in the natural sciences in the work of such physicists as Newton and Leibniz, Einstein, Dirac, Heisenberg, Stephen Hawking, and others. It is very much a back and forth process. Once a good fit is made between a physical phenomenon and applied mathematical system tailored to its corresponding scientific needs, however, then it is a matter of course that the mathematics seems presciently to "know" previously unsuspected things and to predict or retrodict otherwise unexpected facts about the relevant phenomena.

---

[15] Steiner [43].

For the same reason, it follows in an Aristotelian inherentist philosophy of mathematics that formal pen and pencil or high-speed computer calculations of the appropriate mathematical equations, purely formal or "abstract" in themselves—once they have been determined to be appropriate, the right applied mathematics for the right applied mathematics job—should enable mechanics and engineers in real time to build, correctly predict the behavior of, manipulate, and in other ways control physical objects and events to which the calculations are applied. There is in any case no further philosophical, semantic, ontological, or epistemic problem to be overcome in understanding how applications of arithmetic, algebra, geometry, calculus, and probability theory, among others, in fluid dynamics, ballistics, kinematics generally, or quantum mechanics, can be used to explain and make predetermined things happen in the empirical world. Mathematics works so well in physics because mathematical properties nominalized as entities and relations are embodied and embedded in and ultimately derive all their meaning from the physical phenomena to which applied mathematics of the appropriate kind is applied.

Mathematics on the present theory is literally *in* the natural world; it inheres in or is embodied and embedded as the mathematical properties of physical reality. So, *of course*, mathematical physics, once we have the right applied mathematical methods in hand, *must* work. That is the proper goal for applied mathematics in the sciences, to *identify* the requisite applied mathematical language for each physical phenomenon under the aegis of each natural science. It is the goal toward which we find scientists as applied mathematicians striving throughout the history of the exact sciences and among their contemporary practitioners today.

3.5.2 Inapplicable Pure Mathematics—Consequences for the Philosophy of Applied Mathematics

What is left over? What remains after we have accounted for the applicable part of mathematics that can actually be used in the theoretical physical sciences, in mechanics and engineering of all types, as inhering in the physical world of primary substances to which applied mathematics is correctly and successfully applied? What remains are all those branches of mathematics that ostensibly at least are altogether inapplicable to the real empirical world of actual physical entities and actual physical phenomena. Are there any such legitimate genuine parts of mathematics? Can there be such languages and mathematical methods according to an inherentist philosophy of *mathematics*? What should a self-respecting inherentist philosophy of mathematics say about such developments in mathematics?

We must distinguish at the outset between mathematics, for which, as it happens, there has thus far been no scientific physical application and those that are absolutely and in principle inapplic*able*, or for which as a matter of logical, mathematical, or causal physical necessity, there is and can be no possible application. While the direction of discovery in mathematics has often and even paradigmatically been from perceptions of what is needed in a formal system for real-world applications to innovations in mathematics, the opposite line of progression has and can obviously on reflection also and equally occur. The classic example is probably the originally applicationally unmotivated elaboration of non-Euclidean geometries. These, it is frequently remarked, were genuine mathematical theories with genuine mathematical theorems even prior to Einstein's finding an appropriate application for them in relativity physics, in which for the first time applied mathematics required a rigorous mathematical model of the curvature of spacetime determined by large gravitational fields.

Such episodes in the history of applied mathematics are no embarrassment for an inherentist philosophy of mathematics. The inherentist can say that all along the mathematical structures inhered in the physical universe, but that it took some time for scientists to recognize the fact. We simply did not know that Riemannian geometry was needed for astrophysics until Einstein opened our eyes to the fact. There is a difference between a mathematical system's being applicable to physical reality and our *knowing* that it is applicable. Now, we ask, how do we know that the same is not true of many another if not finally of all of what currently pass for supposedly inapplicable mathematical languages and methods? If that should turn out to be the case for a projection of the path of natural science and its reliance on hitherto unexploited branches of "pure" mathematics into the indefinite future, then the inherentist philosophy of mathematics would perfectly comprehend all that legitimately deserves to be styled mathematics, with no overlap of recalcitrant counterexamples. It could conceivably happen that every supposedly pure inapplicable mathematical system will eventually get its obligatory fifteen minutes of fame (or considerably longer) by being applied to some physical phenomenon for which no one previously suspected it would ever have such a use. The inherentist can then say that the mathematical properties of apparently inapplicable pure mathematical languages had inhered in the relevant physical phenomena all along, as fallible scientists and applied mathematicians only belatedly began to appreciate.

That expectation, for a variety of reasons, is probably unrealistic. There might and are even likely to be developments within "pure" mathematics—perhaps the only sort properly so called—of mathematics for mathematics's sake—that will never be applicable even in the modally weakest sense, because in the end they do not describe mathematical properties that actually inhere in physical phenomena anywhere in the physical universe. What would be an example of such? They are not hard to find. The much higher-order cardinals of Cantor's transfinite set theory quickly come to mind; particularly for cardinals greater than $2^{2^{\aleph_0}}$, and particularly if the physical universe is finite and closed in dimension and if quantum phenomena should turn out to be fundamentally and irreducibly discrete. Both of these assumptions, incidentally, would have found eager acceptance by Aristotle and other empirically-minded natural philosophers such as David Hume.[16]

---

[16] Aristotle, *Physics* 263b3–9: "To the question whether it is possible to pass through an infinite number of units [i.e. intervals] either of time or of distance we must reply that in a sense it is and in a sense it is not. If the units [intervals] are actual it is not possible, if they are potential, it is possible." Hume [21, especially pp. 27–65]. See Jacquette [23].

3.6 Metatheoretical Choices for an Inapplicable "Pure" Mathematics from an Inherence Perspective

What are the choices for an inherentist philosopher of mathematics in responding to the putative mathematics of Cantor's paradise if these propositions about the metrical limitations of the physical universe should turn out to be true? What should an inherentist say if it happens that the best scientific cosmologies conclude that the physical universe is finite and discrete? There would appear in that case to be three basic alternatives.

Before we proceed to provide specific details, we should comment briefly and in general terms on the advantages and disadvantages that two of these options entail. There are pros and cons in ascribing to a unified as opposed to a diversified theory of any kind, and more especially within the philosophy of mathematics. A unified account is generally neater, more principled, simpler, and possibly more likely to be regarded as true. This is only the case, however, when a unified theory is also fully adequate to the relevant data. When the data themselves are complex and categorically diversified, then an adequate theory often needs to be correspondingly complex and diversified at the risk otherwise of being oversimplified, blind to essential differences, and incapable of accounting for all the factors essential to the theory's explanatory burden. What happens when we approach the unified/diversified dichotomy from the standpoint of placing a high premium on understanding applied mathematics in the natural sciences? It all depends on informed opinion as to the nature of the data; in this case, whether in fact the universe is finite or infinite, discrete or continuous.

With these words of caution concerning scientific judgment that has yet to be finally rendered, the basic choices for an inherentist philosophy of mathematics in light of the conceivability of there being ultimately inapplicable putatively mathematical languages and formal mathematical methods are these (Table 3.1).

We can now consider all the possibilities in their respective categories and move toward a preferred interpretation, it any should present itself:

Choice (1)—Uncompromising Prohibitive Inherentism
Choice (2)—Conciliatory Inherentism + Intensionalism
Choice (3)—Conciliatory Inherentism + Formalism

Table 3.1 Metatheoretical choices for an inapplicable "pure" mathematics from an inherentist perspective

	Uncomporomising UNIFIED	Concilatory DIVERSIFIED
Austere	NO INHERENTLY INAPPLICAPLE "PURE" MATHEMATICS	CONCILATORY INHERENTISM + INTENSIONALISM
Opulent		CONCILATORY INHERENTISM + FORMALISM

Choice (1) is simply to deny that there are inherently inapplicable systems of pure mathematics. If Cantor's transfinite set theory fails to have physical application, if infinity and higher-order infinities do not inhere in and are not exemplified, embodied or embedded in the natural world, and we can know this, then despite the beauty of Cantor's formal syntax, it is, according to choice (1), not mathematics. What is it then? An inherentist can describe transfinite set theory as a sign system superficially similar to some genuine mathematical languages, but no more mathematics than a historical novel is history. It is significant in this regard that Cantor himself regarded even denumerable or countable infinity as a fiction; it is only later mathematicians and philosophers of mathematics, relying on a default Platonic realism, that have blurred these distinctions and treated higher-order cardinalities as existent mathematical entities on a par with any others.[17]

Choice (2) sacrifices unity, offering separate kinds of component subtheories for applicable and inherently inapplicable "pure" mathematics. An intensionalist semantics for mathematical terms and sentences allows such sentences to count as mathematical, but, in its austerity, the theory does not extend ontic status to corresponding putative mathematical entities, or, even, depending on the exact nature of the superstructural truth value semantics provided (there are several possibilities), to the truth of relevant mathematical sentences.

Choice (3), cutting across some of these major metatheoretical classifications, is opulent rather than austere, permissive rather than prohibitive, and diversified rather than unified. Formalism allows inherently inapplicable but still genuinely mathematical languages and methods to flourish without ontic commitment to the existence of mathematical entities or semantic commitment to the truth of mathematical sentences beyond those forms inherent in the formal properties of mathematical sentences themselves. We reject formalism generally in philosophy of mathematics, for reasons previously explained, particularly because of its inability to account for the usefulness of applied mathematics. Where inherently inapplicable "pure" mathematics is concerned, this is obviously not a problem. Indeed, the one-sided diet of examples that has malnourished formalist philosophy of mathematics is precisely this kind of ethereal inherently inapplicable category of mathematical results to which Cantor's set theory might be said to belong, together with an unwarranted drive to force all of the philosophy of mathematics, contrary perhaps to its nature, into a single unified metatheoretical mold. Seen for what it is with its limitations on its sleeve, formalism represents a perfectly viable choice for one-half of a diversified approach to an otherwise more fundamentally Aristotelian inherentist philosophy of mathematics embodied and embedded in the empirical world of physical phenomena.

Choice (1) is unified, resolute, but prohibitive and austere, perhaps excessively so. Its advantages are potentially outweighed by its implications for the reform of ordinary ways of speaking about mathematics if we can no longer talk about Cantor's formal accomplishments among conceivably unlimitedly many other

---

[17] See Cantor, *Grundlagen einer allgemeinen Mannigfaltigkeitslehre* [10, pp. 181–82].

examples that might be given, as mathematics. This might be judged too high a price to pay for a unified pure and uncompromisingly Aristotelian inherentism in the philosophy of mathematics. It might therefore be dispreferred in comparison with either of the following two choices, which are equally acceptable, depending on one's attitude toward intensional or nonexistent mathematical objects as mere (objective) objects of thought versus the sterility of a formalist philosophy of mathematics.

References

1. Allen, R.E. 1961. "The Argument from Opposites in *Republic* V." *The Review of Metaphysics* 15:325–35.
2. Aristotle. 1995. *Physics*. The Revised Oxford Translation, edited by Jonathan Barnes. Princeton/Bollingen Series LXII.2, Volume 1. Princeton, NJ: Princeton University Press.
3. Azzouni, Jody. 1994. *Metaphysical Myths, Mathematical Practice*. Cambridge: Cambridge University Press.
4. Balaguer, Mark. 1988. *Platonism and Anti-Platonism in Mathematics*. Oxford: Oxford University Press.
5. Benacerraf, Paul. 1965. "What Numbers Could Not Be." *The Philosophical Review* 74:47–73.
6. Benacerraf, Paul. 1973. "Mathematical Truth." *The Journal of Philosophy* 70:661–80; reprinted in Benacerraf and Putnam [7], 403–20.
7. Benacerraf, Paul and Hilary Putnam, eds. 1983. *Philosophy of Mathematics: Selected Readings*. 2nd edition. Cambridge, MA: Cambridge University Press.
8. Boehmer, Philotheus. 1946. "The Realistic Conceptualism of William Ockham." *Traditio* 4:307–35.
9. Brouwer, L.E.J. 1913. "Intuitionism and Formalism." *Bulletin of the American Mathematical Society* 20:81–96.
10. Cantor, Georg. 1966. *Gesammelte Abhandlungen mathematischen und philosophischen Inhalts, mit erluternden Anmerkungen sowie mit Ergngzungen aus dem Briefwechsel Cantor-Dedekind*. Edited by Ernst Zermelo. Hildesheim: Georg Olms Verlag.
11. Chihara, Charles S. 1990. *Constructibility and Mathematical Essence*. Oxford: Oxford University Press.
12. Chihara, Charles S. 2004. *A Structural Account of Mathematics*. Oxford: Oxford University Press.
13. Detlefsen, Michael. 1993. "Hilbert's Formalism." *Revue internationale de philosophie* 47:285–304.
14. Field, Hartry. 1980. *Science Without Numbers*. Princeton, NJ: Princeton University Press.
15. Field, Hartry. 1985. "Comments and Criticisms on Conservativeness and Incompleteness." *The Journal of Philosophy* 82:239–60.
16. Field, Hartry. 1989. *Realism, Mathematics, and Modality*. Oxford: Blackwell.
17. Field, Hartry. 1992. "A Nominalistic Proof of the Conservativeness of Set Theory." *Journal of Philosophical Logic* 21:111–23.
18. Heyting, Arend. 1956. *Intuitionism: An Introduction*. Amsterdam: North-Holland.
19. Hilbert, David. 1926. "Über das Unendliche." *Mathematische Annalen* 95:161–90.
20. Hilbert, David. 1928. "Die Grundlagen der Mathematik." *Abhandlungen aus dem Seminar der Hamburgischen Universität* 6:65–85.
21. Hume, David. 1978 (1739–1740). *A Treatise of Human Nature*. Edited by Selby-Bigge; 2nd edition revised by P.H. Nidditch. Oxford: Oxford University Press.
22. Jacquette, Dale. 2001. *David Hume's Critique of Infinity*. Leiden: Brill Academic Publishers.

23. Jacquette, Dale, ed. 2002. *Philosophy of Mathematics: An Anthology*. Oxford: Blackwell Publishing.
24. Jacquette, Dale. 2004. "Mathematical Fiction and Structuralism in Chihara's Constructibility Theory." (Review of Charles S. Chihara, *A Structural Account of Mathematics*). *History and Philosophy of Logic* 25:319–24.
25. Lee, Edward N. 1966. "On the Metaphysics of the Image in Plato's *Timaeus*." *The Monist* 50:341–68.
26. Maddy, Penelope. 1980. "Perception and Mathematical Intuition." *The Philosophical Review* 89:163–96.
27. Maddy, Penelope. 1990. *Realism in Mathematics*. Oxford: Oxford University Press.
28. Maddy, Penelope. 1997. *Naturalism in Mathematics*. Oxford: Oxford University Press.
29. Maurer, Armand. 1999. *The Philosophy of William of Ockham in the Light of Its Principles*. Rome: Pontifical Institute of Medieval Studies.
30. Mill, John Stuart. 1941 (1843). *A System of Logic, Rationative and Inductive: Being a Connected View of the Principles of Evidence and Methods of Scientific Investigation*. London: Longmans, Gree & Co.
31. Nehamas, Alexader. 1982. "Participation and Predication in Plato's Later Thought." *The Review of Metaphysics* 36:343–74.
32. Ockham, William (of). 1974. *Ockham's Theory of Terms, Part I of the Summa Logicae*. Translated by Michael J. Loux. Notre Dame: University of Notre Dame Press.
33. Plato. 1971. *Gorgias*. Translated with an introduction by Walter Hamilton. Harmondsworth: Penguin Books.
34. Plato. 1982. *Philebus*. Translated with an introduction by Robin A.H. Waterfield. Harmondsworth: Penguin Books.
35. Putnam, Hilary. 1967a. "Mathematics Without Foundations." *The Journal of Philosophy* 64:5–22.
36. Putnam, Hilary. 1967b. "The Thesis that Mathematics Is Logic." In *Bertrand Russell: Philosopher of the Century*, edited by Ralph Schoenman, 273–303. London: George Allen & Unwin.
37. Quine, W.V.O. 1986. "Reply to Charles Parsons." In *The Philosophy of W.V. Quine*, edited by L. Hahn and P. Schilpp, 396–403. LaSalle: Open Court.
38. Resnik, Michael. 1981. "Mathematics as a Science of Patterns: Ontology and Reference." *Noûs* 16:529–50.
39. Resnik, Michael. 1988. "Mathematics from the Structural Point of View." *Revue internationale de philosophie* 42:400–24.
40. Resnik, Michael. 1997. *Mathematics as a Science of Patterns*. Oxford: Oxford University Press.
41. Shapiro, Stuart. 1997. *Philosophy of Mathematics: Structure and Ontology*. Oxford: Oxford University Press.
42. Shapiro, Stuart. 2000. *Thinking About Mathematics*. Oxford: Oxford University Press.
43. Steiner, Mark. 1998. *The Applicability of Mathematics as a Philosophical Problem*. Cambridge, MA: Harvard University Press.
44. Sweeney, Leo. 1988. "Participation in Plato's Dialogues: *Phaedo, Parmenides, Sophist, Timaeus*." *The New Scholasticism* 62:125–49.
45. Van Atten, Mark. 2004. *On Brouwer*. Belmont, CA: Wadsworth Philosophers Series.

Chapter 4
The Philosophical Impact of the Löwenheim-Skolem Theorem

Miloš Arsenijević

4.1 The Historical Philosophico-Mathematical Background of the Löwenheim-Skolem Theorem

4.1.1 The Relation Externalism

In his Intellectual Biography [30, Ch. V], Bertrand Russell named the year 1889 as a turn, which he relates not only to his own philosophical development but also to the beginning of an era, in which, contrary to the opinion of Leibniz and Hegel, relations between objects started to be treated as equally real as and not reducible to the properties of objects between which they hold. For instance, if a and b are two objects, then a and b plus a relation holding between them make up a relational structure that is equally real as a and b themselves, and in addition—which is a consequence particularly important for our present purposes—objects a and b would remain the very same objects if they ceased to stand in a given relation and started being in a different relation.

4.1.2 Referring to Objects, Properties and Relations According to the Theory of Meaning Holism: Frege, Wittgenstein and Hilbert

Frege was the first who explicitly introduced the theory of meaning holism by stating that a concept is something unsaturated [13, p. 24] [16, I.1. pp. 33–34], which can become a reference only by being ascribed to an object. So, for instance, if the concept horse occupies the place of the grammatical subject in a sentence, it does not function as a concept [14].

M. Arsenijević (✉)
Department of Philosophy, University of Belgrade, Belgrade, Serbia
e-mail: marsenij@f.bg.ac.rs

As for the way in which we refer to objects, Frege applied his distinction between sense and reference (*Sinn* and *Bedeutung*) in order to show that we normally, if not always, refer to an object through some mode of its representation [15, pp. 57, 62, 67]. So, for instance, while "Venus" directly refers to Venus in the representation independent way, the expressions "the Morning Star" and "the Evening Star", when functioning as names are two different ways in which we refer to Venus (independently of whether it shines in the morning or in the evening). But there are cases in which there is nothing like "Venus" in the given example. "The centre of the circle inscribed in an equilateral triangle" and "the centre of the circle circumscribed about the same equilateral triangle" are two different ways of referring to one and the same point, but there is no name that would refer directly to it. And if we refer to this point by "the centre of gravity", it is clear that this is just another mode of representation of the same object to which "the centre of the circle inscribed in an equilateral triangle" and "the centre of the circle circumscribed about the same equilateral triangle" refer.

Wittgenstein radicalized the theory of meaning holism by stating that names have no reference at all outside sentences in which "state of affairs" are stated [40, 3.3], for the world is, according to Wittgenstein, "the totality of facts, not of things" [40, 1.1].

And finally, it was Hilbert who stated that there is no reference, either in view of names (constants or, indirectly, individual variables) or of relations (relation constants) or of the statements (about relations holding between objects which the constants refer to or the variables range over) outside a whole formal theory. So, according to Hilbert, it is only a whole system of axioms (a formal theory) that implicitly defines objects and relations which the theory is about [20, 21]. Consequently, the whole formal theory gets its reference through a simultaneous interpretation of all its basic symbols and well-formed formulae, and this reference is a relational structure in which the theorems of the theory are satisfied, i.e. true.

4.1.3 Consistency, Completeness and Categoricalness

According to Hilbert's Programme, the ideal formal system should be consistent, complete and categorical [12, Ch. V, §4].

Syntactically, an axiom system is consistent if and only if there is no formula A of the system for which both A and its negation can be proved. Semantically, a system is consistent if there is an interpretation such that its axioms are true. As a consequence, later formulated as a theorem of the Model Theory, an axiom system (a formal theory) is consistent if and only if it has a model. So, in order to prove that a system is consistent it would be sufficient to show that it has a model. However, for doing this, one should have a well-established meta-theory concerning the existence of a model. That's why Hilbert wanted to have a purely formal consistency proof without relating it to a model. However, in many interesting cases such a proof is not of elementary nature and requires always stronger and stronger theories, as it follows from Gödel's Second Incompleteness Theorem [18]. This problem of Hilbert's Programme is, however, irrelevant for our main concern.

The question concerning syntactical completeness is indirectly relevant to our topic. A formal system is syntactically complete if and only if there is no pair of sentences—a sentence and its negation—such that neither of the two sentences is a theorem of the system.

The demand concerning the categoricalness of a system will be of crucial importance for our main concern. An axiom system (a formal theory) is categorical if and only if all its models are isomorphic, i.e. if and only if all the relational structures in which the system is interpretable are such that there is a structure preserving one-one mapping between the elements of their basic sets.

4.1.4 The Set Equipotency and Higher-Order Infinities

One of the central things that are going to be questioned by the Löwenheim-Skolem Theorem concerns Cantor's theory of higher-order infinities, which is based on the conception of the power of a set [12, pp. 95ff].

Two finite sets are equipotent if and only if all the elements of one of them can be brought into 1–1 correspondence with all the elements of the other one. That's why, for instance, the set of four people has the same power as the set of four apples. By generalizing this idea, two infinite sets are also said to be equipotent if and only if all the elements of one of them can be brought into 1–1 correspondence with all the elements of the other one. Now, a set has less power than some other set if and only if all its elements can be brought into 1–1 correspondence with the elements of some proper subset of the latter set but, at the same time, there are not enough elements of the former with which all the elements of the latter could be brought into 1–1 correspondence. That's why a set of five apples has a greater power than a set of four people. And that's also why, according to several proofs that Cantor has offered, the set of natural numbers is equipotent with the set of rational numbers but has a less power than the set of real numbers. Cardinal numbers are numbers that denote set powers. So, $\aleph_0$ denotes the power of all the infinite sets that are equipotent with the set of natural numbers, and these sets are the weakest infinite sets. Cardinal numbers $\aleph_1, \aleph_2, \aleph_3, \ldots$ denote infinite sets of always greater and greater power. Cantor had stated and believed to have proven [5, p. 333] that the power of the set of real numbers is $\aleph_1$, namely, that there is no infinite sets whose power would be greater than the power of the set of natural numbers but lesser than the power of the set of real numbers, but since his proof has turned out to be inconclusive, this statement of his was later called the Continuum Hypothesis.

4.1.5 The Set Orderings

In order to get a relational structure, we have to start with a basic set and then define at least one relation on it. The most important relation is the ordering relation, i.e. either < or ≤, where the latter can be defined via the former and the identity relation. However, it is important to notice that, by starting with different basic sets, we can get different orderings—in accordance with the Cantorian procedure—by using the allegedly same ordering relation. So, for instance, the three relational structures, $\langle \mathbb{N}, \leq \rangle$, $\langle \mathbb{Q}, \leq \rangle$, $\langle \mathbb{R}, \leq \rangle$, where $\mathbb{N}$, $\mathbb{Q}$ and $\mathbb{R}$ are the set of natural numbers, the set of rational numbers and the set of real numbers, respectively, are not ordered in the same way: the first structure is discrete, the second one is dense but not continuous, and the third one is continuous.

Concerning the order of $\langle \mathbb{N}, \leq \rangle$, it will be very important, for the understanding of an apparent paradox of the Löwenheim-Skolem Theorem, that, in the metatheory, the ordering relation of the standard model can be introduced in two seemingly equivalent ways, whose difference, however, can be exemplified by using a model of Non-Standard Arithmetic. Namely, since the well-order of the intended model is well-founded and total, it seems that any of the following two pairs of conditions is sufficient for its definition. We can either stipulate that (1) there is an element which is the minimal element of the structure; and that (2) for any element, there is a unique element that is his immediate successor, or, alternately, we can retain the first condition and add: (2') any non-empty subset of the basic set has a unique minimal element. But, as we shall see below (see Section 4.3.2), there are structures in which conditions (1) and (2) are satisfied, whereas (2') is not. This means that (1) and (2) are not sufficient for defining, in a categorical way, the order of natural numbers in Standard Arithmetic, whereas (1) and (2') are.

As for the difference between $\langle \mathbb{Q}, \leq \rangle$ and $\langle \mathbb{R}, \leq \rangle$, it consists only in the fact—which Cantor held to be the first who had discovered and defined it clearly [5, p. 190]—that while each element of $\langle \mathbb{Q}, \leq \rangle$ is an accumulation point of an infinite number of elements, it is true only in $\langle \mathbb{R}, \leq \rangle$ that each accumulation of an infinite number of elements has as its accumulation point the element that is an element of the basic set itself. The lesson, which will be very important for an interpretation of the Löwenheim-Skolem Theorem, is that the allegedly same ordering relation functions differently in view of $\mathbb{N}$, $\mathbb{Q}$ and $\mathbb{R}$, so that the difference between structures which are discrete, dense but not continuous, and continuous depends on how they are structured partly independently on how they are ordered according to the $\leq$ relation. In particular, if a structure is well-ordered according to the second definition, its basic set is countable, but it is a question, as we shall see below, whether it is so in the case in which a structure is well-ordered according to the first definition only.

And finally, from the Hilbertian point of view, the difference between discrete, dense but not continuous, and continuous structures is to be obtained only through different axioms defining implicitly the meaning of the $\leq$ relation. This means that, according to the Hilbertian meaning holism, the $\leq$ relation cannot be said to be the same in each of the three cases. More concretely, though it might seem that the same ordering relation holds between elements of the otherwise differently structured elements of discrete, dense but not continuous, and continuous structures, the very difference between these structures is based on the fact that the ordering relation is implicitly defined in three different ways relating to these three structures.

4.1.6 Intuitionism and Platonism

Though Intuitionists were not directly involved in the discussion concerning the Löwenheim-Skolem Theorem due to the fact that the Intuitionist Programme remained untouched either by the Theorem itself or by its consequences, the concept of constructability [12, pp. 61, 104, 108], though not in the sense in which Intuitionists understand it, will appear in some important examples concerning the problem of changing cardinalities [25].

Intuitionists reject the Cantorian concept of the actual infinity and use only the Aristotelian concept of the dynamic (or potential) infinite. So they always start with a finite number of constructed objects that may then get greater and greater unboundedly but never becomes actually infinite [4, pp. 270ff.]. This treatment enables them to prove various statements about the objects introduced in such a way whenever they have a recursive control over what they speak about and an inductive way to prove a theorem, but they do not allow us to speak of infinite sets or classes as "finished entities" [4, p. 433] but only of "spreads" as entities "in statu nascendi" [39, p. 52]. For instance, we may speak of natural numbers as a species, without restricting our discourse to a finite number of them, and can also prove, by using mathematical induction, that any of these numbers must be odd or even, but we mustn't speak of "the set of all the natural numbers (whose cardinal number is $\aleph_0$)."

An important consequence is that we cannot use the Weierstrassian concept of real numbers according to which any complete decimal expansion defines a unique real number. We may say, for instance, that $0.33\ldots$, where 3 is supposedly going to occur at any place of the decimal expansion, defines the unique number, i.e. $\frac{1}{3}$, but we mustn't take that the decimal expansion of π defines π as the unique real number, because, firstly, there is no recursive way according to which such an expansion would be defined, and, secondly, there is no mathematical object such as the complete infinite decimal expansion.

Due to the given restriction under which one is allowed to speak of the existence of mathematical objects and to prove the existence of their properties and relations holding between them, the use of many classical logical principles and derivation rules is also to be restricted. It is so in the case of the principle of excluded middle, the counterposition, the double negation, the reductio ad absurdum and so on. In particular, this prevents all the Cantorian proofs concerning the existence of various types of infinity and the uncountability of the set of real numbers.

Now, I shall call Platonists all those who do not accept the intuitionist rigors concerning the existence of mathematical objects and their way in which the theorems are only allowed to be proved. This means that Platonism will be taken in a much broader sense than as denotation of the mathematical programme contrasted to Logicism, Intuitionism and Formalism. In particular, Hilbert's Programme will not be contrasted to Platonism, since the rigor of Hilbert's foundation of mathematics concerns the syntactical finitism and recursive control that should govern the introduction of basic symbols and formation and derivation rules [23, pp. 137ff], which is, as such, not directed against the transfinite mathematics that lies on the semantical part of a formal theory. As Hilbert put it himself, "No one shall drive us out of the paradise which Cantor has created for us" [23, p. 141].

4.2 The Löwenheim-Skolem Theorem and Its Generalization

4.2.1 What Is the Löwenheim-Skolem Theorem About?

The essential statement of what is now called the Löwenheim-Skolem Theorem as well as its proof—in spite of some errors and slopps [38, p. 156]—are to be found in Löwenheim's famous paper [26]. However, due to the fact that Skolem, in his four papers [31, 32, 34, 35], removed all gaps and omissions from Löwenheim's proof, got rid of any use of the Axiom of Choice, strengthened and extended the Theorem, analyzed profoundly its meaning, formulated the Theorem related Paradox and offered its first resolution, his name was later rightly attached to the name of Löwenheim when referring to the Theorem itself. Some go even further on and call it the Skolem-Löwenheim Theorem [12, p. 302].

The Theorem is nowadays highly estimated as the first great result in what was later called the Model Theory [38, p. 154], viz. as a contribution that proved something substantially important and seemingly paradoxical about the relation between a formal theory and its interpretation.

Since, perhaps contrary to, say, Gödel's Incompleteness Theorem, the understanding of the Löwenheim-Skolem Theorem and its consequences represents a problem per se that does not depend essentially on the understanding of its proof, we shall turn directly, after giving its main formulation, to the clarification of its meaning.

4.2.2 The Main Formulation of the Löwenheim-Skolem Theorem and the Straightforward Meaning of Its Strong Version

Löwenheim's original formulation [26] was about a first-order sentence σ that has a model. However, since σ can be a conjunction, we may speak, instead of σ, of a set Σ of first-order sentences. In particular, Σ can be the set of axioms of a formal theory. As for the model, since no qualification is indicated, the basic set of the relational structure the Theorem is about can be an infinite set of any cardinality whatsoever.

Theorem 1 *If Σ has a model whose basic set is infinite, then Σ has a model whose basic set is countable.*

Let us explain the straightforward meaning of the Strong Version of the Theorem, where, given that A is the basic set of the original structure and B the basic set of a countable model B, $B \subseteq A$. Let S be a structure which consists of (1) an infinite set A whose cardinal $|A|$ is greater than $\aleph_0$, and (2) a finite or denumerable number of relations $R_1, R_2, \ldots$ defined on it. Then, there is a structure S' that consists of (1) the basic set B whose cardinal is $\aleph_0$, and of (2) the relations $R'_1, R'_2, \ldots$ that are just the relations $R_1, R_2, \ldots$ of S restricted to the set B, so that for every sentence σ of the first-order language which corresponds to S, i.e., whose extra-logical symbols are just relation-symbols which refer to the relations $R_1, R_2, \ldots$ of S, σ is true in S' if and only if σ is true in S. In particular, if **T** is a first-order theory and S is a model of **T**, then S', too, is a model of **T**.

4.2.3 The Generalized Versions of the Löwenheim-Skolem Theorem

In 1928, Tarski presented in his seminar a form of what is now called the Upward Löwenheim-Skolem Theorem [38, p. 160]. However, this result was never published and was only mentioned in the editor's note of Skolem's paper that appeared six years later [36]. So, the proof is to be found only in the famous paper of Malcev [27].

Theorem 2 *If Σ is countable and has a model whose basic set is infinite, then Σ has a model in each infinite power greater than the power of the original basic set.*

Since the Theorem can be generalized so as to state that Σ has a model in each infinite power lesser than the power of the original basic set—which is its version called the Downward Löwenheim-Skolem Theorem—the most generalized form states that:

Theorem 3 *If Σ is countable and has a model whose basic set is infinite, then Σ has a model in each infinite power.*

However, since, from a philosophical point of view, the original version of the Theorem is sufficient for the formulation and understanding of the most intriguing questions and the most interesting examples related to its consequences, we shall in what follows focus our attention to this form of the Theorem and refer to it, unless necessary, by using its name without qualification.

4.3 The Far-Reaching Consequences of the Löwenheim-Skolem Theorem

4.3.1 The General Problem Concerning Hilbert's Programme Caused by the Löwenheim-Skolem Theorem

As it is said above (Section 4.2.1), the Löwenheim-Skolem Theorem concerns the relation between a first-order formal theory and its interpretation. Now, we have to remember that at the time when the Löwenheim Theorem appeared one of the main concern of mathematicians was to formulate, as first-order formal theories, the set theory, the theory of elementary arithmetic, the theory of real numbers and of the continuum in general (within the formalized set theory or independently of it). These theories were expected to be in accordance with Hilbert's Programme, i.e., to be consistent, complete and categorical, expressing formally and unequivocally all the truths discovered informally or semi-formally in the respective mathematical theories, i.e., in the Cantorian set theory, the Fregean or Dedekindian Arithmetic and in the general theory of the continuum applicable in the theory of real numbers as well as in geometry. For this "paradise state," in which a real breakthrough concerning the formal foundation of the most important mathematical theories was expected, the Löwenheim's Theorem and Skolem's analysis of its consequences represented a real disaster.

In the first place, the Löwenheim-Skolem Theorem implies the existence of non-intended models of all the mentioned formal theories that are non-isomorphic with the intended models. This means that these theories are necessarily not categorical.

The non-categoricity of a theory means that we cannot formally distinguish what is distinguishable in the corresponding informal or semi-formal theory. In particular, the cardinality becomes something relative [11, pp. 108ff], for, according to the generalized version of the Löwenheim-Skolem Theorem, the structure in which the theory is interpreted can be taken to be of any cardinality whatsoever. This relativeness of the cardinals was very disturbing both to Skolem [32, pp. 223ff] and von Neumann [28, pp. 239–240]. For von Neumann, it suggests a kind of unreality of cardinals and therefore serves as the argument in favour of Intuitionism.

And finally, one can make one step more, which Skolem did, and raise the question about a possible paradox [33], since, as we shall see, a sentence stating the existence of uncountable sets can be true after being interpreted in a structure whose basic set is denumerable.

4.3.2 The Non-categoricalness and the Formal Indistinguishability of the Informally Distinguishable

In order to illustrate the problem of the non-categoricity of a formal theory, I shall start with the formal theory of elementary arithmetic as the simplest and most obvious case.

4 The Philosophical Impact of the Löwenheim-Skolem Theorem

The objects of the basic set of the relational-operational structure that is the intended model of the fully formalized elementary arithmetic are numbers 0, 1, 2, 3, ... for which the so-called Archimedes Axiom holds and which are all finite in spite of the fact that there is an infinite number of them. As it is standardly defined, "an Archimedean model of arithmetic is a model in which for every number N and for every [positive] number ϵ there is a finite number n such that $\epsilon + \epsilon + \ldots + \epsilon > N$, where ϵ is taken n times" [1, pp. 926f].

Let us imagine, however, a structure that does not differ from the intended model in any other respect except that in it the Archimedes Axiom does not hold. This means that in the basic set of this structure, in addition to finite numbers, there are numbers that are infinite in the sense that they cannot be reached in a finite number of steps by starting from any number that is finite in the sense in which all members of the basic set of an Archimedean model are finite. It is evident that this non-Archimedean structure is not isomorphic with the structure that is the intended model of the formal theory of elementary arithmetic.

However, though in such a non-Archimedean model there are numbers a and b such that there is no n that is finite and such that $a \times n \geq b$, the structure supposedly does not differ from an Archimedean structure in no other respect. So, every number, be it finite or infinite, has its unique immediate successor.

Now, given that there is an infinite number of infinite numbers just as there is an infinite number of finite numbers, the fact that there is no maximal element of the set of finite numbers in the given non-Archimedean structure is completely analogues to the fact that there is no minimal element of the set of infinite numbers. This means, in effect, that there is an infinite subset of the set of elements of the basic set of the given non-Archimedean structure that does not have a minimal element, which means, consequently, that, in view of two pairs of conditions cited in Section 4.1.5, conditions (1) and (2) are satisfied, whereas the condition (2') is not.

One would certainly like that, in accordance with Hilbert's programme, the formal theory of elementary arithmetic grasps the difference between the Archimedean and the non-Archimedean arithmetic so that if the former is a model of the formal theory, the latter is not. Unfortunately, this cannot be done if the formal theory is a first-order theory.

The problem is that the axioms that would be formulated in the style of Dedekind and Peano do not enable us to preclude the existence of infinite (or hyper-finite) numbers in the basic set of the intended model of the theory. For instance, it will be true that for any two a and b such that $0 < a$ and $a < b$, it holds that there is n such that $a \times n \geq b$, independently on whether we interpret the formal theory in an Archimedean or in a non-Archimedean structure, for if b is a hyper-finite number, n can be a hyper-finite number as well. One could try to impose a limitation to standard numbers, as Fraenkel did in a similar context [10, pp. 233–34], by adding the Axiom of Restriction to Peano's arithmetic, say of the form

$$\forall x [x = 0 \vee x = 0' \vee x = 0'' \vee \ldots],$$

but this expression is of infinite length and is, therefore, not legitimate within the framework of the standard first-order theory. And there is no way of reformulating it within the standard framework.

If one tries to use the fact that in the non-Archimedean structures there are infinite sets that have no minimal element whereas in the Archimedean structures it is not so in order to make the difference between the two, this would also lead nowhere, since the variables of the formal theory of arithmetic range over the numbers and not over their sets. To express the difference, one would need a second-order language.

All in all, there is no way to avoid the non-categoricalness by interpreting the first-order formal theory of arithmetic in such a way that it becomes also possible to distinguish formally what is distinguishable in the meta-theory.

4.3.3 Skolem's Paradox

It was only in 1928 that Hilbert and Ackermann formulated quite precisely the concept of the completeness of a logical syntax with respect to a given semantic theory [22]. Only two years later, Gödel was quick to prove, in his doctoral dissertation, his famous Completeness Theorem [17], which is now called simply Gödel's Completeness Theorem, in contrast to his Incompleteness Theorem [19], which concerns the question of the syntactical incompleteness (see Section 4.1.3 above). Gödel's Completeness Theorem says that:

Theorem 4 *A sentence σ of a first-order formal theory Σ is true in all the models of Σ if σ is a theorem of Σ.*

By using this theorem, it is easier to reach the point of Skolem's Paradox than in the way in which it was done by Skolem himself, who, for this purpose, could use only the Löwenheim-Skolem Theorem itself.

By Gödel's Completeness Theorem, if a first-order formulation of the Zermelo-Fraenkel Set Theory (**ZF**) is consistent, then each theorem of **ZF** is true in any of its models. Now, by the Löwenheim-Skolem Theorem, one of the models of **ZF** is denumerable. Let S be such a model and let A be the basic set of S, and R a binary relation formulated in **ZF** and interpreted in S as $\in$ defined on A. For the sake of convenience, let us take that, if a member c of A stands in the relation R to a member b of A, c is a member of b in S, i.e., we shall speak of b as if it were the set $\{c \mid cRb\}$ (of all the members c such that cRb). In addition, let us denote by ω the only member x of A that satisfies in S the formula "x is the least infinite ordinal." Now, on the one hand, it is a theorem of **ZF** that there are uncountable sets, so, (1) the set A must have a member a such that it is true in S that a is not denumerable. On the other hand, however, (2) all the members b of a in S are members of A, which is supposedly a denumerable set. (1) and (2) are seemingly inconsistent, and this is what is known as Skolem's Paradox [12, p. 303].

Since, as mentioned above, (1) and (2), taken together, seem to imply the relativization of the cardinality, Skolem's Paradox is sometimes also understood as referring to this fact, if, namely, one is prone to believe, as von Neumann was, that the relativeness of cardinality is inconsistent with the way in which the very concept of cardinality is to be understood.

4.4 The Positive Reactions to the Löwenheim-Skolem Theorem: To Blame the Language or to Re-investigate Structures?

Confronted with all the unpleasant consequences of the Löwenheim-Skolem Theorem and of Skolem's Paradox in particular, one can try, in view of the fact that the Theorem concerns the relation between a formal theory and its interpretation, to find one of the following two ways out of the situation: to blame the first-orderness of the language in which formal theories are supposedly formulated and use a stronger language to formulate them or to re-investigate the very structures the theories are about in order to re-define at least some of the key concepts underlying their understanding. Or perhaps, as the third possibility, one can find that it is necessary to do both.

4.4.1 The Weakness of the Language

As a consequence of the so-called linguistic turn in philosophy that happened at the beginning of twentieth century, one could reasonably expect that the first option was ready to be endorsed, both by mathematicians as well as by philosophers. A general lesson of the linguistic turn has been that very many, even if not all, problems and apparent paradoxes which we are confronted with by dealing with reality have their origin in the language we use to speak of it. Isn't it so also in the philosophy of mathematics, where, at those days, the stubborn practice to stick to first-order theories was nearly canonized?

The idea of blaming the language of formal theories for the disastrous consequences of the Löwenheim-Skolem Theorem may arise quite naturally by analysing the informal or semi-formal theories themselves which the main formal theories were to formalize. The point is that the axiom systems used by mathematicians were formulated within theories—such as informal set theory in the first place—which were essentially second-order theories, so that one had indeed categorical axiom systems for natural numbers theory, for real numbers theory and for geometry. It is a bit strange that this fact had not been earlier anticipated as a possible source of the problem that later emerged as a consequence of the Löwenheim-Skolem Theorem. Let me give an example.

As mentioned in Section 4.1.5, Cantor was the first to clearly realize that there are two conditions which have to be met if a structure is to be continuous. A set of elements makes up a continuum if and only if (1) it is perfect, and (2) coherent (*zusammenhängend*) [5, p. 190]. The first condition is easy to formulate within a first-order language, because the density axiom, if added to the rest of axioms defining a linearly ordered structure, implies that in any model there is an infinite number of elements accumulating about any of its elements. So, $\langle \mathbb{Q}, \leq \rangle$ as the standard perfect structure, is implicitly defined by the following eight axioms:

$$\forall \alpha_n \; \neg \alpha_n < \alpha_n \tag{4.1}$$

$$\forall \alpha_l \forall \alpha_m \forall \alpha_n ((\alpha_l < \alpha_m \wedge \alpha_m < \alpha_n) \rightarrow \alpha_l < \alpha_n) \tag{4.2}$$

$$\forall \alpha_m \forall \alpha_n (\alpha_m < \alpha_n \vee \alpha_n < \alpha_m \vee \alpha_m = \alpha_n) \tag{4.3}$$

$$\forall \alpha_l \forall \alpha_m \forall \alpha_n ((\alpha_l = \alpha_m \wedge \alpha_l < \alpha_n) \rightarrow \alpha_m < \alpha_n) \tag{4.4}$$

$$\forall \alpha_l \forall \alpha_m \forall \alpha_n ((\alpha_l = \alpha_m \wedge \alpha_n < \alpha_l) \rightarrow \alpha_n < \alpha_m) \tag{4.5}$$

$$\forall \alpha_m \exists \alpha_n \; \alpha_m < \alpha_n \tag{4.6}$$

$$\forall \alpha_m \exists \alpha_n \; \alpha_n < \alpha_m \tag{4.7}$$

$$\forall \alpha_m \forall \alpha_n (\alpha_m < \alpha_n \rightarrow \exists \alpha_l (\alpha_m < \alpha_l \wedge \alpha_l < \alpha_n)) \tag{4.8}$$

where the last axiom is the density axiom.

However, the second condition cannot be formulated within a standard first-order theory. Namely, in order to say that the basic set is not only perfect but also coherent (*zusammenhängend*), we have to mention explicitly an infinite number of elements, for, according to Cantor, a set is coherent only if any accumulation of an infinite number of elements has the accumulation point that is an element of the basic set itself. In other words, any infinite accumulation from the left to the right must have the least upper bound that is an element of the basic set itself just as any infinite accumulation from the right to the left must have the greatest lower bound that is an element of the basic set itself. This can be expressed only in the second-order language or in the extended first-order language, which is now known as the infinitary language $L_{\omega_1\omega_1}$. For the reasons that will be mentioned below (in Section 4.5.4), let me formulate the two necessary axioms in the language $L_{\omega_1\omega_1}$ [2]:

$$\forall \alpha_1 \forall \alpha_2 \ldots \forall \alpha_i \ldots$$
$$(\exists \beta_1 \bigwedge_{1 \leq i < \omega} \alpha_i < \beta_1 \Rightarrow \exists \gamma_1 (\bigwedge_{1 \leq i < \omega} \alpha_i < \gamma_1 \wedge \neg \exists \delta_1 (\bigwedge_{1 \leq i < \omega} \alpha_i < \delta_1 \wedge \delta_1 < \gamma_1))) \tag{4.9}$$

$$\forall \alpha_1 \forall \alpha_2 \ldots \forall \alpha_i \ldots$$
$$(\exists \beta_1 \bigwedge_{1 \leq i < \omega} \alpha_i > \beta_1 \rightarrow \exists \gamma_1 (\bigwedge_{1 \leq i < \omega} \alpha_i > \gamma_1 \wedge \neg \exists \delta_1 (\bigwedge_{1 \leq i < \omega} \alpha_i < \delta_1 \wedge \delta_1 > \gamma_1))) \tag{4.10}$$

(where $\alpha_m > \alpha_n \leftrightarrow_{def} \alpha_n < \alpha_m$). Notice that the antecedents in these two axioms are unavoidable because in $\langle \mathbb{R}, \leq \rangle$, which is the intended model of the system representing a linear continuum, there are infinite subsets of $\mathbb{R}$ without an upper and/or a lower bound, so that what we want to say is that if there is an upper (lower) bound at all, there is also the least upper (greatest lower) bound.

But now, though the above axiom system is formulated in the extended first-order language, the last two axioms contain infinite conjunctions, which was not legitimate at the time at which the continuum theory was to be formulated as a formal theory.

Generalizing the point of the previous example and turning to Skolem's Paradox and all the related problems concerning the non-categoricity of formal theories proposed at the time we are speaking about, we can simply say that the language used in the formulation of these theories was blind for making all the differences expressible only in a non-standard language. In particular, this means that, bearing on mind the meaning of Skolem's Paradox, there can be a relation between the elements of the basic set which is uninterpretable as any relation of a given formal theory but which makes the statement of the uncountability of the basic set true, in spite of the fact that all the relations envisaged by the theory are such that they make the very same basic set countable.

So, one might say that the allegedly paradoxical consequences of the Löwenheim-Skolem Theorem represent nothing else but just a striking example of the weakness of the first-order language for describing the structures in which they are interpreted.

Some mathematicians were ready to accept this as the end of the story. So, already in 1930, Zermelo formulated the set theory in the second-order language [41]. More than three decades later, Abraham Robinson offered a second-order formulation of the non-Archimedean arithmetic and real numbers theory, which contain infinite numbers and infinitesimals [29].

The semantics of the second-order logic is far less clear than the semantics of the first-order logic and, in addition, many philosophers are reluctant, for various reasons, to accept the ontological commitments that follow from the ontology of classes, properties and relations implied by the second-order mathematics. But this is not the matter of our concern. So, let us turn directly to the second strategy of dealing with the consequences of the Löwenheim-Skolem Theorem, which assumes that the Theorem tells us something important about the very relational structures in which formal theories are interpreted.

4.4.2 Changing Cardinalities: The Relativeness of Cardinality as a Language-Independent Property

If the lesson concerning the weakness of the first-order language in view of mathematicians' attempts to use it by trying to formalize informal set theory, natural numbers theory, real numbers theory, etc. were all that the Löwenheim-Skolem Theorem contributed to, it would certainly be a big result which got rid mathematical and philosophical community of a prejudice that characterized the naïve and ill-founded hope of the "paradise state" in the first three decades of twentieth century. But it would not be what it is now believed to be [11, p. 106]—one of the greatest results in the history of the twentieth century mathematics, which threw a new light on some basic concepts of the set theory and the concept of relational structures in general. The meaning of this latter result became clearly visible only much later through some revolutionary results of Paul Cohen, Solomon Feferman and Azriel Lévy in the seventh decade of twentieth century. But, before turning to these results, I shall try to elucidate the main point by analyzing in a more detailed way Skolem's Paradox itself and by using a quite simple example.

Those who, by resolving Skolem's Paradox, stress the weakness of the first-order formalization of informal set theory for distinguishing cardinalities of different models in which the formal theory is interpretable do not have to stop at this defeatist conclusion, and normally they don't. The *explanation* of the blindness of a formal theory consists in the fact that there can be a relation "invisible" by the theory which makes a countable model uncountable or an uncountable model countable.

As for the first possibility, it is sufficient that one is reminded of the example concerning the second Cantor's condition for the continuity of an ordered structure (see Section 4.4.1). Though, in accordance with Hilbert's Programme, the difference between the ordering relation of only dense and continuous structures should be grasped axiomatically (see Section 4.1.5 above), and though this can be done by the use of the language $L_{\omega_1\omega_1}$ (as suggested in Section 4.4.1), it cannot be done within a standard first-order theory, and it is exactly the formal indistinguishability between these two ordering relations that makes it possible that the theorem of **ZF** about the existence of uncountable sets is true even if the ordering relation of a structure in which the first-order formalization of **ZF** is interpreted makes its basic set denumerable.

The second possibility is more intriguing. How could it be that a supposedly uncountable model becomes countable?—Let us start with quite a simple case. Suppose that we have a formal theory interpretable in a structure that is dense but not continuous. Is this model also countable? The immediate response will be: "Yes, of course! The set of rational numbers is dense, but it is also countable." However obvious this answer might be, there is a fact that can be easily overlooked, but which is of crucial importance. We know that there are several functions which define mappings of the set of rationals in such a way that the set of images is directly countable. For instance, we can "arrange" the set of positive rational numbers as follows:

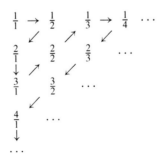

and then pick them up following directions indicated by arrows, obtaining the 1–1 mapping onto the set of natural numbers, which is directly countable. Since knowledge implies truth, the positive answer to the question of countability of rational numbers seems self-evident. But this "self-evidence" may hide the fact that, independently of our knowledge or ignorance, it is yet the case that the model is denumerable only because there are mappings such as the given one. If, counterfactually, we hadn't known that there are such mappings, it would have been far from evident that it is so.

The point could be considered philosophically perverse if there were no other, much more interesting cases in which the same phenomenon appears. The most interesting one concerns the denumerability of the set of real numbers.

As his most famous result, Cohen proved 1963 that if **ZF** is consistent, it remains consistent when the Axiom of Choice and the Generalized Continuum Hypothesis are added [6, 7]. Using the model of Cohen's type applied in this proof, Feferman and Lévy proved that, by omitting the Axiom of Choice, "if **ZF** is consistent, it stays consistent after addition of the following axiom: the set of real numbers is a denumerable union of denumerable sets" [9, p. 593].[1] And then, since it can be proved that the set of elements of a denumerable union of denumerable sets is itself denumerable, it follows that, under given assumptions, the set of real numbers is denumerable!

Ironically, the fact that the set of elements of a denumerable union of denumerable sets is itself denumerable can be proved by the very same method that I have just used above for showing that the set of rational numbers is denumerable, and which was originally used by Cantor himself! Namely, let $B_1, B_2, B_3, \ldots$ be members of a denumerable union and $a_{11}, a_{12}, a_{13}, \ldots$ elements of B_1, $a_{21}, a_{22}, a_{23}, \ldots$ elements of B_2, $a_{31}, a_{32}, a_{33}, \ldots$ elements of B_3, and so on. Now, by "arranging" the elements of $B_1, B_2, B_3, \ldots$ as follows:

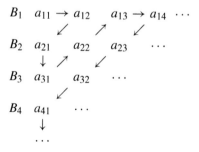

and picking them up following directions indicated by arrows, we obtain the 1–1 mapping onto the set of natural numbers, which is directly countable.

Further elucidation concerning the significance of the omission of the Axiom of Choice lies outside the scope of this paper. So, we shall turn directly to general philosophical aspects concerning the mentioned consequences of the relativization of cardinalities.

---

[1] See also [8, p. 146] and [24, p. 142]

4.5 Concluding Logico-Ontological Considerations

Even for the hardest Platonists, the realm of higher order infinities transcending $2^{\aleph_0}$, however interesting it may be for mathematicians, seems unsurveyable from an ontological point of view. So, by dealing with philosophically interesting consequences of the Löwenheim-Skolem Theorem and Skolem's Paradox in particular, we shall focus our attention to discrete, dense and continuous structures that are sufficiently close to reality in a common sense of the word, but which involve, at the same time, the relevant difference between the countable and the uncountable.

4.5.1 Cardinality as a Non-absolute Property

As we have just seen (in Section 4.4.2), the resolution of Skolem's Paradox that has had the most important impact in mathematics demands the relativization of cardinalities. This relativization seems to be in a blatant contradiction with the very concept of cardinal number as it was originally defined by Cantor (see Section 4.1.4). Though the status of the Continuum Hypothesis allows us to take that $2^{\aleph_0} = \aleph_1$ but also that it is not so (some mathematicians have suggested that we should rather take that $2^{\aleph_0} = \aleph_2$ [37]), this does not mean that we may assume both to be the case at the same time. So, we need some reconceptualization of cardinality if it should be allowed to be non-absolute.

Now, the above consideration and the cited examples suggest a clear way in which the concept of cardinality is to be re-defined. Instead of speaking of the cardinality of a set as such, we should rather speak of the cardinality in a qualified sense, namely, of the cardinality of the basic set of a structure. In the literature, it is quite common to speak of the countability or uncountability of a model. This is not correct strictly speaking, but it can be accepted as a *façon de parler*. It is yet a set which is countable or uncountable, but it is always a basic set of a structure, which also contains relations, and the countability or the uncountability of such a set depends essentially on relations defined on it. So, instead of simply saying that a set is countable, we should always say that it is countable in view of this or that relation. Then, it becomes consistent to say that a set is uncountable in view of this but countable in view of that relation. Even the simplest example shows what this means. The set of rationals is not countable in view of the way in which the rationals are ordered by the standard precedence relation. But if we order them in a different way, by using one of the well-known functions, their set becomes countable. However trivial this may seem, it ceases to be trivial when we turn to real numbers, where under certain conditions they can be mapped onto a structure in such a way that they start to be countable (see Section 4.4.2). So, as suggested, it is not the set as such which is countable or uncountable but the set structured in a certain way.

4.5.2 Changing Cardinalities: Relation-Dependence Without Re-structuring the Structures

There is one thing that can be said to remain ambiguous in the just given explanation of the relativity of cardinality. It is said that the cardinality of a set can change depending on different relations that can be defined on it as the basic set. Can these different relations be assumed to hold simultaneously in a relational structure? The question is very important, for if the answer were negative, one could say that, in fact, one and the same basic set as the set of a relational structure cannot *be* uncountable and countable *at the same time*. We should say instead that, if uncountable, it can only be mapped onto a structure which is countable.

The question is tricky. On the one hand, we want to say that the set of rational numbers and (under certain conditions) the set of real numbers are countable. On the other hand, if we admit that they become countable only after appropriate re-structuring of their elements, one could say that after such a re-structuring the elements cease to be rationals or reals and become natural numbers.

I do not see any other way out but to distinguish between two senses of countability, direct and derivative, and say that the set of rational numbers and the set of real numbers are countable because there is a different structure whose basic set is directly countable and, at the same time, such that its elements can serve as images of the elements of the basic set of the original structures. After all, it is a function that maps all the rationals or reals onto a set of their images that gives the meaning to the statement that the set of rationals and the set of reals are countable. We mustn't detach the meaning of countability from the existence of such a function, because it is actually only the set of images that is directly countable. This seems to be the only way in which we can continue to speak of rationals as rationals and of reals as reals, and to say, at the same time, that their sets are countable.

By generalizing the given example, we can say that the relativity of cardinality concerns the change of cardinality of the basic set of a structure in view of its possible mapping onto the basic set of a different structure. So, the set of real numbers does not cease to be uncountable in spite of the fact that there is a model in which the set of their images is denumerable.

4.5.3 The World and Its Substance: Relation Externalism and the Problem of Referring to Objects by Re-structuring the Structures

According to Wittgenstein's Tractatus, the substance of the world is just the set of its objects [40, 2.021], whereas the world itself is a complex relational structure involving all the actual relations between objects [40, 2.022].

Now, I suggested above (in Section 4.5.2) that rational or real numbers would cease to be what they are if they were structured as natural numbers and that this represents the reason for using their images when speaking of their countability (in a derivative sense). This seems to be in a direct contradiction to Russell's relation externalism (see Section 4.1.1), according to which the objects remain what they are after having changed their relation to other objects. I think that relation externalism fails in this case only because numbers are not entities like ordinary objects in space and time.

Let us speak, however, of the so-called rational points of a line segment, so that 0 refers to the left end-point, 1 to the right end-point, $\frac{1}{2}$ to the mid-point of the segment, and so on. Now, if we accept, at least *arguendo*, that points are basic elements of the real world, as Cantor did [5, pp. 275ff], we can imagine a real re-structuring of the points of the given line segment such that the set of its former rational points becomes directly countable. But in this case we only use rational numbers to pick out the objects (points) that supposedly exist in reality independently of how we refer to them, while in the case in which we speak of numbers themselves it is not so. By using the theory of meaning holism, we should say that we cannot refer to $\frac{1}{2}$ as an element of a relational structure by ignoring its position in the given relational structure. There is nothing like "Venus" that could be used here to refer to $\frac{1}{2}$ directly (see Section 4.1.2).

The difference between the above two cases—numbers versus points—may become crucial when we try to apply the relativity of cardinality to the analysis of reality in a sense that is stronger that the sense in which we speak of reality of numbers. Namely, it seems that, in view of the possibility of an actual re-structuring of the continuum, there is a sense in which it could be possible that the cardinal number of the basic set actually becomes $\aleph_0$. And then again, starting from the elements of such a decomposed continuum as a pure "substance of the world," God could build up, in the inverse order, the world such as it actually is. The possibility of this scenario, which is based on the relativity of cardinality, shows that, however complex the world may be, for its constitution, it might be sufficient that its "substance" is of cardinality $\aleph_0$.

4.5.4 How to Apply Hilbert's Programme in the Formalization of God's Re-structuring the Elements of the Space-World

As I have just suggested, if the process of changing cardinalities could have been understood as the process of a real downward decomposition of the world, it should be also possible to suppose that God, in an inverse process, has structured the real space-world by starting from a set of its basic elements whose cardinality is $\aleph_0$. The natural question is, then, how we are to proceed when trying to formalize each of the higher-order structures obtained in the process of God's re-structuring the world.

If we restrict our attention up to the stage at which one-dimensional continua have been created, the question will be reduced to the formal distinction between discrete, dense and continuous structures. However poor this might seem in view of other structures envisaged in the transfinite mathematics, it will be enough for understanding what the application of Hilbert's Programme would generally look like.

4 The Philosophical Impact of the Löwenheim-Skolem Theorem

The first important question concerns language. As we saw above (see Section 4.4.1), the standard first-order language would not do the job. This means that we have to choose between some of stronger languages. For several reasons, I suggest that we use the language $L_{\omega_1\omega_1}$ [3]. One of these reasons is that we would not have to add anything to our basic assumption that the "world substance" is a set of an infinite number of elements whose cardinal number is $\aleph_0$ and would also not have to refer directly to any set at all. So, the variables will range, during the whole process of the world construction, only over the elements of one and the same basic set. The second important reason is that we shall be able to treat any of the theories formalizing a higher-order structure as a direct axiomatic extension of the lower-order theory, which will explain the relation between the non-categoricalness and incompleteness of a theory in an interesting way. This should be one of the most interesting results concerning the question we are dealing with.

The second important question concerns the Hilbertian idea that the difference between the structures we are dealing with should be a consequence of the difference in the meaning of the ordering relation, which is to be grasped only axiomatically (see Section 4.1.5). This means that, contrary to Cantor, we do not have to add anything else concerning the cardinality of the basic set as such if we find that a model of the theory formalizing a higher-order structure is non-denumerable, because (as stated in Section 4.5.1) the cardinality of a structure does not concern the basic set as such but its cardinality in view of a certain relation.

Now, if we want to formalize the linear structure that is only dense, we shall naturally add the density axiom to the rest of axioms defining implicitly a linearly ordered structure (see Section 4.4.1). The problem is, however, that the obtained formal theory has non-isomorphic models, as we can see by anticipating the next step of God's re-structuring the world. Moreover, the models will differ just in view of their cardinality!

The standard model of a dense structure is the set of rational points, whose cardinal number is $\aleph_0$. However, let us start with the unit continuum [0, 1] (supposedly already created by God) and delete, in addition to its two end-points, all the open intervals $(\frac{1}{3}, \frac{2}{3})$, $(\frac{1}{9}, \frac{2}{9})$, $(\frac{7}{9}, \frac{8}{9})$, $(\frac{1}{27}, \frac{2}{27})$, $(\frac{7}{27}, \frac{8}{27})$, $(\frac{19}{27}, \frac{20}{27})$, $(\frac{25}{27}, \frac{26}{27})$, ... and so on analogously. Now, since $\frac{1}{3} + \frac{2}{9} + \frac{4}{27} + \ldots + \frac{2^{n-1}}{3^n} + \ldots = 1$, the length of the deleted intervals is metrically equal to 1, while the remaining points make up a discontinuum, which is a set metrically equal to zero. This set, which is known as Cantor's ternary set, is dense (i.e., perfect in Cantor's terminology), which is easy to see. But, since the cardinal number of all the deleted intervals is supposedly greater than $\aleph_0$, the cardinal number of such a discontinuum should also be greater than $\aleph_0$, which means that it represents a non-standard model of the system containing just first eight axioms cited above (in Section 4.4.1).

Ignoring metrical differences between the basic sets of the two models—the set of rational points and Cantor's discontinuum—which can be treated as something external and irrelevant for the basic isomorphism between the models of the axiom system that contains the density axiom, the question concerning the difference in cardinality remains unsolved. Given the relativity of cardinality, on the basis of which we have supposed that the cardinal number of the basic set of elements of God's construction of the world that contains the structures of higher cardinalities is not greater than $\aleph_0$, as well as the assumption that the introduction of a higher cardinality can mean nothing else but a change of the holistic meaning of the ordering relation, we must try, by pursuing the Hilbertian approach, to grasp this change axiomatically.

Contrary to standard dense but not continuous structures, Cantor's discontinuum as a specific, non-standard discontinuous structure, which contains "wholes" that are continuous, can be expressed only in a system that contains axioms 4.9 and 4.10 (see Section 4.4.1), which implicitly define structures of a higher cardinality. This means that the system containing just first eight axioms must be said to be incomplete, since it is non-trivially extendable through the introduction of new axioms. So, the specific non-categoricalness of the system defining dense structures can be overcome if we complete it in one way or another by using axioms 4.9 and 4.10 or their negations. Let us mention that we can get interesting non-standard models by adding only one of the two axioms [3, 3.3].

But again, if we add axioms 4.9 and 4.10 that are necessary for obtaining linear continua, we obtain a formal theory that is further completable in different ways! In particular, the system containing 10 axioms cited above (in Section 4.4.1) can be extended through the introduction of the large-scale and the small-scale Archimedean axiom as well as through the introduction of the non-Archimedean ones. So, for instance, we can preclude the non-standard interpretation by introducing the following two axioms [3, p. 42]:

$$\exists \alpha_1 \exists \alpha_2 \ldots \exists \alpha_n \ldots (\alpha_2 < \alpha_1 \wedge \bigwedge_{1 \leq i < \omega} \alpha_{2i-1} < \alpha_{2i+1} \wedge \bigwedge_{1 \leq i < \omega} \alpha_{2i+2} < \alpha_{2i} \wedge$$
$$\wedge \forall \beta \bigwedge_{1 \leq i < \omega} ((\alpha_i < \beta \wedge \beta < \alpha_{i+2}) \rightarrow \bigwedge_{1 \leq k < \omega} \neg \beta = \alpha_k) \wedge \qquad (4.11)$$
$$\wedge \forall \gamma \bigvee_{1 \leq i, j < \omega} (\alpha_i < \gamma \wedge \gamma < \alpha_j))$$

and

$$\exists \alpha_1 \ldots \exists \alpha_n \ldots$$
$$(\forall \beta \bigvee_{1 \leq i, j < \omega} (\alpha_i < \beta \wedge \beta < \alpha_j) \wedge \forall \gamma \forall \delta (\gamma < \delta \rightarrow \bigvee_{1 \leq i < \omega} (\gamma < \alpha_k \wedge \alpha_k < \delta)))$$
(4.12)

where the first of them precludes the hyper-finite elements, while the second one precludes infinitesimals.

And so on, and so forth. It is clear in which way we are to cope with the problem of non-categoricalness. Though it is not possible to settle this problem once for ever, whenever it can be reduced to the incompleteness question, we can apply the *pay-as-you-go* strategy and preclude the unintended non-isomorphic models by a concrete extension of the theory. And in a possible case in which it were not possible to proceed in this way any longer, the problem should be re-considered as the question concerning the weakness of the formal language we have used.

And finally, as for the question about cardinalities of different structures we come across by following God's re-structuring the world, it must be admitted that it cannot be answered in a straightforward way, since it is not clear how exactly mathematicians themselves use the concept of cardinality after its re-conceptualization in view of the Löwenheim-Skolem Theorem and the cited results of Cohen, Feferman and Lévy. As I suggested above, only discrete structures like $\langle \mathbb{N}, \leq \rangle$, should be said to be directly denumerable. But this does not mean that there are not special reasons for distinguishing various kinds of countability in the derivative sense. Mathematical reality is more complex than the reality of the Cantorian space-world we have been talking about. It would be interesting to see which reasons have led some of mathematicians to assume that $2^{\aleph_0} = \aleph_2$ [37], but such an investigation lies outside the scope of this paper.

Acknowledgments I am very much thankful to Miloš Adžić for discussions about the topic and an anonymous referee for useful comments on an earlier draft of the paper.

References

1. Arkeryd, Leif. 2005. "Nonstandard Analysis." *The American Mathematical Monthly* 112:926–28.
2. Arsenijević, Miloš, and Miodrag Kapetanović. 2008. "The 'Great Struggle' Between Cantorians and Neo-Aristotelians: Much Ado About Nothing." *Grazer Philosophische Studien* 76:79–90.
3. Arsenijević, Miloš, and Miodrag Kapetanović. 2008. "An $L_{\omega_1\omega_1}$ Axiomatization of the Linear Archimedean Continua as Merely Relational Structures." *WSEAS Transactions on Mathematics* 7:39–47.
4. Brouwer, Luitzen Egbertus Jan. 1975. *Collected Works I*. Amsterdam: North-Holland and Elsevier.
5. Cantor, Georg. 1962. *Gesammelte Abhandlungen mathematischen und philosophischen Inhalts*. Edited by Ernst Zermelo. Hildesheim: Georg Olms.
6. Cohen, Paul. 1963. "The Independence of the Continuum Hypothesis." *Proceedings of the National Academy of Sciences of the USA* 50:1143–48.
7. Cohen, Paul. 1964. "The Independence of the Continuum Hypothesis II." *Proceedings of the National Academy of Sciences of the USA* 51:105–10.
8. Cohen, Paul. 1966. *Set Theory and the Continuum Hypothesis*. New York, NY: W.A. Benjamin.
9. Feferman, Solomon, and Azriel Lévy. 1963. "Independence Results in Set Theory by Cohen's Method II." *Notices of the American Mathematical Society* 10:592–93.
10. Fraenkel, Abraham Adolf. 1922. "Zu den Grundlagen der Cantor-Zermeloschen Mengenlehre." *Mathematische Annalen* 86:230–37.
11. Fraenkel, Abraham Adolf, and Yehoshua Bar-Hillel. 1958. *Foundations of Set Theory*. Amsterdam: North-Holland.
12. Fraenkel, Abraham Adolf, Yehoshua Bar-Hillel, and Azriel Levy. 1973. *Foundation of Set Theory*. 2nd revised edition. Amsterdam: North-Holland.

13. Frege, Gottlob. 1960. "Fuction and Concept." In *Translation from the Philosophical Writings of Gottlob Frege*, edited by Peter Geach and Max Black, 21–41. Oxford: Blackwell.
14. Frege, Gottlob. 1960. "On Concept and Object." In *Translation from the Philosophical Writings of Gottlob Frege*, edited by Peter Geach and Max Black, 42–55. Oxford: Blackwell.
15. Frege, Gottlob. 1960. "On Sense and Reference." In *Translation from the Philosophical Writings of Gottlob Frege*, edited by Peter Geach and Max Black, 56–78. Oxford: Blackwell.
16. Frege, Gottlob. 1964. *Basic Laws of Arithmetic*. Edited by M. Furth. Berkeley, CA: University of California Press.
17. Gödel, Kurt. 1930. "Die Vollständigkeit der Axiome des logischen Funktionenkalküls." *Monatschriften für Mathematik und Physik* 37:349–60.
18. Gödel, Kurt. 1930/1931. "Über Vollständigkeit und Widerspruchsfreiheit." *Ergebnisse eines mathematischen Kolloquiums* 3:12–13.
19. Gödel, Kurt. 1931. "Über formal unentscheibare Sätze der Pricipia Mathematica und verwandter Systeme I." *Monatschriften für Mathematik und Physik* 38:173–98.
20. Hilbert, David. 1918. "Axiomatisches Denken." *Mathematische Annalen* 78:405–19.
21. Hilbert, David. 1922. "Neubegründung der Mathematik: Erste Mitteilung." *Abhandlungen aus dem Seminar der Hamburgischen Universität* 1:157–77.
22. Hilbert, David, and Wilhelm Friedrich Ackermann. 1928. *Grundzüge der theoretischen Logik*. Berlin: Springer.
23. Hilbert, David. 1964. "On the Infinite." In *Philosophy of Mathematics*, edited by Paul Benacerraf and Hilary Putnam, 134–54. Upper Saddle River, NJ: Prentice-Hall.
24. Jech, Thomas. 1973. *The Axiom of Choice*. Amsterdam: North-Holland.
25. Lévy, Azriel. 1963. "Independence Results in Set Theory by Cohens method I." *Notices of the American Mathematical Society* 10:592–93.
26. Löwenheim, Leopold. 1915. "Über Möglichkeiten in Relativkalkül." *Mathematische Annalen* 76:447–70.
27. Malcev, Anatoly. 1936. "Untersuchungen aus dem Gebiet der mathematischen Logik." *Recueil Mathématique* 43:323–36.
28. von Neumann, John. 1925. "Eine Axiomatisierung der Mengenlehre." *Jahrschrift für Mathematik* 154:219–40.
29. Robinson, Abraham. 1966. *Non-standard Analysis*. Amsterdam: North-Holland.
30. Russell, Bertrand. 1997. *My Philosophical Development*, revised edition 1995. London: Routledge.
31. Skolem, Thoralf. 1920. "Logisch-kombinatorische Untersuchungen über die Erfüllbarkeit oder Beweisbarkeit mathematischer Sätze nebst einem Theoreme über dichte Mengen." *Skrifter utgit av Videnskapselkapet i Kristiania I, Matematiska-Naturvetenskap Kl* 4:1–36.
32. Skolem, Thoralf. 1922. "Einige Bemerkungen zur axiomatischen Begründung der Mengenlehre." *Wissenschaftliche Vorträge gehalten auf dem 5. Kongress der skandinavischen Mathematiker in Helsingfors* 4:217–32.
33. Skolem, Thoralf. 1923. "Begründung der elementaren Arithmetik durch die rekurrierende Denkweise ohne Anwendung scheinbarer Veränderlichen mit unendlichem Ausdehnungsbereich." *Skrifter utgit av Videnskapselkapet i Kristiania I, Matematiska-Naturvetenskap Kl* 6:1–38.
34. Skolem, Thoralf. 1928. "Über die mathematische Logik." *Norsk. Mat. Tidsk.* 10:125–42.
35. Skolem, Thoralf. 1929. "Über einige Grundlagenfragen der Mathematik." *Skrifter uigit av det NorskeVid. Akad. i Oslo I* 4:73–82.
36. Skolem, Thoralf. 1934. "Über die Nicht-Charakterisierbarkeit der Zahlenreihe mittels endlich oder abzählbar unendlich vieler Aussagen mit ausschliesslich Zahlvariablen." *Foundations of Mathematics* 23:150–61.
37. Todorčević, Stevo. 1997. "Comparing the Continuum with the First Two Uncountable Cardinals." In *Logic and Scientific Methods*, 145–55. Dordrecht: Kluwer.
38. Vaught, Robert Lawson. 1974. "Model Theory Before 1945." In *Proceedings of the Tarski Symposium*, edited by Leon Henkin et al., 153–72. Providence, RI: American Mathematical Society.

39. Weyl, Hermann. 1949. *Philosophy of Mathematics*. Princeton, NJ: Princeton University Press.
40. Wittgenstein, Ludwig. 1955. *Tractatus Logico-Philosophicus*. London: Routledge and Kegan Paul.
41. Zermelo, Ernst. 1930. "Über Grenzzahlen und Mengenbereiche." *Foundations of Mathematics* 16:29–47.

Chapter 5
Debating (Neo)logicism: Frege and the Neo-Fregeans

Majda Trobok

5.1 Introduction

The problem of the internal structure and the basis of our mathematical knowledge is a fundamental one in the philosophy of mathematics. It is often tied to the related issue of its epistemological source. These two issues are often presented together and labelled as "knowledge-of-sources rationale." However we have to keep distinct, within the rationale itself, its two prongs: the normative foundationalist project in mathematics and the more factual question of grasp of mathematical knowledge. This thought is going to guide the present paper. Since it is often assumed that Frege's original route addresses both sub-issues, in this paper I will try to argue against this construal of his theory.

Firstly, an interpretation of Frege's original route will be presented and defended, which is more limited in its scope, and incompatible with the narrow epistemological reading of his theory. Secondly I shall critically concentrate on the Neo-Fregeans' programme that is supposed, in the context of epistemic significance, to be following the Fregean's one (the neo-Fregean's logicist version I find most appealing and whose work I shall try critically to address here, is Hale's and Wright's neo-logicist account).[1]

As for Frege himself, I shall abide by his distinction between the narrowly epistemological query and the task of determining the foundations for mathematics; and argue that his motivation is focused upon the latter one, even to the point of exclusivity. My aim is not to de-philosophise his effort and portray him as just an ingenious mathematician, but instead to locate his philosophical interest in an adequate fashion. In particular, as regards Hume's principle, the main target of the present-day debate, I will argue that Frege does not come to grasp and does not

---

[1] See e.g., Hale and Wright [8, 9].

M. Trobok (✉)
Department of Philosophy, University of Rijeka, Rijeka, Croatia
e-mail: trobok@ffri.hr

invite the reader to grasp natural numbers through Hume's Principle, so that to say that Hume's Principle offers an epistemological route is to reverse the order of things. In short, Hume's Principle has only a logico-semantic priority, not a genetic, source-related, epistemic one.

Neo-Fregeans, in contrast, talk about Hume's Principle and Frege's theorem in strongly epistemic terms as offering "one clear a priori route into a recognition of the truth of...the fundamental laws of arithmetic (...)."[2]

I shall argue, albeit very tentatively, for a pessimistic conclusion to the effect that the ultimate result of all these worthy efforts might be the failure in both Frege's aims, taken at face value: proving the analyticity of arithmetic and hence determining the foundations of mathematics to be uncontentiously solid since based of logic. In the last section I very briefly evaluate a possible escape route for the neo-Fregean logicist, namely to sustain that we could truly stipulate Hume's principle, posit certain concepts and then check their having non-empty extensions. Such a way of stipulation tout court would not ask for numbers to be known in advance and would be close to the Hilbert-style implicit definition. In that case Hume's Principle would represent an epistemic path for the knowledge of arithmetic and analysis. Such a project would unfortunately be far away from Frege's goals, given his negative attitude toward Hilbert-style definitions. I thus limit myself to the issue of fidelity of neo-logicism to its original paradigm; I leave it open that neo-logicism might have independent high qualities that would recommend it as the best course to take.

5.2 Frege's Logicism

Let me start from Frege as seen by contemporary commentators who stress the knowledge-of-sources rationale, in order to proceed to his own pronouncements a few paragraphs later. In Frege's theory the knowledge-of-sources rationale would motivate the goal of establishing a variant of logicist view, i.e. the theses of epistemic dependence of mathematical knowledge on logical one and thus determining the epistemological source of the former.

> According to Frege, mathematical objects were logical objects. Hence a knowledge of numbers calls for nothing beyond knowledge of logic and definitions. (Hale and Wright [8, p. 1, Intro.])

So, as far as Frege's logicist programme is concerned, in the neo-Fregeans' interpretation, it allegedly shows or aims to show how mathematical knowledge is based on our capacity to grasp mathematical objects by the specifically reasoning faculties of the mind. Following a well known tradition, they take Frege's insistence on the semantic primacy of the sentential context as crucial, in conjunction with consideration of Hume's Principle:

---

[2] Wright, On the philosophical significance of Frege's theorem, p. 210.

5 Debating (Neo)logicism: Frege and the Neo-Fregeans

Where neo-Fregeanism principally differs from Frege is in its taking a more optimistic view than Frege himself came to hold of the prospects for the kind of contextual explanation of the fundamental concepts of arithmetic and analysis—the concepts of cardinal number and real number—which he considered and rejected in the central sections (§§60–68) of *Grundlagen*. The proposal there under consideration is that the concept of (cardinal) number may be explained, in accordance with Frege's context principle, by fixing the sense of identity-statements linking canonical singular terms for its instances—terms of the form "the number belonging to the concept F", or more briefly "the number of Fs"—and that this may be done by means of what is now widely called Hume's Principle (Hale and Wright [8, Intro., pp. 1–2])

Are we to accept such a reading of Frege's logicist project? Let us start with few historical remarks. Following Bolzano's and his successors' steps in aiming to remove intuition and visual representation from arithmetic and analysis (if anything else, because it is misleading), Frege goes one step further. Historically, the demand of getting a strongly rigorous proof for mathematical statements while ignoring the intuitionally based results and denying the role of our hunches goes back to the beginning of nineteenth century and continue through the work of primarily Bolzano and Weierstrass. In 1872 Weierstrass famously discovers the existence of functions being continuous at each point of their domain but not being differentiable in any, which has contradicted most shockingly the mathematicians' intuitions about continuous functions. And he proceeds with the elimination of self-evidence and intuition from mathematical proofs in—what Lakatos labels as—"the Weierstrassian revolution of rigour" (Lakatos [12, p. 55]).

Following such demand for rigour in mathematical proofs, Frege's further step consists in aiming to determine the justification and foundation for the basic mathematical proof-steps. He nicely confronts (*Grundlagen*, §2) his demand for vigour independently from the deductive confirmation of certain mathematical results with the demand for the improvement of Euclidean rigour, which brought to the additional study of the V Euclidean axiom and the consequently results:

> ...it lies deep in the nature of mathematics always to prefer proof, wherever it is possible, to inductive confirmation. Euclid proved many things that would have been granted him anyway. And it was the dissatisfaction even with the Euclidean rigour that led to the investigation of the Axiom of Parallels.[3]

Frege's further and deeper step leads him to the very foundation of mathematics. He is not however just interested in the groundwork of mathematics in the sense of determining the justification of mathematical statements, but also with the rational order by which such justification should proceed:

> After we have convinced ourselves that a boulder is immovable, by trying unsuccessfully to move it, there remains the further question, what is it that supports it so securely? (Frege, *Grundlagen*, §2)

---

[3] Wherever possible, the *Grundlagen* quotations are taken from (Beaney [1]); alternatively they are from Austin's translation.

It is not just that mathematicians should be rigorous in their search for subjective certainty, they should also, indeed primarily, be concerned with the **objective** foundations of mathematical knowledge. It is not enough any more to reduce a mathematical proof into rigorous, self-evident steps in order to be sure not to have based them on intuition—as Frege nicely points out to in *Grundlagen*'s paragraph 2—it is vital to determine the objective base, the foundations of mathematics. Since even what seems to be uncontentiously true, like the case with the fifth Euclid's axiom was, could turn out to be open to discussion and further analyses, and reveal the possibility of a different outcome (in the case of Euclid's axioms, of a different geometry based on the negation of his Axiom of Parallels). The aim is hence to determine what it is that supports the arithmetical-boulder so securely, what makes the truth of arithmetical statements *objectively* "immovable."

Event though such a demand for reliable, objective foundations is not original (Descartes having famously stated it in his *Meditations*, in his search for the true order of knowledge), the way in which Frege tries to answer it **is** novel. His main idea is to show that mathematical theorems are truths of logic, "analytic", i.e. derivable from general laws of logic and definitions. And since logic is the arbiter of all things, in the sense that everything existing objectively has to obey the laws of logic, by proving arithmetic to be reducible to logic, we prove it to be securely grounded, objectively true. The question to point out to is the one that concerns the existence of epistemic connotation of such a project. I will try to argue for a negative answer. Many authors (e.g. Dummett, Kitcher, Martin-Löf, Shapiro, to a certain extent) find analyticity to be for Frege an **epistemic** concept, turning on how a proposition is knowable.[4] I think the two aspects, foundationalism and epistemology, are to be distinguished, the former being Frege's main concern, the latter not being one at all. I will argue for it in several steps. I will distinguish the less usual notion of justification, namely the logico-semantical one from its more usual counterpart, i.e. the subject's justification, and argue that Frege is interested in the former one, relying on an analyses of the main *Grundlagen* passages; along the way I will briefly take a critical look on the work of those more recent authors who endorse the view that Frege's programme is epistemological in their, justification centred meaning of the term.

The upshot will be that Frege's logicist project concentrates on the justificatory links between arithmetic and logic, where the notion of justification is logico-semantical (in the sense of objective grounding), not subjectively epistemological. More particularly, in connection with Hume's principle, I will endorse the view that the factual and subjective-normative query about our mathematical knowledge does not find its answer in the grasp of the Principle, since its function is limited to its logico-semantic aspect, leaving the canonically epistemic one open.

Let us start with the definition of analyticity, which is a clearly semantic notion, classified by Frege together with the notion of apriority, exactly as the proposed

---

[4] See Dummett [4], Kitcher [11], Martin-Löf [13] and Shapiro [15].

5 Debating (Neo)logicism: Frege and the Neo-Fregeans

reading would predict, to the complete surprise of a present-day mainstream epistemologists. In *Grundlagen* (§3), Frege says:

> When ... a proposition is called a priori or analytic (italics mine) in my sense,... it is a judgment about the ultimate ground upon which rests the justification for holding it to be true ... The problem becomes ... that of finding the proof of the proposition, and of following it up right back to the primitive truths. If, carrying out this process, we come only on general laws and on definitions, then the truth is an analytic one ... if, however, it is possible to give the proof without making use of truths which are not of a general nature, but belong to the sphere of some general science, then the proposition is a synthetic one.

Although Frege uses terms like justification, which to the contemporary reader may sound explicitly epistemic, his actual description of the object of his interest reduces it to logical semantic relations and their patterns. Contrary to what contemporary epistemologist would choose to do,[5] Frege explicitly places together the notions of aposteriori and analytic (the distinction being notably introduced in paragraph 3) and clearly distinguishes

> The question of how we arrive at the content of a judgment from the question as to how we provide the justification for our assertion. (*Grundlagen*, §3)

The notions of analyticity and aposteriority are joined in the context of determining "the ultimate ground on which the justification for holding (a proposition-MT) to be true rests." Frege hence does not follow the contemporary habit of locating the aposteriori into the epistemic domain and the analytic to the logico-semantical one, thus assigning them to completely disjoint fields of investigation. Moreover for Frege, the notion of justification clearly belongs to mathematics rather than to the matters concerning cognizer's mind, and is thus logico-semantical.

> In this case the question (of apriority-MT) is removed from the domain of psychology and assigned to that of mathematics, if it concerns a mathematical truth. (*Grundlagen*, §3)

This suggests that we should distinguish two notions of justification. The quotation above exemplifies the first one, objective logico-semantical notion of justification. The more usual notion of justification is less concerned with the nature of truths and more with the cognizers's thinking process, it is subject's justification that sometimes has to do with the structure of his belief-system and sometimes with the normative aspects of the very genesis of his beliefs. The two notions are independent, or so I shall argue.

I want to take Frege's move seriously, and following what I see as his intention, contrast the logico-semantical notion of justification, in the sense of objective grounding, with this second one, more at home on contemporary epistemology, that I shall call genetic, source-related.

One could object that there is an intermediate domain of judgement available, the one of epistemic normativity which is neither psychologicalin the naturalist sense,

---

[5] See e.g., Burge [3].

nor purely non-epistemic in the radical sense of being independent from cognizer's justification. Ironically, for the present context, such normativity has been taken by Burge [3] as being central for Frege's project. I do not however see elements of epistemic normativity as being central to Frege's programme, the latter being about reducing mathematics to logic with the aim of proving its being "immovable." The reduction of mathematics to logic is not an epistemic result, in any possible sense of the word. It may have epistemic consequences, for instance, helping mathematicians by enhancing the clarity of their grasp of fundamental mathematical notions, but it is itself not an epistemic move. After all, the epistemic path taken by the great mathematicians did very well in the history of mathematics without being logicist in its root, nor Frege criticizes it as such except for its not being sufficiently well founded, lacking the needed rigour.

We shall need the distinction between logico-semantical and genetic, source-related notions of justification a few lines below, in connection with the crucial move—the appeal to Hume's Principle. The move will be introduced by providing some background.

The lynch-pin of Frege's logicism is clearly the claim that mathematics—more precisely arithmetic and analysis—is reducible to logic. Since mathematical statements are reducible to logic, we can determine their foundations via logic alone. And the task of reducing arithmetic, i.e. defining basic arithmetical terms such as numbers in logical terms only has, as such, no epistemic connotations. Shapiro, for example, even though he initially represents the programme as an epistemic one, at one point concludes by saying that:

> Perhaps this notion of foundation is as metaphysical as it is epistemic, despite the use of notions like "proof" and "justification". It is not a question of whether we know, for example, that $7 + 5 = 12$, to take Frege's (and Kant's) own example. There is really no question but that we do know that. Nor is it a question of how we know that $7 + 5 = 12$. We knew that proposition long before the foundational work began. Moreover, our own knowledge did not need to go, and in fact did not go, via the proposed founding definitions. We just did the sum. Frege was interested in objective grounding relations among propositions, perhaps something along the lines of Bernard Bolzano's ground-consequence relation. This seems to drive a wedge between the state of being justified and the ultimate ground or justification of a proposition. (Shapiro [15, pp. 22–23])

I would add that such a notion of foundation in which, as Shapiro rightly points out, the main task is to determine objectively based relations among arithmetical and logical truths is clearly and exclusively logico-semantical, i.e. metaphysical.

The thesis that numbers are logical objects as well as the logico-semantical analyses of basic arithmetical truths and definitions have, as such, no epistemic connotations in the sense of determining how we perceive such relations and, more importantly, how the basic mathematical concepts and truths are epistemically accessible in the first place.

What about the epistemic aspect of analyticity? Frege himself points out to the distinction between the epistemological query and the problem of determining the foundations for mathematics; he namely asserts:

> It frequently happens that we first discover the content of a proposition and only then provide a rigorous proof in another, more difficult way, by means of which the conditions of its validity can often also be discerned more precisely. Thus in general the question as to how we arrive at the content of a judgement has to be distinguished from the question as to how we provide the justification for our assertion. (*Grundlagen*, §3)

> ...This would make them analytic judgments, despite the fact that they would not normally be discovered by thought alone; for we are concerned here not with the way in which they are discovered but with the kind of ground on which their proof rests; or in LEIBNIZ'S words, "the question here is not one of the history of our discoveries, which is different in different men, but of the connexion and natural order of truths, which is always the same." (*Grundlagen*, §17)

The aim of a proof is to "place the truth of a proposition beyond all doubt" (§3); in the case of mathematics it amounts to demanding "that the fundamental theorems of arithmetic, wherever possible, must be proven with the greatest rigour; since only if the utmost care is taken to avoid any gaps in the chain of inference can it be said with certainty upon what primitive truths the proof is based" (§4).

And we get to the requested proofs through our reason alone; doubting here makes no sense,

> for what are things independent of the reason? To answer that would be as much as to judge without judging, or to wash the fur without wetting it. (Frege, *Grundlagen*, §26)

It is interesting to contrast Frege's detailed articulation of logico-semantical relations with his very short, and to many interpreters puzzling remarks that do concern epistemic matters. He offers little in the way of explicit argument on how we actually grasp mathematical objects, the solution of the riddle concerning what sustains the "mathematical boulder" so securely being the objective of his logicist project. This solution is to be found with no appeal to our intuitions or representations, but relying exclusively on reason. However, and this might suggest the direction towards a future solution of the epistemic puzzle, the laws of reason are the laws of logic. Ultimately, the rules of logic being for him those of reason, he foreshadows the epistemic route for grasping the rules of logic, encompassing arithmetic as well.

I would like to illustrate and further document this reading of Frege by applying it to one of the central topics of Frege's project, indeed the one that has been turned into the central topic by the neo-Fregeans.

In the route of proving in the Grundlagen that natural numbers are reducible to logical laws and definitions, Frege introduces (what Boolos names) Hume's Principle.[6]

---

[6] The principle has been called Hume's Principle by Boolos (in "The consistency of Frege's *Foundations of Arithmetic*", in [2]). Boolos gave it this title because it recalls a remark in Hume's *Treatise* (Book I, Part iii, Section 1, par. 5), and because Frege quotes Hume in *Grundlagen* (§63):

> when two numbers are so combin'd, as that the one always as unite answering to every unite of the other, we pronounce them equal ...

Hume's Principle (HP):
$\forall F \forall G (n(F) = n(G) \Leftrightarrow F \approx G)$
F, G—concepts;
$n(G)$—the number of G's;
$\approx$—equinumerosity relation

Let us apply our distinctions to this crucial move. Hume's Principle represents for Frege a possible step in his logicist project. How we grasp Hume's Principle remains in *Grundlagen* without an answer. What is certain is that Frege's aim is to characterize the already known (mathematical) objects—natural numbers, more precisely to offer the criterion for their identity.

In the paragraphs introductory to Hume's Principle, i.e. the last paragraphs of the *Grundlagen* (in particular §62), one well-known reading is that the mode of presentation that Frege introduces is intrinsically an epistemic concept, as many authors have pointed out (most famously Dummett). That, if actually the case, would colour Frege's logicist project with epistemic connotations. In an alternative construal though, the mode of presentation is not related to the query of grasp of mathematical knowledge. The fact being that for centuries mathematicians have grasped and managed to grasp properties of mathematical objects without knowing their mode of presentation endorsed by Frege. The mode of presentation in Frege's terms is objective, mathematicians can either fail to grasp it (as they did for centuries) or succeed in doing so (as in Frege's case).

We might take as an example the Earth and its mode of presentation as an object that is a planet through the property of being visible by virtue of the light from a star reflected off its surface and that is (not-perfectly) spherical in its shape. Notwithstanding this mode of presentation and the fact that mankind has known since Pythagoras' formulation that the Earth is spherical, the Earth had been perceived as flat by astronomers again and again in the Middle Ages (failing to grasp its mode of presentation).

The mode of presentation thus, construed as the way an object present itself to the world, does not reveal per se its epistemic accessibility. In this sense, it does abide by a reading of Frege's project that lacks epistemic connotations.

Frege's example with Venus might look as a counter-example to my argument but, Frege characterizes the object itself merely as heavenly body; the component "star" in the "Morning star" and "Evening star" is, at least for Frege himself, a semantically inert part of the two proper names.

Having endorsed the view that Frege's project lacks an epistemic overtone, I wish to elucidate it further by additionally refining the proposed picture of the role of Hume's Principle in Frege's logicist programme of getting a description of arithmetic based on logic, thereby giving mathematics the grounds for security and truth it needs. I would like to claim that Frege does not grasp and does not invite the reader to grasp natural numbers through Hume's Principle, so that to say that Hume's Principle offers an epistemological route is to reverse the order of things. To put it in above introduced terminology, Hume's Principle has a logico-semantic priority, not a genetic, source-related, epistemic one. Let me briefly argue for this. Firstly,

Hume's Principle got formulated after twenty centuries of mathematical development. From a purely mathematical point of view, mathematicians from ancient Greeks to modern number theorists have developed the theory of numbers to its full extent. Of course, as Frege points out, there are still philosophico-mathematical problems concerning "a concept that is fundamental to a great science" that remain open, and such an investigation of the concept of number is a task that mathematicians and philosophers should share. But, his approach is "more philosophical that many mathematicians may deem appropriate" (*Grundlagen*, Intro.). Frege is able to introduce Hume's Principle due to his knowledge of mathematics in details; what he does is to encapsulate in Hume's Principle the criterion of identity for mathematically well known objects. That Frege depicts, instead of stipulating, natural numbers is also implicit both in the Caesar problem and in Frege's approach toward the so-called Hilbert-style implicit definition. Firstly, when Frege says we know Cesar is not a number, this proves that in thinking of numbers he has in mind very specific (abstract) objects, because he talks about identities of the form: the number of F $= x$, where x is not a number. But in order to know that x is not a number, i.e. that the identity is a mixed one, we have to know what numbers are, and this is something we could have not possibly come to know just by positing Hume's Principle. His asking whether Caesar is a number is a picturesque way of inquiring whether Hume's Principles leaves the truth value and hence the meaning of so-called "mixed" identities (like Caesar $= 0$) undetermined. His positive answer to it suggests that positing Hume's principle is not a way to actually get the "extreme example" clarified. However, we know too well that Caesar is *not* a number. As Frege points out, "naturally, no one is going to confuse [Caesar] with the [number zero]..." (§62).

So contrary to what someone might suspect, there is no vicious circle involved here, since Cesar's not being a number is a fact uncontentiously known by us prior to positing Hume's Principle.

Secondly, part of the argument that Frege depicts natural numbers instead of stipulating their definitions can also be recovered from Frege's negative stance toward Hilbert-style implicit definition (usually presented as a set of axioms) and his derogatory view of what the aim of a (implicit) definition amounts to:

> ...axioms and theorems can never try to lay down the meaning of a sign or word that occurs in them, but it must already be laid down

Standardly, in implicit definitions the reference of the terms (definienda) is determined solely by the fulfilment of requested conditions; once they are fullfiled the nature of the objects satisfying them is irrelevant, as Hilbert famously proclaims "One must be able to say at all times—instead of points, straight lines and planes—tables, chairs and beer mugs." Hence, the axioms, stated in an implicit definition and the conditions imposed (or properties requested by them) are what determines the primitive concepts and their extensions. And this is precisely the proposal of a proper characterization of the role of a definition that Frege rejects in the above quotation. I shall return to the issue of implicit definitions when discussing neo-logicism.

Before the section on neo-logicism, let me briefly pass to the notion of apriority in general. By Frege's own elucidation in §3, apriority amounts to the ability to "provide a proof from completely general laws, which themselves neither need nor admit of proof" (and from definitions not belonging to some specific area of knowledge—as Frege points out in the same paragraph). Hence, this concept concerns the ultimate ground on which the logico-semantic justification for holding a (mathematical) proposition to be true rests upon—and as such is not epistemic. It is not about "the psychological, physiological and physical conditions that have made it possible to form the content of the proposition in our mind." After all, prior to determining the proof we have to know what is the assertion whose truth we want to establish. Frege hence (not just in *Grundlagen*) settles the question as to whether analyticity is an epistemic concept in the negative. Hume's Principle does not offer an epistemic route for grasping (natural) numbers, but rather a way for knowing/determining the ground for taking mathematical propositions to the true.

5.3 What About Neo-Fregean Logicism?

Contemporary neo-Fregean logicism attempts to vindicate the spirit, if not the letter, of the basic doctrines of Frege's logicism, by developing a systematic treatment of arithmetic that fulfils the requirements of Frege's doctrine while avoiding the contradictoriness of Basic Law V. The aim of neo-logicism is to develop branches of mathematics from abstraction principles and it is primarily an epistemological programme. As Shapiro points out:

> Neo-logicism is, at root, an epistemological program, attempting to determine how mathematical knowledge can be grounded. We can know facts about *the natural number* by deriving them from HP. (Shapiro [14, p. 99])

Neo-Fregeans are themselves explicit on this one:

> The neo-Fregean thesis about arithmetic is that knowledge of its fundamental laws (essentially, the Dedekind-Peano axioms)—and hence of the existence of a range of objects which satisfy them—may be based a priori on Hume's Principle (Wright, "Is Hume's Principle Analytic", in Hale and Wright [8, p. 321])

Neo-Fregeans maintain that it is possible, following Frege himself, to define by stipulation abstract sortal concepts—that is concepts whose instances are abstract objects of a certain kind.[7] What has to be stipulated is the truth of an abstraction principle.

The general form of an abstraction principle is the following one:

$$\forall f \forall g (\Sigma(f) = \Sigma(g) \Leftrightarrow f \approx g)$$

---

[7] See e.g., Hale [7].

5 Debating (Neo)logicism: Frege and the Neo-Fregeans

f and g—variables referring to entities of a certain kind (objects or concepts usually), Σ—a higher-order operator which forms singular terms when applied to f and g, so that $\Sigma(f)$ and $\Sigma(g)$ are singular terms referring to objects, and $\approx$—an equivalence relation on entities denoted by f and g.

It is abstraction principles which are supposed to bear the main burden of the task of reconciling logicist or neo-Fregean logicist thesis that arithmetic and analysis are pure logic. In so far as they are stipulations they can aspire to explain in one stroke both how logic can be committed to abstract objects, and how it is possible to have knowledge of these objects.

The neo-logicists claim that

> ...we can account for the necessity of at least the basic arithmetic truths and how these truths can be known a priori. (Shapiro [16, p. 71])

In particular, the principle neo-logicists concentrate on is our already discussed Hume's Principle.

> If such an explanatory principle ...can be regarded as analytic, then that should suffice at least to demonstrate the analyticity of arithmetic. Even if that term is found troubling... it will remain that Hume's Principle like any principle serving implicitly to define a certain concept will be available without significant epistemological presupposition to one who has mastery of the concept it configures... So one clear a priori route into a recognition of the truth of... the fundamental laws of arithmetic... will have been made out.
>
> ...
>
> So, ...there will be an a priori route from a mastery of second-order logic to a full understanding and grasp of the truth of the fundamental laws of arithmetic. Such an epistemological route... would be an outcome still worth describing as logicism... (Wright, On the philosophical significance of Frege's theorem, in Hale and Wright [8, pp. 279–80])

According to the neo-Fregeans, following Frege's priority of syntax thesis, the required condition for singular terms to refer is they occur in true statements (leaving aside for the moment some well known qualifications).

The idea that abstraction principles are a legitimate way of introducing mathematical theories is problematic, since some of them, as the infamous Basic Law V, are inconsistent. I shall concentrate in this talk on the epistemic aspect of it. My main worry about the programme is the possibility that the burning epistemic problems of neo-logicism are being projected back upon Frege; in other words that Frege is being wrongly credited with something he does not actually assert, and for which he would never ask any credit (in fact I will argue that the possibility has turned out to be very much actual). In contrast, neo-Fregeans themselves insist on the epistemic route so that they are, differently form Frege, explicit in taking their programme to be fundamentally an epistemic one.

They begin in a modest way talking in terms of explanation:

> ...by stipulating, that the number of Fs is the same as the number of Gs just in the case the Fs are one-one correlated with the Gs, we can set up number as a sortal concept, i.e. that Hume's Principle *suffices* to explain the concept of number as a sortal concept. (Hale and Wright [8, p. 15])

However, they also propose a stronger claim of an a priori route for grasping the concept of number and deriving the basic laws of arithmetic via Frege's theorem. The problem of distinguishing the fundationalist project from the epistemological one appears more acute in the neo-Fregean's programme since they state it explicitly. Hume' Principle allegedly gives us reasons for treating mathematical knowledge as being a priori, by offering an a priori route for acquiring mathematical knowledge, germane to the rationalist epistemology. According to neo-Fregean logicists Frege's logicism was correct in all main respects except for two points: Frege overestimated the significance of Caesar problem and underestimated the significance of Frege's theorem (the derivation of the axioms of arithmetic from Hume's Principle in second-order logic) In order to avoid appealing to the disastrous Basic Law V, neo-Fregean logicists famously do not follow Frege all the way, they advocate instead adding Hume's Principle to the second-order logic as a supplementary axiom, sustaining that Frege's theorem gives reason for grounding the claim that arithmetic is analytic in Hume's Principle. As I have said at the outset, the result is the failure in both Frege's aims, taken at face value: proving the analyticity of arithmetic and hence determining the foundations of mathematics to be uncontentiously solid since based on logic. Neo-logicism does not prove (Frege's) analyticity of arithmetic since Hume's Principle is **not** a law of logic, as Boolos pointed out long time ago. Instead, they say that the fact that adding Hume's Principle to second-order logic results in a consistent system that suffices for a foundation of arithmetic (all the basic laws of arithmetic are derivable within the system) and that this "constitutes a vindication of logicism, on a reasonable understanding of that thesis."[8] But if Hume's Principle is not a law of logic, in what sense is logicism vindicated? Next, what about the apriorist epistemology? Neo-Fregeans sustain that

> ... the case for the existence of numbers *can* be made on the basis of Hume's Principle, and it is important to the neo-Fregean that this should be so, precisely because it provides for a head-on response to the epistemological challenge posed by Benacerraf's dilemma.

> ... provided that facts about the one-one correlation of concepts—in the basic case, sortal concepts under which only concrete objects fall—are, as we may reasonably presume, unproblematically accessible, we gain access, via Hume's principle and without any need to postulate any mysterious extrasensory faculties or so-called mathematical intuition, to corresponding truths whose formulation involves reference to numbers. (Hale and Wright [10, p. 172–73])

Even though Wright insightfully emphases that in every epistemic project there are presuppositions that have to be assumed on trust, without evidential justification (in order to avoid an infinite regress), I find the question of how we grasp Hume's Principle legitimate and unpalatable for the neo-Fregean's programme. By leaving it without an answer, the epistemic project does not offer an alternative to the mysterious extrasensory faculties or so-called mathematical intuition, it just shifts the mysterious part upon the presupposed unproblematic grasp of Hume's Principle.

---

[8] Hale and Wright [10, p. 169].

Hale and Wight invite us to consider an analogy. We come to know when the directions of two lines are the same through the Direction Principle ($\forall a \forall b (d(a) = d(b) \Leftrightarrow a \parallel b)$).

The Principle seems to be stipulated, and seems to give us the meaning the direction in virtue of pure stipulation. Hale and Wright apply the same assumptions to the epistemology of Hume's Principle. "The number of" receives its meaning from stipulation in the same way in which "direction" does. However, the analogy does not hold in the epistemic sense since the introduction of directions of lines does not presuppose any determine objects (what do we know about properties of objects corresponding to directions of lines besides what is determined by the Direction Principle alone?!) or any theory about directions determined intuitively or in any other way prior to the stipulation itself. We truly **stipulate** directions of lines. The analogy, upon which **Frege** rests, is that we understand what directions of lines are through the Direction Principle, in the same sense in which we can know what numbers are through Hume's Principle—but, as I have been pointing out, this is not an epistemic route *tout court*, as neo-Fregeans (and others) sustain.

Here is my final worry: the only way out for the neo-Fregean logicist might be to sustain that we could truly stipulate Hume's principle, posit certain concepts and then check their having non-empty extensions. Such a way of stipulation *tout court* would not ask for numbers to be known in advance and would be close to the Hilbert-style implicit definition. As Shapiro explains (Ebert and Shapiro [5]) there are important differences between Hilbert-style and neo-Fregeans logicists' stipulations the crucial one in this context being that

> With the exception of logical terminology (connectives, etc.), no term in a Hilbert-style implicit definition comes with the previously established meaning or extension.
>
> ...
>
> For Hilbert, the satisfiability (or relative consistency) of the set of axioms is sufficient for their truth, whereas for the neo-logicist, a crucial issue is the uniqueness of the objects referred to by the relevant terms involved.

Could Hilbert-style reading of Hume's Principle help?

The acceptance of a Hilbert-style implicit definition would raise a new version of Julius Cesar worry: by using Hume's Principle as a **Hilbert-style** implicit definition, it would not be possible to depict certain, unique objects; remember Hilbert's quip that "table, chairs and beer mugs" could be taken as satisfiers of axioms normally taken to refer to points and lines. No Hilbert-style implicit definition can uniquely determine the objects it refers to and it's not its aim either. As Ebert and Shapiro rightly notice: "the connection to intuition or observation is broken for good."[9] On the other hand, the history of mathematics shows examples that did work this way. Let us remember, e.g. Cardano's stipulation of "imaginary numbers" (1545, *Ars Magna*)—at first they here stipulated as numbers whose square was a negative number and it took almost 300 years before Gauss determined

---

[9] Ebert and Shapiro [5, p. 421].

their geometrical interpretation and hence explained "the true metaphysics of the imaginary numbers" (1831). Maybe a similar, truly stipulative, positing route might be open for Hume's principle and natural numbers as well. In that case Hume's Principle would represent an epistemic path for the knowledge of arithmetic and analysis.

Such a project would unfortunately be far away from Frege's goals, given his approach toward Hilbert-style definitions, and the corresponding meta-theory according to which singular terms do not have to uniquely determine the objects they refer to.

With the adapted concept of analyticity and Hilbert-style implicit definition, however, the essential core of Frege's logicist programme—contrary to the neo-Fregeans' aim—would **not** to be preserved.

5.4 Conclusion

I have started from the contrast between two concepts of justification: genetic and foundationalist. In contrast to the lot of mainstream contemporary work I have argued that Frege's interest is far from the genetic-epistemological and is limited to the philosophical-mathematical task of determining the foundations for mathematics.

Consequently, I offer an interpretation of Frege's original route, which is more limited in its scope, and incompatible with the mainstream epistemological reading of his theory. I have argued for such an interpretation through the analyses of relevant passages of *Grundlagen* and some mathematico-logico-historical data. I emphasise the logico-semantical nature of Frege's view of justification, and the priority of the notion of analyticity. Analysing the implicit definition of numbers in Hume's Principle, I hope to have shown that Frege's aim was to determine the objective justificatory connections between arithmetic and logic, which are normative foundational in their roots. Going one step further, I argue that in Frege's project these connections, like any other central items for that matter, have no source-related epistemic priority. I hence contrast the logico-semantical notion of justification, from the subject's justification as its more usual counterpart and propose the idea that Frege's project is not about the latter one at all.

More specifically, in my analysis I firstly concentrate on Frege's aim of finding out the objective justification of mathematical statements and the order in which such a justification should be carried on, holding such an aim not to be related to determining the epistemic path of mathematical knowledge. Secondly, I point to Frege's not following the contemporary habit of locating the aposteriori into the epistemic domain and the analytic to the logico-semantical one, thus assigning them to completely disjoint fields of investigation, but grouping them together under what I see as the common logico semantic heading. I thirdly examine the discrepancy between the logico-semantical and the genetic, source-related notions of justification, illustrating it in the context of the discussion of Hume's Principle.

I then concentrate on the modes of presentation, taken to be paradigmatically epistemic by many authors, most importantly by Dummett. I offer an alternative reading according to which the notion of the mode of presentation is not to be allied to the actual epistemic grasp of arithmetical statements. Finally, I return to Hume's Principle debate in the context of the query of depicting vs. stipulating mathematical items and the relation to the implicit definition; the aim is to show that, given Frege's project, Hume's Principle does not represent an epistemic path for the grasp of (natural) numbers; instead, it offers a way for determining the ground for taking arithmetical statements to the true. Witness the fact that Frege himself does not pretend to grasp natural numbers through Hume's Principle. The Principle has only a logico-semantic priority, not a genetic, source-related, epistemic one.

In the second part of the paper, I critically concentrate on the Neo-Fregeans' programme, more precisely on the neo-logicists' version that I find most appealing, which is Hale's and Wright's neo-logicist account. This project is supposed to be following the original Fregean's one in the matters of epistemic significance, and I argue that the suggestion is misleading: the Neo-Fregeans do not manage to fulfil either of Frege's aims, taken at face value: proving the analyticity of arithmetic and hence determining the foundations of mathematics to be uncontentiously solid since based of logic. I do not however analyse those features, which are legion, that makes neo-Fregean logicism a worthwhile project.

Acknowledgments Portions of this were presented at the conference in Dubrovnik in May 2010. Many thanks to the participants for their comments: Stewart Shapiro, Per Martin-Löf, Alan Wier, Berislav Žarnić, Stephen Reed. Many thanks as well to Nenad Smokrović and especially to Nenad Miščević.

References

1. Beaney, Michael. 1997. *The Frege Reader*. Oxford: Blackwell Publishing.
2. Boolos, George. 1998. *Logic, Logic and Logic*. Cambridge, MA: Harvard University Press.
3. Burge, Tyler. 2005. *Truth, Thought, Reason—Essays on Frege*. Oxford: Clarendon Press.
4. Dummett, Michael. 1991. *Frege : Philosophy of Mathematics*. Cambridge, MA: Harvard University Press.
5. Ebert, Philip, and Stewart Shapiro. 2009. "The Good, the Bad and the Ugly." *Synthese* 170:415–41.
6. Frege, Gottlob. 1884. *Die Grundlagen der Arithmetik*. Translated by Austin, J.L., 1953, *The Foundations of Arithmetic*. New York, NY: Harper & Brothers.
7. Hale, Bob. 1999. "Intuition and Reflection in Arithmetic II." *Proceedings of the Aristotelian Society* 73:75–98.
8. Hale, Bob, and Crispin Wright. 2001. *The Reason's Proper Study—Essays Towards a Neo-Fregean Philosophy of Mathematics*. Oxford: Clarendon Press.
9. Hale, Bob, and Crispin Wright. 2002. "Benacerraf's Dilemma Revisited." *European Journal of Philosophy* 10:101–29.
10. Hale, Bob, and Crispin Wright. 2005. "Logicism in the Twenty-First Century." In *The Oxford Handbook of Philosophy of Mathematics and Logic*, edited by Stewart Shapiro, 172–73, Oxford University Press, New York.
11. Kitcher, Philip. 1979. "Frege's Epistemology." *The Philosophical Review* 88:235–62.

12. Lakatos, Imre. 1976. *Proofs and Refutations*. Cambridge: Cambridge Universtity Press.
13. Martin-Löf, Per. 1996. "On the Meaning of the Logical Constants and the Justifications of the Logical Laws." *Nordic Journal of Philosophical Logic* 1:11–60.
14. Shapiro, Stewart. 2000. "Introduction to the Abstraction and Neo-Logicism Special Issue." *Philosophia Mathematica* 8(II):99.
15. Shapiro, Stewart. 2004. "Foundations of Mathematics: Metaphysics, Epistemology, Structure." *The Philosophical Quarterly* 54:22–23.
16. Shapiro, Stewart. 2009. "The Measure of Scottish Neo-Logicism." In *Logicism, Intuitionism, and Formalism*, edited by Linström et al., Synthese Library 341. Springer Dordrecht; London.
17. Wright, Crispin. 1983. *Frege's Conception of Numbers as Objects*. Aberdeen: Aberdeen University Press.

Part II
Epistemology and Logic

Chapter 6
Informal Logic and Informal Consequence

Danilo Šuster

6.1 Introduction

My reflections on the so-called informal logic were provoked, initially, by the practice of teaching logic to undergraduate students of philosophy. Contemporary formal logic offers a well worked out theory; the old educational problem is simply how to make it relevant to philosophical or even everyday reasoning. Informal logic as an attempt to develop a logic to assess, analyse and improve ordinary language (or "everyday") reasoning is by definition closely tied to general educational goals and critical inquiry. The core notion in a course of informal logic and critical thinking is usually the notion of the argument and questions such as: What distinguishes good from bad arguments? What makes a good argument succeed? What makes a bad argument fail? It seems sensible to combine classes of standard formal logic with classes which outline various non-formal techniques of argument analysis.

Now, by the end of a typical "combined" course almost all of the students will have mastered the required symbolic manipulations (natural deduction, axiomatic proofs). However, when required to informally and critically analyse a piece of "ordinary" reasoning many of them fail badly. Elementary logical "calculi" are apparently much easier to master than the informal techniques of applied logic. What then should we do with informal logic? What should we teach and how should we test the results? (Mis)achievements are difficult to evaluate—is failure to be explained by lack of knowledge in some specific field of everyday argumentation (not something to be taught in the *logic* class) or by lack of some special logical knowledge (something one *should* master in the logic class)? Are there any *special* skills of informal logic at all? Is it all just a matter of general intelligence and the depth of one's knowledge?[1]

---

[1] I was not the first to be puzzled. Books are now written on this topic. Cf. Sobocan and Groarke [28].

D. Šuster (✉)
Department of Philosophy, University of Maribor, Maribor, Slovenia
e-mail: danilo.suster@uni-mb.si

Peter Medawer, a Nobel laureate in medicine, gave the following comment on scientific method and philosophy of science in general: "If the purpose of scientific methodology is to prescribe or expound a system of enquiry or even a code of practice for scientific behaviour, then scientists seem to be able to get on very well without it. Most scientists receive no tuition in scientific method, but those who have been instructed perform no better as scientists than those who have not. Of what other branch of learning can it be said that it gives its proficients no advantage; that it need not be taught or, if taught, need not be learned?" (Medawar [23, p. 8]). Well, informal logic sprang naturally to my mind. Not surprisingly—informal logic, or logic in a broad sense, is basically just elementary scientific methodology, or so I will argue. Medawer also added: "Of course, the fact that scientists do not consciously practice a formal methodology is very poor evidence that no such methodology exists" (Medawar [23, p. 9]). So, all hope for a more theoretical approach is perhaps not lost.

The educational puzzlements lead to more general philosophical questions. What is informal logic—is it "logic" at all? If the notion of consequence is at the heart of logic, does it even make sense to speak about "informal" consequence? Soundness—premise truth and deductive validity of an inference is a classical standard in argument evaluation. Informal logicians replace the standard of soundness with a broader notion of argument *cogency*. An argument is cogent if and only if (i) its premises are rationally acceptable, (ii) its premises are relevant to its conclusion and (iii) its premises provide sufficient reason to accept the conclusion or its premises constitute grounds adequate for accepting the conclusion (the "ARG" conditions according to Govier). I will argue that the ARG criteria proposed by informal logicians characterize a certain broad kind of a consequence relation. But let me start with some general, programmatic observations on informal logic.

6.2 Informal Logic

Informal logic, variously called the logic of "real" arguments, the study of the practice of argumentation, critical thinking, argumentation theory, theory of practical reasoning, applied logic ..., is a blooming field of theoretical and practical activity. In their survey article Johnson and Blair [20] describe informal logic as (a) the theory of fallacies and (b) the theory of (actual, natural) arguments. The questions investigated by informal logic are not new, Aristotle already addressed many of them. But,

> What is new is the central focus on argumentation in natural language, as an interpersonal, social, purposive practice. What is new too, at least in comparison to other philosophical investigations of arguments and reasoning in the last 100 years, is the skepticism about the value of formal logic as a tool for analyzing and evaluating natural-language arguments. This skepticism is implicit in the very name "informal logic", with all its unfortunate connotations of sloppiness and lack of rigour (Hitchcock [14, p. 130]).

There really is a strong tendency to associate in-formal not only with non-formal:

> By "informal logic" we mean to designate a branch of logic whose task is to develop non-formal standards, criteria, and procedures for the analysis, interpretation, evaluation, critique and construction of argumentation in everyday discourse (Johnson and Blair [19, p. 148]).

but with anti-formal. The growing disenchantment with the capacity of formal logic to set the standards of good reasoning has led to informal logic being described as any approach in logic which either avoids or minimizes the use of formal logic as the theory of analysis (the notion of logical form) and as the theory of evaluation (the notions of validity and soundness) of arguments. Nothing new, though. Present-day informal logicians share a dislike for mathematical formalism with J.S. Mill. Mill was aware of the work of Boole, De Morgan and Jevons, but for him "[Jevons'] speculations on Logic, like those of Boole and De Morgan, and some of those of Hamilton, are infected with this vice, a mania for encumbering questions with useless complication, and with a notation implying the existence of greater precision in the data than the question admit of" (Mill [24], quoted in Wilson [37, p. 280]). And this vice "is one preeminently at variance with the wants of the time, which demand that scientific deductions should be made as simple and as easily intelligible as they can be made without being scientific" (Mill [24], quoted in Wilson [37, p. 280]). These remarks anticipate objections from those informal logicians who claim that the formalism of formal logic sometimes obscures the tools needed to critically analyze real life arguments rather than contrived examples.

In the emphasis on investigations of natural arguments in their actual settings as opposed to formal techniques of contemporary logic one may detect the remnants of the old divide: ideal language vs. ordinary language theorists. Formal plays the role of the "Ugly, Dirty and Bad." Another opposition often found in characterizing the distinction between the two approaches is the one between syntax *cum* semantics and pragmatics:

> Formal logic has to do with the forms of argument (syntax) and truth values (semantics)... Informal logic (or more broadly, argumentation, as a field) has to do with the uses of argumentation in a context of dialogue, an essentially pragmatic undertaking (Walton [34, pp. 418–19], quoted by Johnson and Blair [20, p. 362]).

> From the pragmatic point of view, any particular argument should be seen as being advanced in the context of a particular dialogue setting. Sensitivity to the special features of different contexts of dialogue is a requirement for the reasoned analysis of an argument (Walton [35, p. 2]).

To be fair—not all theoreticians subscribe to the view that informal is simply anti-formal. In his survey article on informal logic Hitchcock remarks:

> In any case, the research programme of informal logic does not preclude the use of formal methods or appeal to formal logics. Its distinctiveness consists in its consideration of a set of questions that are not addressed in the specialist journals of formal logic, such as the Journal of Symbolic Logic and the Notre Dame Journal of Formal Logic, or in such histories of formal logic as that by William and Martha Kneale (1962). It might in fact better be called "theory of argument." Its questions have however traditionally been regarded as

part of logic, broadly conceived. The name can thus be taken to refer to that part of logic as traditionally conceived that is not covered by contemporary formal logic (Hitchcock [15, p. 101]).

I agree with the spirit of this paragraph, although it does not offer much in the way of a definition of informal logic ("that part of logic that is *not* covered by formal logic"). Problems with the very definition of the discipline should give us cause for concern. According to Walton and Brinton ([36, p. 9], quoted in Johnson and Blair [20, p. 352]): "Informal logic has yet to come together as a clearly defined discipline, one organized around some well-defined and agreed upon systematic techniques that have a definite structure and can be decisively applied by users." Woods remarked that the bar has been set too high. If these were the conditions under which something is a discipline "we would know disciplinary impoverishment on a grand scale. We would have lost philosophy, for starters, to say nothing of economics and psychology ... (Woods [38, p. 159])." I can not judge the situation in economics and psychology, I agree that philosophy is (and has always been) unique, but at least compared to modern formal logic, informal logic is a "pre-science."

In his analysis of the structure of science Kuhn introduced a notion of "pre-science" which, so it seems to me, fits the theoretical situation of informal logic well. Before a scientific discipline develops into "normal" science, there is normally a long period of somewhat inchoate, directionless research into a given subject matter. There are various competing schools, each of which has a fundamentally different conception of what the basic problems of the discipline are and what criteria should be used to evaluate theories about that subject matter. Some disciplines never reach the status of a "normal" science. If we take, now, the *Fundamentals of Argumentation Theory* (van Eemeren et al. [5]) as our guide in the theory of argument, the following approaches are listed: theory of fallacies, new rhetoric, critical thinking, dialogue logic and formal dialectics, pragma-dialectics, theory of dialogue, game theory ... A variety of approaches signals foundational problems. What exactly is informal logic? Is it really a branch of logic? Is it, or ought it to be, a distinct discipline? How, if at all, is informal logic to be marked off from neighboring subjects such as critical thinking, dialogue logic, and argumentation theory as a branch of rhetoric?

Some of the problems with were noticed long ago, at the very beginning of the discipline, first canonized in Aristotle's *Organon* which contains elementary deductive logic and principles of argumentation, the study of fallacies, philosophy of language, the basic principles of definition and explanation, the basic principles of scientific methodology and epistemology,... Sextus Empiricus in his *Outlines of Pyrrhonism* presented what I would call the dilemma of the dialectician (mentioned briefly by Walton [31, p. 303]):

> Perhaps it will not be out of place briefly to consider the topic of sophisms, since those who glorify logic say that it is requisite for explaining them away. Thus, they say, if logic has the ability to distinguish true from false arguments, and if sophisms are false arguments, logic will be capable of discerning these as they abuse the truth with their apparent plausibilities. Hence, the logicians, pretending to be giving assistance to tottering common sense, try earnestly to give us instruction about the concept, the types, and the solutions of sophisms.

6 Informal Logic and Informal Consequence

> In the case of those sophisms that logic seems particularly capable of refuting, the explanation is useless; while as regards those for which explanation is useful, it is not the logician who would explain them away but rather those in each art (techné) who have got an understanding of the facts (*Outlines* II: 236; Mates [22, p. 167]).

This sounds like Medawer on philosophers of science teaching scientific method! Sextus, a physician himself, gave the following example:

> In the abatement stage of disease, a varied diet and wine are to be approved. In every type of disease, abatement occurs before the first three days are up. Therefore, it is necessary for the most part to take a varied diet and wine before the first three days are up. The logician would have nothing to say toward explaining the argument away, useful though such an explanation would be; but the doctor will do so, knowing that "abatement" is ambiguous and refers either to that of the entire disease, or to the tendency to betterment, after crisis, of each particular attack; and knowing also that the abatement of the particular attack occurs for the most part before the first three days are up but that it is not in this abatement but in the abatement of the whole disease that we recommend the varied diet.
>
> Whence he will say that the premises of the argument are incoherent, with one kind of abatement—of the whole disease—taken in the first premise, and another kind—of the particular attack—taken in the second. And thus, in the case of the sophisms that can be usefully explained away, the logician will have nothing to say, but instead he will propound to us such arguments as these: Snow is frozen water. But water is dark in color. Therefore, snow is dark in color. And, when he has gathered together a collection of such nonsense, he knits his brow and takes logic to hand, trying very solemnly to establish for us by means of syllogistic proofs that ... snow is white.
>
> If, then, logic fails to explain away such sophisms as might usefully be solved, while in the case of those that somebody might suppose that it does explain, the explanation is useless, then logic is simply of no use in the solution of sophisms (*Outlines* II: 236; Mates [22, pp. 167–68]).

We may take "logic" in this text as logic of *Organon* or logic in the broad traditional sense mentioned by Hitchcock. So here is our dilemma: (informal) logic is either trivial or powerless on its own (field expertise is needed). And to follow the lead of Sextus in contemporary terminology: the analysis of reasoning is either "contentful", but this is done by experts, or topic neutral. Concentrating on topic neutral reasoning skills will only bring us back to formal logic, supposedly hardly applicable in matters of real life. But learning to reason substantively involves learning about actual subject areas and thus requires expert knowledge. The dilemma is reflected nicely in contemporary textbooks on informal logic (critical thinking): on one side there are general introductions to scientific methodology, enlightened "common sense," with long passages and detailed analyses of scientific articles. Woods remarks that with these works (such as Fisher [7]) informal logic lies closest to the bosom of philosophy and he sees them as continuous with the Commentaries of times gone by (Woods [38, p. 156]). I see them more as works of scientific apprenticeship—working laboriously through the material one slowly acquires the knowledge of an expert. On the other side there is an open market in literature ("How to Win Every Argument in 10 Steps") introducing readers to the wonderful power of how to tell a good argument from a bad one and influence people by being able to put a label in Latin on short snippets from the press.

Johnson and Blair [20, p. 352] remarked that formal logic began as a revolution at the level of theory that later filtered down into logic textbooks. Textbooks are instruments for passing the latest theory on to the next generation and hence the theoretical developments found in textbooks normally represent the precipitate from the theoretical controversies that occurred earlier in journal and monograph literature. In informal logic developments at the theoretical level were largely motivated by the attempt to teach students how to assess arguments in use. "Be clear about what tools are needed or need to be designed to do the job properly, then develop the theory needed to support the toolkit" (Johnson and Blair [20, p. 352]). But this "do-it-yourself" theory does not help much with the problems of foundations and our dilemma of the dialectician!

Not everybody would claim that the divide formal/informal is insurmountable. Jacquette proposes a different line of division—natural language versus symbolic language:

> I propose that a logical theory or procedure is formal if and only if it adopts a specialized symbolism for representing logical forms that does not occur in ordinary nonspecialized nonsymbolic thought and language. Although I acknowledge that all of logic has to do with logical form, I do not agree that all expressions of logical form must themselves be formal. This distinction captures much of the received concept, since it includes all of symbolic logic and excludes nonsymbolic evaluations of validity or invalidity. As we might expect, formal logic by the proposed distinction will roughly include everything belonging to what has become the de facto criterion for formal logic in relations expressed by means of standard and nonstandard notational variations and extensions of the propositional and predicate-quantificational calculus. The definition additionally includes schematic and graphic treatments of syllogistic logic that have traditionally been regarded as more properly within the aegis of informal logic and critical reasoning. Informal logic by contrast on the present proposal is limited to the consideration of a proposition's or argument's logical form by discursive reconstruction within natural language, the use of counterexamples to discredit inferences, identification of arguments as committing any of the so-called rhetorical fallacies, and the like (Jacquette [18, p. 134]).

I do not see a sharp line of division along these lines, though. There is the practical value of "formal" patterns recognized by informal theoreticians devising symbolic representations—diagrams, schemes, letters, ... True, this is not a "pure" symbolic language—but these representations are on a par with, say, graphic treatments of syllogisms in traditional "formal" logic. Frege compared the use of symbolic language instead of natural language in logic to the use of a microscope instead of the naked eye in biology. But even in biology one does not always need a microscope and sometimes too much precision is an "over-kill." Jacquette adds:

> The relegation of syllogistic logic, square of opposition, and argument diagramming methods to the genus of informal logic can now be seen as a kind of historical accident. Were it not for the emergence of more powerful algebraic methods of formal logic ..., there is little doubt that the logic of syllogisms, Venn and other styles of diagramming, etc., would constitute the whole of formal logic as opposed to purely informal nonspecialized nonsymbolic logical methods (Jacquette [18, p. 134]).

Yet it is difficult to see where the line should be drawn between an approach that uses argument diagramming methods and one that uses reconstructions within natural language—both will be used in a typical course on informal logic, though neither of them will find a place in a course on mathematical logic. Venn (or Euler) diagrams are sometimes useful in "informal" analysis, but they are, typically, also part of more formal approaches. And who would deny that, say, a disjunctive syllogism is not a useful tool in "informal" analysis of complex patterns of argumentation, but the difference between using "or" and "∨" in its representation seems to be of minor importance.[2]

Well, perhaps this is exactly Jacquette's point. In any case, I am sympathetic to his starting point—"all of logic has to do with logical form." Informal logicians disagree, or to put it guardedly, the attitude of the practitioners and "fathers" of informal logic towards formal logic is ambivalent. Thus (Johnson and Blair [20, p. 360]):

> How does informal logic differ from formal logic? In our view, the difference is partly one of subject matter. The social, communicative practice of argumentation can and should be distinguished from both inference and implication. In even the simplest such argument, the arguer proposes to the addressee that a set of propositions supports another, and thereby invites the addressee to infer the latter from the former. The relation of support may, but need not be, one in which the supporting propositions purportedly deductively imply the supported proposition. Part, though not all, of the normative theory of argumentation has as its subject-matter the answer to the question, "What sorts of support relationship are logically cogent?" We take it that one subset of logically cogent support relationships are ones in which the supporting propositions logically imply the supported proposition, and we take the subject matter of formal deductive logic to consist (inter alia) of the study of forms of entailment, that is, valid implication relationships among propositions or sentences.

And they add:

> We take informal logic to be the study of all the conditions under which an addressee ought to infer the target proposition from those adduced by the arguer as support for it. Thus the subject matter of informal logic is different from that of formal logic. Informal logic has the task of developing norms for the evaluation of arguments; formal logic has the task of developing the norms for formally valid implication relations (Johnson and Blair [20, p. 360]).

I would think that the subject matters of informal logic and formal logic at least overlap, classical logic, after all, is also the science of correct reasoning! Johnson and Blair sometimes deliberately go against a use of "argument" according to which logical proofs or demonstrations are counted as arguments. I agree that the sets of unrelated sentences or propositions *they* quote as an example of classically valid arguments should not be counted as arguments (of the type "The moon is not made of green cheese. So, 2 + 2 is 4."). Relevant logicians share this opinion, for that matter. But why could a (strictly deductive) proof that the square root of two is irrational not be a good and persuasive argument? And what is wrong with more mundane reasoning that uses deductions, say: "The player who won both Wimbledon and the US Open in 1982 was the greater player in that year. Connors won

---

[2] Of course, one should be aware of problems with different understandings of "or" in a natural language, but these differences will be reflected in different symbolisms.

both. Therefore, Connors was the greater player," (suppose I am wondering whether McEnroe or Connors was the greater player in 1982 and a friend of mine offers me this argument, cf. Jackson [16, p. 102]). The reasoning offered is a perfect logical deduction, but this does not undermine the act of propounding this obviously valid argument.

For Johnson and Blair an argument is a set of reasons, that is, has been, or might be, offered to another person or other persons with the intention of persuading them, or some audience, to modify their beliefs, attitudes or behavior (Johnson and Blair [20, p. 360]). This seems to be too narrow—the "teasing-out" function of propounding arguments is ignored. As Jackson notes: "The act of propounding an argument may have brought a half-buried piece of information to the surface, may have alerted me to the relevance of certain facts to my final concern, or may simply have enabled me to see how to get it altogether, so as to make transparent what I want to know" (Jackson [16, p. 102]). Well, Johnson and Blair might point out that reasoning about the greater player in 1982 and a demonstration that the square root of two is irrational are good pieces of *reasoning* but not arguments (complex social, speech activities). The "teasing-out" function allegedly pertains to proper reasoning and not to proper argument.

We may grant that argumentation is a social and public speech activity involving more than one party, with practical goals (persuasion). One cannot argue without at least an imaginary audience or interlocutor. Reasoning, on the other hand, is a mental activity that can be performed privately and much reasoning is done before and outside the context of argument. Argumentation requires that its participants reason, so reasoning is necessary for argumentation. At the heart of the activity of argumentation is the offering of and response to arguments in the more narrow sense of reasons offered in support of or against claims. According to Blair [2, p. 372], and perhaps not entirely consistent with other characterizations offered by Blair and Johnson, informal logic is restricted to the normative study of the cogency of argument, which is only one part of critical thinking and argumentation theory. I agree with this restriction. The relationship between reasoning proper and arguments within informal logic is complex, but, to be brief—since reasoning is necessary for argumentation, standards of good reasoning should be respected in argumentation and good reasoning includes deductions.

Some theoreticians, most notably Walton [32, 35], understand informal logic as essentially pragmatic. For Johnson and Blair argumentation is a social activity paradigmatically carried out in the medium of a natural language. But even their approach to informal logic is described by Walton as a narrow, text-based, product-oriented approach to argument. In pragma-dialectics, as one of the influential theoretical models of informal logic, argumentative discourse is conceived of as a certain activity (a critical discussion) aimed at resolving a difference of opinion by putting the acceptability of the "standpoints" at issue to the test by applying criteria that are both problem-valid as well as intersubjectively valid.

Pragmatics is sometimes characterized as dealing with the use of language and effects of context. But this has various meanings—features of the context can be epistemic features indexed to the audience or the arguer (their belief systems, reasons, doubts, justifications...), or conversational features of a dialogue. In argument analysis, should we consider *epistemic* norms or *conversational* norms? According to the first interpretation we should look at the beliefs of the audience (and/or the arguer). According to the second we should look at the conversation itself—what the audience has said, not what they think. Fallacies are explained as breaking the rules of proper dialogue. Circular arguments, for instance, are fallacious because they violate normative rules of dialogue which demand consensual starting points (cf. van Eemeren and Grootendorst [4]).

I think that the pull toward the pragmatic in the conversational sense should be taken with great caution in informal logic. In a critical discussion the initial conflict of opinions could be resolved, but both parties might still be wrong. But taking the *probative* function of an argument as our starting point—the use of an argument to remove doubts about the conclusion, to make it knowable, rationally believable or acceptable, we should be interested in the truth of the matter (or acceptability if truth is a notion which seems ill suited to many informal contexts). And not just in justifying our thesis and questioning or refuting the other party's thesis, by reasoned means, using accepted standards of evidence. Pragma-dialectics sometimes looks like a theory of conflict resolution through argumentative discussion and some wonder whether this is a theory of argumentation at all (cf. Wreen [39, p. 302]). Still, the relationship between reasoning and argumentation is complex. As Parsons [25] has noticed, arguments first have to be extracted from the texts analysed and interpreted, filled with steps that are not articulated in the "ur-argument" that are overtly present in the text. In the interpretative process we then have to establish the setting of an argument—a set of statements that are taken for granted and assumed principles of inference. The fallaciousness of an argument as analysed by informal logic is *not* an inherent property of a reasoning structure apart from the setting. Dialectical schools operate with commitments in a dialogue or initial acceptances, but the point is the same.

As I said, I am sympathetic to Jacquette's starting point—"all of logic has to do with logical form." Let me restate it slightly differently. A good argument has traditionally been the one whose conclusion *follows* from its premises. And logical form has always played an important role in explaining the concept of logical consequence. So, what can we say about "formal" and "informal" consequence? Does it even make sense to speak about "informal consequence"?

6.3 Informal Consequence

The most basic intuition about what it is for a conclusion to follow logically from the premises is that a valid inference is truth preserving: if the premises are true, so is the conclusion. According to Prawitz [26, p. 672] two further conditions must also be satisfied: (i) it is because of the logical form of the sentences involved and not because of their specific content that the inference is truth preserving; (ii) it is necessary that if the premises are true, then so is the conclusion.

Soundness—premise truth and deductive validity of an inference is a classical standard in argument evaluation. There is a wide agreement within informal logic on the inadequacy of soundness as a criterion of a good argument. Johnson and Blair replace the standard of soundness with a broader notion of argument *cogency*. An argument is cogent if and only if (i) its premises are rationally acceptable, (ii) its premises are relevant to its conclusion and (iii) its premises provide sufficient reason to accept the conclusion (the so called "R. S. A." criterion). Some prefer the notion of groundedness to that of sufficiency—premises in a cogent argument constitute grounds adequate for accepting the conclusion. The distinction is not important for my purposes so I will follow Trudy Govier [11] in calling conditions (i)–(iii) the "ARG" conditions for cogent arguments, to use an acronym (*a*cceptance, *r*elevance, *g*roundedness). These three criteria are sometimes augmented with a fourth: (iv) that there are no known better reasons for an opposite conclusion. Fallacies are explained as being violations of one or more of these criteria. And an additional preliminary condition for cogency has to be satisfied—premises and conclusions should be free of expressions whose meaning is ambiguous or indeterminate (cf. Freeman [9, p. 127]).

What kind of a consequence relation, if any, do ARG conditions specify? It is clear from the first criterion of ARG (premise *acceptability*) that a cogent argument does not (necessarily) preserve *truth*. But this alone does not discredit the notion of "informal" consequence. Van Benthem [1, p. 72] has remarked that:

> The idea that logic is about just one notion of "logical consequence" is actually one very particular historical stance. It was absent in the work of the great pioneer Bernard Bolzano, who thought that logic should chart the many different consequence relations that we have, depending on the reasoning task at hand. A similar rich view of the subject matter of the discipline is still found in the work of Mill, and especially, C. S. Peirce, who studied combinations of deduction, induction, and "abduction."

Something weaker than truth is preserved in good reasoning studied by an informal logician. But still, if the premises are acceptable (or whatever) and other criteria are met, then so is the conclusion.

How about the classical form—content distinction, does it make any sense in informal logic? I think it does, but it is not fixed in advance. Fallacies are common patterns of poor reasoning which can usefully be identified in the evaluation of informal reasoning. Some informal logicians introduce a special notion of an *argumentation scheme* as a stereotypical pattern of *defeasible* reasoning that typically occurs in common, everyday arguments. Standard accounts of argumentation schemes describe them as representing different types of plausible arguments which, when successfully deployed, create presumptions in favor of their conclusions and thereby shift the burden of proof to an objector. But, as one might expect, there is not much of an agreement in classifications and typologies used. The pragma-dialectical school recognizes a symptomatic relation (e.g., argument from sign), a relation of comparison (e.g., argument by analogy), and a causal relation (e.g., causal argument and means-end argumentation). According to Walton [33] common patterns of reasoning employed in everyday argumentation are argument from sign, argument from example, argument from position to know, argument from expert opinion, argument from cause to effect, argument from analogy, argument from precedent, etc. And there is yet another classification of schemes according to the type of warrant involved in the argument.

Argumentation schemes are subject to default contextually in a given case, and in this respect they differ from the context-free types of classical deductive arguments. But classical soundness by itself was never a sufficient standard in the evaluation of arguments. In a good argument one should not beg the question, so we are told. Now, begging the question is often said to be including one's conclusion in one's premises. But the argument does not beg the question just in case the conclusion explicitly appears in the premises, for then a mere reformulation of premises would be enough to avoid the charge. Surely, if "Since firefighters must be strong men willing to face danger every day, it follows that only a man can be a firefighter," begs the question, then so does "Since firefighters must be strong men willing to face danger every day, it follows that no woman can be a firefighter." Inclusion has to be understood more widely, the argument begs the question if the conclusion *implicitly* appears in the premises. But then, as noted by Jackson [16, p. 100], it is difficult to avoid the result that the argument begs the question when it is impossible for premises to be true and the conclusion false. So all valid arguments are question-begging? Not so, but one has to invoke some extra-formal considerations to explain the difference.

On the other hand, informal logic requires an eye for pattern and form in a certain very general sense. Informal logic uses counterexamples to discredit inferences—but is this not a general logical ability to move in the modal space? *Non-sequitur* as the most general type of logical fallacy is a violation of form insofar as it represents a possibility for your premises to be true and your conclusion false. The procedure of resolving questions of form is always the same: keep something fixed (logical "constants" in classical logic) and vary the other parts. But what is fixed is not given in advance and the possibility involved is not logical—only *relevant* options are to be considered and it is notoriously difficult (context-dependent) to explicate the notion of relevance. And of course, imagination is restricted by knowledge: if you know nothing about a certain field, then abstract patterns alone will rarely be of help (the moral from Sextus Empiricus).

By way of an example consider a famous paragraph from Descartes [3, p. 29] and a comment by Leibniz[3]:

> Next, examining attentively what I was, I saw that I could pretend that I had no body and that there was no world or place for me to be in, but that I could not for all that pretend that I did not exist; ... I thereby concluded that I was a substance whose whole essence or nature resides only in thinking, and which, in order to exist, has no need of place and is not dependent on any material thing. Accordingly this "I", that is to say, the Soul by which I am what I am, is entirely distinct from the body and is even easier to know than the body; and would not stop being everything it is, even if the body were not to exist.

---

[3] I got this example years ago from Peter Smith in Sheffield.

For Leibniz [21, p. 385] this is a mere sophism:

> It is not valid to reason: "I can assume or imagine that no corporeal body exists, but I cannot imagine that I do not exist or do not think. Therefore I am not corporeal, nor is thought a modification of the body." I am amazed that so able a man could have based so much on so flimsy a sophism... No one who thinks that the soul is corporeal will admit that we can assume that nothing corporeal exists, but he will admit that we can doubt (as long as we are ignorant of the nature of the soul) whether anything corporeal exists or does not exist. And since we nevertheless see clearly that our soul exists, he will admit that only one thing follows from this: that we can still doubt that the soul is corporeal. And no amount of torture can extort anything more from this argument.

Descartes's reasoning has the following *form*: "I can imagine that X does not exist, but I cannot imagine that I do not exist. Therefore I am not X." *Non sequitur*, according to Leibniz, inconceivability of a difference establishes doubt only and no categorical conclusions follow.[4] A counterexample is easy to find, take the case of amnesia and put a video recording of your past self for "X." Something is fixed (X) and something is variable, but one cannot give a recipe for a concrete analysis in advance. This explains one of the discrete charms of formal logic: even if ignorant of the topic, look for the (classical) logical form of an argument and calculate the result (whether the conclusion follows). But this would be more or less useless in the case at hand.

The last characteristics of logical consequence mentioned by Prawitz is necessity. Classically, if B follows from A, then it is necessary that if A is true, then so is B. No such necessity in the case of cogency—according to the ARG criteria premises should provide sufficient reason or adequate grounds to accept the conclusion. But a gap between the two approaches might look greater than it really is.

Relations of support studied by an informal logician seem to be a subject matter of epistemology. Some would even claim that "we may say that informal logic—the theory of it at least—is a field within epistemology, that field concerned with the norms and criteria of acceptability of claims arising within the polis" (Freeman [9, pp. 121–22]). Several authors have argued for the thesis that informal logic is included within epistemology or is epistemology done with a particular aim in view. Fisher [8] emphasizes connections between the empirical studies of real-life argumentation and naturalised epistemology. For Goldman [10] the theory of good argumentation is a special case of social epistemology since norms of good argumentation flow from the epistemic situation of cognizers, a situation that gives rise to certain conversational norms. These norms are best seen as a social quest for true belief and error avoidance. And according to Toulmin [30] argument analysis is just applied epistemology—in a successful argument sufficient evidence is given to support the conclusion, but the criteria of sufficiency depend on the nature of problems at issue.

And here is the bridge. Philosophically, logic was always the study of correct reasoning and reasoning is an epistemic, mental activity. In order to accommodate

---

[4] Kripke and Chalmers would disagree, but that is not the point here.

6 Informal Logic and Informal Consequence

for the role of logical consequence in organizing and extending knowledge Shapiro [27, p. 659] proposes the following definition of logical consequence:

> Φ is a logical consequence of Γ if it is irrational to maintain that every member of Γ is true and that Φ is false. The premises Γ alone justify the conclusion Φ.

It is difficult to explicate the notion of (ir)rationality properly, but this characterization of logical consequence could very well be spelled out as "G" in the "ARG": "the premises Γ constitute grounds adequate for accepting the conclusion Φ." One may also say that the conclusion classically follows by rational "necessity," if we believe the premises, we must believe the conclusion, on pain of contradiction. On the other hand one might say that the conclusion in a cogent argument follows by rational "necessity," if we believe the premises, we must believe the conclusion. Perhaps not on pain of contradiction but on pain of some weaker, contextual notion of implausibility.

Despite Shapiro's attempt to incorporate (epistemological) criteria of correct reasoning in the classical definition of logical consequence one may still protest against "informal consequence." Woods opens his inspiring discussion of informal logic (Woods [38]) with the following quote from Hintikka [12]: "I have a great deal of sympathy with the intentions of those philosophers who speak of 'informal logic', but I don't think that any clarity is gained by using the term 'logic' for what they are doing."

In the spirit of van Benthem [1] this is like saying that no clarity is gained by using the term "logic" for what researchers in "non-monotonic logics" are doing. Well, an informal logician could just shrug her shoulders and say with Shakespeare's Juliette—what is in name? "That which we call a rose by any other name would smell as sweet." But I think she can do better than that. The ARG criteria do not score so badly as a characterization of a certain *broad* kind of a consequence relation. We do not (in general) have truth preservation in cogent arguments but if the premises are acceptable and other criteria are met, then so is the conclusion. We can speak about form in informal analysis as well and this is not an oxymoron (argumentation schemes, patterns of fallacies, counterexamples), form in a loose sense, but still form. And finally, there is rational necessity of the grounding or support relation. Not quite the classical consequence relation, but still, I think that a certain broad notion of consequence emerged from the comparison. So, contrary to Hintikka, the term "logic" is not out of place. And to quote van Benthem [1, p. 80] again:

> My view is that there remains one logic, but not in any particular definition of logical consequence, or any favoured logical system. The unity of logic, like that of other creative disciplines, resides in the mentality of its practitioners, and their modus operandi.

Informal logic insofar it is *logic* is concerned with the traditional task of logic—standards of correct reasoning. We could also speak about broad logical consequence or logic in a broad sense. This logical core might be developed in different directions, to use ARG as our starting point: what is for a certain audience to accept premises—questions of rhetoric, dialectics, pragmatics, theory of dialogue;

problems of relevance and form—theory of fallacies, argumentation schemes; groundedness—induction, abduction, epistemology. Still, the most natural placement for the logical core specified by ARG is an epistemological enterprise in which argument is seen as embodying reasoning within a process of inquiry or of belief formation.

6.4 An Example

In a sense, informal logic is a theoretical retro movement. Fallacies, inductive logic and scientific method have been routinely discussed in the much despised elementary logic textbooks since the nineteenth century. Standards were set by Aristotle—recall that Aristotle regarded logic as a tool for every science. This conception is reflected in the collective title Organon that we still use to refer to Aristotle's logical writings. Another great work in this tradition is "*A System of Logic*, written by the greatest informal logician to date, unless the nod goes to Aristotle himself," (Woods [38, p. 162]). Mill developed a system of logic suitable for every bit of reasoning—for him logic of ordinary reasoning (vital moral issues included) was possible and this same logic was logic of science.

Woods remarks that in this respect Mill's connection with present-day informal logic is called into question. Unjustifiably so, I think—the present-day practitioners should learn from Mill. Are the ARG conditions not just the ideals of enlightened common sense or elementary scientific methodology which require a respect for available evidence and "reasonable" inference, awareness of alternatives and a willingness to modify or reject those beliefs that fail to conform to the evidence? The logical core of informal logic is most naturally placed in (basic) scientific methodology applied to matters of "polis" and everyday life. Mill would agree, and he would disagree with those who oppose the very logical core of scientific method.

Let me analyse—as a *practical* illustration of informal logic—an example of this type of animosity to logic in the broad sense and then draw some final morals. Consider Paul Feyerabend's drastic views that science is just one of the many ideologies that propel society and that it should be treated as such. Feyerabend claims that negative opinions about astrology and other alternative practices are not justified by scientific research. I think that informal logic should be embedded in elementary scientific methodology applied to subject areas accessible to every informed intellectual. The alternative practices so vigorously defended by Feyerabend (herbalism, alternative medicine, judgments based on intuition, rain dances...) very often fail to meet precisely the standards of this basic methodology. So what are Feyerabend's *arguments* for his astonishing claims?

In his plea for democratic relativism Feyerabend dismissed the predominantly negative attitudes of scientists towards such phenomena as elitist or racist. In "The Unusual Story of Astrology" [6] he critically analyses "Objections to Astrology," a statement by 192 leading scientists (first appeared in *The Humanist* of September/October 1975). The scientists declare that concepts of modern astronomy and physics undermine the principles of astrology. Feyerabend first interprets the principles of astrology as a claim that celestial events (positions of planets, the Moon and the Sun,...) exert influence on human life. This is a very broad interpretation of astrology—a different, narrower and much more common definition is implied in the text of the 1975 statement: "It is simply a mistake to imagine that the forces exerted by stars and planets at the moment of birth can in any way shape our futures." This statement is now interpreted by Feyerabend as: "It is simply a mistake to imagine that celestial events (positions of planets, the Moon and the Sun...) have any influence on human life." And there is yet a third meaning of astrology in Feyerabend's text, namely the thesis that celestial events (positions of planets, the Moon and the Sun,...) exert influence on life (in general) on Earth.

Nelson Goodman once wrote that the practical scientist does the business but the philosopher keeps the books. So let us do some book keeping. We have astrology-narrow (and interesting): the forces exerted by stars and planets at the moment of birth can shape the futures of human beings (their characters, personalities). Next we have astrology-broad: celestial events exert influence on human life. And finally we have astrology-empty (and largely uninteresting): celestial events exert influence on life (in general) on Earth. And here is the trick: compile a mass of evidence against the denial of astrology-empty and present this evidence as a counter-argument to the denial of astrology-narrow. Feyerabend meticulously surveys various research reports (the influence of the activities of the Sun on life on Earth, correlations between organic and inorganic processes on Earth and various parameters of the Sun and the Moon; he quotes articles such as "Possible Effects of Extra Terrestrial Stimuli on Colloidal Systems and Living Organisms", etc.) A lot of respect for scientific results and scientific methodology from someone so strongly opposed to "objective" scientific standards! After being bombarded with this counter-evidence, we read (as a *minor* objection, according to Feyerabend) that the scientists in the statement also complain that psychologists have not found the slightest evidence that astrology is of any, or even minimal value as an indicator of the past, present or future features of one's life. Feyerabend's reply would exhilarate every PR agency advising politicians in pre-election campaigns: "This argument (against astrology, D.Š.) has no value, when we remember that astronomers and biologists were not even able to find the evidence already published and contributed by their own professions," (presumably the articles quoted in length by Feyerabend).

For starters: first replace astrology-narrow ("the claim that knowledge of the apparent relative positions of celestial bodies is useful in understanding, interpreting, and organizing information about personality and human affairs and other terrestrial matters" is suggested by *Wikipedia*; "type of divination that involves the forecasting of earthly and human events through the observation and interpretation of the fixed stars, the Sun, the Moon, and the planets" according to *Encyclopædia Britannica*) with astrology-broad. Next refute a denial of astrology-empty (celestial events exert influence on life on Earth) and ignore powerful objections to astrology-narrow on the basis that those who objected to astrology-narrow were not able to find any evidence for astrology-broad. They were not even looking for it, but this will not prevent Feyerabend from switching over to the offensive. PR agencies advising political parties on how to win the elections prescribe the following rule: defense is for losers, when under attack (and justifiably so) do not, *ever*, retreat but make an assault. So Feyerabend, when faced with a decisive argument against his position (no evidence for astrology-narrow), drops in an offensive ad hominem: scientists are incompetent and they are unable to find any evidence.

Basically we have obliterating different senses of a single term (astrology-broad-narrow-empty) and suppressed evidence (no significant correlations) spiced with *ad hominem*. True, life is short and our cognitive resources are limited, but here we encounter a deliberate selection of information. There is a ready and quite general explanation for this selection. Some of our beliefs are very precious to us, perhaps we have "invested" a lot in them and would like to protect them at all costs. Denunciations of Western imperialism, his critique of science itself, as well as his concern for environmental issues ensured that Feyerabend has become a hero of the anti-technological counterculture. One might sympathize with Feyerabend's idea of a free society in which "all traditions have equal rights and equal access to the centres of power." One attached to those ideals will easily ignore or suppress counter-evidence to the conclusion that "objectively" there may be nothing to choose between the claims of science and those of astrology, voodoo, and alternative medicine. This is the familiar "confirmation bias." And what to make of Feyerabend's claim that theoretical anarchism is more humanitarian and more likely to encourage progress than its law-and-order scientific alternative? Hugh Trevor-Rope once remarked that one of the early effects of the discovery that nature is strictly governed by impersonal laws was to reduce the enthusiasm for burning witches.

6.5 Conclusion

I do not think that there was a great deal of theory involved in spotting fallacious moves in Feyerabend's reasoning. The main features traditionally ascribed to scientific method are a clear statement of a problem, careful confrontation of theory with fact, open-mindedness, and (potential) public availability or replicability of evidence. In the spirit of elementary scientific methodology, the starting points of argument analysis are very simple, almost trivial: first, identify the phenomenon you are dealing with. As always a preliminary condition for cogency has to be satisfied, premises and conclusions have to be free of expressions whose meaning is ambiguous. So, what does *that* ("astrology") mean? What exactly is claimed (conclusion) and what evidence is offered for those claims? The other two elements involved in the analysis were problems of relevance *(ad hominem)* and groundedness (suppressed evidence). The diagnosis of a dialectician remains the old scholastic: *distinguo* (be aware of different senses).

How about our dilemma of the dialectician? Here is what Sextus has to say about *amphiboly*:

In view of these points, then, the logical treatment of sophisms that is so much boasted about by the logicians is useless. We say similar things about the distinguishing of amphibolies. For if an amphiboly is a linguistic expression having two or more meanings, and if linguistic expressions have meaning by convention, then those amphibolies that are worth resolving—such as occur in some practical situation—will be resolved, not by the logician but by the people practiced in each particular art, who themselves have the experience of how they have created the conventional usage of the terms to denote the things signified, as, for example, in the case of the amphiboly "In periods of abatement one should prescribe a varied diet and wine" (*Outlines* II: 256; Mates [22, p. 168]).

What kind of knowledge was required to notice the ambiguity in Feyerabend's definition of astrology and *non sequitur* in his reasoning? Do we have to be experts in the field (astronomers, astrologists)? I do not think so. General alertness, knowing something about different subjects and general education is required, but one need not be a specialist. And knowing something, or better, the access to knowledge about different subjects has never been easier. Informal logic at its core embodies the attitude of basic scientific methodology toward claims, positions, theses in general, including those defended or put forward in the public sphere of knowledge and opinion (usually media and matters of "polis"). To repeat—cultivating respect for available evidence and "reasonable" inference, awareness of alternatives and a willingness to modify or reject those beliefs that fail to conform to the evidence.

For Toulmin logic is "concerned with the soundness of the claims we make" (Toulmin [30, p. 7]), rather than with the task of telling apart valid from invalid inferences, and he adds that this requires more than mere calculations, it requires "experience, insight and judgment". I have argued that the ability to tell valid from invalid inferences apart is a part of logic in the broad sense, but I agree with the stress on practice. I take the gist of Medawer's pessimistic remark on scientific method to be that a typical scientist will absorb the elements and skills of scientific methodology through her education and practice. Something similar is true of informal logic. In certain important aspects "applied" or informal logic includes elements of skill. Memorizing dozens of fallacies, all of them context dependent (not always fallacious), is useless without a "plain" ability to recognize the fact that the conclusion does not follow—never mind the name—and the ability to find an appropriate counterexample. Elements of skill, pattern recognition, practice and general knowledge required to assess arguments on various topics explain the difficulties in teaching and learning this subject. The ability to recognize the same pattern in different contexts and the ability to find an example or the counterexample to the pattern (inference scheme, typical fallacy, analogy...) seem to be important characteristics of a "critical thinker."

The notion of logic in the broad sense, or broad logical consequence which captures general norms of correct reasoning perhaps offers a promising theoretical framework. True, "informal logic" often designates something wider, as a toolbox in the sense of *Organon* it overlaps different disciplines and approaches. In the retro-spirit of *A System of Logic* I propose to incorporate the ARG logical core in elementary scientific methodology extended to subject areas accessible to every informed intellectual. But other packages are also possible (deduction, after all, can be very persuasive, so even a rhetorician will find logic in a broad sense very useful). How about contemporary dialectical schools? Consider the following definition (van Eemeren and Grootendorst [4, p. 1]):

> Argumentation is a verbal, social, and rational activity aimed at convincing a reasonable critic of the acceptability of a standpoint by putting forward a constellation of propositions justifying or refuting the proposition expressed in the standpoint.

The descriptive aspect of this definition lies in the concept of argumentation as a speech act. The normative aspect is represented in the reference to a *reasonable* critic, which adds a critical dimension to the definition. But all you need to incorporate the norms of ARG into this setting is to say that for a reasonable critic an ARG failing is automatically a dialectical or persuasive failing. Jackson [17, p. 472] gives a nice illustration—Galileo's famous thought experiment to make trouble for the view that the heavier a body is, the faster it will fall on being released. Galileo noted that a body weighing three stone can be thought of as two connected bodies, one weighing one stone and the other weighing two stone, and invited questions like, does the lighter body hold back or accelerate the heavier?

> This thought experiment is a wonderful "dialectical or persuasive" success but there's a sense in which no new evidence has entered the picture. What happens is that contemplating the thought experiment "teases out", makes explicit, the bearing of theses we already accept to the question of whether or not heavier bodies fall faster. Don't we want to count this success as an epistemological one, in which case we'd better count the opposite as epistemological failures? (Jackson [17, p. 472]).

The example shows how the "teasing-out" function of an argument can also be part of a proper, persuasive argument. Jackson speaks about epistemological norms, but one could also use the notion of the ARG criteria insofar as they constrain reasoning within a process of inquiry or of belief formation.

According to van Benthem [1, p. 67] logic arose in antiquity from two sources: the study of real argumentation in the dialectical tradition, and that of axiom-based proof patterns organizing scientific inquiry. Both are represented in *Organon*, but they separated and the difference seemed to be insuperable. No longer so. Contemporary research programme of formal logic does not preclude the analysis of real-life arguments. The latest developments in formal logic try to capture the subtleties of natural reasoning (non-monotonic, dynamic, relevant, paraconsistent, preferential logics ...)[5]. One can view informal logic and its ARG logical core as an attempt of reconciliation from the other, dialectical side. The norms of "real argumentation" are norms of elementary scientific methodology in which argument is seen within a process of inquiry or of belief formation in subject areas accessible to every informed intellectual.

---

[5] Some approaches confront "definitory" rules of standard formal logic with strategic-procedure rules which tell you how to win an argument, cf. Hintikka [13].

Acknowledgments An earlier version was presented at the 2009 Rijeka conference, the paper descended from Šuster [29].

References

1. Benthem, Johan van. 2008. "Logic and Reasoning: Do the Facts Matter?" *Studia Logica* 88: 67–84.
2. Blair, John A. 2001. "Walton's Argumentation Schemes for Presumptive Reasoning: A Critique and Development." *Argumentation* 15:365–79.
3. Descartes, René. 2006. *A Discourse on the Method of Correctly Conducting One's Reason and Seeking Truth in the Sciences.* Translated by Ian Maclean. Oxford: Oxford University Press.
4. Eemeren, Frans H. van, and Rob Grootendorst. 2004. *A Systematic Theory of Argumentation: The Pragma-Dialectical Approach.* Cambridge: Cambridge University Press.
5. Eemeren, Frans H. van, Rob Grootendorst, Francisca S. Henkemans, John A. Blair, Ralph H. Johnson, Erik C.W. Krabbe, Christian Plantin, Douglas N. Walton, Charles A. Willard, John Woods, and David Zarefsky. 1996. *Fundamentals of Argumentation Theory: A Handbook of Historical Backgrounds and Contemporary Developments.* Mahwah, NJ: Lawrence Erlbaum Associates Publishers.
6. Feyerabend, Paul. 1978. *Science in a Free Society.* London: New Left Books.
7. Fisher, Alec. 1980. *The Logic of Real Arguments.* Cambridge: Cambridge University Press.
8. Fisher, Alec. 2000. "Informal Logic and Its Implications for Philosophy." *Informal Logic* 2:109–15.
9. Freeman, James B. 2000. "The Place of Informal Logic in Philosophy." *Informal Logic* 20:117–28.
10. Goldman, Alvin I. 1994. "Argumentation and Social Epistemology." *The Journal of Philosophy* 91:27–49.
11. Govier, Trudy. 1987. *A Practical Study of Argument.* Belmont, CA: Wadsworth Publishing Co.
12. Hintikka, Jaakko. 1985. "True and False Logics of Scientific Discovery." *Communication and Cognition* 18:3–14; reprinted in Hintikka, Jaakko. 1999. *Selected Papers*, Vol. 5. Dordrecht and Boston: Kluwer.
13. Hintikka, Jaakko. 2001. "Is Logic the Key to All Good Reasoning?" *Argumentation* 15:35–57.
14. Hitchcock, David. 2000. "The Significance of Informal Logic for Philosophy." *Informal Logic* 20:129–38.
15. Hitchcock, David. 2007. "Informal Logic and the Concept of Argument." In *Philosophy of Logic. Handbook of the Philosophy of Science*, edited by Dale Jacquette, 100–129. Amsterdam: North Holland, Elsevier B.V.
16. Jackson, Frank. 1987. *Conditionals.* Oxford: Basil Blackwell.
17. Jackson, Frank. 2008. "Replies to My Critics." In *Minds, Ethics, and Conditionals – Themes from the Philosophy of Frank Jackson*, edited by Ian Ravenscroft, 387–472. Oxford: Clarendon Press.
18. Jacquette, Dale. 2007. "On the Relation of Informal to Symbolic Logic." In *Philosophy of Logic. Handbook of the Philosophy of Science*, edited by Dale Jacquette, 131–54. Amsterdam: North Holland, Elsevier B.V.
19. Johnson, Ralph H., and John A. Blair. 1977. *Logical Self-defense.* Toronto and New York, NY: McGraw-Hill Ryerson.
20. Johnson, Ralph H., and John A. Blair. 2002. "Informal Logic and the Reconfiguration of Logic." In *Handbook of the Logic of Argument and Inference*, edited by Dov M. Gabbay, Ralph H. Johnson, Hans J. Ohlbach, and John Woods, 339–96. Amsterdam: North Holland, Elsevier B.V.
21. Leibniz, Gottfried W. 1989. "Critical Thoughts on the General Part of the Principles of Descartes." In *Philosophical Papers and Letters.* Translated and edited by Leroy E. Loemker, 383–412. Dordercht: Kluwer.

22. Mates, Benson. 1996. *The Skeptic Way: Sextus Empiricus's Outlines of Pyrrhonism*. New York and Oxford: Oxford University Press.
23. Medawar, Peter. 1969. "Induction and Intuition in Scientific Thought." In *Pluto's Republic*. New York, NY: Oxford University Press. 1982.
24. Mill, John S. 1963. "Later Letters, Vol. 3." In *Collected Works, Vol. 17*, edited by J. Robson, 1862–63. Toronto: University of Toronto Press.
25. Parsons, Terence. 1996. "What Is an Argument?" *The Journal of Philosophy* 93:164–85.
26. Prawitz, Dag. 2005. "Logical Consequence from a Constructivist Point of View." In *The Oxford Handbook of Philosophy of Mathematics and Logic*, edited by Stewart Shapiro, 671–95. Oxford: Oxford University Press.
27. Shapiro, Stewart. 2005. "Logical Consequence, Proof Theory, and Model Theory." In *The Oxford Handbook of Philosophy of Mathematics and Logic*, edited by Stewart Shapiro, 651–70. Oxford: Oxford University Press.
28. Sobocan, Jan, and Leo Groarke, eds. 2007. *Critical Thinking, Education and Assessment: Can Critical Thinking Be Tested?* London, Ontario: Althouse Press, University of Western Ontario.
29. Šuster, Danilo. 2009. "Non Sequitur'—Some Reflections on Informal Logic." *Balkan Journal of Philosophy* 2:91–102.
30. Toulmin, Stephen. 2003. *The Uses of Argument*. Cambridge: Cambridge University Press.
31. Walton, Douglas N. 1987. *Informal Fallacies*. Amsterdam, Philadelphia, PA: John Benjamins Publishing Company.
32. Walton, Douglas N. 1990. "What Is Reasoning? What Is an Argument?" *Journal of Philosophy* 87:399–419.
33. Walton, Douglas N. 1996. *Argumentation Schemes for Presumptive Reasoning*. Mahwah, NJ: Lawrence Erlbaum Associates Publishers.
34. Walton, Douglas N. 1998. *The New Dialectic: Conversational Contexts of Argument*. Toronto: University of Toronto Press.
35. Walton, Douglas N. 2008. *Informal Logic: A Pragmatic Approach*. 2nd edition. Cambridge: Cambridge University Press.
36. Walton, Douglas N., and Alan Brinton, eds. 1997. *Historical Foundations of Informal Logic*. Farnham: Ashgate Publishing Company.
37. Wilson, Fred. 2008. "The Logic of John Stuart Mill." In *Handbook of the History of Logic Volume 4, British Logic in the Nineteenth Century*, edited by Dov M. Gabbay and John Woods, 229–82. Amsterdam: North Holland, Elsevier B.V.
38. Woods, John. 2000. "How Philosophical Is Informal Logic?" *Informal Logic* 20:139–67.
39. Wreen, Michael J. 1994. "Look, Ma! No Frans!" *Pragmatics & Cognition* 2:285–306.

Chapter 7
Logical Consequence and Rationality

Nenad Smokrović

7.1 Introduction

One of the most salient goals of logical theory is to characterize the relation of logical consequence. Whatever the characterization, it should characterize the most abstract candidate relation between premises and the conclusion. Although the logical consequence relation has been characterized as a mathematical formal theory, from the middle of the nineteenth century on, various less rigorous, informal attempts to articulate it were at work since the time of Aristotle. It is also possible that a consequence relation is somehow accessible to ordinary thinkers and expressed in natural languages. In this way, we have at least three different notions of logical consequence which have been given a common name, namely, first, a mathematically formalized one, then second, "pre-theoretic," in fact sophisticated but pre-formal notion expressed more or less in natural language resources (but possibly appealing, perhaps under some other name, to philosophical categories such as modality and formality), and third and finally, the notion of logical consequence that corresponds to whatever is responsible for ordinary correct reasoning performed by ordinary people (Nenad Miščević has suggested to me, in a half-kidding way, the term "anthropo-logical consequence" for this third notion). To anticipate, I will ecumenically call the second as well as the third notion, i.e. the sophisticated and the ordinary ones, "pre-theoretical notions of logical consequence". The second one is weakly, and the third one is strongly and literally pre-theoretic.

A significant number of contemporary logicians see the theoretical articulation of the logical consequence dependent on the pre-theoretic notion. The problem arising here is that in the contemporary debates, theoreticians, talking sometimes about pre-theoretic, sometimes about ordinary or intuitive notion of the logical consequence, do not sufficiently clearly distinguish between "pre-theoretic," in the sense of pre-mathematical, but often very sophisticated and in this sense non-ordinary, and the ordinary notion that even a naïve thinker might turn out to possesses.

N. Smokrović (✉)
Department of Philosophy, University of Rijeka, Rijeka, Croatia
e-mail: nenad@ffri.hr

In this paper I will scrutinize the notion(s) underlying the term "pre-theoretic logical consequence" distinguishing between a stronger and weaker notion and arguing that both of them, each having its own role, should be considered in accounting for the relation between those notions and mathematically formalized articulations of logical consequence. To depict the relation, I will offer a very programmatic outline according to which a formal logician is in the position of the translator in analogy with Quine's translation schema. The general structure of the idea will be given in the short indication of the research program based on a variant of Putnamian theory.

Contemporary formal logical theory characterizes logical consequence (above all in its formal guise) in two different, sometimes competing ways, the proof-theoretical and the model-theoretical one. The model-theoretic approach, on the one hand, focuses upon *interpretations* of forms of statements. In terms of validity, a formula is model-theoretically valid just in case it is true in all structures for (or satisfied by) its language, and this reading then generalizes up to the consequence relation. On the other hand, in the proof-theoretic approach the formal consequence relation is seen as explicable in terms of *inferential rules*. It could be said that a sentence A is inferable (or provable) from (set of sentences) X by means of the collection R of inference rules if there is a proof of A from X. Also, on the contemporary scene the model-theoretic approach is most frequently embedded in classical logic while the proof-theoretic approach is mostly based on constructive and intuitionist logic.

The logical theory, setting aside diversities, as a mathematical formalized language and calculus seems to be expert logicians' concern, whose scientific discourse is over and above the ordinary inferential practice. This appearance is misleading. Tarski, who first introduced the semantic, model-theoretic account of logical consequence in the field, strongly emphasized that his (and, probably, any other) account should correspond, remain faithful to the intuitive, ordinary conception "from which we borrow the name," as Etchemendy [4, p. 2] puts it. Tarski does not specify whether it is our second, sophisticated pre-formal, or third, hypothetically ordinary conception. In his seminal paper "On the Concept of Logical Consequence," he wrote:

> The concept of logical consequence is one of those whose introduction into the field of strict formal investigation was not a matter of arbitrary decision on the part of this or that investigator; in defining this concept, efforts were made to adhere to the common usage of the language of everyday life.

The idea that the formalized, theoretical articulation of the logical consequence should correspond, or in mathematical terms, model the ordinary, pre-theoretic conception of logical consequence (the one taken from "the common usage of the language of everyday life") has become rather prevalent among contemporary logicians and philosophers of logic.[1] Thus, the prevailing view is that theoretical

---

[1] A distinguished representative of the opposite view is Michael Resnik who denies any relevant connection between formal logic and pre-theoretic inferential practice [16].

articulations of logical consequence are significantly determined by and answerable to its pre-theoretic notion, in either of the two senses we distinguished. Some, notably Shapiro, holds that they are mutually co-determined [18, p. 155]. Even those who otherwise criticize Tarski's approach, most radically Etchemendy [4] and Field [5] take his aiming at ordinary concept of logical consequence at face value, and only object that his account failed because of its alleged inability to stay true to this ordinary concept. Similarly, Gómez-Torrente, talking of logical truth and, derivatively, of logical consequence, says in the footsteps of Tarski:

> On most views, with a mathematical characterization of logical truth we attempt to delineate a set of formulae possessing a number of non-mathematical properties. Which properties these are vary depending on our pre-theoretic conception of, for example, the features of modality and formality.

One of the most influential authors in the field, Stewart Shapiro, commenting the relation between great fields of mathematical logic (proof theory, model theory, set theory and computability) and its philosophical ramification, says in the same vein:

> Our main question here concerns how that wonderful mathematics relates to the philosophical targets: correct reasoning, valid thought, inference. [19, p. 651]

The underlying idea behind those considerations is that "logic is the study of correct reasoning" [18, p. 135]. Correct reasoning is carried out in natural languages (or, alternatively, in a "language of thought") as its vehicle, and indeed by ordinary reasoners. The term covers a broad range of logically naïve thinkers that are nevertheless engaged in making inferences, from those without any particular theoretical knowledge to experts in a particular scientific domain (but without special (meta-)logical training), economists, lawyers, even practicing mathematicians. What makes their reasoning patterns correct is presumably an intuitively, pre-theoretically accessible consequence relation obtaining among natural language sentences (or, for that matter, propositions of the language of thought). On the other hand, a theoretical (formal, i.e. model-theoretic or proof-theoretic) logical consequence is "rigorously defined only for *formal* languages" [18, p. 135]. Given this dual allegiance of the logical consequence relation, poised between the formal and the pre-formal, the question arises how to account for the relationship between those of its aspects that are expressed in formal language, on one side, and those pertaining to the natural language(s) on the other.

Accordingly, the program, of the kind I am myself also interested in, having a goal of connecting the theoretical logical consequence with the intuitive or pre-theoretic logical consequence in the way that former models or captures the later, could be confirmed if there is a kind of correlation between the formal language and the natural language (or language of thought), most plausibly a fragment of it (say, declarative sentences) that comes closest to the formal logical discourse. Let me name this kind of program *the modeling program*.

Unfortunately, in spite of taking the relation between two concepts of logical consequence, the ordinary and the mathematically formulated one, to be crucial to the philosophy of logic, theoreticians, including prominently Tarski himself, followed by the contemporary proponents of his kind of approach (as well as his opponents, accusing him for not capturing the ordinary notion of logical consequence), do not say much about the real nature of the pre-theoretic, ordinary or intuitive conception of logical consequence.[2] Their use of the expression "pre-theoretic notion of logical consequence" remains vague and in need of further clarification. This is strange given the importance they ascribe to the latter.

The ambiguity to be mentioned first is that it is not clear whether the discussion about intuitive or pre-theoretic notion of logical consequence concerns theoretician's notion previous to formal, mathematical formulations of logical consequence (our number two, sophisticated pre-formal notion), or the ordinary, naïve thinker's concept(ion) or even faculties (that she has independently of any theoretical activity) needed for her mastering of characteristic ingredients of the logical consequence relation, i.e. the items embraced by our third category. Let me illustrate the ambiguities in the otherwise inspiring and interesting literature. Gómez-Torrente in his fine *Stanford encyclopedia* article on logical truth [6] addresses the problem and offers the solution in favor of the former aspect, riding roughshod over the Tarskian concerns about "the common usage of the language of everyday life":

> By "pre-theoretic" it's not meant "previous to any theoretical activity;" there could hardly be a "pre-theoretic" conception of logical truth in this sense. In this context what's meant is "previous to the theoretical activity of mathematical characterization." [6]

For him, the pre-theoretical concept as "previous to the theoretical activity of mathematical characterization" is a concept one possesses previous to the formalization of the logical theory. Accordingly, even Aristotle's concept of the logical consequence falls into the category. Keeping the taxonomy in the frame of these two broad categories: "previous to any theoretical activity" and "previous to the theoretical activity of mathematical characterization," we have expert logicians engage in doing formalized theory, on one side, and expert logicians engaged in not yet formalized logical theory, on the other. All other people, according to such taxonomy, *do not have access to any conception of logical consequence whatsoever*. It seems that thus connecting the theoretical, fully formalized concept, merely to the one immediately preceding the formalization (our number two, sophisticated pre-formal notion) is not such a great theoretical gain for at least two reasons.

The first one concerns the programmatic view that formal characterization of logical consequence should model an ordinary, and thereby strongly pre-theoretic notion. If the point is simply that formalized mathematical theory should correspond to not-yet-formalized logical theory leaving aside any interest in ordinary inferential practice, and ordinary incipient reflections about it, the proposal seems to fall short of an account of ordinary correct reasoning that proceeds roughly but reliably in accordance with what formalized as well as not-yet-formalized but sophisticated theoretical characterization prescribe. This leaves the sophisticated theory and its

---

[2] Exemptions are Robert Hanna [7] and Jodi Azzouni [1], although their concerns are logical abilities in general.

formalization in an epistemic vacuum, depriving it from connections that Tarski and others have wisely insisted upon.

The other reason is related to the fact that ordinary people also have certain logical abilities and a kind of logical knowledge that enables them to recognize the instances of the consequence relation, possibly, even more specifically, the instances of the logical consequence relation as well. At least, taking into account that the expression "logical consequence" is a term of art we should ascribe to them the ability to recognize that "something implies something" or that "something follows from something". It is not to say that ordinary thinkers, being able to recognize that "something follows from something," ipso facto are in the possession of the notion of logical consequence (ordinary or some other). The focus is on the claim that ordinary thinker's logical capacities might be a resource rich enough for grasping a logical consequence relation. As we pointed out the term "ordinary thinker" covers a broad spectrum, from people without any particular theoretical knowledge to experts in a particular scientific domain who are, without any doubt, able to recognize (more or less correctly) that a conclusion follows from particular set of sentences. If only the highly sophisticated logical practices were the subject matter of the theoretical activity, a theoretician embracing the modeling program could simply list various plausible not-yet-formalized characterizations of the logical consequence and investigate the relation between them and theoretical articulations, honoring them with the epithet of "pre-theoretical," emptied from any connection with ordinary practices (as some logician actually do). So, we need the strongly pre-theoretical, i.e. ordinary items to guide our thinking about logical consequence.

In Section 7.2 I will present those two aspects, the weakly and the strongly pre-theoretical one in some more details.

7.2 How Should the Pre-theoretic Conception of Logical Consequence Be Understood?

As I said, my approach to the pre-theoretic conception of the logical consequence will suggest holding unavoidable both its aspects. The first one is concerned with determining plausible standards, given by the pre-formal, but sophisticated and professional characterizations of the logical consequence relation, according to which something could count as an inference token satisfying the (logical) consequence relation.

Starting from Aristotle, the concept of the pre-theoretic logical consequence has been formulated in various ways. Most often, these ways appeal to the categories such as modality, formality, or to some epistemic requirements. Whatever the basic category chosen, it is almost universally accepted that a minimal requirement on pre-theoretic or ordinary correct reasoning should be truth-preservation. It is equally universal that truth preservation could be considered either in terms of *modality* (strengthening it up to the necessary preservation), or of the *form* (limiting it to the cases of a particular logical kind). As Shapiro sums it up talking about the slogan of truth-preservation:

> The slogan could reflect the *modal component* (my italics) of logical consequence, in the sense that if the premises of the good argument were true, then the conclusion would have to be. Or it could reflect an intuition that the argument has a *valid form* (my italics), assuming that one can delimit the form-content distinction in natural language, or whatever the vehicle of reasoning is. [18, p. 153]

To sort out the positions and rehearse them let me remind you of the general distinction between metaphysic or ontic and epistemic approaches to the characterization of the logical consequence. The former approach aims to determine what is for two sentences to stay in the logical consequence relation. Inside this category, formulations differ regarding different general categories that are supposed to basically characterize the reasoning in the natural language or the language of thought. Those categories are modality, formality and semanticity (as a sub-species of formality). The epistemic approach shifts the focus from the question about the nature of the logical consequence to the question of "how we come to know" that particular relation is a logical consequence relation. In the terms of justified believes, if we believe the premises, we must believe the conclusion on the pain of contradiction, or on the pain of irrationality. The taxonomy follows up Shapiro's exhaustive list of characterizations.

Ontic Formulations The most usual way to determine the logical consequence is modal characterization:

(1) If Φ is a logical consequence of set of the sentences Γ [19, p. 655], it is not possible for every member of Γ to be true and yet Φ false.

In terms of possible worlds, characterization states:

(2) If Φ is a logical consequence of set of the sentences Γ, Φ holds in every possible world in which every member of Γ holds.

Traditional but in the contemporary discourse contentious formulation is in terms of formality.

It is usual to hold that an argument is valid iff every argument with the same (logical) form is valid. The answer of how to characterize the logical form turns out to be the answer to the question of logical terms, since logical form is characterized as containing only logical terms. In this way, the issue of formality is sorted out in terms of the truth and the meaning of "logical terms".

Semantic Characterization

(3) The truth of the members of Γ guarantees the truth of Φ in virtue of the meanings of a special collection of the terms, the "logical terminology."

Neither of these two modes of characterizing the pre-theoretical notion of logical consequence, taken separately, is entirely satisfactory. The problem with the modal characterization is that it is too broad to specifically delineate logical consequence

7 Logical Consequence and Rationality   127

relation. Namely, according to this formulation, (taken together with the very wide semantic formulation, according to which the truth of the members of Γ guarantees the truth of Φ in virtue of the meanings of the terms in those sentences) analytic or conceptual consequence relation could satisfy it. For example, the sentence "Jim is shorter than Bill" is a necessary consequence of the sentence "Bill is taller than Jim". Nevertheless, the argument

"Bill is taller than Jim; therefore Jim is shorter than Bill"

does not expresses a logical consequence relation because its validity depends on the meaning of non-logical terms, namely on the converse meaning of the expressions "to be taller then" and "to be shorter then". The strengthened semantic formulation (3) requires exact characterization of the terms that could count as logical terms. Logicians disagree on such characterization, but I will hold that Tarskian model-theoretic criterion for logical terms (the term is logical if its extension is invariant under any permutation of the domain) is a necessary condition on this terms.

On the other hand, here are the most usual epistemic articulations of logical consequence.

Epistemic Aspect

(4) There is a deduction of Φ from Γ by a chain of legitimate, gap-free (self-evident) rules of inference.
(5) It is irrational to maintain that every member of Γ is true and Φ is false.
(more specifically, "The truth of Φ follows by necessity of thought from the truth of all the sentences of Γ").

The epistemic aspect shifts the perspective in the sense that it transforms the modal and semantic statements of what the logical consequence is into the statements of how one comes to know that things are as modal and semantic formulations state. A central account for the grasping of logical consequence in those formulations is given in terms of "necessity of thought," "having it on the pain of irrationality," "legitimate, gap-free (self-evident) rules of inferences," and similar. The problem with epistemic characterization is that it, stating the normative conditions on an epistemic agent considers agent's epistemic capacities as ideal. Concerning normative conditions, the formulation (5) demands that a rational agent should "maintain that every member of Γ is true and Φ is false," otherwise, the agent is irrational. Rationality of the agent consists in his ability to recognize and/or perform "a deduction of Φ from Γ by a chain of legitimate, gap-free (self-evident) rules of inference." Of course, such demands on rationality are highly idealized. This negligence of actual, more limited cognitive faculties leaves the possibility that the set of rational human beings be empty.

Shapiro's answer to the problem is a "blended sense" formulation of the logical consequence. Binding together characterizations (1) and (3), "blended sense" gives a highly plausible notion of the pre-theoretic model of correct reasoning. Here is the formulation:

(BS) "Let us say that a sentence Φ (in natural language) is a consequence of a set Γ of sentences in a blended sense if it is not possible for every member of Γ to be true and Φ false, and this impossibility holds in virtue of the meaning of the logical terms." [19, p. 663]

All these formulations (from (1) to (3) and (BS)) concern our second item, the sophisticated pre-formal (and only in this weak sense pre-theoretical) notion of logical consequence. This brings us to the leading idea of the paper, namely that all such pre-formal articulations of the logical consequence should in one way or another concern themselves with ordinary thinker's inferential behavior. The nice way to establish the connection between sophisticated pre-formal characterizations of logical consequence and naïve thinker's abilities to manage those characterizations is to bring into discussion Robert Hanna's notion of "proto-logic" [7]. Namely, he formulates four meta-logical principles that, among other things, underline the ordinary logical capacity. As Hanna said:

> I now want to propose that the protologic is innately contained in a cognitive faculty for logical representation, namely, the logic faculty. [7, p. 45]

What is interesting enough is that two (first and third ones) of those four principles correspond to Shapiro's "blended sense" formulation. I am presenting here those corresponding principles:

1. *The weak principle of validity*: An argument is valid if it is impossible for all of its premises to be true and its conclusion false.
2. *The weak principle of logical truth*: A sentence is logically true if it comes out true under every possible uniform reinterpretation of its non-logical terms.

The "validity of the argument" in the weak principle 1 is synonymous with "... is a logical consequence of ...". Regarding the second part of (BS) formulation, I hold that the principle 2 corresponds to it and also expresses a weak and informal version of Tarski's criterion for logical terms, which possibly corresponds to ordinary thinker's actual logical faculties. In this way, the link between sophisticated, pre-formal aspect of pre-theoretic notion of logical consequence and the ordinary one concerning naïve thinker's inferential practices and their cognitive abilities is indicated.

7.3 The Program: From Theoretical Through Pre-formal to the Ordinary

To determine the relation between theoretical formulations of logical consequence and what those formulations are aiming to capture, the outline of the research program for finding "this something" that we named with the term pre-theoretic notion, (both in the stronger and in the weaker sense) of logical consequence should be indicate. Succinctly formulating in an illuminating way the program that connects

7 Logical Consequence and Rationality

formal language articulation of logical consequence and natural language deductions, S. Shapiro says:

> ...models correspond to something concerning correct reasoning, and this something is related to whatever it is that natural language deductions must answer to. [18, p. 141]

And adds in the footnote:

> A programme is confirmed if "intuitive consequence" relations among the natural language sentences are *translated* (my italic) as model-theoretic consequences in the formal language. [18, fn. 3]

A program Shapiro is talking about is a realist program, which, to be confirmed, at least some features of the mathematical model must correspond to features of the reality. Such features Shapiro calls "representors", in contrast to artifacts that are theoretical constructs that not correspond to anything in the reality. The way I read him he enjoins us to bind the theoretical concept through pre-formal one to the ordinary conception or epistemic kind, the last two being the two kinds of the pre-theoretical item. This ordinary pre-theoretic logical consequence is precisely the (somewhat idealized) aspect of reality, i.e. of our ordinary inferential practices that the mathematical theory of logical consequence is aiming to model.

I will argue that there is something like the pre-theoretical conception of logical consequence instantiated in ordinary inferential practice. To start explaining this "something" I will take translation as a "key word."

Namely, the analogy of the above Shapiro's quotation with Quine's translation schema irresistibly comes to one's mind. The relation that holds between the formal, Frege's pure language, and the natural language conceived as a medium for correct reasoning is much the same as the relation between the translator's language and an unknown language. Quine's famous formulation is this:

> Take the ...case of trying to construe some unknown language on the strength of observable behavior. If a native is prepared to assent to some compound sentence but not to a constituent, this is a reason not to construe the construction as conjunction. If a native is prepared to assent to a constituent but not the compound, this is a reason not to construe the construction as alternation. We impute our orthodox logic to him, or impose it on him, by translating his language to suit. We build the logic into our manual of translation. Nor is there cause here for apology. We have to base translation on some kind of evidence, and what better? [15, p. 82]

We now introduce our crucial analogy, applying the translation schema to our question at hand. According to it, our formal logician is in the position of the translator looking at the naïve inferential practice expressed in a natural language (observable behavior in Quine's case). As the Quine's translator reads off the correctness of her translation from the native's behavior, so the logician seeks to confirm her mathematical theory finding "representors" in reality, i.e. in the natural language deductions (where deduction, I think, should be understood both, as an inferential form and as an act of reasoning). Also, as the Quine's translator imputes his own logic to the native, so the formal logician measures naïve thinker's correctness in reasoning imputing him her preferred logic.

Remember that according to Quine, in order to check whether her translation is correct, the translator should obtain strong evidence that the native understands the sentence of the form "*p&q*". She understands the sentence if she, assenting to the conjunction, assents to (all) conjuncts (or, in negative, does not understand the sentence, if assenting to the compound sentence, she is not prepared to assent to some of the conjuncts). Imputing his own logic to the native, the translator finds on the native's part the (implicit) understanding of the truth conditions. At this stage of Quine's translation schema the sameness of underlying logical principles in the translator's and in the native's language, based on the native's observable behavior, is established. The successful translation can go on when the native is recognized as a competent reasoner having the same pre-theoretic conception of logical connectives as the translator has.

In the case of logical consequence, the program of "translation" is vindicated if there is (in the naïve inferential practice) something that "is related to whatever it is that natural language deductions must answer to." Whether there is something in the ordinary inferential practice that corresponds to the theoretician-translator's required standard for correct reasoning is an empirical question (as it is in the Quine's case as well, since the translator is looking for the evidence in native's behavior). In the case of logical consequence the logician should rely on the work of the cognitive scientist to obtain the required evidence. Therefore, the program of "translation" would be confirmed if we were to obtain the evidence that basically there is the same set of fundamental logical principles present in "pure" logical language as it is in the natural language, where it plays the role of foundations underlying the logical formalization.

Let me now briefly formulate a tentative idea concerning the generalization of the above sketched outlook. I want to appeal to Putnam's famous theory of reference. Criticizing Russell's theory and offering a new theory of reference and meaning for general terms (kinds terms in his theory, which is more appropriate in the context of our discussion), Putnam says (taking the example of the kind term "gold"):

> The use of a word such as "gold" depends on our possessing paradigms, standard examples that are agreed to be model members of the kind ... What makes something gold is having the same nature as the paradigms.

And several lines above it:

> A term refers to something if it stands in the right relation to ... sameness of "nature" in the case of kind words. [14, p. 73]

Due to the limited length of the paper, I will only indicate the plausible route of investigation.

I am inclined to read Shapiro's formulation of the program in a Putnamian way. The elements of Shapiro's program read in my proposed way are: (a) something in the human world answerable to the natural language deductions; (b) our sophisticated pre-formal characterization of a logical consequence that states criteria for correct reasoning, and (c) mathematically formulated logical consequence that aims

7 Logical Consequence and Rationality

to model or capture both ingredients, first, our (b), i.e. the standards for correct reasoning and second, our (a) i.e. what is supposed to correspond to those standards. Of course, it is possible that there is nothing "in the human world" that fits the theoretical requirements, that ordinary inferential practice simply does not correspond to standards established by the pre-formal notion of a logical consequence. In this way, the final answer relies on the empirical findings of cognitive science. In the nutshell, according to our picture, the full theoretical and formal articulation of a logical consequence would be achieved if it managed to model, as Putnam said, "existentially given things," approaching it through, in Putnam's words, a paradigm that directs us to the referent, while the paradigm itself is successful if it has the same nature as the referent. This element "in the human world," that is responsible for the ordinary inferential practice, should be "observed" through the pre-formal articulation of a logical consequence. In this way, in the Putnamian spirit if not the letter, the program does not determine the extension of the term in question in advance, dictating the set of necessary and sufficient conditions, but leaving that the extension be partly fixed by the world. Viewed in this way, the theoretical articulation of the logical consequence would be achieved in the best way by establishing a fruitful and firm collaboration between logic and cognitive science.

What is supposed to be the contribution of cognitive science? Shapiro's blended sense formulation of the pre-formal notion of logical consequence, gives us a clear standard for counting an instance of ordinary deduction as an instance of logical consequence relation, if we take it to be our appropriate "paradigm." On the other hand, Hanna's weakened version of the "proto-logic" principles, gives us the criteria for finding required logical faculties that might meet the standard. Remember, he claims "that the protologic is innately contained in a cognitive faculty for logical representation, namely, the logic faculty." These criteria clearly point to at least two cognitive capacities: the capacity for recognizing modal terms and their role as well as to the capacity for distinguishing those terms in natural language that correspond to logical terms in formal language, from non-logical terms. The first capacity, the one concerning modality, is relatively unproblematic. The claim that the ordinary thinker will find the sentence "Jim is shorter than Bill" as a necessary consequence of "Bill is taller than Jim," is fairly uncontentious, and this kind of reasoning of course falls into conceptual or analytic consequence relation, not the strictly logical one. So, since modal characterization of consequence does not uniquely determine logical consequence relation, further empirical evidence that would witness for the possession of the other capacity by ordinary thinkers, namely the one for distinguishing those terms in natural language that correspond to logical terms in formal language, should be searched for, and if found added to the one concerning the first capacity.

Within a broad area of rationality theory, which is also in the business of offering an account of the capacities we are looking for, and can and should be harnessed for our logical purposes, two general theoretical outlooks have been at the center of the debate in the last two or three decades. Those well-known theories are mental logic theory,[3] and mental models theory.[4] Both turn to be unsatisfactory for the task at hand. My modest alternative proposal would be to rely on the relatively new and promising theory developed by K. Stenning and M. van Lambalgen in their book "Human Reasoning and Cognitive Science" [20]. In the nutshell, the idea is that the reasoning process is initiated by interpretation of the (non-logical and logical) expressions based on the understanding of the expression. The reasoning process inevitably contains understanding-based interpretation of these expressions (or, in the more complex case, the scenario), and once their meaning is fixed, the interpretation determines the reasoning process. Those statements provide a good basis for promising investigation of the ordinary thinker's capacity for discriminating non-logical terms from logical ones. The development of this idea is a task for another paper.

Acknowledgments The paper has profited enormously from the discussions with professors Dag Prawitz and Stuart Shapiro at the IUC conference in Dubrovnik 2010; I want to thank them for inspiration and support. I am particularly grateful to my friends and colleagues, Nenad Miščević and Majda Trobok, for their enormous patience and most valuable advice.

References

1. Azzouni, Jody. 2006. *Tracking Reason: Proof, Consequence, and Truth*. New York, NY: Oxford University Press.
2. Braine, Martin, and David O'Brien, eds. 1998. *Mental Logic*. Mahwah, NJ: Lawrence Erlbaum.
3. Craik, Kenneth. 1943. *The Nature of Explanation*. Cambridge: Cambridge University Press.
4. Etchemendy, John. 1990. *The Concept of Logical Consequence*. Cambridge, MA: Harvard University Press.
5. Field, Hartry. 1989. "Introduction: Fictionalism, Epistemology, and Modality." In *Realism, Mathematics, and Modality*, 1–52. Oxford: Basil Blackwell.
6. Gómez-Torrente, Mario. 2010. "Logical Truth." *The Stanford Encyclopedia of Philosophy (Summer 2010 Edition)*, edited by Edward N. Zalta, http://plato.stanford.edu/archives/sum2010/entries/logical-truth/
7. Hanna, Robert. 2006. *Rationality and Logic*. Cambridge, MA: MIT Press.
8. Johnson-Laird, Philip. 1983. *Mental Models*. Cambridge, MA: Harvard University Press.
9. Johnson-Laird, Philip. 1995. "Inference and Mental Models." In *Perspectives on Thinking and Reasoning*, edited by Stephen Newstead and Jonathan Evans, 115–46. Hove: Lawrence Erlbaum Associates.
10. Johnson-Laird, Philip. 2001. "Mental Models and Deduction." *Trends in Cognitive Science* 5: 434–42.
11. Johnson-Laird, Philip, and Ruth Byrne. 1991. *Deduction*. Hillsdale, NJ: Lawrence Erlbaum.
12. Johnson-Laird, Philip, and Ruth Byrne. 1993. "Models and Deductive Rationality." In *Rationality*, edited by Ken Manktelow and David Over. London: Routledge.
13. Macnamara, John. 1986. *A Border Dispute: The Place of Logic in Psychology*. Cambridge, MA: The MIT Press.

---

[3] For the prominent representatives of "Mental logic" theory, see: Braine [2]; J. Macnamara [13].
[4] The first who in the initial form proposed "Mental model" theory was K. Craik [3]. Johnson-Laird developed the theory in its present form. See [9–12].

14. Putnam, Hilary. 1983. *Realism and Reason*. Cambridge: Cambridge University Press.
15. Quine, Willard Van Orman. 1986. *Philosophy of Logic*. Cambridge, MA: Harvard University Press.
16. Resnik, Michael. 1985. "Logic: Normative or Descriptive? The Ethics of Beliefs or a Branch of Psychology." *Philosophy of Science* 52:221–38.
17. Rips, Lance, 1994. *The Psychology of Proof : Deductive Reasoning in Human Thinking Cambridge*. Cambridge, MA: The MIT Press.
18. Shapiro, Stewart. 1998. "Logical Consequence: Models and Modality." In *The Philosophy of Mathematics Today*, edited by Matthias Schirn. Oxford: Oxford University Press.
19. Shapiro, Stewart. 2005. "Logical Consequence, Proof Theory, and Model Theory." In *The Oxford Handbook of Philosophy of Mathematics and Logic*, edited by Stewart Shapiro, 651–70. Oxford: Oxford University Press.
20. Stenning, Keith, and Michiel van Lambalgen. 2008. *Human Reasoning and Cognitive Science*. Cambridge, MA: MIT Press.

Chapter 8
Logic, Indispensability and Aposteriority

Nenad Miščević

8.1 Introduction

Logic is the heart of rational thinking. But how can and should one justify logical reasoning and logical intuitions? Can it be done at all, and if yes, can it be done purely a priori, or is there an important a posteriori aspect to the justification? The issue has been very much alive in contemporary analytic debate at least since Quine, who embraced the answer fully in favor of the a posteriori alternative and argued for it on the grounds that "logic is handmaiden of all the sciences, including mathematics" [31, p. 98]. The two sides in the debate, the apriorist and the aposteriorist one, are still at loggerheads.[1] In this paper I want to propose and briefly argue for a more moderate and "centrist" answer, combining the two extremes: the full justification cannot be had on purely a priori grounds, since there is an important a posteriori element characterizing it, derived from the unavoidability and indispensability of logic for any kind of cognitive project. This a posteriori justification is best located at the internal but reflective, second level: in spontaneous correct reasoning one is justified at the first level both internally by the obviousness and compelling nature of one's inferential steps and externally by their ultra-reliability, but once the skeptical doubts set in and the philosophical questioning begins, one needs to appeal to the evidence that lies at least partly outside of the narrow circle of purely logical considerations. It is this appeal at the reflective level that introduces logic-external, more holistic considerations, and "infects" the justification (and the reasoner's ultimate entitlement) with an a posteriori component, distantly reminding one of the original Quinean approach.

---

[1] A terminological note: since the considerations to be adduced are only distantly related to the traditional empiricism(s), and since the issue is purely normative epistemic, I will call the two opposing camps "apriorists" and "aposteriorists" (instead of rationalists and empiricists, to avoid terms charged with ambiguities).

N. Miščević (✉)
Department of Philosophy, University of Maribor, Maribor, Slovenia
e-mail: vismiscevic@ceu.hu

Appeals to unavoidability and indispensability have been extremely prominent in the revival of interest for a priori justification in the last decade, most prominently in the work of Paul Boghossian, Crispin Wright and, to a lesser extent, Paul Horwich (see references). The appeals combine in an interesting way ideas from Quine and late(r) Wittgenstein. My strategy in arguing will be to join these apriorist-rationalist (potential) opponents in their appeals and then briefly try to show that the appeals lead outside of the circle of the a priori. The intended conclusion is that unavoidability and indispensability of logic for any kind of cognitive project are important reflective justifiers of logical and inferential propensities, perhaps the most important one, and that they are a posteriori.

Let me now set the stage for the main argument. What does typical simple logical reasoning look like? Consider conjunction elimination. Suppose a person, call her Thinker, receives a piece of information about some particular conjunction, of the form $p \land q$, being true. She quickly passes from this information to the decision to act upon one of the conjuncts, for instance q. Her implicit handling of elimination of conjunction can be brought to light by explicitly asking her a question, e.g. whether is it possible that p and q but not q. The "Of course, not" answer would confirm the impression that she does have a mastery of the rule governing conjunction. Call this knowledge instance-knowledge. It seems that knowledge manifested in such spontaneous inferences is knowledge how. However, when a naïve thinker begins to reflect, the inferential step seems obvious. This story which is to follow is neutral between various explanatory proposals, proof-theoretic, model theoretic, mental-model centered etc.

The typical inference pattern of conjunction, encompassing its introduction and elimination rules is critical for it. Being able to follow the rules, and finding them compelling just is to posses the concept $\land$ (conjuction).[2] Now, the sense, captured by rules, determines reference or semantic value, in this case truth value. Nothing else counts. So, once the Thinker has the concept $\land$, she will find the transition from particular instances of p plus q to "the $p \land q$" unproblematic and compelling. Consider now the semantic values, i.e. truth or falsity of these sentences. The truth-table for $\land$ tells us, in complete harmony with the introduction rule, that the later sentence is true iff the two former ones are. So, there is a simple determination principle, going from the sense of $\land$ to the truth-value (reference) of the composed sentence, as captured by the truth table. Now, being able to follow the rules, and finding them compelling entails believing the truth of the compound sentence if you believe that its constituents are true. This is knowable from the armchair, so to speak.

Not everybody agrees that naïve reasoners use logic; the relevant literature is rife with proposals of heuristics that are meant to replace all or some of logical rules (Gigerenzer et al. [19], also Bishop and Trout [6], and the excellent reader by Adler and Rips [1]). Anti-logicism sees the standard logic is an artificial invention almost unrelated to our natural cognitive system. This entails separate justificatory accounts for logic and for ordinary reasoning strategies. For the view we might

---

[2] The relevant rules are, of course, the familiar ones: $\frac{P, Q}{P \land Q}$ and $\frac{P \land Q}{P}$, $\frac{P \land Q}{Q}$

call minimal logicism the standard logic is part of our cognitive system but not its core. Finally, full logicism (Rips [33]) sees the standard logic is the core of our natural cognitive system. Unfortunately, I have to set this disagreement aside, since arguing for the logic-focused picture is a long and arduous task given the richness of alternative proposals. I shall therefore proceed dogmatically, assuming that some form of elementary logic (rule or model-based, including mental-model based) is being used in naïve reasoning; for a defense of the dogma see for instance (Rips [33]).

Another question naturally arises: which logic do people use, if any? I will not address it here, and assume instead some minimal set of rules, common to various logical systems. A few words about justification. I shall use the term in the most general way to indicate the positive epistemic status of a belief, and the consequent blamelessness of the believer. Traditional internal(ist) justification, together with externalist justification and/or warrant and entitlement should be taken as subspecies of this most general normative kind.[3] I will here formulate our question in terms of justifying as doing, and ask whether it is purely a priori, or is there an important a posteriori aspect to the justification? Alternatively, for those who think of justifiedness as the property of beliefs or inferences independent of one's reflective doings, we may rephrase the question: are justifiedness and/or entitlement just had by the given act of reasoning, are they purely a priori, or is there an important a posteriori aspect to them?

Here is the plan. The next section introduces the issue of apriority, and rehearses the skeptical doubts about immediate justifiers for logical practice and beliefs. The third section is the heart of the paper, and is dedicated to indispensability argument. Its first sub-section looks at naturalistic variant, and the second, most important, to the neo-Wittgensteinian appeal to hinges and "cornerstones". The strategy is endorsed, and then turned against its usual apriorist reading. The final brief

---

[3] The literature abounds with proposals. Boghossian [10], in his paper says he will "use the terms 'justification', 'warrant' and 'entitlement' interchangeably." (p. 236). Peacocke in his "The Realm of Reason" writes: "The notion of entitlement also conforms to the following principles. A transition to which a thinker is entitled is a rational transition. A judgment is knowledge only if it is reached by a transition to which the judger is entitled. A thinker may be entitled to make a judgment without having the capacity to think about the states which entitle him to make the judgment. A child may be entitled to make an observational judgment by his perceptual experience without his having the concept of perceptual states." [10, p. 7]. And he offers a largely reliability account for the case of logic:

PRINCIPLE I: The Special Truth-Conduciveness Thesis
A fundamental and irreducible part of what makes a transition one to which a thinker is entitled is that the transition tends to lead to true judgements (or, in case the transition relies on premisses, tends to do so when its premisses are true) in a distinctive way characteristic of rational transitions. [10, p. 11]

Burge defines entitlement as an epistemic warrant to accept something and adds the crucial waiver: "Entitlements are epistemic rights or warrants that need not be understood nor even accessible to the subject." [15, p. 458] C. Wright follows the suggestion that warrant is that property, whatever it is, that makes the difference between knowledge and mere true belief.

sub-section is a short appendix, in which we apply the result to yet another attempt to justify logic, the one due to Paul Boghossian. The Conclusion suggests that the justification of our logical intuitional beliefs and practices (and perhaps other armchair beliefs in) is plural and structured, with a priori and a posteriori elements combined in a complex way.

8.2 The A Priori and the Beautiful Mind

Let us return to our Thinker, who finds the transition from an instance of $p \wedge q$ to q obvious and compelling. One important epistemological question is the following: is she justified in trusting their otherwise compelling intuitions? Are reasoners in general thus justified? This is the common ground shared among philosophers of various persuasions. My take here is to propose a distinction of levels (in fact, joint various authors who propose such a move, see below): place upon the first level the source of beliefs in question, e.g. intuition. Place upon a second, meta-cognitive level thinker's reflective awareness about the quality of her first-level source, e.g. one's reflective questioning of or trust in one's intuitions. Such a two-level view of justification has been probably implicit in classical epistemology (Plato, Descartes, and Spinoza), and is nowadays proposed by various authors, most prominently E. Sosa [34, 35] but also W. Alston [2, 3] and J. van Cleve (with a lot of difference of detail). It can therefore serve as a suitable common ground between the explanationist and the anti-explanationist (the naturalist-explanationist will do well to present the epistemic rules as goal-based, grounded in the naturalistically acceptable truth-goal). I shall follow the most generous variant (of the kind favored by Sosa): the thinker may on the second level of reflexive questioning use all the available sources in order to assess the reliability (and other virtues) of a given first-order source, in this case of intuition or reason.

Within such a picture one can distinguish degrees of reflective, meta-cognitive achievement on the second, reflective level. The lowest degree is guaranteed by the immediate compellingness of contents, i.e. of intuitional propositions. If the thinker psychologically cannot doubt some such proposition, then she is prima facie allowed to believe it: epistemic ought implies epistemic can. Still, a more conscientious thinker would want to have a coherent meta-cognitive perspective on deliverances of her cognitive abilities, and an explanatory view on functioning of abilities. Again, we may distinguish immediate or folk view (of e.g. perception or intuition ability) from theoretical perspective on these abilities.

Finally, let us distinguish two directions of reflection: 1st person type and 3rd person type. Call the person doing first level logical reasoning Thinker, and the philosopher judging it Epistemologist. In the first direction, the Thinker is reflecting about her own first-level moves, whereas in the second, the Epistemologist is reflecting about Thinker's moves. My own view is that 1st person reflective justifiedness is necessary for being completely justified; the Thinker has to philosophize at least a bit about her own spontaneous practice in order to become fully justified in accepting its results. However, even if you disagree, you might think that completely blind spontaneous thinking is not sufficient for justification. Only most simple reliabilists think it is. Others, for instance, think that some sort of availability of the 3rd person type justification is needed. Peacocke and Boghossian might be among them.

Let us start from the first level. Externally, we may hope that logic is ultra-reliable, and this would yield externalist justification. On the internal side, most thinkers, including ourselves, spontaneously find their intuitions obviously true in very compelling manner, and those among them who reach the reflexive level, consider their intuition-capacity and their reason generally de facto reliable. Nowadays, clarity and distinctness is mostly associated with obviousness in the sense of subjective obviousness, where the notion of obviousness is characterized thus "Proposition p is obvious to agent A at time t if and only if solely in virtue of grasping p at t, p seems to be true to A" (Jeshion [26, p. 955]). Subjective obviousness is a descriptive property. We obtain the corresponding normative concept by demanding that grasping p yield actual justification: "Clear grasp of a self-evident proposition is sufficient and compelling basis for justified recognition of the proposition's truth by a rational agent" (Jeshion [26, p. 956]). More optimistic and more normative account of self-evidence add that understanding a self-evident proposition reveals its truth. "p is self-evident provided an adequate understanding of it is sufficient for being justified in believing it and for knowing it if one believes it on the basis of that understanding" (Audi [4, p. 208]).

The reliability of first-order source, if available, yields an external, 3rd person justifiedness. In contrast, the reflexive or meta-cognitive, second-order trust in one's own reliability, if justified, would make us, the thinkers, reflectively justified on the second level. As reflective creatures aiming at truth, we need both levels of justification.

What kind of justification can we have? Traditionally, logic has been firmly associated with apriority: the kind of justification available for logical practices and intuitions is a priori. So, let me say a few words about the a priori/ a posteriori contrast. Here is Lawrence BonJour, joining and explicating the classical view of it:

> In summation, I propose to count a proposition P as being justified a priori (for a particular person, at a particular time) if and only if that person has a reason for thinking P to be true that does not depend on any positive appeal to experience or other causally mediated, quasi-perceptual contact with contingent features of the world, but only on pure thought or reason, even if the persons ability to understand P in question derives, in whole or in part, from experience. [14, p. 11].

And he continues:

> it is apparent rational insight (and, correlatively, apparent self evidence, that provides the basis for a priori epistemic justification. (p. 113)

> ...a priori justification, if we set aside the rare or non-existent case of direct experiential challenge, is incapable of being undermined or overridden by experience alone. [14, p. 123]

Similar views have been expressed by others, prominently G. Bealer [5]. I think the traditional view is the best option for the apriorist. However, I don't want to beg the question against those more modest recent proposals that see a priori as being compatible with empirical revisability. (D. Summerfield [36] thus stressed the irrelevance of immunity). Let me quote B. Hale's formulation of the same moderate stance:

> we know a priori that p if our true belief that p is justified, and our justification makes no appeal to empirical evidence. Justified belief can be open to revision without thereby forfeiting its claim to amount to knowledge a priori—what is needed to defeat that claim is ... argument that it is revisable in response to empirical evidence. [21, p. 147]

Back to the logical matters. On purely externalist grounds logic is justified since it is ultra-reliable. But let us also allow for a first-level internal justification: obviousness and immediate compellingness does provide some good reason Intuition is prima facie a priori justified, period; why is this not enough? J. Pust [30] has been asking. Well, because many beliefs that are prima facie justified (virtuous) turn out to be unjustified (virtuous) on closer reflection. To return to our initial example, our unsophisticated Thinker is to a large extent justified in trusting the obviousness of her intuition. But sophisticated, reflective justification cries for more: how does she, or how do we, epistemologists know that she is not being eccentric in performing her reasoning step?

Not all obvious and compelling beliefs and procedures are justified. Some people are eccentric. The famous mathematician Nash once explained that he is receiving messages from extraterrestrials which come to him with the same degree of persuasiveness (and he probably meant obviousness and immediate compellingness) as his mathematical theorems. Since this phrase is printed on the cover of the paperback edition of the "Beautiful mind", let me call the problem The Beautiful mind problem. It introduces the need for second level, reflective justification: why do I trust my use of Conjunction elimination, if geniuses like Nash found their logical reasoning as persuasive as messages from extraterrestrials? It is a more moderate problem than the related extreme Cartesian problem of madness which C. Wright uses as part of the motivation for his proposal for the appeal to indispensability, to be discussed in the next part of the paper. In short, if a Nash could fall in for extraterrestrials, obviousness and compellingness are not enough.

In a discussion of an early version of this paper in Dubrovnik Tim Williamson has remarked that taking the Beautiful mind or madness problem concedes too much to the skeptic. Don't even start such a discussion with the skeptic, otherwise you will loose it. Well, discussion with the skeptic has been essential for epistemology. Logical practice and beliefs stand in need of entitlement and justification. And in the particular case, to stay for the moment with Williamson's views, the ultimate result of refusing to discuss with the skeptic demands stressing not only the unassailability of the main body of our beliefs, but also the role reasoning plays in obtaining it. Logic beliefs are not merely one area of one's doxastic structure which can be to a large extent isolated from the rest, like, for instance, religious convictions. But this line is almost a replay of the indispensability argument, which is our main topic here, only it would use indispensability in order to silence the skeptic, not to try to convince him.[4] In short, and with apologies for brevity, there is a need for second level, reflective justification at which obviousness itself is being questioned and discussed. What is left, if ultra-reliability is too external, and obviousness is questioned? This is the topic of our next section.

8.3 Logic as Unavoidable and Indispensable

As we said at the beginning, the remaining and central family of arguments for ultimate justification of our logical practice(s) and intuitions concerns the following facts: simple rules of logic are compelling and unavoidable for humans, they enable the very having of beliefs and constitute the rationality of reasoning. Because of this, they are both unavoidable and indispensable for our thinking, and for any sort of cognitive projects we might engage in. This unavoidability and global indispensability secure the third-person justification (sometimes, as we mentioned, called warrant or entitlement) for the naïve reasoner, and justification for sophisticated, reflective

---

[4] There is an alternative way to save apriority, by redefining it in a more modest manner: neither reflective "purity" nor immunity to empirical refutation are necessary for apriority, the recipe goes. We mentioned the later change, and here we document the attempts to the former. Albert Casullo [16] and G. Rey [32] concentrate on sufficiency of spontaneous level and allow for a posteriori justification on reflective level. To illustrate, Casullo has raised the issue of reflective access: how can we come to be informed about the status of our beliefs? Casullo proposes an a posteriori inquiry at the second level: it is empirical research that will tell us which, if any, of our beliefs are justified a priori. The main line of Casullo's final overall picture has quite a lot in common with the naturalistic picture sketched by G. Rey in his papers on a priori, but arrived at from the opposite direction (e.g. Rey [32]). Rey starts from a naturalist computationalist account of roughly analytic a priori beliefs, and then looks for a way to make the notion of a priori precise. He ends up by denying immunity, immediate second level access, and by insisting on an a posteriori account of the a priori. Rey's account is very sketchy on analysis of a priori, but it nicely supplements Casullo's in matters of cognitive psychological account, on which Casullo is practically silent, in spite of recommending it in principle.

In fact, such minimalistic views like Casullo's finely illustrate the progressive weakening of the idea of pure apriority. First, the immunity from empirical refutation is gone. This adds weight to the a posteriori considerations: if one believes that p on a priori grounds, one's belief is still threatened by potential a posteriori defeaters. The originally a priori glass is getting filled with a posteriori liquid. Step two. You wonder if your belief that two plus three equals five is a priori? Well, consult your cognitive psychologist. Gone is the second level a priori accessibility. This adds another sip of a posteriori liquid into the glass. And here is the last drop, but not the least one: you may not rest content with your candidate a priori belief, say about two plus three, before you have an explanation of your hoped for reliability! And the explanation will be an a posteriori one, since the identification of the belief as a priori is already an a posteriori one. If Casullo is right, not much is left of apriority indeed. The most we can have is justification that has its source in a non-experiential natural cognitive capacity, but that itself stands in need of a lot of a posteriori support and underpinning. This line yields a less then minimal apriority. If a belief is justified (virtuous) partly because it has not been empirically defeated, then it automatically has some a posteriori negative justification. Add the empirical support it can get from reflective explanation and it will have a structured justification with a strong a posteriori component, not very different from the view we are proposing.

thinker. The apriorists add that these two, entitlement and justification, are a priori. I shall argue that they are, on the contrary, a posteriori.

Let me put my cards on the table, in the form of a schema for my strategy. I want to go along with the apriorist in agreeing about the following initial claims:

(0) Logical practice and beliefs stand in need of entitlement and justification.
(1) Simple rules of logic are compelling and unavoidable for humans, therefore
(2) they are both unavoidable and indispensable for our thinking, and for any sort of cognitive projects we might engage in.

However, I would proceed by arguing the following:

(3) The use of unavoidable and indispensable tools can derive its justification from projects whenever the projects are themselves meaningful.

If the argument is successful, as I hope it is, it brings in a posteriori considerations:

(4) Our most general cognitive project has been at least minimally successful, and therefore, it is meaningful and we are justified in believing that it is, and the naïve thinker is entitled to her logical reasoning.
(5) This justification and entitlement are to a large extent a posteriori.
(6) The meaningfulness of our general cognitive project(s), guaranteed by our success up to now, secures the entitlement for the naïve reasoner, and justification for sophisticated, reflective thinker.
(7) Because of (5), these are both a posteriori.
(8) The reflective justification of logical beliefs and the entitlement to naïve logical reasoning have at least one strong a posteriori component. (from (7))

Our proposal is distantly inspired by Quine, but it differs essentially from his view. Quine simply dismisses obviousness, to which many practitioners—mathematicians and logicians—are happy to appeal. Our proposal allows for apriority at immediate, non-reflective level, and is thus not open to charges for implausibility and self-defeating disdain for the actual practice. It is moderately holistic, and this only on the second, reflective level, so it does not import implausible and uncontrollable holism into the first level.

In reality, (1) fuses together some ideas that have been separately stressed and developed by various authors, so we have to address them separately. Some of the authors stress that compellingness of simple rules of logic, and then disagree about its nature. P. Horwich has been stressing a kind of naturalistic inevitability, Boghossian a more transcendental kind. Finally, C. Wright offers a Wittgenstein-inspired account of their indispensability. We shall briefly summarize and comment the first approach, then concentrate upon the Wittgensteinian line; finally we briefly, all to briefly, apply the results from the discussion of it to Boghossian's project. Again, apologies for brevity; I discuss Horwich and Boghossian in more detail elsewhere (Miščević [27, 28]).

Before proceeding further, let me distinguish the issue of a particular episode of the use of logic from the more general issue of justification of logic as such. If a mathematician uses a logical strategy for finding out about a theorem, and we are asked whether she is justified in doing so, on the natural reading of the question the focus is on a particular strategy. If it is logically impeccable, and this is relevant at this juncture, she is thereby justified; we do not need any more general story (thanks go to Nenad Smokrović for pressing the point). The context of the discussion changes if our interlocutor raises a more general question: well, her strategy is logically correct, but why rely on logic at all? Here, a different kind of answer is needed, and the proposals which we will discuss now attempt to come to grips with the task.

8.3.1 Naturalistic Inevitability (P. Horwich)

Paul Horwich has proposed a naturalistic computationalist argument for a priori justification of the use of classical logic in reasoning, that combines in an original way considerations from Quine and post-Tractatus Wittgensein (later he backed from it, and didn't include it in reprint in the book [25]; in a discussion of my objections at a conference in Pecs he told the audience that he has some reservations about his proposal). I find the proposal worthy of discussion, so I proceed with a short reconstruction of it (from Horwich [24, p. 168]). Horwich starts with the contrast between science and ordinary assertoric practices. He renders unto Quine what he thinks belongs to him: the logic, arithmetic, and geometry of science are a posteriori. But the ordinary assertoric practices are less subject to revisability. Take the sentence: "If London is larger than Paris, then Paris is not larger than London". It is unthinkable for us that it does not hold. So, in non-scientific assertoric practices "we will continue to rely on classical logic, on standard arithmetic, and on Euclidean geometry". "They are a priori", he adds. The result: there are two logics, an a priori one and an a posteriori one. Presumably also two epistemically disparate kinds of arithmetic, one a priori and the other a posteriori. Here is his story about the a priori part.

Suppose that each human being is born with, and stuck with, a simple language of thought (i.e. mentalese) containing, amongst other things, certain symbols whose intrinsic nature is such that the principles of classical logic are obeyed. (A scientifically plausible assumption, that can be extended to arithmetic, geometry, and innate concepts in many areas). This commits humans to classical logic as their natural reasoning system underpinning their rationality. This commitment derives neither from experience nor is revisable in light of it. This commitment is inevitable, humans cannot get rid of it. Call this Inevitability Claim. Now, norms are constrained by possibilities: ought implies can, so if one cannot believe p one is not rationally required to believe it (Impossibility implies lack of obligation). Therefore, (under assumption that it is the case that certain beliefs are innate and irremovable) we can understand why they would be amongst those beliefs that we treat as unconditionally rational. Therefore, we have an a priori commitment to classical logic. The final conclusion follows: Therefore, the innate structure of our minds is a potential source of a priori knowledge. Before starting the discussion, let me mention that Horwich accepts the truth-goal as the main epistemic goal: the revisions aim at capturing truth.

Now the discussion. The crucial problem is posed by the Inevitability Claim and the bipartite picture, separating science and commonsense. Innate beliefs seem to be inevitable in a weak sense: we find them natural, we normally don't question them and we find it very difficult to doubt them. Naïve physics and Euclidean geometry are very good examples. But also some reasoning heuristics seem compelling to most people. Unfortunately for the argument, this weak sense is not sufficient. The idea that impossibility implies lack of obligation (converse of the Ought-implies-can principle) and takes "cannot" and "inevitable" in a much stronger sense of "being humanly impossible". However, Euclidean geometry is not any more firmly and literally believed by educated people. A good high-school student can get rid of her innate naïve physics with the help of a good teacher. Scientific revision of ordinary beliefs usually trickles down into commonsense, this is what science classes and "Scientific American" are here for. In short, *if humans can revise their innate beliefs when it comes to science, then they can revise them simpliciter*. If Quine can demand so much of scientist, he can demand something similar from those acquainted with the results of science. The bipartite picture, separating science from all other assertoric practices is false.

Science-driven reflective revisability gives some assurance against blind epistemic luck. It is a matter of such luck that some of our innate beliefs are true and reasoning strategies correct. But we should not rely on luck if we don't have to. And the fact that we indeed can revise our native frames of mind is a great asset: it reduces the power of blind luck. Just consider the problem posed by innate "garbage", the realistic possibility of their being innate material that is cognitively pathological. Some of us believe that racist or religious beliefs can be a case in point, others that some possibly innate reasoning heuristics are one. Again, such a "garbage" might be weakly inevitable, in the sense of requiring a lot of effort even to get rid of in some people for some time, but being ineradicable in general, for most people and forever. The justification bestowed by such circumstances is not what we would like to have as a rational justification for a priori beliefs.

Science-driven reflective revisability therefore has an enormous normative significance. So, if humans can revise their innate beliefs when it comes to science, then they can revise them *simpliciter*, and if they can revise them, they should do so.

All this brings us back to the truth-goal. Since the relevant practices are assertoric, they produce truth-evaluable, true or false items. Truth is an important goal in production of most such items. Therefore, the relevant practices have truth as an important goal, so truth is an important common goal of science and of the relevant assertoric practices. Now, if a "theory" that has been innate is revised in and by science in search of truth, it is reasonable to inform other practices about this rejection. Further, it seems that innate beliefs are de facto revisable. And it is hard to live with double epistemic standards. So, if humans can revise their innate beliefs when it comes to science, then the revision should influence all the assertoric practices in which they play a role. Then, the beliefs would stop being a priori. The same would be reasonable in the case of logic, should the need arise. In short, *if*

8 Logic, Indispensability and Aposteriority 145

humans can revise their innate beliefs when it comes to science, then they can revise them simpliciter, so they ought to do so.

Suppose that we have accepted the conclusion: innate beliefs are difficult to revise, but can be revised if the need arises. Second, science is much more into the kind of business that can lead to revision, ordinary assertoric practices are not. So, there is a duality, but much weaker than needed for Horwich's strategy. We also retain Horwich's partly internalist idea of justification with which we have been implicitly working until now. What are the alternatives for accounting for candidate a priori beliefs? We might then assume that two sorts of justification are better than two mutually isolated (kinds of) belief systems. So our candidate a priori beliefs could enjoy prima facie spontaneous justification from their obviousness and immediate compellingness, i.e. from "can't do otherwise" considerations, featuring the weak and ordinary meaning of "can't". In this sense, I can't imagine logic and arithmetic to go wrong. Similarly with ordinary analytic claims: I can't imagine that spinsters are married (though I can think of two "classical" spinsters united in a marriage, namely a homosexual one). I can't conceive of state of affairs where London is larger than Paris, and Paris is also larger than London (Unless "larger" means "has more inhabitants" in the antecedent, and "has a bigger area" in the consequent of our sentence). I believe that if John persuaded Mary to go, then Mary intended to go. (Unless Marry only thought she formed an intention, but self-deceived herself. Some people would still say John was successful in persuasion, only Mary spoilt things by self-deception.) But my inability to conceive otherwise is still hostage to what one day we can discover. So, my relevant beliefs are weakly a priori, not immune to empirical revision. Where does the threat of aposteriority come in? Maybe in a second order, reflective coherentist justification which has an a posteriori component, namely that science has until now lived happily with classical logic and arithmetic, and that there is no known counterinstance of the non-symmetry of "larger than" and so on. I would be quite happy with such an alternative, and I think it would preserve much that is valuable in Horwich's original proposal. I now proceed to argue for it in a dialogue with the Wittgensteinian tradition, bringing in the global indispensability of logic.

8.3.2 The Global Indispensability Argument (The Wittgensteinian Tradition)

Let me now, for our next step, borrow one central element from the Wittgensteinian tradition, namely the idea of hinges or cornerstones. I will take it in the form developed in one of Crispin Wright's answers to the problem of warrant (as he puts it) of logical practices and beliefs, with apology for using it against aprioristic intentions of Wittgenstein and his followers.[5] It is the idea of the unearned warrant;

---

[5] In fact, we can distinguish two components in Wrigth's discussion. First, in his earlier work he brilliantly shows that the Madmen (and for that matter also Dreamers) Argument in a way destroys

logic is presupposed in every cognitive activity. Wright revives the Wittgensteinian conception of hinges and enriches it with his own idea of "cornerstones":

> Call a proposition a cornerstone for a given region of thought just in case it would follow from a lack of warrant for it that one could not rationally claim warrant for *any* belief in the region. The best—most challenging, most interesting—sceptical paradoxes work in two steps: by (i) making a case that a certain proposition (or restricted type of proposition) that we characteristically accept is indeed such a cornerstone for a much wider class of beliefs, and then (ii) arguing that we have no warrant for it. [39, pp. 167–68]

If a cognitive project is "rationally non-optional", i.e. indispensable in rational enquiry and in deliberation, then we may rationally take for granted the original presuppositions of such a project without specific evidence in their favor. The absence of defeating information is sufficient. So, Wright proposes to combine two warrant providers: the first is a rule-circular justification, reminiscent of justification from constitutiveness, that answers the first order question: how might the knowledge of the validity of basic logical laws be arrived at? The second-order problem about such knowledge is "that of explaining with what right we claim it?" [39, p. 174]. This "second-order problem has a chance of being addressed by invoking the notion of entitlement of cognitive project" (Ibid.).

Wright claims that our acceptance of hinges and cornerstones is warranted by cognitive projects they enable. But this seems to take us from Wittgenstein to Quine and Putnam. If one's early encounter with philosophy of logic was through Quine's "Philosophy of Logic," one would probably be reminded of the famous passages on universal use of logic. For Wright the acceptance of logic is warranted by its being indispensable to each and every cognitive project, each and every "region of thought." Quine, for his part, famously speaks of "lack of special subject matter: logic favors no distinctive portion of the lexicon, and neither does it favor one subdomain of values of variables over another." And then passes to "the ubiquity of the use of logic. It is a handmaiden of all the sciences, including mathematics ... We might say at the risk of marring the figure that it is their promiscuity, in this regard,

---

or "implodes" itself. For the Madman's (our Beautiful Mind person's) thinking he uses the word "maundering". If the reasoner in the scenario is "maundering", she cannot be correctly inferring from her maunderings. So, the skeptical argument does not show that the thinker has no warrant.

> If, as I earlier suggested, an effective argument from Dreaming, or from Brain-in-a-Vathood, etc., cannot proceed without all these elements—if our analysis does indeed capture the essential implicit detail of this kind of sceptical train of thought—then we may indeed draw a large but negative conclusion: that there is actually no method of sceptically undermining our right to rely on any of our cognitive faculties using a fantasy, whatever its exact nature, of first-personally undetectable impairment. [37, p. 116]

> We thereby conclude that ... it is not true that x has no warrant at t to believe that she is not then dreaming, and hence that the impossibility of earning a warrant to believe that one is not now dreaming—if that is what ... argument showed—does not imply that no such warrant is ever possessed. (pp. 107–8)

However, and this is the crucial point, the Argument does suggest that the warrant cannot be earned by any kind of reasoning. The solution is to accept the possibility of an unearned warrant.

that goes far to distinguish logic and mathematics from other sciences. Because of these last two traits of logic and mathematics—their relevance to all science and their partiality toward none—it is customary to draw an emphatic boundary separating them from the natural sciences" [31, p. 98]. I recommend to take Quine's quote with a Putnamian grain of salt, as supporting a realist reading. Then, we seem to be back to indispensability argument: logic and mathematics are to be accepted because they are indispensable to our widest cognitive projects in virtue of their admirable "versatile ancillarity." The general background suggested by ancillarity and indispensability seems to be a means-end framework: logic and its acceptance are warranted as means for an end, not as valid in themselves, in stark contrast to the usual apriorist claims about autonomy.

Now, Cartesian skepticism "challenges knowledge of any external domain, whether abstract or spatiotemporal," as Novak and Simony friendly suggested to me. Indeed, in the debate with the absolute skeptic no-one has a good chance, as Williamson has been pointing out in his remark discussed above. But the present point is different: if, instead of wanting to refute the skeptic in his own terms, you are involved in a "modest anti-skeptical project that just aims to set our own minds at ease," then the question of the comparative value of various indispensability considerations becomes interesting. And here the Quine-Putnamian ones seem to be in better shape than Wittgensteinian ones, simple because of being less restrictive.

However, this is only the beginning. There is an important contrast: in Wittgenstein-inspired views the justification is fully antecedent to the project, and this seems to guarantee apriority to logic. Along the same lines, Tom Stoneham has objected at the presentation of an early version of this paper in the conference in Dubrovnik that in the project under considerations it is the generality of logic that saves it from the need of empirical confirmation.

But does it really do it? Let us approach the answer in a series of steps. First, is indispensability for any kind of large cognitive project by itself warrant-bestowing? To see that it is not, consider the following piece of reasoning. Belief in extraterrestrials is needed in order to embark upon a mega-project of re-interpreting a huge mass of recorded emission from outer space as their messages. Therefore, if one has the project, one is warranted to believe in extraterrestrials. If you don't find the reasoning convincing, this suggests that the acceptance of hinges and cornerstones is justified by the meaningfulness of cognitive projects they enable, and is sensitive to it. The acceptance of logic is warranted by its being indispensable to each and every cognitive project, and is thus sensitive at least to the meaningfulness of major cognitive projects, and to the totality, say, "total inquiry" into what the world is like. Now, clearly impossible, stupid and bad goals do not justify the use of means. "If we want to square the circle, we need theorem Θ; therefore Θ." is not a piece of good reasoning. Of course, the epistemic situation has parallels elsewhere, for example in prudential considerations and in ethics. Impossible whole-life projects do not justify dramatic decisions that would further them if they were possible. Morally bad projects don't contribute to justification. A means (an electric device, a supply of chemicals) can be indispensable for a very bad project (torturing, massive killing by poisoning), but his would not make the procurement of it permissible; the end has to be independently acceptable for the means even to come into consideration.

To return to epistemic issues, consider the following scenario and its consequences, that could be called "Mr. Magoo argument." Mr. Magoo has a very defective cognitive apparatus. His inductive propensities are idiotic, to use politically incorrect vocabulary, his senses most often deceive him, and his "heuristics" are ridiculous. (He lives in a super-hospitable environment, but hardly manages to survive). His idiotic inductive propensities and ridiculous "heuristics," plus his misplaced uncritical trust in his senses are indispensable for his ever forming any belief. Therefore, he is warranted in taking them as unquestioned and unquestionable starting points. If you don't find the reasoning convincing, this suggests that the acceptance of hinges and cornerstones is justified by the quality of cognitive projects they enable, and is sensitive to the chances of their success. But these chances are revealed by trying. Therefore, our best access to our own warrant involves information about the chances success of the relevant cognitive project. Of course, what counts as success should be made clear (thanks go to David Davies, who in discussion in Rijeka reminded me of this); otherwise the considerations would seem to make the final justification just pragmatic. (Wright has already been accused of smuggling in pragmatic considerations.)[6] In contrast to all this, by "success" we mean purely epistemic success, not merely and not at all the pragmatic one. It doesn't matter how the epistemic success is spelled out in detail, for instance in terms of reaching important truths, that enable explanation and understanding, and of avoiding error; other versions will do as well. It is the rational possibility of purely epistemic success that is a reasonable or perhaps even a necessary condition for the means for it being warranted.

I am saying "a reasonable or perhaps even a necessary condition," because I want to point out two lines of argument for my claims stated above:

(3) The use of unavoidable and indispensable tools can derive its justification from projects whenever the projects are themselves meaningful.

If the argument is successful, as I hope it is, it brings in a posteriori considerations:

(4) Our most general cognitive project has been at least minimally successful, and therefore, it is meaningful and we are justified in believing that it is, and the naïve thinker is entitled to her logical reasoning.

One line is a more radical one, claiming that a project is meaningful only if it has a reasonable chance for success, the other is less radical, but acceptable to a wider audience: if a project is successful, then it is meaningful; our most general cognitive project is to an impressive extent successful, so it is meaningful.

Let me first remind you that even the more radical line is quite plausible. I will introduce two actual opponents, both of them my friends and colleagues, in the discussion. First, David Davies once pointed to the possibility that a project

---

[6] For instance, by Duncan Prichard in section 3 of chapter 9 of his [29].

8 Logic, Indispensability and Aposteriority 149

can be meaningful without having a chance of success. This can be taken in two ways, objective and subjective. Indeed, some epistemic project might be objectively doomed to failure, but this does not make one's trying irrational, as long as one has some ground to be optimistic. But it the project is due to failure in one's best judgment, one is not warranted in trying to implement it. The two interact in a complicated way, but we need not worry about this here.

What about daring projects? Majda Trobok has in the discussion pointed to a fine and amusing example from Apostolos Doxiadis's novel "Uncle Petros and Goldbach's Conjecture." So, let us enjoy a bit this witty fiction. In the story, uncle Petros is courageously trying to prove Goldbach's conjecture, but the father of the main character warns his son that one should not aim for what is not attainable: "The Secret of Life is always to set yourself attainable goals. They may be easy or difficult, depending on the circumstances and your character and abilities, but they should always be at-tai-na-ble! In fact, I think I'll hang your Uncle Petros' portrait in your room, with a caption: EXAMPLE TO BE AVOIDED!" (Doxiadis [17, 18], p. 21). And of course, the warning seems opportunistic and narrow minded. Although this consideration is in itself quite important, it does not threaten our line of thought; it concerns criteria of what is reasonably to be expected, and encourages taking a more risky attitude. Our line does not forbid this; as long as there is a reasonable chance, one may be justified in procuring oneself the means needed. Things get more difficult with the next relevant episode in the book, as Trobok has pointed out to me. The friend of the hero, Sammy, has discouraging news:

> So, you think it's impossible that Goldbach's Conjecture is unprovable?
> 'Man, what does "impossible" mean in this context?' Sammy sneered. 'As your uncle correctly told you, there is, thanks to Turing, no way of telling with certainty that a statement is a priori unprovable ...' (p. 157)

Of course, the challenge rests on the possibility of actual, objective unprovability. Mere knowledge that "no way of telling with certainty that a statement is a priori unprovable" does not make the attempt to prove it or disprove it irrational. And Sammy takes exactly this line:

> But if mathematicians involved in advanced research started invoking Gödel, no one would ever go near the interesting problems ... 'Why, it's like not going out in the street for fear that a brick might fall on your head and kill you!' (pp. 157–58)

No terrible threat after all. One might disagree with Sammy, but I hope to have made plausible the useful radical claim that meaningfulness is not independent of chances of success.

Now, what about an epistemic romantic, who disagrees with Sammy and claims that odds against the mathematician are in this case much greater than the odds of a brick falling on one's head, and that the mathematician is still reasonable in his endeavor? That meaningfulness is independent of chances of success?

Well, the radical claim of non-independence is not strictly necessary for our argument. If you are an epistemic romantic, like Uncle Petros is depicted to be, you might still agree with the following two claims: first, that our general cognitive project has de facto been quite successful, and second, that this success is a reasonable device for justifying the means used for implementing the project. In other words, why take heroic line and claim that the project is only a "romantically" meaningful one, if one has enough evidence that it is successful-meaningful? On this second line, the success is a handy and welcome device for justifying our epistemic project, and logic as it means; in line with the claim (3) to the effect that "the use of unavoidable and indispensable tools can derive its justification from projects whenever the projects are themselves meaningful."

Let me then conclude the discussion of meaningfulness-success link. On the one hand, the more radical claim that a project is meaningful only if it has a reasonable chance for success seems plausible to many. On the other hand, even if does not hold, a weaker claim does: if a project is successful, the success can be used for justifying it. In the case of our general cognitive project, the romantic alternative of success-independent justification is too problematic to overweight the availability of the impressive success-linked alternative: it is eminently reasonable for the epistemologist to justify our general cognitive project by its very probable up-to date success.

We can now pass to a slightly more specific issue. It is not clear that success-meaningfulness is completely independent of empirical considerations. Think of projects that would have sounded meaningful to an educated and intelligent Greek, or an Indian from the time of Mahabharata, and that do not sound meaningful to us any more. This brings us back to the main issue of the epistemic point of our cognitive project and the role of logic in it. The warrant for logic is sensitive at least to the chances of success of our "total inquiry," and our awareness of it depends on the information about the success. Now, success of our total inquiry is to a large extent an empirical matter. Therefore, our awareness of it depends in the large measure empirical information. Such information is a posteriori, which to the rationalist looks like a threat. How serious is it? On the aposteriorist line, some assumptions may be pragmatically antecedent to a cognitive project, but they are, firstly, justified by the success of the project, and secondly, revisable in the light of some advanced stage of the project. So, is the epistemic status of logic a priori, and can logic be revised on a posteriori grounds? First question first. We have seen that there is a touch of aposteriority present in the considerations of meaningfulness, and much more in our coming to know about our warrant. Now, officially, Wright can be unconcerned about it. It is the having of the warrant that is a priori, not knowing about it. But things are not that clear. First, this view seems to come very close to the aposteriorist view just mentioned: both theorists, our apriorist and our aposteriorist, accept a kind of warrant antecedent to the project, only give different names to the antecedence: the first takes it as bestowing serious apriority, the second, as bestowing only a kind of "vanilla" apriority, to use Harman's ironical idiom ("The Future of the A priori," title of section 1). Further, there is a problem about full reflective justification that goes beyond entitlement-warrant. How does the cognizer arrive at justified beliefs about herself being warranted? Well, partly by relying on relative success of her total project. And this reflective justification might therefore be seriously a posteriori, in a way that precludes purely a priori justification of logic.

8 Logic, Indispensability and Aposteriority

What about a scenario that is a converse of the Mr. Magoo one, call it Egghead scenario? In it, our hero, Egghead, with his impeccable logic, is extremely successful in abstract reasoning but hopeless in the real world down-to-earth issues. Well, cognitive success in abstract reasoning might be enough; remember we are not pragmatist here, but interested in truth and avoidance of error.

One might accuse us of circularity. After all, we need logic in order to judge the cognitive success of our total inquiry. And a skeptic might go even further, and question our ability to do the judging. This last point is the least worrisome: normally, in discussing armchair matters, we assume that its empirical counterpart is relatively reliable. The circularity issue is a bit worse, but the standard reply here is the only one available: the circle is big enough, huge in fact. We work with the widest possible reflective equilibrium, in which we consider, of course using logic, the harmony between logic and the rest of our belief or, hopefully, knowledge system. If this is not allowed, nothing is.

But is such full reflective justification really needed? Notice that Wright is in no position to deny the need for it, so we have at least an *ad hominem argument*, if not also an appeal to authority. Here is his suggestion about the role of intellectual integrity and good conscience, which point precisely in the direction of reflective thought:

> Descartes' project in the *Meditations* was one of harmonisation of his beliefs with the requirements of rational conscience and its timeless appeal is testimony to the deep entrenchment of virtues of intellectual integrity in our cognitive lives. The *right to claim knowledge*, as challenged by scepticism, is something to be understood in terms of—and to be settled by—canons of intellectual integrity. The paradoxes of scepticism are paradoxes for the attempt at a systematic respect of those canons. They cannot be addressed by a position which allows that in the end thoroughgoing intellectual integrity is unobtainable, that all we can hope for is fortunate cognitive situation. When good conscience fails, there are still, indeed, other good-circumstantial-qualities which our beliefs may have. But what is wanted is good conscience for the claim that this possibility is realised on the grand scale we customarily assume. [39, p. 211]

So, for Wright, the right to claim knowledge is inseparable from having good conscience for the claim that there is a realized possibility of knowledge on the grand scale (compare also Wright [38, p. 70]). And this claim is clearly reflective. Now, if reflection on warrant involves important a posteriori elements, having to do with success of our cognitive project, than our full reflective justification is a posteriori.

Can one avoid aposteriority by making less demands on the logical reasoner? We have distinguished two directions of reflection: 1st person type and 3rd person type. Calling the person doing first level logical reasoning Thinker, and the philosopher judging it Epistemologist. I have proceeded here assuming that 1st person reflective justifiedness is necessary for Thinker being completely justified. However, this is not essential. Even if you go with extreme externalist, and allow the Thinker justification-warrant from ultra-reliability, you would want to have some assurance as Epistemologist that logic is justified, and for this assurance you would, in the present context, appeal to indispensability. The formulation would then be: the Thinker is externalistically justified a priori, but the assurance that this is so comes from global indispensability and is a posteriori. The whole story would still be to a large extent a posteriori. We thus conclude with our

(8) The reflective justification of logical beliefs and the entitlement to naïve logical reasoning have at least one strong a posteriori component.

The remaining question is one of a posteriori revisability, but we have to be brief. How much is written into the warrant? Does it preclude revision? Consider the analogy with the beliefs into the Material world. Here is what we are antecedently entitled to in the case of beliefs about material world, according to Wright: There is a material world, broadly in keeping with the way in which sense-experience represents it [39, p. 187]. Now, this material-world hinge, as we might call it, is very vague. And it imposes very, very weak constraints. For instance, our sense-experience represents the material world as being to a large extent composed of solid, dense matter. But, if we discovered that the ultimate stuff were just "atoms and void," this would not unhinge our sense-experience; nor would a still more dramatic revision, namely the discovery that it is fields of forces, very much unlike ordinary matter, that ultimately make up "material world." In other words, the material-world hinge is minimal, it offers a broad umbrella statement, qualified with the clause "broadly in keeping," that allows for dramatic revisions in interpretation. Exactly what one would expect from an antecedent assumption, open to all sorts of modifications.

Is there any reason built into the nature of entitlement why the logic-hinge should be any different? If its only *raison d'être* is indispensability for the cognitive project, then it is in the same boat with the material-world hinge. If not even less secure. Logic is needed for every "region of thought," so it should be adaptable to each one of them as well. Is there any reason to think at this stage that our initial logic, the one we find natural and obvious, is so universally applicable without a least revision? Of course not. Antecedently to experience, there is no reason to think that the initial logic, and our initial inability to imagine counterexamples to it, will be that successful. Our final rational confidence in logic might derive partly from the fact that it has never let us down, and this would be in keeping with its ancillary role, stressed by both Wright and Quine.[7] The success of our "total inquiry" is thus to a large extent an empirical matter. Therefore, our awareness of it depends in the large measure on empirical information. Such information is a posteriori. On the aposteriorist line, some assumptions may be pragmatically antecedent to a cognitive project, but they are, firstly, justified by the success of the project, and secondly, revisable in the light of some advanced stage of the project.

---

[7] I am leaving aside a related line that denies the need for justification or warrant, since it has not been prominent in accounting for apriority.

8.3.3 Appendix: The Constitutiveness Argument—A Brief Remark

Let me now briefly apply our conclusion to another prominent attempt to justify logic; we shall not go into details, but just reiterate the main morals of the story told so far. Boghossian's attempt and his line of defense, which we may call The Constitutiveness Argument is that logic can be justified in a rule-circular manner, due to its indispensability for thinking almost any contents whatsoever. Without dispositions to reason in accordance with logic we could not even have the general belief whose justification is supposed to be in question, i.e. the belief about inferential potentials of a given logical constant. The crucial point for him is that the mere fact that the thinker grasps S's meaning entails that the thinker is justified in holding S to be true. (The epistemological consequences of the proposal are developed in "How are objective epistemic reasons possible?" reprinted as a chapter in Boghossian's [11].) Take conditionals. If I don't follow *Modus Ponendo Ponens*, I can't have if-thought at all. So, if I do follow it, with "p" and "if p, then q" as my premises, I cannot be blamed, so, I am entitled to follow it.

> If inferring from those premises to that conclusion is required, if I am to have the ingredient propositions, then, as a matter of metaphysical necessity, I cannot so much as consider the question whether the inference is justified without being disposed to reason in that way. Under those circumstances, then, it looks as though inferring according to MPP cannot be held against me, even if the inference is, as I shall put it, blind—unsupported by any positive warrant. (Boghossian [12, p. 230])

The chapter concludes by stressing that according to the "Constitutive model" the most fundamental relation between grasp of meaning and entitlement occurs when a thinker is entitled to reason in accord with a certain rule simply by virtue of the fact that this rule is constitutive of a concept of his. The author expresses his hope that the model can be extended from reasoning to beliefs, if they are similarly constitutive of the possession of a concept (which has to be non-defective, and we shall come to this in a moment). He proposes that this will solve the issue, famously raised by Aristotle (in *Metaphysics* Γ), about our entitlement to accept the principle of non-contradiction. Argument. Here is his argument in a nutshell:

1. Certain of our inferential dispositions fix what we mean by our logical words (in the language of thought), therefore
2. without those dispositions there is nothing about whose justification we can intelligibly raise a question about.
3. Moreover, without those dispositions we could not even have the general belief whose justification is supposed to be in question. Therefore
4. We are entitled to act on those inferential dispositions prior to, and independently of, having supplied an explicit justification for the general claim that they are truth-preserving. (Boghossian [8, p. 250])

Boghossian has been developing the first line, on meaning-constitutiveness as a priori justifier, combined in his "Knowledge of Logic," with occasional remarks on compellingness, i.e. on the alleged fact that "it is not open to us to regard our fundamental logical beliefs as unjustifiable" (in Boghossian and Peacocke

[13, p. 253]). For instance, in the same paper Boghossian argues for the warrantedness of logical rules mainly from negative compulsion, i.e. from deeply felt unacceptability and inconceivability. He does not offer any causal or psychological explanation of compulsion, which is, after all, a felt item. Here is the relevant quote:

> ...we cannot accept the claim that we have no warrant whatsoever for the core logical principles. We cannot conceive what such a warrant could consist in ...if not in some sort of inference using those very core logical principles', and further: It is not open to us to regard our fundamental logical beliefs as unjustifiable. [13, p. 253])

I agree that the argument is persuasive: no general beliefs unless we use logic, so, nothing much to justify. And we need general beliefs, need reasoning and cannot do without it if we want to come to know about the world. Logic is unavoidable, and also indispensable for our most general project of coming to know. However, this line again raises the same issue: the use of unavoidable and indispensable tools can derive its justification from projects whenever the projects are themselves meaningful.

However, we are justified to think that our most general cognitive project is meaningful, and justified partly of the basis of its up to date success; and this basis is a posteriori. Therefore, the whole reflective justification from compellingness and unavoidability is a posteriori, whereas the more immediate one is a priori. This suggests that the justification of our intuitional armchair beliefs and practices in general is plural and structured, with a priori and a posteriori elements combined in a complex way. It seems thus that a priori/ a posteriori distinction is useful and to the point. What is needed is refinement and respect for structure, not rejection of the distinction. This brings us to our conclusion.

8.4 Conclusion: The Structured Justification

In this paper I have joined philosophers who claim that unavoidability and indispensability of logic are its important justifiers, but have diverged from the recent mainstream, which finds the justification or warrant from unavoidability and indispensability to be a priori. I have argued briefly (all too briefly) for the first, shared claim, and in more details for the presently unorthodox claim for aposteriority.

To summarize the main line once more, I started from the idea that logical practice and beliefs stand in need of entitlement and justification. For various reasons internal obviousness and external ultra-reliability are not sufficient for full reflective justification. Fortunately, simple rules of logic are compelling and unavoidable for humans, therefore they are both unavoidable and indispensable for our thinking, and for any sort of cognitive projects we might engage in. However, the use of unavoidable and indispensable tools also has to be further justified, otherwise the use of such tools for meaningless or abominable projects would be automatically justified. Since our general cognitive project of coming to know about the world is in itself quite valuable, and has been at least minimally successful, it is in the clear and meaningful and we are justified in believing that it is. So, the naïve thinker is entitled to her logical reasoning, and the more sophisticated one can come to know reflectively that she is justified. This justification and entitlement are to a large extent a posteriori. The meaningfulness of our general cognitive project(s), guaranteed by our success up to now, secures the entitlement for the naïve reasoner, and justification for sophisticated, reflective thinker. Because of the importance of empirical element, these are both a posteriori. Therefore, the reflective justification of logical beliefs and the entitlement to naïve logical reasoning have at least one strong a posteriori component.

I have spent less time arguing for the initial moves and for the need of justification for unavoidability and indispensability, assuming that it is widely recognized in the literature. None of the arguments is final, as no philosophical argument is. But all of them converge on unavoidability and indispensability. If you are more of a naturalist, Horwich's computationalist argument might seem more attractive, if anti-naturalist, then the Consitutivity Argument might appeal to you. And if you find Wittgenstein most congenial, on some of many readings of his text, then the Global Indispensability Argument will probably convince you. So, there are good reasons to accept the line. If you disagree, then I hope at least to have established the conditional thesis: *if logic is justified by being unavoidable and indispensable than it is to a large extent justified a posteriori*. If you agree with the antecedent, as I hope you do, you can detach the conclusion: the final, reflective justification of logic is to a large extent a posteriori.

This would then lead to a picture of structured justification and structured aposteriority. Warrant is just a complex and multi-dimensional affair, says A. Goldman [20, p. 48], and then proceeds to criticize the a priori/ a posteriori contrast. It is a bad idea, I think: we need to distinguish and recognize structure. For instance, our Thinker's immediate justification is certainly a priori. But the reflective is not since there is more than a touch of aposteriority present in the considerations of meaningfulness, and much more in our coming to know about our warrant.

How should we then characterize the structured whole? Is justification of ordinary logical reasoning more a priori or more a posteriori? At least since Kant many philosophers thought of the a priori in a rather purist manner: a drop of aposteriority infects any available a priori justification. We may call the idea "The Traditional Principle": If justification (or entitlement) contains a posteriori elements, then it is ultimately a posteriori (e.g. if it is mixed and contains one a posteriori element, it is ultimately a posteriori).

If you accept the Traditional Principle, you might talk about structured aposteriority. If not, just about structured justification and entitlement with a priori elements at the first level, and a powerful a posteriori component on the second, reflective level. I leave the choice open, since it seems more verbal than substantial. Finally, a suggestion: given that logic is a central and paradigmatic candidate a priori field, the idea of structured justification can be generalized from it to the whole of armchair knowledge. But this is the task for future.

Acknowledgments Earlier versions of the paper have been presented at conferences in Rijeka, in May 2009 and in Dubrovnik in August the same year. Thanks go to Majda Trobok, Nenad Smokrović, Zsolt Novak, Andras Simony, Tom Stoneham, Tim Williamson, David Davies and Miša Arsenijević. The paper develops ideas sketched in Miščević [28], and there is a bit of overlap.

References

1. Adler, Jonathan Eric, and Lance J. Rips, eds. 2008. *Reasoning: Studies of Human Inference and Its Foundations.* Cambridge: Cambridge University Press.
2. Alston, William Payne. 1993. *The Reliability of Sense Perception.* Ithaca, NY: Cornell University Press.
3. Alston, William Payne. 1996. *Epistemic Justification: Essays in the Theory of Knowledge.* Ithaca, NY: Cornell University Press.
4. Audi, Robert. 1999. "Self-Evidence." *Noûs* 33:205–28.
5. Bealer, George. 1999. "A Theory of the A Priori." *Noûs* 33:29–55.
6. Bishop, Michael A., and J.D. Trout. 2005. *Epistemology and the Psychology of Human Judgment.* Oxford: Oxford University Press.
7. Boghossian, Paul. 1996. "Analyticity." In *A Companion to the Philosophy of Language,* edited by Robert Hale and Crispin Wright. Oxford: Blackwell, pp. 331–369.
8. Boghossian, Paul. 2000. "Knowledge of Logic." In [13].
9. Boghossian, Paul. 2001. "How Are Objective Epistemic Reasons Possible?." *Philosophical Studies* 106:1–40; reprinted in [11].
10. Boghossian, Paul. 2003. "Blind Reasoning." *Proceedings of the Aristotelian Society Supplementary Volume* 77:225–48.
11. Boghossian, Paul. 2008. *Content and Justification.* Oxford: Oxford University Press.
12. Boghossian, Paul. 2008. "Epistemic Analyticity: A Defense". In [11].
13. Boghossian, Paul, and Christopher Peacocke, eds. 2000. *New Essays on the A priori.* Oxford: Clarendon Press.
14. BonJour, Laurence. 1998. *In Defense of Pure Reason.* Cambridge: Cambridge University Press.
15. Burge, Tyler. 1993. "Content Preservation." *Philosophical Review* 102:457–88.
16. Casullo, Albert. 2003. *A Priori Justification.* Oxford: Oxford University Press.
17. Doxiadis, Apostolos. 1992. *Uncle Petros and Goldbach's Conjecture.* New York, NY: Bloomsbury.
18. Doxiadis, Apostolos. 2002. *Uncle Petros and Goldbach's Conjecture.* New York, NY: Bloomsbury.
19. Gigerenzer, Gerd, and Peter Todd, and the ABC Research Group. 1999. *Simple Heuristics That Make Us Smart.* Oxford: Oxford University Press.
20. Goldman, Alvin. 1999. "A Priori Warrant and Naturalistic Epistemology." *Noûs* 33:1–28.
21. Hale, Bob. 1988. *Abstract Objects.* Oxford: Blackwell.
22. Hale, Bob, and Crispin Wright. 2000. "Implicit Definition and the A priori." In [13].
23. Harman, Gilbert. February 15, 2003. "The Future of the A priori." Available at http://www.princeton.edu/~harman/Papers/FutureAP.html, Gilbert Harman Princeton University. Last accessed October 2, 2011.
24. Horwich, Paul. 2000. "Stipulation, Meaning, and Apriority." In [13].
25. Horwich, Paul. 2005. *Reflections on Meaning.* Oxford: Clarendon Press.
26. Jeshion, Robin. 2001. "Frege's Notion of Self-Evidence." *Mind* 110:955.
27. Miščević, Nenad. 2009. "Can We Save A Priori Knowledge?." *Balkan Journal of Philosophy* 2:103–16.
28. Miščević, Nenad. 2011. "Conceptualism and Knowledge of Logic, A Budget of Problems." In *Truth, Reference and Realism,* edited by Zsolt Novak and Andras Simony, pp. 77–124. Budapest and New York, NY: CEU Press.

29. Pritchard, Duncan. 2005. *Epistemic Luck*. Oxford: Oxford University Press.
30. Pust, Joel. 2000. *Intuitions as Evidence*. New York, NY: Garland.
31. Quine, Willard Van Orman. 1970. *Philosophy of Logic*. Cambridge, MA: Harvard University Press.
32. Rey, Georges. 1998. "A Naturalistic A Priori." *Philosophical Studies* 92:25–43.
33. Rips, L.J. 1994. *The Psychology of Proof: Deduction in Human Thinking*. Cambridge, MA: MIT Press.
34. Sosa, Ernest. 2007. *A Virtue Epistemology: Apt Belief and Reflective Knowledge Vol. 1*. Oxford: Oxford University Press.
35. Sosa, Ernest. 2009. *Reflective Knowledge: Apt Belief and Reflective Knowledge Vol. 2*. Oxford: Oxford University Press.
36. Summerfield, Donna. 1991. "Modest A Priori Knowledge." *Philosophy and Phenomenological Research* 51:39–66.
37. Wright, Crispin. 1991. "Skepticism and Dreaming: Imploding the Demon." *Mind* 100:87–116.
38. Wright, Crispin. 2001. "On Basic Logical Knowledge." *Philosophical Studies* 106:41–85.
39. Wright, Crispin. 2004. "Warrant for Nothing (And Foundations for Free)?." *Aristotelian Society Supplementary Volume* 78:167–212.

Part III
Dynamic Logical Models of Meaning

Chapter 9
Extended Game-Theoretical Semantics

Manuel Rebuschi

9.1 Introduction

Game-theoretical semantics (hereafter, GTS) was created by Hintikka during the 1960s and intended as a formalization of Wittgenstein's remarks on language games. Like other formal connections drawn between logic and game theory, it embodies several philosophically relevant features into semantics: the dynamics of language, language as an activity, language as a collective matter. A specific insight is offered by GTS through the notion of *strategic meaning*. I will propose to use this notion in order to account for linguistic interpretation, to be contrasted with meaning constitution. It will yield solutions to several issues every theory of linguistic meaning is confronted with, especially those involving an epistemic dimension.

My proposal will be based on two moves: (1) the extension of semantic games to the subatomic components of sentences, and (2) a shift in our usual criteria of individuation of functions. The resulting conception of meaning is a two-component theory, but it does not use entities such as Frege's senses or Montague's functions defined on possible worlds. The main idea can be summed up as follows: in addition to the truth-conditions of a sentence, which are given by the existence of a winning strategy for the initial verifier of some semantic game, one should also consider the particular (implemented) strategies employed by concrete speakers. Such strategies correlated with the non-logical expressions of a given natural language consist in functions that pick up their extension relative to a given context.[1] However, they need not realize winning strategies in every context, what is required being that they reach socially acceptable approximations of the extension at stake. Sets of such functions are what is mastered by the agents to understand linguistic expressions. This informal account of truth-conditional *meaning* and strategy-based *interpretation* will get a more precise working out within the framework of GTS.

---

[1] Like Fodor's [5] narrow content. See [17] for an elaboration of the connection between narrow content and the conception developed in the present paper.

M. Rebuschi (✉)
L.H.S.P. – Archives H. Poincaré, Nancy University, France
e-mail: manuel.rebuschi@univ-nancy2.fr

In the next section I will briefly sketch the required technical apparatus: standard and extended GTS for first-order formal languages, and the conception of Skolem functions as components of winning strategies. In Section 9.3 I will look into the application of GTS to natural language, and deal with the question of how to use and individuate Skolem functions in extended GTS. Two notions will be defined: that of *eGTS meaning*, as a set of implemented Skolem functions, and that of *eGTS stereotype* (more or less regimenting Putnam's idea of idiolectal meaning) as a set of implemented (but not always winning) strategies. Next, Section 9.4 will be devoted to examining a few puzzles of the philosophy of language.

9.2 Game-Theoretical Semantics and Skolemization

Semantic games are here introduced both in their standard and extended versions. Standard GTS games are played on complex formulas, assuming that atomic truths are already given. By contrast, eGTS games go on with atomic formulas.

9.2.1 Usual GTS in a Nutshell

Semantic Games The general idea of GTS[2] is to associate to each first-order (FO) sentence φ evaluated relative to some structure $\mathbf{M} = \langle D, I \rangle$ a semantic game, denoted by $G(\varphi, \mathbf{M})$ and played between two abstract players, the initial verifier $\exists loise$ and the initial falsifier $\forall belard$, s.t. the first player (resp. the second one) has a uniform winning strategy iff the formula is true (resp. false) in $\mathbf{M}$. Such evaluation games are played according to the following rules:

- **(R.At)** If α is a true atomic sentence (or identity) in $\mathbf{M}$, then the verifier wins $G(\alpha, \mathbf{M})$, and the falsifier loses. If α is a false atomic sentence (or identity), the reverse obtains.
- **(R.∨)** In the game $G(\varphi_1 \vee \varphi_2, \mathbf{M})$ the verifier picks out an index $i \in \{1, 2\}$. The rest of the game is as in $G(\varphi_i, \mathbf{M})$.
- **(R.∧)** In the game $G(\varphi_1 \wedge \varphi_2, \mathbf{M})$ the falsifier picks out an index $i \in \{1, 2\}$. The rest of the game is as in $G(\varphi_i, \mathbf{M})$.
- **(R.∃)** The game $G(\exists x \varphi(x), \mathbf{M})$ starts with the verifier choosing a member $d \in D$ and a new name $\mathbf{c}$ to designate it; the rest of the game is as in $G(\varphi(\mathbf{c}), \mathbf{M})$.
- **(R.∀)** The game $G(\forall x \varphi(x), \mathbf{M})$ is similar, except that the choice is made by the falsifier.
- **(R.¬)** The game $G(\neg \varphi, \mathbf{M})$ is like $G(\varphi, \mathbf{M})$, except that the roles of the two players (as defined by the rules) are interchanged.

---

[2] See [11] for an overview.

9 Extended Game-Theoretical Semantics

With such rules, one can define truth and falsity according to GTS:

$\mathbf{M} \vDash_{GTS}^{+} \varphi$ (φ is GTS-true in $\mathbf{M}$) iff there is a winning strategy for the initial verifier ($\exists loise$) in $G(\varphi, \mathbf{M})$.

$\mathbf{M} \vDash_{GTS}^{-} \varphi$ (φ is GTS-false in $\mathbf{M}$) iff there is a winning strategy for the initial falsifier ($\forall belard$) in $G(\varphi, \mathbf{M})$.

Skolemization Assertion of the GTS truth-conditions for a sentence, i.e. of the existence of a winning strategy for $\exists loise$ in the associated game, is expressible in the Σ_1^1 fragment of second-order logic. Each strategy can be represented by a finite sequence of Skolem functions corresponding to the moves made by the verifier (rules (R.$\exists$) and (R.$\vee$)) relative to those played by the falsifier. This will yield e.g.:

$$\begin{aligned} \mathbf{M} \vDash_{GTS}^{+} \forall x \exists y R(x, y) &\iff \mathbf{M} \vDash \exists f \forall x R(x, f(x)) \\ \mathbf{M} \vDash_{GTS}^{+} \forall x (\varphi_1 \vee \varphi_2) &\iff \mathbf{M} \vDash \exists f \forall x ((f(x) = 0 \wedge \varphi_1) \vee \\ &\qquad (f(x) \neq 0 \wedge \varphi_2)) \end{aligned} \qquad (9.1)$$

(In the second example one assumes that the model contains at least two elements, and that one of them is denoted by "0".)

Skolemization is in fact a well-known transformation of FO formulas: In a formula in prenex normal form, replace each existential quantifier $\exists x_i$ by a (new) function symbol $\mathbf{f}_i$ whose variables are those bound by the universal quantifiers of which $\exists x_i$ is within the scope. Following Hintikka, extend the introduction of function symbols to disjunctions (for models with at least two elements.) In what follows, $\mathbf{Sk}[\varphi]$ will denote a formula resulting from φ through such a transformation[3]:

$$\begin{aligned} \mathbf{Sk}[\forall x \exists y R(x, y)] &= \forall x R(x, \mathbf{f}(x)) \\ \mathbf{Sk}[\forall x \exists y \forall z \exists u \varphi(x, y, z, u)] &= \forall x \forall z \varphi[x, \mathbf{f}_1(x), z, \mathbf{f}_2(x, z)] \\ \mathbf{Sk}[\forall x (\varphi_1 \vee \varphi_2)] &= \forall x ((\mathbf{f}(x) = 0 \wedge \varphi_1) \vee (\mathbf{f}(x) \neq 0 \wedge \varphi_2)) \end{aligned} \qquad (9.2)$$

A *second-order Skolem form* of a given formula φ, hereafter symbolized by $\mathbf{2Sk}[\varphi]$, obtains from a (first-order) Skolem form of φ in which each Skolem function symbol is replaced by an existentially quantified functional variable:

$$\mathbf{2Sk}[\forall x \exists y R(x, y)] = \exists f \forall x R(x, f(x)) \qquad (9.3)$$

---

[3] Starting with a given FO formula there is no unicity in the upshot in the general case since several prenex normal forms can sometimes be available. This is the case with $\exists x A x \to \exists y B y$ which leads us to two prenex forms, $\forall x \exists y (Ax \to By)$ and $\exists y \forall x (Ax \to By)$, thus to two distinct skolemizations: respectively $\forall x (\neg Ax \vee B\mathbf{f}(x))$ and $\forall x (\neg Ax \vee B\mathbf{a})$, where $\mathbf{a}$ is a constant (function) symbol.

Assuming the Axiom of Choice and the standard "full" semantics of second-order logic, φ and $\mathbf{Sk}[\varphi]$ are equisatisfiable, and φ and $\mathbf{2Sk}[\varphi]$ are equivalent.

Truth-Conditions Assuming the Axiom of choice and the standard interpretation of second-order logic, the GTS truth-definition is equivalent to the standard one:

$$\mathbf{M} \vDash^+_{\text{GTS}} \varphi \iff \mathbf{M} \vDash \varphi. \tag{9.4}$$

The equivalence between GTS and Tarski-like semantics leads to the inescapable fact that for any FO sentence there is always a winning strategy for one of the players: bivalence corresponds to the determination of the semantic games.

GTS provides a nice and intuitive interpretation of Skolemization: the Skolem functions occurring in $\mathbf{Sk}[\varphi]$ are conceived of as the components of $\exists loise$'s winning strategies in $G(\varphi, \mathbf{M})$. For example in $\mathbf{M} = \langle D, I \rangle$, where $D = \mathbb{N}$ and "<" gets its usual interpretation, the formula $\varphi = \forall x \exists y (x < y)$ is obviously true. It admits of one skolemization, $\mathbf{Sk}[\varphi] = \forall x (x < \mathbf{f}(x))$, where the newly introduced symbol $\mathbf{f}$ can receive several values, each of which corresponds to a winning strategy available to $\exists loise$: $\mathbf{f}_1(x) = x + 1$, $\mathbf{f}_2(x) = 2x + 1$, etc. The GTS-truth-conditions of φ are given by $\mathbf{2Sk}[\varphi] = \exists f \forall x (x < f(x))$.

9.2.2 Extending GTS to Non-logical Constants

In standard GTS, Skolem functions replace existential quantifiers and disjunctions. From a meta-semantic point of view, they correspond to what is taken into account by the assignments in Tarski-like semantics. What I will put forward now is extending such a role of Skolem functions to what is dealt with by the interpretation function I of the model-theoretic structure $\mathbf{M} = \langle D, I \rangle$. To put it in another perspective: whereas GTS game rules are associated with logical constants, extended GTS (eGTS hereafter) will associate new rules with the non-logical vocabulary.[4] The notion of semantic game is thus extended to atomic sentences (and identities).

Atomic Games In eGTS, every sentence φ evaluated relative to a structure $\mathbf{M}$ is associated to a game $eG(\varphi, \mathbf{M})$. This new game is identical to the game $G(\varphi, \mathbf{M})$ played according to the standard GTS rules when it is a *molecular game*, i.e. when φ is a complex formula. If φ is an atomic formula or an identity, one reaches an *atomic game*. The original game rule for atomic sentences (R.At) must then be replaced by four new rules (see Appendix 1.)

First of all, if either $\exists loise$ is the current verifier and the atomic sentence is false, or she is the current falsifier and the sentence is true, then $\forall belard$ wins and $\exists loise$

---

[4] Such an extension is actually suggested by Hintikka himself, see [9, p. 51]. However, this suggestion is essentially connected with applications in first-order epistemic logic, and no extended version of GTS is provided. Already in 1985 Hintikka and Kulas [10] argued that game rules must be associated with NL individual constants.

9 Extended Game-Theoretical Semantics

loses. If it is not the case,[5] then ∀*belard* chooses one of its non-logical constants, an individual constant a_i, a function symbol f_j or a relation symbol R_k, and the game goes on.[6] When ∀*belard* chooses an individual constant a_i, ∃*loise* has to pick out an object in the domain; if she has selected the right value, i.e. the very extension of a_i, then she wins the play and ∀*belard* loses. When ∀*belard* chooses a n-ary function symbol f_j, he furthermore picks out a n-tuple of objects in the domain and ∃*loise* must select an object in the domain: if it is identical to the value of f_j for the given tuple then ∃*loise* wins and ∀*belard* loses. When ∀*belard* chooses a n-ary relation symbol R_k, he furthermore picks out a n-tuple of objects in the domain and ∃*loise* must check whether R_k applies to this tuple; if ∃*loise* succeeds, i.e. if she answers "yes" when R_k applies to the tuple and "no" when it doesn't, then she wins the play and ∀*belard* loses.

In eGTS, we thus have new truth and falsity definitions relative to a structure $\mathbf{M} = \langle D, I \rangle$:

$\mathbf{M} \vDash^+_{\text{eGTS}} \varphi$ (φ is eGTS-true in $\mathbf{M}$) iff there is a winning strategy for the initial verifier (∃*loise*) in $eG(\varphi, \mathbf{M})$ played according to the eGTS-rules.

$\mathbf{M} \vDash^-_{\text{eGTS}} \varphi$ (φ is eGTS-false in $\mathbf{M}$) iff there is a winning strategy for the initial falsifier (∀*belard*) in $eG(\varphi, \mathbf{M})$ played according to the eGTS-rules.

It is worth noticing that according to the eGTS game rules, only individual objects are handled by the players—i.e., no higher-order entity is involved. The situation would have turned out differently if ∃*loise* were required to pick out the very extensions of function and relation symbols.

Extending Skolemization to Non-logical Constants An extended version of skolemization which matches eGTS is straightforwardly definable: not only existentially quantified variables and disjunctions, but now individual constants a_i as well as relation symbols R_j can be replaced by existentially quantified functions (for simplification I will no longer consider function symbols at the object language level.) In what follows we will consider a simple example—a precise definition is given in an appendix. Let us recall what are the first- and second-order Skolem forms $\mathbf{Sk}[\varphi]$ and $\mathbf{2Sk}[\varphi]$:

---

[5] Atomic game rules could be formulated independently from the atom truth-value: atomic games would thus be played according to the other rules, and the winner would be the player winning both molecular and atomic game. The outcome regarding ∃*loise*'s winning strategies would be exactly the same.

[6] When an atomic game is reached there is no residual individual variable in the formula: as eGTS games are played for sentences only, every variable is bound and next replaced by a new constant during the molecular game. GTS could of course be defined for open formulas with a slight complication—games relative to a formula, a model and an assignment. However it is not necessary for the objectives of this paper.

$$\varphi = \forall x \exists y R_4(x, y, a_2)$$
$$\mathbf{Sk}[\varphi] = \forall x R_4(x, \mathbf{f}(x), a_2) \qquad (9.5)$$
$$\mathbf{2Sk}[\varphi] = \exists f \forall x R_4(x, f(x), a_2)$$

Let's now introduce some new notations. In $\mathbf{eSk}[\varphi]$ the non-logical constants are replaced by function symbols: one corresponding to a choice function $\mathbf{g}$ for the individual constant a_2, and another, $\mathbf{h}$, for the indicator function[7] of the relation symbol R_4; since we want $\mathbf{eSk}[\varphi]$ to be equivalent to $\mathbf{Sk}[\varphi]$, the newly introduced symbols are equated with their intended values[8]:

$$\mathbf{eSk}[\varphi] = \forall x[\mathbf{h}(x, \mathbf{f}(x), \mathbf{g}) = 1] \wedge [\mathbf{g} = a_2] \wedge [\mathbf{h} = \mathbf{1}_{R_4}] \qquad (9.6)$$

Then in $\mathbf{2eSk}[\varphi]$ the new function symbols are existentially quantified:

$$\mathbf{2eSk}[\varphi] = \exists g \exists h \exists f [\forall x[h(x, f(x), g) = 1] \wedge [g = a_2] \wedge [h = \mathbf{1}_{R_4}]] \qquad (9.7)$$

Assuming the standard semantics for second-order logic any first-order formula $\varphi = \Phi(R_1, \ldots, R_k, a_1, \ldots, a_l, x_1, \ldots, x_m)$ is equivalent to $\mathbf{2eSk}[\varphi]$. (For more details, see Appendix 2.)

Truth-Conditions Prima facie the new game rules do not add any interesting moves to the plays since they say that a play should end in the same manner as was indicated in the original rule (R.At): the verifier wins if the atom is true, while the falsifier wins if it is false. And in fact the following equivalence is trivially inferred from the truth-definitions:

$$\mathbf{M} \vDash^+_{\text{eGTS}} \varphi \iff \mathbf{M} \vDash^+_{\text{GTS}} \varphi. \qquad (9.8)$$

However the specific benefits of GTS were not obvious either since it was shown to be equivalent to Tarski-like semantics. Regarding eGTS, relevant differences will appear at the level of the initial verifier's power, since mastering a winning strategy is now a more complex task than it was in standard GTS. The underlying intuition of atomic games is an extra requirement for $\exists loise$: she must be able to determinate

---

[7] Here again, one has to assume that the domain contains at least two elements, one of which is denoted by 1. As was suggested by a referee, using relations symbols and predicate variables rather than indicator functions and function symbols would provide much more readable Skolem forms. However, the uniform use of (Skolem-like) functions at a metalinguistic level appears to be consistent with the fact that games are played with no higher-order entities. Incidentally, this uniform treatment would allow us to translate the resulting Σ^1_1 formulas into IF logic in the usual way.

[8] Both kinds of functions are linked to *choice functions* in the strict sense: the individual constant functions $\mathbf{g}_{a_i}$ could be defined relative to a domain D s.t. $\mathbf{g}_{a_i}(D) \in D$; the indicator functions for relations $\mathbf{h}_{R_j}$ completely determine functions $\mathbf{h}'_{R_j}$ s.t. $\mathbf{h}'_{R_j}(D^n) \in D^n$.

the semantic values of the expressions involved in the assertions she argues for. This is made clear if we are to describe her winning strategies[9]:

> A winning strategy for $\exists loise$ in some (unextended) GTS game $G(\varphi)$ is an array of Skolem functions related to each choice to be made by her through the game $\overline{\mathbf{f}_\varphi} = \langle \mathbf{f}_\varphi^1, \mathbf{f}_\varphi^2, \ldots \mathbf{f}_\varphi^n \rangle$; correspondingly, a winning strategy for $\exists loise$ in the eGTS game $eG(\varphi)$ is an array $\overline{e\mathbf{f}_\varphi} = \langle \mathbf{f}_\varphi^1, \mathbf{f}_\varphi^2, \ldots \mathbf{f}_\varphi^n, [\mathbf{f}_{\text{atom}}] \rangle$ where $[\mathbf{f}_{\text{atom}}]$ is the set of Skolem functions correlated with the individual constants and relation symbols occurring in φ: $[\mathbf{f}_{\text{atom}}] = \{\mathbf{g}_{a_1}, \ldots, \mathbf{g}_{a_k}, \mathbf{h}_{R_1}, \ldots, \mathbf{h}_{R_l}\}$.

Considering formula φ of example (9.5), its eGTS truth-conditions are given by (9.7) whereas the winning strategies for $\exists loise$ are provided by each interpretation of the function variables $\mathbf{f}$, $\mathbf{g}$ and $\mathbf{h}$ in (9.6). Of course, as long as the players of semantic games are ideal, infinitary and omniscient agents the requirement cannot trigger any fatal issue: the extensional constraint occurring onto the functions of $[\mathbf{f}_{\text{atom}}]$ is that their values coincide with those of the interpretation function I of the structure. More accurately, each function $\mathbf{h}_{R_i} \in [\mathbf{f}_{\text{atom}}]$ must be extensionally equivalent to 1_{R_i}, so $\mathbf{h}_{R_i}$ is completely determined by $I|_{\{R_i\}}$; and similarly each (constant) function $\mathbf{g}_{a_j} \in [\mathbf{f}_{\text{atom}}]$ must be completely determined by $I|_{\{a_j\}}$. The union of the elements of $[\mathbf{f}_{\text{atom}}]$ thus gives exactly the same values as the restriction of the interpretation function I to the non-logical constants involved in φ.

The particular insight offered by Skolem functions will then be to provide a new point of view on the interpretation of a language. Whereas I is a static mapping given once and for all, the Skolem functions of $[\mathbf{f}_{\text{atom}}]$ are expected to encode the devices used by the initial verifier to reach the semantic values of the language constants. The specific contribution of eGTS will thus be made apparent when some restrictions on the agents' powers are introduced. The situation is analogous to that of (unextended) GTS, which gives rise to a genuine account when imperfect information comes into play.[10,11]

---

[9] In what follows I do not give any strict definition. However strategies are recursively definable: the syntax of a given formula completely determines the set of possible plays or histories, which in turn determines the set of strategies for $\exists loise$. Hence the arrays of functions here mentioned are expected to be structured. See [15] for an exact definition.
[10] Imperfect information semantic games provide a new logic which has been developed by Hintikka and Sandu since the 1980s, *independence-friendly* logic (*IF* logic for short). It is a slight extension of first-order logic equivalent to the Σ_1^1 fragment of second-order logic.
[11] Jackson [12] provides another extension of GTS to atomic formulas in the context of knowledge-base management: new game rules are introduced to check whether the atom in question is a proof-theoretic consequence of the knowledge base under consideration. The theory departs from the model-theoretic ground and admits of indeterminate formulas. Such an account can be seen as an implementation of non-omniscient players, where the initial verifier's knowledge is restricted to the content of the knowledge base.

9.3 An Account of Meaning and Interpretation Based on Game Strategies

I define two semantic values for each linguistic expression E in terms of game strategies. The first one is the *eGTS meaning* $||E||$, which is a set of Skolem functions; the second one is the *eGTS stereotype*, †E†$_i$, which is a set of *Dig* functions.

9.3.1 Meaning: Implemented Skolem Functions

Using Strategies to Refine Meaning It has been suggested by van Benthem [1] to use game-semantics in order to account for (hyper)fine-grained meanings: two logically equivalent sentences in FOL can diverge in their syntactic structure so that the corresponding evaluation games require different strategies. It would thus be possible to define the meaning of a sentence φ not only as the set of possible worlds where φ is true, but as the set of pairs ⟨**M**, ws⟩ such that **M** is a possible world where φ is true, and ws is the set of winning strategies for ∃*loise* in $G(\varphi, \mathbf{M})$.

However, whereas the situation is fine with logical constants and unextended GTS, it is different with non-logical constants and eGTS atomic games: now, every component of the winning strategies should coincide with the interpretation function. Then if two predicates (or individual constants) are coextensive in every possible world, adding their eGTS correlated winning strategies cannot add any distinctive information. So no straightforward refinement of meanings can be expected from these strategies.

How to Individuate Skolem Functions? What is required is an intensional characterization of functions. This is the first issue eGTS has to face in order to avoid collapsing into standard GTS. Coextensive functions will be considered distinct whenever they are associated with different processes to determine their values. Of course, the identity conditions of processes are worth defining,[12] but what is required here is only the *possibility* of an intensional characterization of functions based on the idea of process, whatever it is.

The idea meets Moschovakis' [13] conception of Fregean sense as an algorithm, which is also elaborated by Muskens in [14]. What is specific here is the nature of the functions, which are winning strategies in games. However, we are not committed to sticking to the algorithm or program approach. Skolem functions are what is expected to be at least partially mastered by competent speakers and they can be realized by many distinct devices. We will be concerned with *implemented Skolem functions* in general—even though I might speak of "*algorithms*" in a loose way.

Let us introduce a new symbol for extensional identity—$f \equiv g$ for $\forall \vec{x}\, f(\vec{x}) = g(\vec{x})$—and retain the identity symbol for intensional identity between functions, i.e. for identity between implemented functions. The truth-conditions of a sentence φ would be now expressed by the formula coming from **2eSk**[φ] after a shift of the

---

[12] And this is not an easy task, see [2].

identity statements into coextensivity statements, for the Skolem functions correlated with constants ($[g_i \equiv a_i]$) as well as for those linked to relations ($[h_i \equiv \mathbf{1}_{R_i}]$). Such a requirement is weaker than that of identity of implemented functions.

eGTS Meaning Why not simply endorse Musken's theory and get rid of atomic games? But we would then lose the unifying framework of semantic games and of Skolem functions. Several NL semantic theories employ choice and Skolem functions to account for indefinites or anaphoric pronouns [19, 23]. Schlenker [21] and Clark [4] even provide explicit connections between choice or Skolem functions uses in NL semantics and GTS. In fact the very idea was already developed by Hintikka with branching quantifiers. The proposal in this paper is then to extend the use of Skolem functions to NL semantics—and of the correlative GTS games—to the vocabulary, i.e. to names and predicates. It entails that Musken's intensionally characterized functions correlated with names and predicates are naturally interpreted as implemented strategies or Skolem functions.

Since in general linguistic expressions E are correlated with many such implemented functions, I will denote by $||E||$ the set of implemented Skolem functions associated with E, and I will call it the *eGTS meaning* of E. For example, if there were two mechanisms (i.e., concrete devices) to identify dogs, the corresponding functions $\mathbf{h}_1$ and $\mathbf{h}_2$ would be elements of $||Dog||$. The concept of eGTS meaning so defined is model relative, and it will be used as implicitly relative to the actual world.

9.3.2 Interpretation: Implemented Dig Functions

"Strategic Meaning" As was said above, for any FO formula φ there is an equivalence between $\mathbf{2eSk}[\varphi]$ and $\mathbf{2Sk}[\varphi]$ and this implies that no specific insight on the truth-conditions can be given by our new (atomic) games. A new perspective obtains if we examine closer what is expected from the initial verifier. Her winning strategies for molecular games are now enriched with functions for the atomic games involved. As was already noticed, there is no change of the conditions for her to have such strategies: there is a winning strategy for ∃*loise* in the molecular game iff there is a winning strategy for her in the whole (including the atomic) game.

Atomic games are relevant insofar as one wants to know *which particular functions* are involved in a winning strategy. This is the case when bounded players are assumed to play the semantic games or, better, when some (human, concrete) agent is expected to know something about, or to use part of the winning strategy of one (abstract) player. Roughly said the issue is then no longer to know *de dicto* whether there is a winning strategy but to know *de re* which strategy will be a winning one.

Such knowledge is that of what Hintikka [8] labelled "*strategic meaning.*" It is involved in semantic analysis when the "*abstract meaning*" (i.e., the truth-condition) is no longer enough, such as in cases of ambiguity resolution, or in anaphora resolution. According to Hintikka, many features can play a role in the determination of the winning strategies: contextual data, background knowledge, syntactical clues, etc. Strategic meaning is a free extra offered by GTS, beyond the more usual truth-conditional content. It can sometimes be handled by speakers for the interpretation of particular occurrences of sentences in discourse or conversation. Hence strategic meaning can be considered as belonging to the pragmatic side of language. However, as Hintikka deservedly insists, strategic meaning is just a by-product of a semantic theory and must be considered as such.

Adding One Dimension: Interpretation The idea of strategic meaning suggests making a move from meaning constitution to linguistic interpretation (or understanding), not only at the level of complex sentences but also at the level of atomic ones. Meaning constitution is accounted for by semantic games played by the abstract players in a model-theoretic structure. Linguistic interpretation is another type of game: it is concerned with real, limited speakers in concrete contexts. This will lead us to a relativization of the notions of eGTS to contexts and to approximations of Skolem functions. As requiring a total grasp of meaning (hence of extensions) by competent speakers is not realistic, it is necessary to modify the theory developed up to now, and regiment the following three ideas about *linguistic knowledge*: (*i*) It is *contextual* knowledge: there is an elimination of algorithms in the general case; (*ii*) It is *partial* knowledge: there is a specific elimination of algorithms relatively to the agent; (*iii*) It is *approximate* knowledge: linguistic knowledge might involve functions which are not always winning strategies, i.e. not always Skolem functions.

(i) Contextual Knowledge The ability to determine the extension of expressions in order to understand an utterance is relative to its context. Both the way the context is modeled, and the question why what in the context that counts as important does the job in the interpretation process, are issues that go beyond the purpose of this section. I will rather claim in a very general manner that contexts are expected to play a specific role regarding Skolem functions: *contexts should restrict the class of the relevant, hence available, Skolem functions.*

Indeed, my claim highlights a role of contexts which is very often emphasized in the literature, namely quantifier domain restriction (see [22] for a general overview.) Semantic theories more specifically employing Skolem functions usually also take contextual restrictions into account. This is the case of Hintikka's [8] conception of strategic meaning according to which the context restricts the set of available winning strategies. Von Heusinger [6] provides a uniform semantic representation for pronouns: "Pronouns are understood as referring to the most salient individual in the context so far, and are represented as indexed epsilon terms that are interpreted by a choice function [which] reconstructs the salience structure of the context." Therefore, the role played by the context in the setting of the relevant choice functions appears to be a pervarsive feature of NL semantic theories involving such functions.

(ii) Partial Knowledge There are in general connections linking the speaker to the individuals and properties she refers to in her utterance. In eGTS, these connections correspond to the Skolem functions of [f_{atom}]. If such connections are individuated at the level of their implementations, they may become dependent of the context: some algorithm or other is available in such or such a context, but not in another. For

instance, as the speaker is an element of the context, complexity considerations can occur and imply some restriction on the available devices. More generally speaking the location of the utterance can play an important role on the selection of a device to determine the extension of an expression. One can ponder over the calculation of the extension of "*Water*" in a desert $\mathbf{h}_{\text{water}}^{c_1}$ which may diverge from the corresponding calculation in a kitchen $\mathbf{h}_{\text{water}}^{c_2}$.

For the framework of eGTS, what all this means is that relative to a given context c, there are contextual restrictions $||E||^c$ on the set of (implemented) winning strategies of the initial verifier $||E||$ generally available for a given concrete speaker. Some of these restrictions are due to the location of the speaker, but not necessarily all of them. For some utterances of a sentence, there might be no available Skolem function at all even though the sentence is true in the model—i.e. even though there actually are such functions for the initial verifier of the corresponding semantic game.

(iii) Approximate Knowledge Speakers are far from omniscient. In his well-known paper [16] Putnam argued that a speaker who could not discriminate between "*Elms*" and "*Beeches*" might nonetheless be considered a competent English speaker. A fixed amount of approximation is indeed acceptable according to the linguistic community—the exact amount being of course conventionally determined. For instance, a speaker who could not discriminate between "*Snowball*" and "*Tiger*" would not be considered competent.

So competent speakers can employ implemented functions (i.e., concrete devices) to determine the extension of predicates that do not necessarily coincide with the interpretation function of the underlying model. Consequently such functions are not necessarily Skolem functions of eGTS, even though *some* of them can be. I will call these functions *Dig functions*. They are those strategies used by concrete speakers if they were to calculate the extensions of the predicates and names they employ, sometimes winning, sometimes losing.

eGTS Stereotype The set of Dig functions eventually associated with an expression E by a competent speaker i can thus strongly diverge from the eGTS meaning $||E||$: it can come from both a contraction of the set of Skolem functions, and an enlargement to many losing strategies. Following Putnam's ideas let us call this set the *stereotype of* E for i and denote it by $\dagger E \dagger_i$. As for the corresponding set of Skolem functions, we must use the restriction $\dagger E \dagger_i^c$ to model the stereotype of an agent i in a context c. Stereotypes are specific to the agents' idiolects. Some of them are acceptable, others not, depending on social conventions. What counts as a socially acceptable stereotype is a matter of empirical research.

We finally reached a two-dimensional account of "meaning" (in a broad sense), *eGTS meaning* and *eGTS stereotype*, with no resort to possible-world semantics. Intensionality intervenes at the level of the individuation of functions, and a second refinement comes from the interpretation level. In the next section, I will give a few applications of the two notions.

9.4 Application and Philosophical Consequences

This section is devoted to applications. I first consider the eGTS meaning and the eGTS stereotype of NL sentences taken from a concrete example. Distinctions will be introduced regarding the minimal requirement for a speaker to be competent, depending on the syntactic categories of expressions at stake. My GTS-based framework will then be confronted to some classical philosophical puzzles.

9.4.1 Contrasting Meaning and Interpretation

Meaning It is now time to consider how eGTS handles concrete cases. Let us consider a simple discourse:

A man walks. He kicks Nicolas

Its analysis according to GTS is quite standard (see [4, 10, 20]); according to eGTS, the game should go deeper. It is roughly played as follows:

Example 1 The whole game eG is played relative to a given model $\mathbf{M} = \langle D, I \rangle$. It is cut into two subgames, one for each sentence—i.e., $eG = eG(S_1, \mathbf{M}); eG(S_2, \mathbf{M})$, where S_1 stands for "A man walks", and S_2 for "He kicks Nicolas." In $eG(S_1, \mathbf{M})$ ∃*loise* chooses an individual in D for the initial indefinite "A", say b, and puts it in the *choice set CS*; then the game goes on as $eG(b$ is a man and b walks, $\mathbf{M})$. ∀*belard* chooses a conjunct, say b *is a man*, and the game continues as $eG(b$ is a man, $\mathbf{M})$. We have now reached an atomic formula: if it is true, i.e., if ∃*loise* actually chose a man with b, then ∀*belard* cannot do anything clever[13] but choose the predicate "man", and pick out an arbitrary individual, say b', from the domain D; ∃*loise* answers **yes** if b' is a man, and **no** if it isn't—a task she can successfully achieve since she is omniscient. Moving to $eG(S_2, \mathbf{M})$, ∃*loise* chooses an individual *in the choice set CS* to process the anaphoric pronoun "He". So she picks out b, and the game goes on as $eG(b$ kicks Nicolas, $\mathbf{M})$. This is an atomic formula. If it is true, i.e. if the individual chosen by ∃*loise* in the previous subgame actually kicks Nicolas, then ∀*belard* chooses one of its two non-logical constants, say *Nicolas*. ∃*loise* must then find the bearer of the name in D, a job she easily does as an omniscient player.

Assuming that the above discourse is true, there is a winning strategy for ∃*loise* in eG. What would such a strategy look like? It is a sequence of (sets of) implemented Skolem functions:

$$\langle \mathbf{f}_1, \{\mathbf{h}_1, \mathbf{h}_2\}, \mathbf{f}_2, \{\mathbf{h}_3, \mathbf{g}_1\} \rangle$$

---

[13] Strictly speaking, ∀*belard* could also choose the individual constant b and lose immediately.

9 Extended Game-Theoretical Semantics

where: $\mathbf{f}_1 \equiv \mathbf{f}_2$ pick out a man walking and kicking Nicolas, $\mathbf{h}_1 \in ||\text{Man}||$, $\mathbf{h}_2 \in ||\text{Walk}||$, $\mathbf{h}_3 \in ||\text{Kick}||$, and $\mathbf{g}_1 \in ||\text{Nicolas}||$. Hence, ∃*loise*'s winning strategies directly rely on the eGTS-meanings of the predicates and proper name. The target array for ∃*loise* actually is

$$\langle \mathbf{f}_1, \{||\text{Man}||, ||\text{Walk}||\}, \mathbf{f}_2, \{||\text{Kick}||, ||\text{Nicolas}||\} \rangle.$$

This array provides a basis to construe the eGTS-meaning of the whole discourse. Such an analysis requires adding specific rules to combine elementary meanings (those occurring in the array) in a more subtle, syntax-sensitive way than it is in a mere sequence. But that would lead us beyond the scope of the present paper.

Interpretation While shifting from meaning to interpretation, contexts of utterance, limitations of the agents and approximation enter the scene. As an immediate consequence, one has to address the issue of what minimal amount of linguistic knowledge is expected to be mastered by any competent speaker.

Let us consider the interpretation of the above discourse by an agent i hearing it: differently from ∃*loise*, i need not master *any* winning strategy of the corresponding eGTS game. Her target array looks like

$$\langle \mathbf{f}_1^i, \{\dagger \text{Man}\dagger_i, \dagger \text{Walk}\dagger_i\}, \mathbf{f}_2^i, \{\dagger \text{Kick}\dagger_i, \dagger \text{Nicolas}\dagger_i\} \rangle.$$

where ∃*loise*'s implemented functions $\mathbf{f}_1$ and $\mathbf{f}_2$ have been replaced by a couple of others, $\mathbf{f}_1^i$ and $\mathbf{f}_2^i$ respectively, and the elementary meanings have been changed into the corresponding stereotypes for agent i. Roughly said, i must know that the value produced by $\mathbf{f}_2^i$ should be the same as that selected by $\mathbf{f}_1^i$, i.e. $\mathbf{f}_2^i \equiv \mathbf{f}_1^i$, which corresponds to the understanding of the anaphoric pronoun—but she need not know anything about the function $\mathbf{f}_1^i$ itself, except that it should take its values among male human beings. Furthermore, a competent hearer must have some socially acceptable stereotype $\dagger \text{Man} \dagger_i$, but nothing is required about "*Nicolas*", i.e. $\dagger \text{Nicolas} \dagger_i$ can be empty.

It means that the *minimal* knowledge required of a competent speaker can vary between grammatical categories. Of course, an agent can have more than such a minimal knowledge and use strategic meaning to interpret a discourse. In the example, the agent can know the functions' value (i.e., *who* the man kicking Nicolas is), and her stereotype $\dagger \text{Nicolas} \dagger_i$ can be a proper part of the corresponding GTS-meaning (i.e., it can involve implemented functions that actually pick out the bearer of the name.)

In the remainder of the subsection I will check three categories, namely proper names, relations, and definite descriptions, and examine what corresponding knowledge competent speakers are supposed to possess.

Names An implemented Skolem function correlated to a name a is a mechanism $\mathbf{g}_a$ which produces the referent of the name. It represents any mode of identification of its bearer. However, an assertion making use of a proper name can refer to the bearer of the name even though the speaker who utters it does not master *any* of the corresponding Skolem functions in $||a||$. For a competent speaker i to successfully assert: "*He kicks Nicolas*"—and to successfully refer to Nicolas—it is only required that the truth condition of the statement be realized, namely that the ordered pair made of the individual picked out by *he*, and of the bearer of the name I(Nicolas), whoever they are, be in the extension I(Kick) of the kicking relation, whatever this extension is. If the speaker has no idea who is the bearer of the name, $\dagger\texttt{Nicolas}\dagger_i$ is simply empty.[14] Of course, the knowledge of the bearer of a name would increase one's understanding of the sentence where the name occurs, but it is not required.

The semantics based on Skolem and Dig functions is perfectly compatible with the Kripkean theory of *direct reference* for proper names—as well as for natural kind predicates and other relation symbols. Whereas the interpretation function I intervenes at the level of *meaning constitution*, implemented Skolem and Dig functions play an epistemic role: they encode the mode of recognition of the independently given extension of expressions. Hence different speakers knowing the individual that is the bearer of a proper name usually do not share the same Dig functions. The contrast is exactly the one which holds between abstract meaning and strategic meaning.

Predicates (and Other Relation Symbols) In the actual world, one can have two or more functions to determine the extension of "*Elm*". This is the main reason why stereotypes were defined as *sets* of Dig functions. For instance one function will be based on the agent's knowledge and educated ability to recognize species of trees; another one will consist in asking to an expert what this extension is. For sure, these functions are distinct at an implementation level even though they provide the same values.

The functions involved in the stereotype are clearly distinct from intensions. The latter are usually modelled as functions from possible worlds to extensions. By contrast, Dig functions are defined in one (actual) world, with no a priori idea about their applicability in other possible worlds. Nevertheless, Dig functions can model concepts expressed by predicates. Coextensive predicates, such as *Creature owning a heart* (Hx) and *Creature owning a kidney* (Kx), will obviously give rise to two distinct sets of implemented Skolem functions (or eGTS meanings) $||H||$ and $||K||$. Each function is then expected to encode an operating way to produce the extension, i.e. to determine whether any given object belongs to it or not. They can naturally be conceived of as encoding the correlated *concepts* of *Owning a heart* and *Owning a kidney*, which play an essential role in the speaker's ability to produce the extension of the predicates. And of course, this distinction between two coextensive predicates is made with no resort to any possible-world based device.

As was said before, a competent speaker is expected to possess a stereotype composed of Dig functions which yield a socially acceptable approximation of the extension. For instance a speaker i who cannot discriminate between "*Elms*"

---

[14] If the reader doesn't share my intuition, successful reference is more obvious in cases such as the speaker's assertion: "*I do not know who Nicolas is*".

and *"Beeches"*, i.e. such that †Elm†$_i$ = †Beech†$_i$ can nonetheless be considered a competent English speaker although of course, †Elm†$_{Expert}$ ∩ †Beech†$_{Expert}$ = ∅. By contrast, a speaker j who could not discriminate between *"Elms"* and *"Tigers"*, would not be considered a competent speaker, a minimal requirement being that: †Elm†$_j$ ∩ †Tiger†$_j$ = ∅.[15] Beyond the minimal requirement of the possession of at least one Dig function, the understanding of a predicate will be more acute if the speaker has several Dig functions, if many of them are Skolem functions, if she can use them successfully in many counterfactual situations, and so forth.

Definite Descriptions With definite descriptions we are led back to a case similar to non-extended GTS since quantifiers occur in their formalization. However, the interaction between quantifiers and atomic games deserves careful examination.

Considering a sentence such as *"The 2009 French president is bald"*, the description $\iota x P x$ (*"The 2009 French president"*) is paraphrased by an existential statement and the whole sentence is formalized as follows:

$$\varphi : \exists x (Px \wedge \forall y (Py \rightarrow y = x) \wedge Bx) \tag{9.9}$$

Here the GTS truth-conditions rely on the existence of a winning strategy for the initial verifier, i.e. of a constant Skolem function $\mathbf{f}_x = a$ such that ∃*loise* yields a winning strategy in any of the three games correlated to the conjuncts:

$$Pa \wedge \forall y (Py \rightarrow y = a) \wedge Ba \tag{9.10}$$

∃*loise* has thus to hold two Skolem functions associated with the predicates and coinciding with the interpretation function, $\mathbf{h}_P$ and $\mathbf{h}_B$, so that she is able to win the atomic games Pa and Ba, as well as the game associated with $\forall y(Py \rightarrow y = a)$.[16] Once again, the existence of a winning strategy for the initial verifier of a semantic game—abstract meaning—is independent from the knowledge of any strategy by the speaker—strategic meaning.

A complete knowledge of the strategy corresponding to the definite description in the aforementioned example involves knowledge of the two functions $\mathbf{f}_x$ (= a)

---

[15] To be more precise in the writing down of the constraints, we should relativize the stereotypes to usual contexts, in order to avoid situations where, e.g., an elm and a tiger were both boiled, ground, then mixed with flour and black ink, so that the agent can no longer distinguish them. This relativization is here left implicit.

[16] This subformula is equivalent to $\forall y(\neg Py \vee y = a)$, so that ∃*loise* has a winning strategy if, for any value chosen for y by ∀*belard*, she can select one of the disjuncts, i.e. either deny P of this value or identify it to a; it is of course assumed that the function $\mathbf{h}_P$ does not change during the game. Finally, a winning strategy for the initial verifier in the whole game associated with φ is a tuple where $\mathbf{h}_P$ occurs twice—one time for each occurrence of P in φ: $\overline{\mathbf{f}_\varphi} = \langle \mathbf{f}_x, \langle \{\mathbf{h}_P\}, \langle \mathbf{f}_\vee, \{\mathbf{h}_P\} \rangle, \{\mathbf{h}_B\} \rangle \rangle$.

and $\mathbf{h}_P$. However a competent speaker is not expected to master both functions: having a function that enables one to approximately determine the denotation of the description ($\mathbf{h}_P$)—i.e. possessing an acceptable stereotype $\dagger P \dagger_i$—is enough; knowing who the individual fitting the description ($\mathbf{f}_x$) is increases the understanding of the sentence, although not being absolutely essential. The case is partly similar to that of proper names. As a definite description involves a combination of predicates and quantified variables, the minimal requirements for a competent speaker follow those of its components: no strategic meaning is required regarding quantifiers, whereas a conventionally determined stereotype is expected to be used in the case of predicates.

9.4.2 Philosophical Puzzles

With eGTS meanings and stereotypes, we possess two levers to get solutions to the classical semantic puzzles about informative identities, conceivability of impossibilities, and so forth. In this last subsection, I will briefly survey some of these puzzles.

Informative Identities They can be carried using eGTS meanings. For instance, $||\text{Hesperus}|| \neq ||\text{Phosphorus}||$ since the implemented Skolem functions corresponding to each proper name are not the same, even though they are extensionally equivalent: if $\mathbf{g}_H \in ||\text{Hesperus}||$ and $\mathbf{g}_P \in ||\text{Phosphorus}||$, then $\mathbf{g}_H \equiv \mathbf{g}_P$ but $\mathbf{g}_H \neq \mathbf{g}_P$. Skolem and Dig functions can be understood as carrying a part of the Fregean notion of sense: they represent the devices employed respectively by $\exists loise$ and by ordinary speakers to find the extension. Of course, Dig functions are not Frege's senses: they *do not* determine the extension per se, at the semantic or constitutive level.

The informativeness of the identity is due to the fact that speakers are not expected to know anything about the bearers of the names they employ. Learning an identity is consequently learning a fact about Dig functions and, more basically, about the bearers of the names: learning that Hesperus is identical with Phosphorus leads an agent i to correlate functions $\mathbf{g} \in \dagger\text{Hesperus}\dagger_i$ to functions $\mathbf{g}' \in \dagger\text{Phosphorus}\dagger_i$: $\mathbf{g} \equiv \mathbf{g}'$. By contrast, stating that Hesperus is identical with Hesperus doesn't supply any new information.

Rigid Designation Going into modal matters and following Kripke, we can consider the proper names "*Hesperus*" and "*Phosphorus*" as rigid designators, i.e. as names referring to the same entity in every possible world. How are we then to account for the conceivability of impossible situations where the two names do not refer to the same entity? This puzzle gave rise to several strategies, like two-dimensional semantics (2DS) or rescourse to impossible worlds. On the present account, the structure of possible worlds itself is left intact with no ad hoc supplementary component, and Skolem (or dig) functions suffice to account for conceivable impossible situations.

Let us consider the two implemented functions mentioned above, g_H and g_P. As Skolem functions, they can occur in winning strategies for $\exists loise$ in semantic games $G(\varphi, \mathbf{M})$, where φ is replaced by sentences involving the proper names "*Hesperus*" and "*Phosphorus*", and $\mathbf{M}$ is a first-order model corresponding to *the actual world*. Recall that such functions can diverge in another model $\mathbf{N}$ corresponding to another possible world, i.e. $g_H \not\equiv g_P$ in $\mathbf{N}$, even though the proper names still refer to the same individual in $\mathbf{N}$.

In this respect, Skolem functions behave like Hintikka's world-lines [7] or like individual concepts: they link individuals from world to world according to specific viewpoints, and independently from the very nature of the individuals at stake.[17] This is made possible by the general fact that a winning strategy in a game $G(\psi, \mathbf{M})$ need not be winning in the game $G(\psi, \mathbf{M}')$, i.e. in the game correlated to the same sentence but played in another model.

Empty Names Stereotypes and Dig functions provide a nice solution to the usual puzzles since there is now a way to make a difference between two empty names (e.g. Shrek and Pinocchio), and a means to designate entities in other possible worlds. What is required is only to allow Dig functions to be partial, i.e. to be possibly undefined in some possible worlds. Alternatively, it can be postulated that the gaps are filled in with a null individual. There is no prima facie objection to the consideration of two distinct Dig functions, g_p for Pinocchio and g_s for Shrek, such that they be empty in some worlds and their values coincide in no world in which they are defined: such functions thus account for the meaningfulness of fictional discourse in a natural way.

Synonymy Cases The well-known cases of the ignorance of synonymous predicates and, as a consequence, of the equivalence of sentences involving them, are handled in the present framework in a way similar to that of coreferent proper names: even though their extensions coincide in every possible world, the eGTS meanings for e.g. "*Ophthalmologist*" (O) and "*Eye doctor*" (E), which are sets of *implemented* Skolem functions, do not: $||O|| \neq ||E||$; and the corresponding stereotypes of course do not either: $\dagger O \dagger \neq \dagger E \dagger$. This is enough to account for possible distinctive attitudes towards sentences whose equivalence is due to synonymy. Ralph can believe that George is an eye doctor and simultaneously believe that George is not an ophthalmologist, without being inconsistent: Ralph's first belief involves a device—i.e., an implemented function—from $\dagger E \dagger_R$, whilst the second one involves one from $\dagger O \dagger_R$. Hence the *contents* of the attitudes are not the same.

Twin-Earth The present conception enables one to deal with cases like Putnam's Twin-Earth [16]. E-Oscar and TE-Oscar, the microphysical twins living on Earth and Twin-Earth, are supposed to share the same (narrow) mental state as they think about "*Water*", even though E-Oscar refers to H_2O whereas TE-Oscar refers to

---

[17] This means that in a standard Kripkean structure, the accessibility relation between possible worlds is doubled over by world-lines between entities. However, Hintikka does not agree with such a combination of his own ideas with that of rigid designation. See [18].

XYZ. It can be assumed that the twins share their stereotypes: $\dagger \text{water} \dagger_{\text{E-Oscar}} = \dagger \text{water} \dagger_{\text{TE-Oscar}}$. The Dig functions of E-Oscar enable him to determine the extension of *"Water"* on Earth. They are not necessarily Skolem functions, i.e. functions picking out water *in every context*, but they do so in terrestrial contexts: it is only their restriction to terrestrial contexts which coincides with that of Skolem functions, i.e. $\dagger \text{water} \dagger_{\text{E-Oscar}}^{\text{Earth}} \subseteq ||\text{water}||^{\text{Earth}}$. Using the same stereotype on Twin-Earth, TE-Oscar will select another type of extension, namely XYZ. So the extensions depend on the environment—it is the assumption—whereas the stereotype is shared by the twins.

What's New? Most of the puzzles just presented are handled by competing theories like two-dimensional semantics [3]. However, the advantages of the present frameword are worth noticing:

(i) it is non-modal: eGTS meanings as well as eGTS stereotypes are defined in the actual world, with no resort to possible-world structure;
(ii) it does not idealize competent speakers: language users need not master intensions; what they need are conventionally acceptable stereotypes, i.e., sets of concrete devices leading them to calculate approximate extensions of expressions.
(iii) it takes into account idiolectal variations and inter-individual variations of linguistic competence, thanks to the indeterminate character of stereotypes.

These are not technical advantages, but philosophical insights not accounted for by 2DS. These are indirect benefits coming from Putnam's ideas about meaning.

9.5 Conclusion

I have shown that a slight extension of GTS could yield interesting results for the theory of *meaning*. This can be done provided that one does not stick to the usual static and extensional conception of functions as mappings but adopts some fine-grained criterion of individuation of functions—namely, one must move at the implementation level. Here, concrete devices must be introduced in order to account for *interpretation* by limited agents to be contrasted with the semantic games played by unlimited players. Hence after meaning constitution through eGTS comes the step of linguistic understanding, where context, approximation, and other epistemic issues enter the stage.

The conception put forward in this paper can be viewed as an elaboration on Putnam's ideas about meaning. The key is in the strict separation between meaning constitution and language understanding. Putnam appended the notion of stereotype to that of meaning. In our framework, there is a shift from sets of Skolem functions to sets of Dig functions: limited agents are fallible—as they interpret language, they do not automatically grasp functions that yield the appropriate extensions. This is why the devices are not Fregean senses, but rather make up Putnamian stereotypes.

The resulting conception is a non-modal account of meaning and interpretation: Skolem and Dig functions are defined in one single world. The fine-grained individuation of such functions certainly require intensionality, but it is limited to the metalinguistic level. Moreover, the whole conception is based on an informal interpretation of functions as concrete devices which is a long shot from usual possible-world semantics: here competent speakers are not expected to grasp functions defined on sets of possible worlds, let alone two-dimensional functions.

Appendix 1: eGTS Rules

In eGTS, every FO sentence φ evaluated relative to a structure $\mathbf{M} = \langle D, I \rangle$ is associated to a game $eG(\varphi, \mathbf{M})$. This new game is identical to the game $G(\varphi, \mathbf{M})$ played according to the standard GTS rules when it is a *molecular game*, i.e. when φ is a complex formula. If φ is an atomic formula or an identity, one reaches an *atomic game*. The original game rule for atomic sentences in GTS, (R.At), is replaced by the following specific four rules:

(R.At*) In the *atomic game* $eG(\alpha, \mathbf{M})$, if either $\exists loise$ is the current verifier and α is false in $\mathbf{M}$, or she is the current falsifier and α is true, then $\forall belard$ wins and $\exists loise$ loses; else there are two cases:

  (i) α is of the form $Rt_1 \ldots t_n$, R being a n-ary relation symbol and the t_is being terms: $\forall belard$ picks out an index $i \in \{0, 1, \ldots, n\}$; if $i = 0$ then the rest of the game is as in $eG(R, \mathbf{M})$, else it is as in $eG(t_i, \mathbf{M})$.
  (ii) α is of the form $(t_1 = t_2)$, the t_is being terms: $\forall belard$ picks out an index $i \in \{1, 2\}$; the rest of the game is as in $eG(t_i, \mathbf{M})$.

(R.Rel) In the *relation game* $eG(R, \mathbf{M})$, where R is a n-ary relation symbol, $\forall belard$ chooses a n-tuple $\langle d_1, \ldots, d_n \rangle \in D^n$, and $\exists loise$ answers yes or no. If she answers yes and $\langle d_1, \ldots, d_n \rangle \in I(R)$, or she answers no and $\langle d_1, \ldots, d_n \rangle \notin I(R)$ then $\exists loise$ wins and $\forall belard$ loses; else $\forall belard$ wins and $\exists loise$ loses.

(R.Term) In the *term game* $eG(t, \mathbf{M})$, where t is a term, one of the following three cases occurs:

  (i) t is a new constant previously introduced through the play i.e. not occurring in the original formula; then $\exists loise$ wins and $\forall belard$ loses;
  (ii) t is an individual constant; then $\exists loise$ chooses an object $d \in D$; if $d = I(t)$ then $\exists loise$ wins and $\forall belard$ loses; if $d \neq I(t)$ vice versa;

(iii) t is a complex term involving a n-ary function symbol: $t = f(t_1, \ldots, t_n)$; then $\forall belard$ picks out an index $i \in \{0, 1, \ldots, n\}$. If $i > 0$ then rest of the game is as in $eG(t_i, \mathbf{M})$, and if $i = 0$ it is as in $eG(f, \mathbf{M})$.

(R.Fun) In the *function game* $eG(f, \mathbf{M})$, f being a n-ary function symbol, $\forall belard$ chooses a n-tuple $\langle d_1, \ldots, d_n \rangle \in D^n$, then $\exists loise$ chooses an object $d \in D$. If $d = I(f)(d_1, \ldots, d_n)$ then $\exists loise$ wins and $\forall belard$ loses; else vice versa.

Appendix 2: Second-Order Skolem Forms

There is a simple device to yield a result equivalent to extended GTS with no resort to (sub)atomic games, but only to skolemization. In what follows we will assume that the models under consideration contain at least two distinct elements, and that second-order formulas get a standard (full) semantic interpretation. Let:

$$\Phi(a_1, \ldots, a_k, R_1, \ldots, R_l, x_1, \ldots, x_m) \tag{9.11}$$

be a first-order sentence, where $a_1, \ldots, a_k$ are the k individual constant symbols, $R_1, \ldots, R_l$ the l relation symbols, and $x_1, \ldots, x_m$ the m variables occurring inside Φ. Being first-order Φ can be put into prenex normal form:

$$Q_1 x_1 \ldots Q_m x_m \Phi^{\otimes}(a_1, \ldots, a_k, R_1, \ldots, R_l, x_1, \ldots, x_m) \tag{9.12}$$

with $Q_i \in \{\exists, \forall\}$. Φ can also be skolemized, and is equivalent to:

$$\begin{aligned}\mathbf{2Sk}[\Phi] = \exists f_1 \ldots \exists f_n \forall t_1 \ldots \forall t_p \\ \Phi^{\circ}(a_1, \ldots, a_k, R_1, \ldots, R_l, f_1(\vec{t_1}), \ldots, f_n(\vec{t_n}), t_1, \ldots, t_p)\end{aligned} \tag{9.13}$$

where $\{t_1, \ldots, t_p\} \subseteq \{x_1, \ldots, x_m\}$ is the subset of the universally quantified variables of $\Phi^{\otimes}$, $\vec{t_i} \subseteq \{t_1, \ldots, t_p\}$ is the set of the universally quantified variables of $\Phi^{\otimes}$ on which the existentially quantified variable replaced by f_i depends, and Φ° results from $\Phi^{\otimes}$ by a mere permutation of its arguments so that the Skolem functions appear first.

Now we can replace the relation and individual constant symbols in Φ by second-order quantified variables. So Φ is equivalent to the following formula:

$$\begin{aligned}\exists g_1 \ldots \exists g_k \exists X_1 \ldots \exists X_l [\Phi(g_1, \ldots, g_k, X_1, \ldots, X_l, x_1, \ldots, x_m) \\ \wedge [g_1 = a_1] \wedge \ldots \wedge [g_k = a_k] \wedge [X_1 = R_1] \wedge \ldots \wedge [X_l = R_l]]\end{aligned} \tag{9.14}$$

The same existential generalization can be done within $\mathbf{2Sk}\Phi$, reaching the following formula:

$$\exists g_1 \ldots \exists g_k \exists X_1 \ldots \exists X_l \exists f_1 \ldots \exists f_n \forall t_1 \ldots \forall t_p$$
$$[\Phi^\circ(g_1, \ldots, g_k, X_1, \ldots, X_l, f_1(\vec{t_1}), \ldots, f_n(\vec{t_n}), t_1, \ldots, t_p) \quad (9.15)$$
$$\wedge [g_1 = a_1] \wedge \ldots \wedge [g_k = a_k] \wedge [X_1 = R_1] \wedge \ldots \wedge [X_l = R_l]]$$

Furthermore, let us change each relation variable X_i into a corresponding (indicator) function variable h_i and correlatively modify Φ° into $\Phi^\star$—so that each token of $X_i t_1 \ldots t_{n_i}$ be replaced by one of $h_i(t_1 \ldots t_{n_i}) = 1$. Hence Φ is equivalent to its extended second-order Skolem form:

$$\text{2eSk}[\Phi]_1 = \exists g_1 \ldots \exists g_k \exists h_1 \ldots \exists h_l \exists f_1 \ldots \exists f_n \forall t_1 \ldots \forall t_p$$
$$[\Phi^\star(g_1, \ldots, g_k, h_1, \ldots, h_l, f_1(\vec{t_1}), \ldots, f_n(\vec{t_n}), t_1, \ldots, t_p) \quad (9.16)$$
$$\wedge [g_1 = a_1] \wedge \ldots \wedge [g_k = a_k] \wedge [h_1 = 1_{R_1}] \wedge \ldots \wedge [h_l = 1_{R_l}]]$$

A similar first-order skolemization is then given by:

$$\text{eSk}[\Phi] = \forall t_1 \ldots \forall t_p$$
$$[\Phi^\star(\mathbf{g_1}, \ldots, \mathbf{g_k}, \mathbf{h_1}, \ldots, \mathbf{h_l}, \mathbf{f_1}(\vec{t_1}), \ldots, \mathbf{f_n}(\vec{t_n}), t_1, \ldots, t_p) \quad (9.17)$$
$$\wedge [\mathbf{g_1} = a_1] \wedge \ldots \wedge [\mathbf{g_k} = a_k] \wedge [\mathbf{h_1} = 1_{R_1}] \wedge \ldots \wedge [\mathbf{h_l} = 1_{R_l}]]$$

Another second-order Skolem form, equivalent to (9.16), obtains if we restore the original constants in $\Phi^\star$:

$$\text{2eSk}[\Phi]_2 = \exists g_1 \ldots \exists g_k \exists h_1 \ldots \exists h_l \exists f_1 \ldots \exists f_n \forall t_1 \ldots \forall t_p$$
$$[\Phi^\circ(a_1, \ldots, a_k, R_1, \ldots, R_l, f_1(\vec{t_1}), \ldots, f_n(\vec{t_n}), t_1, \ldots, t_p)$$
$$\wedge [g_1 = a_1] \wedge \ldots \wedge [g_k = a_k] \quad (9.18)$$
$$\wedge [h_1 = 1_{R_1}] \wedge \ldots \wedge [h_l = 1_{R_l}]]$$

which can be written in a condensed form as:

$$\text{2eSk}[\Phi]_2 = \exists g_1 \ldots \exists g_k \exists h_1 \ldots \exists h_l$$
$$[\text{2Sk}[\Phi] \wedge [g_1 = a_1] \wedge \ldots \wedge [g_k = a_k] \wedge \quad (9.19)$$
$$[h_1 = 1_{R_1}] \wedge \ldots \wedge [h_l = 1_{R_l}]]$$

Acknowledgments Previous and partial versions of this work were presented on several occasions during the past years—notably at APLI 2006 (Rijeka, Croatia), at JSM 2007 (Paris, France), and at the Universidade Nova de Lisboa (2008). I wish to thank Denis Bonnay, Paul Egré, Bertram Kienzle, Paul Gochet, Helge Rückert, Anna Sierszulska, and Tero Tulenheimo for their comments on earlier versions of this paper and for many fruitful discussions. All errors remain mine.

References

1. van Benthem, Johan. 2006. "The Epistemic Logic of IF Games." In *The Philosophy of Jakko Hintikka*, The Library of Living Philosophers Volume XXX, edited by R.E. Auxier and L.E. Hahn, 481–512. Chicago and La Salle, IL: Open Court.

2. Blass, Andreas, Nachum Dershowitz, and Yuri Gurevich. 2009. "When Are Two Algorithms the Same?." *The Bulletin of Symbolic Logic* 15(2):145–68.
3. Chalmers, David J. 2004. "Epistemic Two-Dimensional Semantics." *Philosophical Studies* 118:153–226.
4. Clark, Robin. 2007. "Games, Quantifiers and Pronouns." In *Game Theory and Linguistic Meaning*, edited by A.-V. Pietarinen, 139–59. Amsterdam: Elsevier.
5. Fodor, Jerry A. 1987. *Psychosemantics: The Problem of Meaning in the Philosophy of Mind.* Cambridge MA: MIT Press.
6. von Heusinger, Klaus. 2002. "Reference and Representation of Pronouns." In *Pronouns – Representation and Grammar*, edited by H.J. Simon and H. Wiese, 109–35. Amsterdam, Philadelphia, PA: Benjamin.
7. Hintikka, Jaakko. 1969. "Semantics for Propositional Attitudes." In *Philosophical Logic*, edited by J.W. Davis, D.J. Hockney and W.K. Wilson, 21–45. Dordrecht: D. Reidel.
8. Hintikka, Jaakko. 1987. "Language Understanding and Strategic Meaning." *Synthese* 73:497–529.
9. Hintikka, Jaakko. 2003. "A Second Generation Epistemic Logic and Its General Significance." In *Knowledge Contributors*, edited by V.F. Hendricks, S.A. Pedersen, and K.F. Jørgensen, 33–55. Dordrecht: Kluwer Academic Publishers.
10. Hintikka, Jaakko, and Jack Kulas. 1985. *Anaphora and Definite Descriptions: Two Applications of Game-Theoretical Semantics.* Dordrecht: D. Reidel.
11. Hintikka, Jaakko, and Gabriel Sandu. 1997. "Game-Theoretical Semantics." In *Handbook of Logic and Language*, edited by J. van Benthem and A. ter Meulen, 361–410. Amsterdam: Elsevier.
12. Jackson, Peter. 1988. "On Game-Theoretic Interactions with First-Order Knowledge Bases." In *Non-standard Logics for Automated Reasoning*, edited by P. Smets, E.H. Mamdani, D. Dubois, and H. Prade, 27–54. London: Academic Press.
13. Moschovakis, Yannis N. 1994. "Sense and Denotation as Algorithm and Value." In *Lecture Notes in Logic* 2, edited by J. Oikkonen and J. Väänänen, 210–49. Berlin: Springer.
14. Muskens, Reinhard. 2005. Sense and the Computation of Reference. *Linguistics and Philosophy* 28:473–504.
15. Pietarinen, Ahti-Veikko, and Tero Tulenheimo. 2004. *An Introduction to IF Logic*. ESSLLI 2004, Nancy. http://esslli2004.loria.fr/content/readers/45.pdf. Accessed July 16, 2011.
16. Putnam, Hilary. 1975. "The Meaning of 'Meaning'." In *Language, Mind and Knowledge*, edited by K. Gunderson, 131–93. Minneapolis, MN: University of Minnesota Press.
17. Rebuschi, Manuel. 2008. "Contenu étroit, mécanisme et fonctions de choix." *Philosophie* 100:77–94.
18. Rebuschi, Manuel. 2009. "Modalités épistémiques et modalités aléthiques chez Hintikka." *Revue Internationale de Philosophie* 250:395–404.
19. Reinhart, Tanya. 1997. "Quantifier Scope. How Labor Is Divided Between QR and Choice Functions." *Linguistics and Philosophy* 20:335–97.
20. Sandu, Gabriel. 1997. "On the Theory of Anaphora: Dynamic Predicate Logic vs. Game-Theoretical Semantics." *Linguistics and Philosophy* 20:147–74.
21. Schlenker, Philippe. 2006. "Scopal Independence: A Note on Branching & Island-Escaping Readings of Indefinites & Disjunctions." *Journal of Semantics* 23(3):281–314.
22. Stanley, Jason and Zoltán Gendler Szabó. 2000. "On Quantifier Domain Restriction." *Mind & Language* 15(2&3):219–61.
23. Winter, Yoad. 2004 "Functional Quantification." *Research on Language and Computation* 2:331–63.

Chapter 10
Dynamic Logic of Propositional Commitments

Tomoyuki Yamada

10.1 Introduction

A number of systems of dynamic epistemic logic have been developed recently as extensions of static epistemic logic by Plaza [11], Gerbrandy and Groeneveld [5], Gerbrandy [4], Baltag, Moss and Solecki [2], and Kooi and van Benthem [7] among others.[1] In these systems, dynamic changes brought about by various kinds of information transmission including public announcements as well as private communications are studied, and these communicative acts are interpreted as events that update epistemic states of some or all of the agents involved. More recently, inspired by these developments, acts of commanding and acts of promising have been modeled as updators of deontic statuses of various alternative courses of actions available to agents involved in social interactions, and "dynamified" deontic logics have been developed as extensions of multi-agent variants of static deontic logic by Yamada in [16–19]. The same strategy has also been applied in developing dynamic logics of preference change by van Benthem and Liu [13] and Liu [9].

These developments suggest the following general recipe for developing various logics that deal with particular kinds of speech acts:

- first, carefully identify the aspects of the situations affected by the speech acts that you want to study, and find or develop a static modal logic that characterizes the aspects identified,
- next, add dynamic modal operators that stand for the types of the speech acts being studied, and define model updating operations that interpret these speech acts as what update the very aspects,

---

[1] A detailed, state-of-the-art textbook exposition of dynamic epistemic logic can be found in van Ditmarsch, van der Hoek and Kooi [14].

T. Yamada (✉)
Graduate School of Letters, Hokkaido University, Sapporo, Japan
e-mail: yamada@LET.hokudai.ac.jp

- and then finally, if possible, find a complete set of reduction axioms which enables you to derive the completeness of the dynamified logic from the completeness of the static logic.

The purpose of this paper is to describe how the effects of acts of making assertions, acts of making concessions, and acts of withdrawing assertions and concessions can be captured by developing dynamic logics according to this recipe.[2]

As the recipe dictates, our first task is to identify the aspects affected by these speech acts, and find a modal logic that characterizes these aspects. We do this in Section 10.2. Our working hypothesis is that these acts update the sets of so called "propositional commitments" the agents bear, and we develop a static logic, MPCL, which deals with propositional commitments in a multi-agent environment.

According to the above recipe, our next task is to "dynamify" MPCL in order to characterize the logical dynamics of changing propositional commitments. For technical reasons, we do this in two steps. First, in Section 10.3 we extend MPCL into DMPCL, dynamified MPCL, by adding two kinds of modal operators standing for acts of asserting and acts of conceding respectively, and present a complete set of reduction axioms for it. Then, in Section 10.4, we further extend it into DMPCL$^+$, by adding another two kinds of modal operators standing for acts of withdrawing assertions and acts of withdrawing concessions respectively. As may be expected, the effects of acts of withdrawing turn out to be very difficult to capture, and the completeness problem for DMPCL$^+$ is still open. Yet the possibility of withdrawal seems to be a distinguishing characteristic common to a wide range of acts whose effects are conventional or institutional, and so the logical dynamics of withdrawal seem to be of considerable significance to the study of social interactions among rational agents. We make a brief comparison with the AGM approach to belief revision in the same section. And finally, in Section 10.5, we briefly consider an application of DMPCL$^+$ to scorekeeping for argumentation games.

10.2 The Static Base Logic MPCL

In the literature on speech act theory, agents who make assertions are usually said to be committed to the truth of their assertions (for example, see [12]). The kind of commitments incurred are sometimes called "propositional commitments" in argumentation theory. The notion of propositional commitment is introduced into the study of dialogue by Hamblin in [6], and is further studied by Walton and Krabbe in [15] with reference to a particular kind of dialogue called "persuasion dialogue". Walton and Krabbe recognize three types of commitment, namely, (1) commitments incurred by making concessions, (2) commitments called assertions, and (3) participants' dark-side commitments ([15], pp. 186–87). In this paper, we treat acts of

---

[2] This recipe was presented at the XXII World Congress of Philosophy, 30 July–5 August, 2008, Seoul, Korea.

asserting and conceding as updators of the sets of propositional commitments agents bear following Walton and Krabbe, but only consider the first two types of "commitments" as commitments. Since "dark-side commitments" are "hidden or veiled commitments" that are supposed to be fixed, they will not be affected by the kinds of speech acts to be studied; they can be modeled as hidden beliefs. We refer to the first type of commitments as "c-commitments" and the second type of commitments as "a-commitments", reserving the term "assertion" for acts of asserting.

According to Walton and Krabbe ([15], p. 8), propositional commitments constitute a special case of commitment to a course of action. The main difference between c-commitments and a-commitments lies in the fact that an agent who has an a-commitment to the proposition p is obliged to defend it if the other party in the dialogue requires her to justify it, while an agent who has a c-commitment to the proposition p is only obliged to allow the other party to use it in the arguments ([15], p. 186). As anyone who asserts that p will be obliged to allow the other party to use it in the arguments, a-commitments imply c-commitments.

Our next task is to develop a static modal logic that deals with a-commitments and c-commitments. First, we define the language.

Definition 1 Take a countably infinite set *Aprop* of proposition letters, and a finite set I of agents, with p ranging over *Aprop*, and i over I. The language $\mathcal{L}_{\mathsf{MPCL}}$ of the multi-agent propositional commitment logic MPCL is given by:

$$\varphi ::= \top \mid p \mid \neg\varphi \mid (\varphi \wedge \psi) \mid [\text{a-cmt}]_i\varphi \mid [\text{c-cmt}]_i\varphi.$$

Intuitively, a formula of the form $[\text{a-cmt}]_i\varphi$ means that the agent i has an a-commitment to the proposition φ, and a formula of the form $[\text{c-cmt}]_i\varphi$ means that i has a c-commitment to φ. We will also say that the agent i is a-committed and c-committed to φ when we have $[\text{a-cmt}]_i\varphi$ and $[\text{c-cmt}]_i\varphi$ respectively. We use $\langle\text{a-cmt}\rangle_i\varphi$ and $\langle\text{c-cmt}\rangle_i\varphi$ as the abbreviations of $\neg[\text{a-cmt}]_i\neg\varphi$ and $\neg[\text{c-cmt}]_i\neg\varphi$ respectively, in addition to the standard abbreviations such as $\vee$, $\rightarrow$, etc.

Next we examine some general principles captured in the language just defined. As anyone who asserts that p will be expected to believe or know that p, and anyone who concedes that p will be expected not to know or believe that $\neg p$, the logic of propositional commitments may be expected to be similar to epistemic logic and doxastic logic. But there are some differences. First, unlike the knowledge that p (but similar to the belief that p), one's propositional commitment to p does not entail p. Propositional commitments are not veridical. Thus the following formulas are not valid:

$$[\text{a-cmt}]_i\varphi \rightarrow \varphi$$
$$[\text{c-cmt}]_i\varphi \rightarrow \varphi.$$

This means that when we build possible worlds models for interpreting sentences of this language, we should not assume that the accessibility relations for propositional commitments are reflexive. Second, although one's beliefs are often supposed to be consistent in doxastic logic, one's set of propositional commitments can be inconsistent. Thus the following formulas are not valid:

$$\neg[\text{a-cmt}]_i \bot$$
$$\neg[\text{c-cmt}]_i \bot.$$

This means that we should not assume that the accessibility relations for propositional commitments are serial. Moreover, it is not clear whether the following analogues of the so-called positive and negative introspection axioms of epistemic and doxastic logics are valid or not:

$$[\text{a-cmt}]_i \varphi \rightarrow [\text{a-cmt}]_i [\text{a-cmt}]_i \varphi$$
$$\neg[\text{a-cmt}]_i \varphi \rightarrow [\text{a-cmt}]_i \neg[\text{a-cmt}]_i \varphi$$
$$[\text{c-cmt}]_i \varphi \rightarrow [\text{c-cmt}]_i [\text{c-cmt}]_i \varphi$$
$$\neg[\text{c-cmt}]_i \varphi \rightarrow [\text{c-cmt}]_i \neg[\text{c-cmt}]_i \varphi.$$

Leaving the discussion of these introspection principles for further research, we will only assume K-axioms and necessitation rules for a-commitments and c-commitments in addition to the assumption that each a-commitment implies its corresponding c-commitment.

Thus, we define:

Definition 2 An $\mathcal{L}_{\mathsf{MPCL}}$-model is a tuple $M = \langle W^M, \{\rhd_i^M \mid i \in I\}, \{\blacktriangleright_i^M \mid i \in I\}, V^M \rangle$ satisfying the following conditions:

(i) W^M is a non-empty set (heuristically, of "possible worlds"),
(ii) $\rhd_i^M \subseteq W^M \times W^M$ for each $i \in I$,
(iii) $\blacktriangleright_i^M \subseteq \rhd_i^M$ for each $i \in I$,
(iv) V^M is a function that assigns a subset $V^M(p)$ of W^M to each proposition letter $p \in A\text{prop}$.

We sometimes refer to a possible world $w \in W^M$ as a point in W^M or in M as well.

A truth definition for $\mathcal{L}_{\mathsf{MPCL}}$ can be given in a standard way by associating the modal operators $[\text{a-cmt}]_i$ and $[\text{c-cmt}]_i$ with $\rhd_i^M$ and $\blacktriangleright_i^M$ respectively. Thus:

Definition 3 Let M be an $\mathcal{L}_{\mathsf{MPCL}}$-model and w a point in W^M. If $p \in A\text{prop}$, and $i \in I$, then:

(a) $M, w \models_{\mathsf{MPCL}} p$ iff $w \in V^M(p)$
(b) $M, w \models_{\mathsf{MPCL}} \top$
(c) $M, w \models_{\mathsf{MPCL}} \neg\varphi$ iff   it is not the case that $M, w \models_{\mathsf{MPCL}} \varphi$
(d) $M, w \models_{\mathsf{MPCL}} (\varphi \wedge \psi)$ iff $M, w \models_{\mathsf{MPCL}} \varphi$ and $M, w \models_{\mathsf{MPCL}} \psi$
(e) $M, w \models_{\mathsf{MPCL}} [\text{a-cmt}]_i \varphi$ iff   for every v such that $\langle w, v \rangle \in \rhd_i^M$, $M, v \models_{\mathsf{MPCL}} \varphi$
(f) $M, w \models_{\mathsf{MPCL}} [\text{c-cmt}]_i \varphi$ iff   for every v such that $\langle w, v \rangle \in \blacktriangleright_i^M$, $M, v \models_{\mathsf{MPCL}} \varphi$.

A formula φ is true in an $\mathcal{L}_{\mathsf{MPCL}}$-model M at a point w of W^M if $M, w \models_{\mathsf{MPCL}} \varphi$. The semantic consequence relation and the notion of validity can also be defined in the standard way.

Now we define the proof system for MPCL.

Definition 4 The proof system for MPCL consists of the following axioms and rules:

(i) all instantiations of propositional tautologies over the present language,
(ii) K-axioms for the commitment modalities [a-cmt]$_i$ and [c-cmt]$_i$ for each $i \in I$,
(iii) modus ponens,
(iv) necessitation rules for the commitment modalities [a-cmt]$_i$ and [c-cmt]$_i$ for each $i \in I$,
(v) the axiom of the following form for each $i \in I$:

$$\text{(Mix)} \quad [\text{a-cmt}]_i \varphi \to [\text{c-cmt}]_i \varphi.$$

This proof system is easily seen to be sound, and its completeness can be proved in an entirely standard way.[3]

Theorem 1 (Completeness of MPCL) *The above proof system completely axiomatizes MPCL.*

Note that our minimal set of assumptions involves the assumption that the following proposition is true:

Proposition 1 *The set of a-commitments and the set of c-commitments of an agent are both closed under logical consequences.*

The epistemic analogue of this feature is usually called "logical omniscience", and is sometimes criticized as unrealistic. In the case of propositional commitments, however, we find the closure under logical consequences non-problematic. Rational agents should withdraw at least one of their assertions or concessions if some unwanted consequences are derived from what they have explicitly asserted or conceded. They are taken to be responsible for the logical consequences of what they have said at least to this extent.

10.3 The Logic of Acts of Asserting and Conceding DMPCL

The formulas of MPCL can be used to talk about the situations before and after the performance of an act of asserting, an act of conceding, or an act of withdrawing by modeling relevant situations using $\mathcal{L}_{\mathsf{MPCL}}$-models. For example, let $\langle M, w \rangle$

---

[3] Strictly speaking, the necessitation rule for c-commitment is redundant since Mix Axiom enables us to derive it from the necessitation rule for a-commitment. We list it here in order to record the fact that MPCL is normal.

and $\langle N, w \rangle$ be the situations before and after an agent i's act of asserting that p respectively. If i has never committed to the truth of p before, then we have:

$$M, w \not\models_{\mathsf{MPCL}} [\text{a-cmt}]_i p$$
$$N, w \models_{\mathsf{MPCL}} [\text{a-cmt}]_i p.$$

Thus MPCL can be used to characterize the sets of propositions to which agents are committed with respect to each stage of their interactions. But in the above example, neither the difference between the stages before and after i's act of asserting nor i's act of asserting that links them can be talked about in MPCL; they are talked about in the metalanguage. Thus our next task is to dynamify MPCL in order to have an object language that can be used to characterize the logical dynamics of changing propositional commitments. As was said before, we do this in two steps for technical reasons. First, we extend MPCL into DMPCL, dynamified MPCL, by adding dynamic modal operators standing for acts of asserting and acts of conceding in this section. Then, in the next section, we further extend it into DMPCL$^+$, by adding another set of dynamic modal operators standing for acts of withdrawing.

Now we extend the language:

Definition 5 Take the same countably infinite set *Aprop* of proposition letters and the same finite set I of agents as before, with p ranging over *Aprop*, and i over I. The language $\mathcal{L}_{\mathsf{DMPCL}}$ of dynamified multi-agent propositional commitment logic DMPCL is given by:

$$\varphi ::= \top \mid p \mid \neg \varphi \mid (\varphi \wedge \psi) \mid [\text{a-cmt}]_i \varphi \mid [\text{c-cmt}]_i \varphi \mid [\pi]\varphi$$
$$\pi ::= \text{assert}_i \varphi \mid \text{concede}_i \varphi.$$

Note that all the formulas of $\mathcal{L}_{\mathsf{MPCL}}$ are also formulas of $\mathcal{L}_{\mathsf{DMPCL}}$.

A truth definition for this language can be given with reference to $\mathcal{L}_{\mathsf{MPCL}}$-models by expanding the truth definition for $\mathcal{L}_{\mathsf{MPCL}}$ with two additional clauses for the new kinds of formulas as follows:

Definition 6 Let M be an $\mathcal{L}_{\mathsf{MPCL}}$-model and w a point in W^M. If $p \in Aprop$, and $i \in I$, then:

(a) $M, w \models_{\mathsf{DMPCL}} p$ iff $w \in V^M(p)$
(b) $M, w \models_{\mathsf{DMPCL}} \top$
(c) $M, w \models_{\mathsf{DMPCL}} \neg \varphi$ iff   it is not the case that $M, w \models_{\mathsf{DMPCL}} \varphi$
(d) $M, w \models_{\mathsf{DMPCL}} (\varphi \wedge \psi)$ iff $M, w \models_{\mathsf{DMPCL}} \varphi$ and $M, w \models_{\mathsf{DMPCL}} \psi$
(e) $M, w \models_{\mathsf{DMPCL}} [\text{a-cmt}]_i \varphi$ iff   for every v such that $\langle w, v \rangle \in \triangleright_i^M$, $M, v \models_{\mathsf{DMPCL}} \varphi$
(f) $M, w \models_{\mathsf{DMPCL}} [\text{c-cmt}]_i \varphi$ iff   for every v such that $\langle w, v \rangle \in \blacktriangleright_i^M$, $M, v \models_{\mathsf{DMPCL}} \varphi$
(g) $M, w \models_{\mathsf{DMPCL}} [\text{assert}_i \chi] \varphi$ iff $M_{\text{assert}_i \chi}, w \models_{\mathsf{DMPCL}} \varphi$
(h) $M, w \models_{\mathsf{DMPCL}} [\text{concede}_i \chi] \varphi$ iff $M_{\text{concede}_i \chi}, w \models_{\mathsf{DMPCL}} \varphi$,

where $M_{\text{assert}_i \chi}$ is the $\mathcal{L}_{\text{MPCL}}$-model obtained from M by replacing $\rhd_i^M$ and $\blacktriangleright_i^M$ with their subsets $\{\langle x, y \rangle \in \rhd_i^M \mid M, y \models_{\text{DMPCL}} \chi\}$ and $\{\langle x, y \rangle \in \blacktriangleright_i^M \mid M, y \models_{\text{DMPCL}} \chi\}$ respectively, and $M_{\text{concede}_i \chi}$ is the $\mathcal{L}_{\text{MPCL}}$-model obtained from M by replacing $\blacktriangleright_i^M$ with its subset $\{\langle x, y \rangle \in \blacktriangleright_i^M \mid M, y \models_{\text{DMPCL}} \chi\}$. A formula φ is true in an $\mathcal{L}_{\text{MPCL}}$-model M at a point w of W^M if $M, w \models_{\text{DMPCL}} \varphi$. The semantic consequence relation and the notion of validity can also be defined in the standard way.

Note that the truth of the formula of the form $[\text{assert}_i \chi]\varphi$ and that of the formula of the form $[\text{concede}_i \chi]\varphi$ at w in M are defined in terms of the truth of the formula of the form φ at w in the updated models $M_{\text{assert}_i \chi}$ and $M_{\text{concede}_i \chi}$ respectively. Intuitively, the update by $\text{assert}_i \chi$ cuts every accessibility link $\langle x, y \rangle$ of $\rhd_i^M$ and $\blacktriangleright_i^M$ if χ doesn't hold at y in M, and the update by $\text{concede}_i \chi$ cuts every accessibility link $\langle x, y \rangle$ of $\blacktriangleright_i^M$ if χ doesn't hold at y in M. This guarantees that the accessibility relation associated with c-commitments of any agent $i \in I$ will always be a subset of the accessibility relation associated with i's a-commitments, and so the updated models $M_{\text{assert}_i \chi}$ and $M_{\text{concede}_i \chi}$ will also be $\mathcal{L}_{\text{MPCL}}$-models.

Note also that the first six clauses reproduce the corresponding clauses in the truth definition for $\mathcal{L}_{\text{MPCL}}$ faithfully. Thus we have:

Corollary 1 *Let M be an $\mathcal{L}_{\text{MPCL}}$-model and w a point in M. Then for any $\varphi \in \mathcal{L}_{\text{MPCL}}$, we have:*

$$M, w \models_{\text{DMPCL}} \varphi \text{ iff } M, w \models_{\text{MPCL}} \varphi.$$

For each $i \in I$, a formula $\varphi \in \mathcal{L}_{\text{MPCL}}$ is said to be i-free if neither the operator $[\text{a-cmt}]_i$ nor the operator $[\text{c-cmt}]_i$ occurs in it. The following corollary can be proved by induction on the length of ψ:

Corollary 2 *If $\psi \in \mathcal{L}_{\text{MPCL}}$ is i-free, then for any $\varphi \in \mathcal{L}_{\text{MPCL}}$, we have:*

$$M, w \models_{\text{DMPCL}} \psi \quad \text{iff} \quad M_{\text{assert}_i \varphi}, w \models_{\text{DMPCL}} \psi$$
$$M, w \models_{\text{DMPCL}} \psi \quad \text{iff} \quad M_{\text{concede}_i \varphi}, w \models_{\text{DMPCL}} \psi.$$

We also have:

Proposition 2 *If $\varphi \in \mathcal{L}_{\text{MPCL}}$ is i-free, the following three principles are valid:*

$$[\text{assert}_i \varphi][\text{a-cmt}]_i \varphi$$
$$[\text{assert}_i \varphi][\text{c-cmt}]_i \varphi$$
$$[\text{concede}_i \varphi][\text{c-cmt}]_i \varphi.$$

These restricted principles partially characterize the workings of acts of asserting and acts of conceding: though not without exceptions, they usually generate corresponding propositional commitments.[4]

If $\varphi \in \mathcal{L}_{\mathsf{MPCL}}$ is both i-free and j-free, we have

$$[\mathsf{assert}_i\varphi][\mathsf{assert}_j\neg\varphi]([\text{a-cmt}]_i\varphi \wedge [\text{a-cmt}]_j\neg\varphi).$$

This means that if an agent i asserts φ in $\langle M, w \rangle$, and another agent j asserts $\neg\varphi$ after that, we have

$$(M_{\mathsf{assert}_i\varphi})_{\mathsf{assert}_j\neg\varphi}, w \models_{\mathsf{DMPCL}} ([\text{a-cmt}]_i\varphi \wedge [\text{a-cmt}]_j\neg\varphi).$$

Thus, even if two agents jointly make mutually incompatible assertions, we can use DMPCL to represent the resulting situation without falling into a contradiction. While $(\varphi \wedge \neg\varphi)$ is a contradiction, $([\text{a-cmt}]_i\varphi \wedge [\text{a-cmt}]_j\neg\varphi)$ is not. This feature can be important when we design information systems which have to deal with possibly conflicting inputs from multiple agents. We have to be able to accommodate differences of opinions among agents without making the whole system inconsistent.[5]

Note also that even $[\text{a-cmt}]_i(\varphi \wedge \neg\varphi)$ is not by itself a contradiction, although it ascribes a contradictory a-commitment to the agent i. Such commitment will be generated if i asserts both φ and $\neg\varphi$, for example. In such a situation, accessibility relations associated with i's a-commitments and c-commitments will become empty, and i will be both a-committed and c-committed to every proposition. Since a set of propositional commitments an agent has can be inconsistent, we find it important for us to be able to talk about speech acts that lead to such inconsistencies. As the so-called D Axiom would preclude the very possibility of such situations, we have avoided including it in our proof system for MPCL.

The proof system for DMPCL is given by expanding that for MPCL.

Definition 7 The proof system for DMPCL comprises all the axioms and rules of the proof system for MPCL, the necessitation rules for assertion modality $[\mathsf{assert}_i\varphi]$ and concession modality $[\mathsf{concede}_i\varphi]$, and the following axioms:

(A1) $[\mathsf{assert}_i\varphi]p \quad \leftrightarrow \quad p$
(A2) $[\mathsf{assert}_i\varphi]\top \quad \leftrightarrow \quad \top$
(A3) $[\mathsf{assert}_i\varphi]\neg\psi \quad \leftrightarrow \quad \neg[\mathsf{assert}_i\varphi]\psi$
(A4) $[\mathsf{assert}_i\varphi](\psi \wedge \chi) \quad \leftrightarrow \quad [\mathsf{assert}_i\varphi]\psi \wedge [\mathsf{assert}_i\varphi]\chi$
(A5) $[\mathsf{assert}_i\varphi][\text{a-cmt}]_j\psi \quad \leftrightarrow \quad [\text{a-cmt}]_j[\mathsf{assert}_i\varphi]\psi \qquad (i \neq j)$

---

[4] The restriction on φ is motivated by the fact that the truth of φ at w in M does not guarantee the truth of φ at w in $M_{\mathsf{assert}_i\varphi}$ or the truth of φ at w in $M_{\mathsf{concede}_i\varphi}$ if φ is not i-free. For more on this point, see [16, p. 9].

[5] An interesting discussion of the usefulness of explicit treatment of speech acts in such a system can be found in [10].

10 Dynamic Logic of Propositional Commitments

(A6) $[\text{assert}_i \varphi][\text{a-cmt}]_i \psi \leftrightarrow [\text{a-cmt}]_i (\varphi \rightarrow [\text{assert}_i \varphi] \psi)$
(A7) $[\text{assert}_i \varphi][\text{c-cmt}]_j \psi \leftrightarrow [\text{c-cmt}]_j [\text{assert}_i \varphi] \psi \quad (i \neq j)$
(A8) $[\text{assert}_i \varphi][\text{c-cmt}]_i \psi \leftrightarrow [\text{c-cmt}]_i (\varphi \rightarrow [\text{assert}_i \varphi] \psi)$
(C1) $[\text{concede}_i \varphi] p \leftrightarrow p$
(C2) $[\text{concede}_i \varphi] \top \leftrightarrow \top$
(C3) $[\text{concede}_i \varphi] \neg \psi \leftrightarrow \neg [\text{concede}_i \varphi] \psi$
(C4) $[\text{concede}_i \varphi](\psi \wedge \chi) \leftrightarrow [\text{concede}_i \varphi] \psi \wedge [\text{concede}_i \varphi] \chi$
(C5) $[\text{concede}_i \varphi][\text{a-cmt}]_j \psi \leftrightarrow [\text{a-cmt}]_j [\text{concede}_i \varphi] \psi \quad (\text{for any } j)$
(C6) $[\text{concede}_i \varphi][\text{c-cmt}]_j \psi \leftrightarrow [\text{c-cmt}]_j [\text{concede}_i \varphi] \psi \quad (i \neq j)$
(C7) $[\text{concede}_i \varphi][\text{c-cmt}]_i \psi \leftrightarrow [\text{c-cmt}]_i (\varphi \rightarrow [\text{concede}_i \varphi] \psi).$

Axioms (A6), (A8) and (C7) are crucial here. They capture how the acts of asserting and conceding update the model. Consider (A6). The left-hand side of it says that $[\text{a-cmt}]_i \psi$ holds after the update by $\text{assert}_i \varphi$. The right-hand side of it specifies the necessary and sufficient conditions for this in terms of the conditions that hold before the update. Take an arbitrary $\mathcal{L}_{\text{MPCL}}$-model M and an arbitrary world w of M. $[\text{a-cmt}]_i \psi$ holds at w in the updated model $M_{\text{assert}_i \varphi}$ iff ψ holds at every world v that is accessible with respect to i's a-commitment ($[\text{a-cmt}]_i$-accessible, hereafter) from w in $M_{\text{assert}_i \varphi}$. Since the update by $\text{assert}_i \varphi$ cuts every $[\text{a-cmt}]_i$-arrow arriving in non-φ-worlds in M, only the φ-worlds $[\text{a-cmt}]_i$-accessible from w in M remain $[\text{a-cmt}]_i$-accessible from w in $M_{\text{assert}_i \varphi}$. But ψ holds at such world v in the updated model $M_{\text{assert}_i \varphi}$ iff $[\text{assert}_i \varphi] \psi$ holds at v in M. Hence $[\text{a-cmt}]_i \psi$ holds at w in the updated model $M_{\text{assert}_i \varphi}$ iff $[\text{a-cmt}]_i (\varphi \rightarrow [\text{assert}_i \varphi] \psi)$ holds at w in M before the update. Thus (A6) says that the necessary and sufficient condition for $[\text{a-cmt}]_i \psi$ to hold at w in $M_{\text{assert}_i \varphi}$ is that every φ world $[\text{a-cmt}]_i$-accessible from w in M is a world where $[\text{assert}_i \varphi] \psi$ holds in M. Axioms (A8) and (C7) can be understood similarly.

Note that Axioms (A1), (A2), (C1), and (C2) enable us to eliminate each occurrence of assertion modalities and concession modalities prefixed to a proposition letter or the constant $\top$. The other axioms enable us to reduce the length of the subformula to which an assertion modality or a concession modality is prefixed. Thus, these axioms, sometimes called "reduction axioms", enable us to define a translation function that takes a formula of $\mathcal{L}_{\text{DMPCL}}$ and yields a formula of $\mathcal{L}_{\text{MPCL}}$ that is provably equivalent to the original formula.

Definition 8 The translation function that takes a formula of $\mathcal{L}_{\text{DMPCL}}$ and yields a formula of $\mathcal{L}_{\text{MPCL}}$ is defined as follows:

$t(p) = p$
$t(\top) = \top$
$t(\neg \varphi) = \neg t(\varphi)$
$t(\varphi \wedge \psi) = t(\varphi) \wedge t(\psi)$

$t([\text{a-cmt}]_i \varphi)$ $\quad = [\text{a-cmt}]_i t(\varphi)$

$t([\text{c-cmt}]_i \varphi)$ $\quad = [\text{c-cmt}]_i t(\varphi)$

$t([\text{assert}_i \varphi] p)$ $\quad = p$

$t([\text{assert}_i \varphi] \top)$ $\quad = \top$

$t([\text{assert}_i \varphi] \neg \psi)$ $\quad = \neg t([\text{assert}_i \varphi] \psi)$

$t([\text{assert}_i \varphi](\psi \wedge \chi))$ $\quad = t([\text{assert}_i \varphi]\psi) \wedge t([\text{assert}_i \varphi]\chi)$

$t([\text{assert}_i \varphi][\text{a-cmt}]_j \psi)$ $\quad = [\text{a-cmt}]_j t([\text{assert}_i \varphi]\psi) \quad (i \neq j)$

$t([\text{assert}_i \varphi][\text{a-cmt}]_i \psi)$ $\quad = [\text{a-cmt}]_i t(\varphi \rightarrow [\text{assert}_i \varphi]\psi)$

$t([\text{assert}_i \varphi][\text{c-cmt}]_j \psi)$ $\quad = [\text{c-cmt}]_j t([\text{assert}_i \varphi]\psi) \quad (i \neq j)$

$t([\text{assert}_i \varphi][\text{c-cmt}]_i \psi)$ $\quad = [\text{c-cmt}]_i t(\varphi \rightarrow [\text{assert}_i \varphi]\psi)$

$t([\text{assert}_i \varphi][\text{assert}_j \psi]\chi)$ $\quad = t([\text{assert}_i \varphi] t([\text{assert}_j \psi]\chi))$

$t([\text{assert}_i \varphi][\text{concede}_j \psi]\chi)$ $\quad = t([\text{assert}_i \varphi] t([\text{concede}_j \psi]\chi))$

$t([\text{concede}_i \varphi] p)$ $\quad = p$

$t([\text{concede}_i \varphi] \top)$ $\quad = \top$

$t([\text{concede}_i \varphi] \neg \psi)$ $\quad = \neg t([\text{concede}_i \varphi]\psi)$

$t([\text{concede}_i \varphi](\psi \wedge \chi))$ $\quad = t([\text{concede}_i \varphi]\psi) \wedge t([\text{concede}_i \varphi]\chi)$

$t([\text{concede}_i \varphi][\text{a-cmt}]_j \psi)$ $\quad = [\text{a-cmt}]_j t([\text{concede}_i \varphi]\psi)$

$t([\text{concede}_i \varphi][\text{c-cmt}]_j \psi)$ $\quad = [\text{c-cmt}]_j t([\text{concede}_i \varphi]\psi) \quad (i \neq j)$

$t([\text{concede}_i \varphi][\text{c-cmt}]_i \psi)$ $\quad = [\text{c-cmt}]_i t(\varphi \rightarrow [\text{concede}_i \varphi]\psi)$

$t([\text{concede}_i \varphi][\text{assert}_j \psi]\chi)$ $\quad = t([\text{concede}_i \varphi] t([\text{assert}_j \psi]\chi))$

$t([\text{concede}_i \varphi][\text{concede}_j \psi]\chi) = t([\text{concede}_i \varphi] t([\text{concede}_j \psi]\chi))$.

This translation enables us to derive the completeness of DMPCL from the completeness of $\mathcal{L}_{\text{MPCL}}$.[6] Thus,

Theorem 2 (Completeness of DMPCL) *There is a complete axiomatization of DMPCL.*

10.4 A Further Extension DMPCL$^+$

Consider a formula of the form $[\text{assert}_i \chi][\text{assert}_j \xi][\text{assert}_i \eta]\varphi$. It means that φ holds after i asserts η after j asserts ξ after i asserts χ, and it is true at w in M if and only if φ is true at w in the updated model $((M_{\text{assert}_i \chi})_{\text{assert}_j \xi})_{\text{assert}_i \eta}$. Let an expression of the form $\circlearrowleft \text{assert}_i \chi$ and $\circlearrowleft \text{concede}_i \chi$ represent the type of i's acts of withdrawing i's own assertion that χ and i's acts of withdrawing i's own concession that χ respectively. Then what will we get if we update $((M_{\text{assert}_i \chi})_{\text{assert}_j \xi})_{\text{assert}_i \eta}$

---

[6] The outline of the derivation is completely similar to that of the completeness of ECL given in [16].

10 Dynamic Logic of Propositional Commitments

with ◌ assert$_i\chi$, for example? We suggest that what we will get in that situation should be calculated by calculating what we would have in $(M_{\text{assert}_j\xi})_{\text{assert}_i\eta}$, as far as propositional commitments are concerned.

This is not meant to imply that the act of withdrawing could affect the past history. What we are proposing is that the set of propositional commitments an agent i will bear after withdrawing i's own act of asserting that χ in the situation $\langle(((M_{\text{assert}_i\chi})_{\text{assert}_j\xi})_{\text{assert}_i\eta}, w\rangle$, for example, should be the same as the set of propositional commitments i would bear in the situation $\langle(M_{\text{assert}_j\xi})_{\text{assert}_i\eta}, w\rangle$. Intuitively, the set of propositional commitments an agent i will bear after withdrawing her own assertion that χ will be the same as the set of propositional commitments she would bear if she had not asserted that χ but had made all the other assertions and concessions she actually made. We develop a formal treatment of withdrawals which incorporates this intuitive idea as faithfully as possible in this section.

First, we extend the language.

Definition 9 Take the same countably infinite set *Aprop* of proposition letters and the same finite set I of agents as before, with p ranging over *Aprop*, and i over I. The language $\mathcal{L}_{\text{DMPCL}^+}$ of dynamified multi-agent propositional commitment logic with withdrawals DMPCL$^+$ is given by:

$$\varphi ::= \top \mid p \mid \neg\varphi \mid (\varphi \wedge \psi) \mid [\text{a-cmt}]_i\varphi \mid [\text{c-cmt}]_i\varphi \mid [\pi]\varphi$$
$$\pi ::= \text{assert}_i\varphi \mid \text{concede}_i\varphi \mid \circlearrowright \text{assert}_i\varphi \mid \circlearrowright \text{concede}_i\varphi.$$

Note that withdrawals are allowed only for assertions and concessions; we have not allowed withdrawals of withdrawals here. Instead of withdrawals of withdrawals, an agent can assert or concede again the same propositions which she once asserted or conceded but has subsequently withdrawn.[7]

Note also that we only allow agents to withdraw their own assertions or concessions. Although there may be agents who have the authority to withdraw certain speech acts performed by other agents in hierarchical organizations, we leave such complexity for further research.

In order to give a truth definition for the above language, we need to consider the effects of acts of withdrawing performed at the stages we will be in after going

---

[7] Strictly speaking, such acts of re-asserting and re-conceding do not always have the same effects as acts of withdrawals of withdrawals. The effect of the act of withdrawing the act of withdrawing of the form ◌ assert$_i\varphi$, for example, can be different from the effects of re-asserting φ. Consider a case where φ is asserted at stage s_i, withdrawn at a later stage s_j, and re-asserted at a still later stage s_k by an agent. What would happen if, instead of re-asserting φ at s_k, the agent withdrew at s_k her earlier withdrawal of φ at s_j? Her earlier assertion of φ at s_i would become effective again. Now, the effects of re-asserting φ at s_k can be different from the effects of asserting φ at s_i as the former depend on the things said during the discourse between s_i and s_k. To be sure the things said during the discourse between s_i and s_k would also affect the states after her "resurrected" assertion of φ at S_i. But there is no guarantee that they would "neutralize", so to speak, the difference in such a way that the state after the withdrawal at s_K of her earlier withdrawal would be exactly the same as the actual state after her re-asserting of φ at s_K.

through various arbitrary sequences of relevant speech acts involving acts of withdrawing as well as acts of asserting and conceding. We call such sequences commitment affecting act sequences, or caa-sequences for short. Before examining the effects of acts of withdrawing with reference to arbitrary caa-sequences, however, we will consider their effects with reference to somewhat simpler sequences consisting of only acts of asserting and conceding. We call such a sequence a positive commitment act sequence, or a pca-sequence for short. Then the above example suggests that the effects of an act of withdrawing performed at the stage we will be in after going through an arbitrary pca-sequence σ starting from $\langle M, w \rangle$ can be captured by considering the model obtained from M by updating M with another pca-sequence obtained from σ by deleting from σ the assertion or the concession that was withdrawn. Thus, in the above example, we considered the model $(M_{\text{assert}_j \xi})_{\text{assert}_i \eta}$ in order to examine the effects of the act of withdrawing of the form $\circlearrowleft \text{assert}_i \chi$ performed in the situation $\langle ((M_{\text{assert}_j \chi})_{\text{assert}_j \xi})_{\text{assert}_i \eta}, w \rangle$, and the pca-sequence $\langle \text{assert}_j \xi, \text{assert}_i \eta \rangle$ is exactly what we get by deleting the occurrence of $\text{assert}_i \chi$ from the pca-sequence $\langle \text{assert}_i \chi, \text{assert}_j \xi, \text{assert}_i \eta \rangle$.

Note that an arbitrary pca-sequence σ might include two or more occurrences of a given assertion or concession, or might include none of them. For the sake of generality, we will also talk of σ as a sequence even if σ is empty or σ consists of only one speech act. Thus we define:

Definition 10 Let $\sigma = \langle \pi_1, \cdots, \pi_n \rangle$ be a (possibly empty) pca-sequence. We define the reduced pca-sequences $\sigma \upharpoonright \circlearrowleft \text{assert}_i \varphi$ and $\sigma \upharpoonright \circlearrowleft \text{concede}_i \varphi$, to be obtained by deleting from σ every occurrence of the act of type $\text{assert}_i \varphi$ and every occurrence of the act of type $\text{concede}_i \varphi$ respectively, as follows:

$\sigma \upharpoonright \circlearrowleft \text{assert}_i \varphi$

$= \begin{cases} \sigma & \text{if } \sigma \text{ is empty} \\ \langle \pi_1, \cdots, \pi_{n-1} \rangle \upharpoonright \circlearrowleft \text{assert}_i \varphi & \text{if } \sigma = \langle \pi_1, \cdots, \pi_n \rangle, \text{ and } \pi_n = \text{assert}_i \varphi \\ \langle \langle \pi_1, \cdots, \pi_{n-1} \rangle \upharpoonright \circlearrowleft \text{assert}_i \varphi, \pi_n \rangle & \text{if } \sigma = \langle \pi_1, \cdots, \pi_n \rangle, \text{ and } \pi_n \neq \text{assert}_i \varphi \end{cases}$

and

$\sigma \upharpoonright \circlearrowleft \text{concede}_i \varphi$

$= \begin{cases} \sigma & \text{if } \sigma \text{ is empty} \\ \langle \pi_1, \cdots, \pi_{n-1} \rangle \upharpoonright \circlearrowleft \text{concede}_i \varphi & \text{if } \sigma = \langle \pi_1, \cdots, \pi_n \rangle, \text{ and } \pi_n = \text{concede}_i \varphi \\ \langle \langle \pi_1, \cdots, \pi_{n-1} \rangle \upharpoonright \circlearrowleft \text{concede}_i \varphi, \pi_n \rangle & \text{if } \sigma = \langle \pi_1, \cdots, \pi_n \rangle, \text{ and } \pi_n \neq \text{concede}_i \varphi. \end{cases}$

Note that $\sigma \upharpoonright \circlearrowleft \text{assert}_i \varphi$ and $\sigma \upharpoonright \circlearrowleft \text{concede}_i \varphi$ are pca-sequences. Note also that we allow acts of withdrawing to withdraw repeated assertions or repeated concessions in one go, so to speak. For example, we have:

$\langle \text{assert}_i \chi, \text{assert}_j \xi, \text{assert}_k \eta, \text{assert}_i \chi \rangle \upharpoonright \circlearrowleft \text{assert}_i \chi = \langle \text{assert}_j \xi, \text{assert}_k \eta \rangle$.

10 Dynamic Logic of Propositional Commitments

If an agent who insisted that φ by repeatedly asserting that φ comes to wish to withdraw her assertion that φ, it would be strange if she wished to withdraw only some of her acts of asserting φ while keeping others untouched. She would still be a-committed to φ.

We are now in a position to define a special pca-sequence σ^* that can be used to calculate the propositional commitments agents bear after going through an arbitrary caa-sequence σ. We get σ^* from σ by applying the procedures we have just introduced to the occurrences of withdrawals in σ according to the order they occur in σ.

Definition 11 Given an arbitrary caa-sequence σ possibly involving acts of withdrawing as well as acts of asserting and acts of conceding, we define its corresponding pca-sequence σ^* as follows:

$$\sigma^* = \begin{cases} \sigma & \text{if } \sigma \text{ is empty} \\ \langle\langle\pi_1, \cdots, \pi_{n-1}\rangle^*, \text{assert}_i\varphi\rangle & \text{if } \sigma = \langle\pi_1, \cdots, \pi_n\rangle, \text{ and } \pi_n = \text{assert}_i\varphi \\ \langle\langle\pi_1, \cdots, \pi_{n-1}\rangle^*, \text{concede}_i\varphi\rangle & \text{if } \sigma = \langle\pi_1, \cdots, \pi_n\rangle, \text{ and } \pi_n = \text{concede}_i\varphi \\ \langle\pi_1, \cdots, \pi_{n-1}\rangle^* \upharpoonright \circlearrowleft \text{assert}_i\varphi & \text{if } \sigma = \langle\pi_1, \cdots, \pi_n\rangle, \text{ and } \pi_n = \circlearrowleft \text{assert}_i\varphi \\ \langle\pi_1, \cdots, \pi_{n-1}\rangle^* \upharpoonright \circlearrowleft \text{concede}_i\varphi & \text{if } \sigma = \langle\pi_1, \cdots, \pi_n\rangle, \text{ and } \pi_n = \circlearrowleft \text{concede}_i\varphi. \end{cases}$$

This definition enables us to deal with the effects of an act of withdrawing performed at the stage we will be in after going through an arbitrary caa-sequence σ. We just have to work with the reduced pca-sequences $\sigma^* \upharpoonright \circlearrowleft \text{assert}_i\varphi$ and $\sigma^* \upharpoonright \circlearrowleft \text{concede}_i\varphi$.

In order to give a truth definition for DMPCL^+ with the help of these definitions, however, we have to exercise due care. In the notation used in the truth definition for DMPCL, $(\cdots ((M_{\pi_1})_{\pi_2}) \cdots)_{\pi_n}$ represents the model obtained from M by updating it successively with the sequence of speech acts $\langle\pi_1, \pi_2, \cdots, \pi_n\rangle$, which is a pca-sequence in our current terminology. If $\sigma = \langle\pi_1, \pi_2, \cdots, \pi_n\rangle$, we may wish to abbreviate $(\cdots ((M_{\pi_1})_{\pi_2}) \cdots)_{\pi_n}$ as M_σ, and talk of it as the model obtained from M by updating it with σ. Then the model world pair $\langle M_\sigma, w\rangle$ will represent the situation we will be in after going through the whole pca-sequence σ of assertions and concessions starting from $\langle M, w\rangle$. But there can be another $\mathcal{L}_{\text{MPCL}}$-model N and another pca-sequence τ such that $M = N_\tau$. Thus σ can be considered as a partial representation of the whole discourse that leads to $\langle M_\sigma, w\rangle$.

This is unsurprising since agents involved may have non-trivial propositional commitments even in the situation $\langle M, w\rangle$; such commitments can be considered as the products of previous discourse that led to $\langle M, w\rangle$. If we only deal with acts of asserting and conceding, there is nothing problematic about this. But it can lead to a contradiction when we take acts of withdrawing into consideration. The result of updating M_σ with $\circlearrowleft \text{assert}_i \chi$ might not be identical with the result of updating $(N_\tau)_\sigma$ with $\circlearrowleft \text{assert}_i \chi$ since $\text{assert}_i \chi$ might occur in τ. Such a discrepancy is inadmissible since $M = N_\tau$. In order to avoid this problem, we will keep models and sequences of speech acts separate as you will see in the truth definition below.

Definition 12 Let M be an $\mathcal{L}_{\text{MPCL}}$-model, σ an arbitrary caa-sequence, σ^* the corresponding pca-sequence of σ, and w a point in M. If $p \in A\text{prop}$, and $i \in I$, then:

(a) $M, \sigma, w \models_{\mathsf{DMPCL^+}} p$ iff $w \in V^M(p)$
(b) $M, \sigma, w \models_{\mathsf{DMPCL^+}} \top$
(c) $M, \sigma, w \models_{\mathsf{DMPCL^+}} \neg\varphi$ iff   it is not the case that $M, \sigma, w \models_{\mathsf{DMPCL^+}} \varphi$
(d) $M, \sigma, w \models_{\mathsf{DMPCL^+}} (\varphi \wedge \psi)$ iff $M, \sigma, w \models_{\mathsf{DMPCL^+}} \varphi$ and $M, \sigma, w \models_{\mathsf{DMPCL^+}} \psi$
(e) $M, \sigma, w \models_{\mathsf{DMPCL^+}} [\text{a-cmt}]_i \varphi$ iff   for all v such that $\langle w, v \rangle \in \triangleright_i^M \!\upharpoonright\! \sigma^*$, $M, \sigma^*, v \models_{\mathsf{DMPCL^+}} \varphi$
(f) $M, \sigma, w \models_{\mathsf{DMPCL^+}} [\text{c-cmt}]_i \varphi$ iff   for all v such that $\langle w, v \rangle \in \blacktriangleright_i^M \!\upharpoonright\! \sigma^*$, $M, \sigma^*, v \models_{\mathsf{DMPCL^+}} \varphi$
(g) $M, \sigma, w \models_{\mathsf{DMPCL^+}} [\text{assert}_i \chi] \varphi$ iff $M, \langle \sigma, \text{assert}_i \chi \rangle, w \models_{\mathsf{DMPCL^+}} \varphi$
(h) $M, \sigma, w \models_{\mathsf{DMPCL^+}} [\text{concede}_i \chi] \varphi$ iff $M, \langle \sigma, \text{concede}_i \chi \rangle, w \models_{\mathsf{DMPCL^+}} \varphi$
(i) $M, \sigma, w \models_{\mathsf{DMPCL^+}} [\circlearrowleft \text{assert}_i \chi] \varphi$ iff $M, \sigma^* \!\upharpoonright\! \circlearrowleft \text{assert}_i \chi, w \models_{\mathsf{DMPCL^+}} \varphi$
(j) $M, \sigma, w \models_{\mathsf{DMPCL^+}} [\circlearrowleft \text{concede}_i \chi] \varphi$ iff $M, \sigma^* \!\upharpoonright\! \circlearrowleft \text{concede}_i \chi, w \models_{\mathsf{DMPCL^+}} \varphi$,

where

$$\triangleright_i^M \!\upharpoonright\! \sigma^* = \begin{cases} \triangleright_i^M & \text{if } \sigma^* \text{ is empty,} \\ \{\langle x, y \rangle \in \triangleright_i^M \!\upharpoonright\! \langle \pi_1, \ldots, \pi_{n-1} \rangle \mid M, \langle \pi_1, \ldots, \pi_{n-1} \rangle, y \models_{\mathsf{DMPCL^+}} \psi \} \\ & \text{if } \sigma^* = \langle \pi_1, \ldots, \pi_n \rangle \text{ and } \pi_n = \text{assert}_i \psi, \\ \triangleright_i^M \!\upharpoonright\! \langle \pi_1, \ldots, \pi_{n-1} \rangle & \text{if } \sigma^* = \langle \pi_1, \ldots, \pi_n \rangle \text{ and } \pi_n \neq \text{assert}_i \psi, \end{cases}$$

and

$$\blacktriangleright_i^M \!\upharpoonright\! \sigma^* = \begin{cases} \blacktriangleright_i^M & \text{if } \sigma^* \text{ is empty,} \\ \{\langle x, y \rangle \in \blacktriangleright_i^M \!\upharpoonright\! \langle \pi_1, \ldots, \pi_{n-1} \rangle \mid M, \langle \pi_1, \ldots, \pi_{n-1} \rangle, y \models_{\mathsf{DMPCL^+}} \psi \} \\ & \text{if } \sigma^* = \langle \pi_1, \ldots, \pi_n \rangle \text{ and } \pi_n = \text{assert}_i \psi \text{ or } \pi_n = \text{concede}_i \psi, \\ \blacktriangleright_i^M \!\upharpoonright\! \langle \pi_1, \ldots, \pi_{n-1} \rangle \\ & \text{if } \sigma^* = \langle \pi_1, \ldots, \pi_n \rangle, \pi_n \neq \text{assert}_i \psi \text{ and } \pi_n \neq \text{concede}_i \psi. \end{cases}$$

A formula φ is true in an $\mathcal{L}_{\mathsf{MPCL}}$-model M with respect to an arbitrary caa-sequence σ at a point w of M if $M, \sigma, w \models_{\mathsf{DMPCL^+}} \varphi$. The semantic consequence relation and the notion of validity can also be defined in the obvious way.

Note that acts of withdrawing behave very differently from what theorists of belief revision call "contraction". Let $\mathcal{B}$ be the set of beliefs of an agent, say a. Then in the AGM approach, contraction $\ominus$ is supposed to satisfy the postulate that $\varphi \notin \mathcal{B} \ominus \varphi$ if $\nvdash \varphi$, but we have $M, \sigma \!\upharpoonright\! \circlearrowleft \text{assert}_a p, w \models_{\mathsf{DMPCL^+}} [\text{a-cmt}]_a p$ if σ includes $\text{assert}_a q$ and $\text{assert}_a (q \to p)$, for example. Thus, even if a withdraws a's own acts of the form $\text{assert}_a p$ (or of the form $\text{concede}_a p$), if there is a set of propositions jointly implying p in the set of propositions a has asserted (or conceded), a is still a-committed (or c-committed) to p. Acts of withdrawing do not directly nullify propositional commitments but do so only indirectly; we can only withdraw actually performed acts of asserting and conceding. We record this fact as a proposition.

Proposition 3 *Acts of withdrawing do not satisfy the AGM postulates for contraction.*

The AGM postulates, when considered as postulates for theory revision, characterize the desirable properties the revised theory has to have. But in order to have a theory which has such desirable properties, we have to restate the theory explicitly, and the task of restatement might not be so straightforward in some cases. DMPCL$^+$ seems to reflect this difficulty correctly.

10.5 Scorekeeping for Argumentation Games

In DMPCL and in DMPCL$^+$, we have characterized propositional commitments as products of various courses of discourse. This suggests an interesting possibility of applying DMPCL$^+$ to scorekeeping for debates or argumentation games. The notion of scorekeeping is introduced into the discussion of language by Lewis in [8], and used by Brandom in [3] in his attempt to develop a theory of meaning based on Wittgenstein's notion of meaning as use. In Brandom's version, each agent is considered as a deontic scorekeeper, and "the significance of an assertion of p" is considered as "a mapping that associates with one social deontic score—characterizing the stage before that speech act is performed, according to some scorekeeper—the set of scores for the conversational stage that results from the assertion, according to the same scorekeeper" ([3], p. 190). In this paper, however, we will only consider "the official score" kept by an idealized scorekeeper, and examine how DMPCL$^+$ can be applied to such official scorekeeping.

In order to do so, we need to take account of the fact that we may have various propositional commitments in $\langle M, \sigma, w \rangle$ even if σ is empty. Some of them are merely unavoidable commitments; for example, if φ is a tautology, we have $M, \sigma, w \models_{\text{DMPCL}^+} [\text{a-cmt}]_i \varphi$ and $M, \sigma, w \models_{\text{DMPCL}^+} [\text{c-cmt}]_i \varphi$. But there may be other contingent commitments in $\langle M, \sigma, w \rangle$ as well, and, as we have seen, we can think of them as products of the discourse that precedes $\langle M, \sigma, w \rangle$.

This means that only certain special $\mathcal{L}_{\text{MPCL}}$-models can be used to represent the initial stage of a piece of discourse in which no speech acts have been made yet. In order to apply DMPCL$^+$ to scorekeeping for an argumentation game played by two players, for example, we have to define a special model that represents the initial stage of the game, where both players have neither a-commitments nor c-commitments other than the unavoidable ones. Thus we define:

Definition 13 Given a countably infinite set *Aprop* of proposition letters, and the set $I = \{a, b\}$ of players a and b, with p ranging over *Aprop*, and i over I. Then, the initial stage model is the tuple $M^0 = \langle W^0, \{\triangleright_i^0 \mid i \in I\}, \{\blacktriangleright_i^0 \mid i \in I\}, V^0 \rangle$, where:

(i) W^0 is the power set $\mathscr{P}(\textit{Aprop})$ of *Aprop*,
(ii) $\triangleright_i^0 = W^0 \times W^0$ for each $i \in I$,
(iii) $\blacktriangleright_i^0 = W^0 \times W^0$ for each $i \in I$,
(iv) V^0 is the function that assigns a subset $V^0(p) = \{w \in W^0 \mid p \in w\}$ of W^0 to each proposition letter $p \in \textit{Aprop}$.

Note that M^0 is an $\mathcal{L}_{\mathsf{MPCL}}$-model, and that, if σ is empty, for any proposition letter p, any world w, and any agent i, we have $(\neg[\text{a-cmt}]_i\, p \wedge \neg[\text{a-cmt}]_i\, \neg p)$ and $(\neg[\text{c-cmt}]_i\, p \wedge \neg[\text{c-cmt}]_i\, \neg p)$ in M^0 at w with respect to σ.

Thus, if σ is empty and w is the actual world, $\langle M^0, \sigma, w \rangle$ can be used to represent the initial stage of an argumentation game. The scores for subsequent stages can then be calculated according to the updating procedures defined for interpreting assertions, concessions, and their withdrawals, as far as propositional commitments are concerned.

Of course, there must be many other features that the scorekeeper has to record, such as penalties for withdrawing, for example.[8] It should be clear that DMPCL$^+$ only gives us a partial characterization of the scorekeeping function. But the fact that it gives us a partial characterization shows that records of changing propositional commitments belong to the public score that characterizes conversational stages. Thus propositional commitments belong to the dynamic social reality.

10.6 Conclusion

We have shown that acts of asserting and acts of conceding can be modeled as updators of propositional commitments in DMPCL, and presented a complete set of reduction axioms for it. Since the acts of asserting and conceding are exactly the kind of acts with respect to which Austin's notion of conventional effect ([1]) may seem most dubious, having a sound and complete logic that deals with their objective or public effects can be of considerable significance.

We have also given a truth definition for the language of DMPCL$^+$, Dynamified Multi-agent Propositional Commitment Logic With withdrawals. Having formulated the truth definition, the obvious next step is to examine what principles are valid, and whether there can be a complete axiomatization of it or not. Since the effects of an act of withdrawing depend not only on the conditions that hold in the directly preceding situation but also on the earlier updating history, no complete set of reduction axioms seems to be forthcoming. But even the mere truth definition for the formulas with modalities standing for acts of withdrawing assertions and concessions may be said to provide the notion of conventional effects of illocutionary acts of asserting and conceding with further support, as the possibility of withdrawal seems to be a distinguishing characteristic common to a wide range of acts whose effects are conventional or institutional. As we have seen, changing propositional commitments that agents bear are part of the public social reality.[9]

---

[8] Such a feature may require very careful treatment. For example, if an agent a in an argumentation game has withdrawn her earlier assertion or concession after many things have said by her opponent b as well as by her, some of the things said by b may be the kind of things which b would not have said if a had not made the very assertion or concession a has just withdrawn. Should we allow b to withdraw some of his own assertions or concessions for free? And how about a's further withdrawals motivated by b's withdrawals?

[9] For more on Austin's notion of conventional effect, see [18, 19].

Acknowledgments This work has been supported by JSPS Grant-in-Aid for Scientific Research (C) (KAKENHI 19520002). An earlier version of this paper was presented at LENLS (Logic and Engineering of Natural Language Semantics) 2008, 9–10 June, 2008, Asahikawa, Japan. As a fault was found in the truth definition for DMPCL$^+$ in this version shortly after LENLS 2008, it was revised immediately. Various parts of the more recent versions of the paper incorporating the revised truth definition were presented at the 11th Symposium: Contemporary Philosophical Issues, University of Rijeka, 30 May, 2009, Rijeka, Croatia, and at the 4th International Conference on Philosophy, 1–4 June 2009, Athens, Greece, as well as in lectures given at the University of Zagreb, Tsinghua University, and Hokkaido University in 2009. The truth definition for DMPCL$^+$ in the present version is not only revised but also generalized. I thank the participants of these events and the editors of the present volume for their interesting questions and helpful comments.

References

1. Austin, John L. 1955. *How to Do Things with Words. The William James Lectures*. Harvard University. In *How to Do Things with Words*, edited by James O. Urmson and Marina Sbisà. 2nd edition. 1975. Cambridge, MA: Harvard University Press.
2. Baltag, Alexandru, Lawrence S. Moss, and Slawomir Solecki. 1999. "The Logic of Public Announcements, Common Knowledge, and Private Suspicions." *Technical Report* TR534. Department of Computer Science (CSCI). Indiana University.
3. Brandom, Robert B. 1994. *Making It Explicit: Reasoning, Representing, and Discursive Commitment*. Cambridge, MA: Harvard University Press.
4. Gerbrandy, Jelle. 1999. "Bisimulations on Planet Kripke." PhD thesis. *ILLC Dissertation Series* DS-1999-01. University of Amsterdam.
5. Gerbrandy, Jelle and Willem Groeneveld. 1997. "Reasoning About Information Change." *Journal of Logic, Language, and Information* 6:147–69.
6. Hamblin, Charles L. 1970. *Fallacies*. London: Methuen.
7. Kooi, Barteld and Johan van Benthem. 2004. "Reduction Axioms for Epistemic Actions." In Preliminary Proceedings of AiML-2004: Advances in Modal Logic, edited by Renate Schmidt, Ian Pratt-Hartmann, Mark Reynolds, and Heinrich Wansing, 197–211. *Technical Report Series* UMCS-04-9-1. Department of Computer Science. University of Manchester.
8. Lewis, David. 1979. "Scorekeeping in a Language Game." *Journal of Philosophical Logic* 8: 339–59. Reprinted in David Lewis. 1983. *Philosophical Papers*. Volume 1, 233–49. Oxford: Oxford University Press.
9. Liu, Fenrong. 2008. "Changing for the Better: Preference Dynamics and Agent Diversity." PhD thesis. *ILLC Dissertation Series* DS-2008-02. University of Amsterdam.
10. Neuhaus, Fabian and Bill Andersen. 2009. "The Bigger Picture: Speech Acts in Interaction with Ontology-Based Information Systems." In Proceedings of the Second Interdisciplinary Ontology Meeting, February 28th–March 1st, 2009, Tokyo, Japan. *Interdiciplinary Ontology* Volume 2, edited by Mitsuhiro Okada and Barry Smith, 45–56. Open Research Center for Logic and Formal Ontology. Keio University.
11. Plaza, Jan A. 1989. "Logics of Public Communications." In Proceedings of the 4th International Symposium on Methodologies for Intelligent Systems: Poster Session Program, edited by Mary L. Emrich, Marilyn S. Phifer, Mirsad Hadzikadic, and Zbigniew W. Ras, 201–16. Oak Ridge National Laboratory. Reprinted, in 2007. *Synthese*. 158:165–79.
12. Searle, John. 1979. *Expression and Meaning*. Cambridge: Cambridge University Press.
13. Van Benthem, Johan and Fenrong Liu. 2007. "Dynamic Logic of Preference Upgrade." *Journal of Applied Non-Classical Logics* 17:157–82.
14. Van Ditmarsh, Hans, Wiebe van der Hoek, and Barteld Kooi. 2007. *Dynamic Epistemic Logic*. Synthese Library. Volume 337. Dordrecht: Springer.
15. Walton, Douglas N. and Erik C. Krabbe. 1995. *Commitment in Dialogue: Basic Concepts of Interpersonal Reasoning*. Albany, NY: State University of New York Press.

16. Yamada, Tomoyuki. 2007a. "Acts of Commanding and Changing Obligations." In Computational Logic in Multi-Agent Systems, 7th International Workshop, CLIMA VII, Hakodate, Japan, May 2006, Revised Selected and Invited Papers, edited by Katsumi Inoue, Ken Sato, and Francesca Toni, 1–19. *Lecture Notes in Artificial Intelligence.* Volume 4371. Berlin / Heidelburg / New York, NY: Springer.
17. Yamada, Tomoyuki. 2007b. "Logical Dynamics of Commands and Obligations." In New Frontiers in Artificial Intelligence, JSAI 2006 Conference and Workshops, Tokyo, Japan, June 2006, Revised Selected Papers, edited by Takashi Washio, Ken Satoh, Hideaki Takeda, and Akihiro Inokuchi, 133–46. *Lecture Notes in Artificial Intelligence.* Volume 4384. Berlin / Heidelburg / New York, NY: Springer.
18. Yamada, Tomoyuki. 2008a. "Acts of Promising in Dynamified Deontic Logic." In New Frontiers in Artificial Intelligence, JSAI 2007 Conference and Workshops, Miyazaki, Japan, June 18–22, 2007, Revised Selected Papers, edited by Ken Sato, Akihiro Inokuchi, Katashi Nagao, and Takahiro Kawamura, 95–108. *Lecture Notes in Artificial Intelligence.* Volume 4914. Berlin / Heidelburg / New York, NY: Springer.
19. Yamada, Tomoyuki. 2008b. "Logical Dynamics of Some Speech Acts that Affect Obligations and Preferences." *Synthese* 165:295–315.

Chapter 11
Is Unsaying Polite?

Berislav Žarnić

> *'Have some wine,'* the March Hare said in an encouraging tone. Alice looked all round the table, but there was nothing on it but tea. *'I don't see any wine,'* she remarked.
> *'There isn't any,'* said the March Hare.
> *'Then it wasn't very civil of you to offer it,'* said Alice angrily.
> *'It wasn't very civil of you to sit down without being invited,'* said the March Hare.
> —Alice's Adventures in the Wonderland [6, p. 96]

11.1 Two Ways of Negating a Sentence

Wittgenstein and Stenius According to the influential tradition in philosophy of language, advocated inter alios by Erik Stenius [23] in 1967, there are three logico-semantic moods: indicative, imperative and interrogative, and there are two main components in natural language sentences: modal element, which determines sentence's mood, and sentence radical, which carries the descriptive content. Although Wittgenstein had more permissive attitude regarding the number of sentence moods, still the conception of the twofold sentence structure, consisting in *use* of a *picture*, prevails in the later Wittgenstein's philosophy.

> But how many kinds of sentence are there? Say assertion, question, and command?—There are *countless* kinds: countless different kinds of use of what we call "symbols," "words," "sentences." And this multiplicity is not something fixed, given once for all; but new types of language, new language-games, as we may say, come into existence, and others become obsolete and get forgotten. (We can get a *rough picture* of this from the changes in mathematics.) ...
>
> Imagine a picture representing a boxer in a particular stance. Now, this picture can be used to tell someone how he should stand, should hold himself; or how a particular man did stand in such-and-such situation; and so on. One might (using the language of chemistry) call that picture a proposition-radical. [28, p. 11]

Two Negation Positions The two-part sentence structure offers two options for placement of negation. First, it is the modal element that may be negated: *negation*

B. Žarnić (✉)
Faculty of Philosophy, University of Split, Split, Croatia
e-mail: berislav@ffst.hr

[modal element] [radical]. I call this position "external negation position." Second, it is the sentence radical that may be negated: [modal element] *negation* [radical]. I call this position "internal negation position."

Ross Alf Ross, one of the founders of imperative logic, drew a parallel distinction in 1941 [18]. According to Ross, there are imperatives with "negated theme of demand" (i.e. with negated radical) and there are imperatives with "negated factor of demand" (i.e. with negated modal element).

> [This] means that it is necessary to use linguistic expressions which distinguish between negative imperatives in two different senses, i.e. 1) imperatives with a negative theme of demand ($I(\overline{x})$ = you are (not to close the door) = you are to leave it open) and 2) imperatives with a negative factor of demand, expressing that a positive imperative with an identical theme of demand is not valid ($\overline{I}(x)$ = (you are not to) close the door = the imperative "you are to close the door" is not valid).
>
> The use of the imperative mood in colloquial language does not allow this important difference between $I(\overline{x})$ and $\overline{I}(x)$ to be clearly marked. All imperative in the grammatical sense are positive in the sense that they posses a positive factor of demand. For example, "Do not close the door!" can only mean $I(\overline{x})$ not $\overline{I}(x)$. Only by using linguistically indicative mood the difference becomes apparent. For example, "It is your duty not to close the door" ($I(\overline{x})$), and "It is not your duty to close the door" ($\overline{I}(x)$). [18, p. 63]

Ross includes "imperatives with a negative factor of demand" among imperatives, understood in a broad, nongrammatical sense. The difference between externally and internally negated imperatives is clearly visible, since their grammatical forms differ.

Searle Later, the same distinction was made in Searle's speech act theory, where illocutionary force indicator has the role similar to the role of modal element, while propositional indicator corresponds to sentence radical. Searle used the term "illocutionary negation" for external negation, and he classified permissions as directives alongside other speech acts typically performed by uttering an imperative.

> "Permit" also has the syntax of directives, though giving permission is not strictly speaking trying to get someone to do something, rather it consists in removing antecedently existing restrictions on his doing it, and is therefore the illocutionary negation of a directive with a negative propositional content, its logical form is $\sim!(\sim p)$. [20, p. 22]

It seems that Searle needlessly narrows down permissions to those having "negative propositional content." In my opinion, the expression "a negative propositional content" should be replaced with "an opposite propositional content." Then the citation could be interpreted as stating that

(i) $\sim!(\sim p)$ is illocutionary negation of $!(p)$, and
(ii) $\sim!(p)$ is illocutionary negation of $!(\sim p)$.

An example for relation (ii) is given by the pair (iii)–(iv), below.

(iii) You may close the door.
(iv) Don't close the door!

11 Is Unsaying Polite? 203

It should be noted here that "illocutionary negation" operates simultaneously at two negation positions: external negation includes internal negation.

Grice Grice proclaimed the principles of cooperative communication. If a principle is violated, an utterance becomes inappropriate for reasons other than their "truth conditions."

> In my eyes the most promising line of answer lies in building up a theory which will enable one to distinguish between the case in which an utterance is inappropriate because it is false or fails to be true, or more generally fails to correspond with the world in some favored way, and the case in which it is inappropriate for reasons of a different kind. [10, p. 4]

Horn and Tappenden Horn and Tappenden (inter alios) have discussed the difference between the two ways of negation in the special case of indicatives. Horn [13] has pointed out that external, i.e. metalinguistic negation erases some part of the semantic field, like presuppositions, implicatures, points of view, etc.

> I discuss the two uses of negation (descriptive and metalinguistic) in terms of what they generally negate: truth (of a proposition) vs. assertability (of an utterance). [13, p. 122]

> Metalinguistic negation, as we have seen, is used to deny or object to any aspect of a previous utterance—from the conventional or conversational implicata that may be associated with it, to its syntactic, morphological, or phonetic form. [13, p. 144]

In Horn's conception, the external negation takes some previous speech act as its object. Hence, new questions come to fore. Is external negation capable of erasing or canceling the joint effect of two or more previously performed speech acts? Can external negation also take as its object the propositional part of the negated speech act, and, in that way, incorporate internal negation?

> I will argue that negation has both a speech-act indicating and a content-modifying function, and puzzles can be generated by running them together. [24, p. 263]

> [...] how are we to theoretically classify two distinct patterns of use exhibited by sentences containing negation? One of the uses is to be construed in terms of a speech act of denial, the other in terms of asserting a content, [...] So understood, the semantic (content modifying) function is given by the truth table for internal negation if it is given by a truth table at all. The speech act of denial is the commitment to the failure to obtain of the conditions that would have to obtain for S to be true. Though this speech act is correct or incorrect in just the conditions that the assertion of an external negation of S would be correct the speech act differs from the assertion of an external negation in that it bears different relations to embedded sentences. Though one can deny S, it need not be possible to define an external negation operator over the whole language. [24, p. 282]

According to Tappenden [24], the use of the word "deny" is ambiguous. There is a use of the word which covers the cases in which "denying that S" brings in the commitment to "asserting (claiming) that $\neg S$." In the other sense, which Tappenden calls "non-derivative" sense because of its irreducibility to assertion, denial is "the commitment to the failure to obtain of the conditions that would have to obtain for S to be true."

The Problem The concept of the twofold sentence structure is challenged by the fact that external, metalinguistic negation cannot be formalized if the scope of negation is restricted to sentence radical since in this way only speech acts with negated content can be expressed. There is or there should be a logical operator that acts upon the whole "[modal element][radical]" thus producing negated speech act, different from the speech act with negated content. Questions arise: Does (or would) external negation increase the pragmatic power of a language to effect changes in the mind and in the group of minds? Does external negation violate some principles of cooperative communication? The answer to these questions requires a general formal semantic model for positive speech act and its opposite speech acts. It is our thesis that within dynamic logic there are resources to build a variety of explanatory models that are able to cover the basic aspects of logical relations occurring within and between the three broad categories of speech acts: asserting, requesting and asking, which roughly correspond to the three main categories of moods: indicatives, imperatives and interrogatives.

11.1.1 Modeling Two Kinds of Negation in Dynamic Semantics

The second type of negation (e.g. the imperative with negated "factor of demand", the denial as irreducible speech act) is what I call "negated speech act." Within the framework of the dynamic semantics, negated speech act can be modeled as a semantic action that makes it logically or conversationally possible to perform the speech act of the same type but with opposite content. In the simple case, to externally negate speech act $\delta\varphi$ with radical φ means to enable the speech act $\delta \sim \varphi$ with the opposite radical $\sim \varphi$.

The language of dynamic modal logic [3, 17] provides a rich vocabulary that can be used for distinguishing types of speech acts in the way that Speaker's speech act affects Hearer's mental state.

> Let Φ be a set of proposition letters. We define the dynamic modal language $\mathcal{DML}(\Phi)$ [...] Its formulas and procedures (typically denoted by φ and α, respectively) are built up from proposition letters ($p \in \Phi$) according to the following rules
>
> $$\varphi ::= p \mid \bot \mid \top \mid \neg\varphi \mid \varphi_1 \wedge \varphi_2 \mid \mathsf{do}(\alpha) \mid \mathsf{ra}(\alpha) \mid \mathsf{fix}(\alpha),$$
> $$\alpha ::= \mathsf{exp}(\varphi) \mid \mathsf{con}(\varphi) \mid \alpha_1 \cap \alpha_2 \mid \alpha_1;\alpha_2 \mid -\alpha \mid \alpha^{\smile} \mid \varphi?.$$

[17, p. 111]

The underlying idea of dynamic modal logic is to interpret procedures α as relations between valuation points, where formulas φ hold (or, in the approach of that will be followed here, relations between structures where formulas are valid or satisfiable). In this way sentences become treated as speech acts: as procedures resulting in a mental state describable by a formula. The question that interests us here is "Which set of speech act types is expressively complete for the language of imperatives and indicatives?" Later, it will be proved that the operational part of rich vocabulary of dynamic modal logic can be reduced to few operations: testing a property of a mental state, moving towards a more informative information state, sequential composition of moves, and indeterministic choice: $\varphi?$, $\mathsf{exp}(\varphi)$, $\alpha_1;\alpha_2$, $\alpha_1 \cup \alpha_2$.

Using dynamic modal language negated speech act could be provisionally described as

11 Is Unsaying Polite?

$$[\![\mathsf{con}_1(\delta\varphi)]\!] = \{\langle x, y\rangle \mid y \sqsubseteq x \wedge \mathfrak{M}, y \not\models \delta\varphi \wedge \neg\exists z(y \sqsubset z \sqsubseteq x \wedge \mathfrak{M}, z \not\models \delta\varphi)\} \tag{con_1}$$

i.e. as a backward motion along the $\sqsubseteq$ ordering towards the nearest point y in the structure $\mathfrak{M} = \langle W, \sqsubseteq, [\![\cdot]\!], V\rangle$ where $\delta\varphi$ does not hold. The provisional description is too broad since the fact that $\delta\varphi$ is not accepted in y need not guarantee the acceptability of $\delta \sim \varphi$ there.

Example 1 According to con_1 the sentence "It is not your duty to open the door" if used to perform negation of the directive "Open the door" could lead to different mental states. In some of these the addressee may believe that the door has already been open or that her duty is to prevent the door from closing. Such states will neither validate the permission "You may keep the door closed" nor the suggestion "It might be good to keep the door closed."

The phenomenon of contradictory relations cannot be found among imperatives since it is not the case for any future state of affairs that some imperative holds for it. A lot of future state of affairs are "imperative indifferent" and we are not obliged either to produce, sustain, destroy, or prevent them. On the other hand, no imperative holds for the state of affairs that cannot be brought about. Therefore, another type of logical opposition should be brought into the picture. The contrariety seems to be fit for the role. On the one hand, both imperatives "Let it be the case that φ" and "Let it be the case that $\neg\varphi$" cannot be jointly satisfied. On the other hand, it is not the case that one of them must be in force. In my pre-understanding of the matter, the abandonment of imperative opens up a logical space for another, contrary imperative. Let us denote by $\delta\varphi$ and $\delta \sim \varphi$ the speech acts of the same type but with contrary content. Using the notion of contrariety, a more precise description of negated speech act can be given in terms of relation con_2 relying on: test (?), sequential composition (;), and con_1.

$$[\![(\delta\sim\varphi)?]\!] = \{\langle x, x\rangle \mid x \models \delta\sim\varphi\} \tag{?}$$
$$[\![\alpha_1]\!]; [\![\alpha_2]\!] = \{\langle x, y\rangle \mid \exists z(\langle x, z\rangle \in [\![\alpha_1]\!] \wedge \langle z, y\rangle \in [\![\alpha_2]\!])\} \tag{;}$$
$$[\![\mathsf{con}_2(\delta\varphi)]\!] = [\![\mathsf{con}_1(\delta\varphi)]\!]; [\![(\delta\sim\varphi)?]\!] \tag{con_2}$$

Another but equivalent way to define negated speech act of the specific type is to define it as a retreat to a mental state upon which the contrary speech act of the same type can be performed (formally, to a point in the domain do of the corresponding relation).

$$[\![\mathsf{con}_2(\delta\varphi)]\!] = [\![\mathsf{con}_1(\bot)]\!]; [\![(\mathsf{do}(\delta\sim\varphi))?]\!]$$

Example 2 Denial of an indicative $\cdot P$ (where $\cdot$ denotes indicative mood and P is propositional content) as a "non-derivative" act receives the following dynamic interpretation: it is a token of the relation type where the second members of the relation enable update with $\cdot\neg P$.

The proposed downdate modeling for negated speech act shows that its notion depends on the notion of speech act with negated or, for the case of imperatives, with contrary content.

For the purpose of modeling denial, as negated speech act of assertion, we will introduce downdate function into Veltman's update semantics [8, 25].[1] Dynamic modal logic takes the relational approach while update semantics narrows it down to the functional one. A preliminary loose connection between dynamic modal logic and update-downdate variant of Veltman's system can be established by the following propositions: $\langle x, x[\varphi^+] \rangle \in [\![\mathsf{ex}(\varphi)]\!]$, $\langle x, x[\varphi^-] \rangle \in [\![\mathsf{con}(\varphi)]\!]$, $\langle x, x[\varphi^?] \rangle \in [\![\varphi?]\!]$.

A token of contractive relation must be chosen in order to apply the functional approach of update/downdate semantics. In the next section I will introduce semantic reformulation of the principles of AGM contraction and define the preferred contraction type on that basis.

11.2 Contraction Types?

In AGM theory [1, 12] the operation of contraction of set A by a sentence x, $A \div x$ results in maximal subset of A that does not entail x. In general there will be more than one maximal subset of A of the kind, and the set of these is called the remainder set of A by x, $A \perp x$. The remainder set $A \perp x$ contains all and only those sets B such that

(i) $B \subseteq A$,
(ii) $x \notin Cn(B)$, and
(iii) there is no B' such that $B \subset B' \subseteq A$ and $x \notin Cn(B')$.

One of the ways to define contraction $A \div x$ is to say that it is a choice operation γ picking a member of the remainder set: $A \div x \in A \perp x$ or $A \div x = \gamma(A \perp x)$. This function is called maxichoice contraction. The definition of the contraction operation is given in syntactic terms and it has three elements:

1. preservation condition—contracted set is a subset of the original set,
2. not-entailment condition—contracted set does not entail contracted sentence,
3. maximality condition—contracted set retains the maximal number of sentences from the original set.

Note that the definition of the maximality condition invokes the other two conditions, as in (iii).

---

[1] In [26] Veltman develops a semantics for counterfactuals and introduces "retraction function" that shares the same traits as the function presented here. They differ only in technical sense: since Veltman relies on use of partial valuations ("situations") while I use relation of minimal difference between full valuations.

The contraction operation can be defined in semantic terms.[2] First let us recursively define truth-valuation h as a binary function taking a sentence φ and a valuation w and delivering truth-value t or f.

Definition 1 For a propositional language $\mathcal{L}$ built over a finite base set $\mathcal{A}$ of propositional letters, a set $w \subseteq \mathcal{A}$ is a valuation point for all $\varphi \in \mathcal{L}$.

Remark 1 The set of all valuation points for a propositional language $\mathcal{L}$ built over the finite set $\mathcal{A}$ of propositional letters will be denoted by $W = \wp \mathcal{A}$.

Definition 2 Truth valuation is a two-place function $h : \mathcal{L} \times W \to \{t, f\}$. Truth equals membership for atoms: $h(A, w) = t$ iff $A \in w$. Compounds are standardly defined: $h(\neg \varphi, w) = t$ iff $h(\varphi, w) = f$; $h(\varphi \wedge \psi, w) = t$ iff $h(\varphi, w) = t$ and $h(\psi, w) = t$, and so on as in classical propositional logic.

Definition 3 Truth set $\mathrm{tr}_X(T) \subseteq W$ for a set of sentences $T \subseteq \mathcal{L}$ with respect to the set X of valuation points is the set $\mathrm{tr}_X(T) = \{w \in X \mid \forall \varphi (\varphi \in T \to h(\varphi, w) = t)\}$.

Notation For the ease of reading, two notational conventions will be adopted: (i) truth set function will be written down as a one-place function whenever it takes the entire set W of valuation points as its argument, i.e. instead of $\mathrm{tr}_W(\cdot)$ I will write $\mathrm{tr}(\cdot)$; and (ii) the valuation points will be indexed by a string of its elements, e.g. w_{pq} for $\{p, q\}$, $w_\emptyset$ for $\emptyset$, etc.

11.2.1 Contraction Defined Semantically

There is a compelling way to think about contraction operation in semantic terms. First, identify each proposition x with its singleton's truth set $\mathrm{tr}_W(\{x\})$ within an exhaustive valuation space W, with the understanding that the division between truth set and its relative complement reflects the informational content of the proposition. Then, identify the fact of proposition being a member in a theory, $x \in T$ with the fact that truth-set of the theory is included in the truth-set of the proposition, $\mathrm{tr}(T) \subseteq \mathrm{tr}(\{x\})$. The syntactic requirement that a theory is deductively closed set, $T = Cn(T)$ is generally satisfied in the truth-set-semantics translation since for any T it holds that $\mathrm{tr}(T) = \mathrm{tr}(Cn(T))$. Therefore, the semantic variant of the condition (1) is $\mathrm{tr}(T) \subseteq \mathrm{tr}(T \div x)$. Not-entailment condition (2) becomes $\mathrm{tr}(T \div x) \not\subseteq \mathrm{Tr}(\{x\})$. For any set (T) that entails x, $x \in Cn(T)$, it holds that: if there is a valuation $w \notin \mathrm{tr}(x)$, then a minimal extension $\mathrm{tr}(T) \cup \{w\}$ will meet not-entailment condition. Any valuation point v can be characterized by a conjunction of literals $\mathrm{nf}(\{v\})$ (see Definition 22 below), so the set $\mathrm{tr}(T \cup \{\mathrm{nf}(\{w\})\}$ will satisfy not entailment condition. But the choice should not be made in an arbitrary manner if the conservative requirement is to be met: it may well be the case that $\mathrm{nf}(\{w\}) \notin Cn(T)$, violating the condition (1).

---

[2] A more advanced semantics for AGM theory, but without contraction, is given in [22].

Example 3 Let $h(p, w_1) = h(q, w_1) = h(r, w_1) = \text{t}$, $h(p, w_2) = h(q, w_2) = h(r, w_2) = \text{f}$, $W = \wp\{p, q, r\}$, and $\mathcal{T} = Cn(\{p, q, r\})$. Then $\text{tr}(\mathcal{T}) = \{w_1\}$, and $\{w_1, w_2\} \nsubseteq (\text{tr}(\{p\}) \cup \text{tr}(\{q\}) \cup \text{tr}(\{r\}))$. Hence, there is no subset $\mathcal{T}'$ of $\mathcal{T}$ such that $\text{tr}(\mathcal{T}') = \{w_1, w_2\}$. Therefore, an arbitrary enlargement of the truth set, as a semantic counterpart for syntactic contraction, cannot satisfy preservation condition (1).

The preservation condition (1) and, consequently, the maximality condition (3) cannot be given a direct semantic translation. In the syntactic version, the "size" of all theories is the same, $|\mathcal{T}| = \aleph_0$: being a deductively closed set, $\mathcal{T} = Cn(\mathcal{T})$, the cardinality of the theory $\mathcal{T}$ is infinite. Still the relation of proper inclusion of the theory $\mathcal{T}$ in $\mathcal{T}'$, $\mathcal{T} \subset \mathcal{T}'$, is informative enough, showing that there is, so to speak, more knowledge in $\mathcal{T}'$ than in $\mathcal{T}$. Maximal membership condition (3) thus meets the conservative requirement of parsimonious epistemology to preserve as much as possible of the previous knowledge content in the contracted set. On the semantic side, equinumerous truth sets are equally informative, they have the same "degree of uncertainty" but there is an important relation besides inclusion: the degree of similarity between valuations. Valuation points can assign the same truth value to some of the propositional letters: the larger the set of coincident assignments, the greater the similarity of valuations.

Definition 4 "One-way" difference relation df between members of X and Y with respect to proposition φ:

$$\text{df}(\varphi, X, Y) = \{\langle w, v \rangle \in X \times Y \mid h(\varphi, w) = \text{f} \wedge h(\varphi, v) = \text{t}\}.$$

Notation The cardinality of a set X is denoted by $|X|$. The symbol $\triangle$ stands for operation of symmetric difference between sets: $a \triangle b = (a - b) \cup (b - a)$.

Definition 5 The relation μdf of minimal one-way difference between X and Y with respect to proposition φ:

$$\mu\text{df}(\varphi, X, Y) =$$
$$= \{\langle w, v \rangle \in \text{df}(\varphi, X, Y) \mid \forall z \forall u (\langle z, u \rangle \in \text{df}(\varphi, X, Y) \to |w \triangle v| \leq |z \triangle u|)\}.$$

Example 4 For all X and Y it holds that $\mu\text{df}(\top, X, Y) = \mu\text{df}(\bot, X, Y) = \emptyset$.

Example 5 Let $W = \wp\{p, q\}$. Then $\mu\text{df}(p \vee q, W, W) = \{\langle w_\emptyset, w_p \rangle, \langle w_\emptyset, w_q \rangle\}$.

Notation Expressions mem_1 and mem_2 stand for functions that deliver first and second members of a binary relation R, respectively; i.e. $mem_1(R) = \{x \mid \exists y\, Rxy\}$ and $mem_2(R) = \{y \mid \exists x\, Rxy\}$.

Definition 6 Set of "the closest antipodes" of X in Y with respect to φ:

$$\text{ca}(\varphi, X, Y) = \{v \mid \exists w (w \in X \wedge \langle w, v \rangle \in \mu\text{df}(\varphi, X, Y))\}$$
$$= mem_2(\mu\text{df}(\varphi, X, Y)).$$

11 Is Unsaying Polite?

Semantic Interpretation of AGM Contraction Now we can give a semantic interpretation for AGM principles of contraction by using the notion of truth set and notion of closest antipodes.

1. Preservation condition: $\text{tr}(\mathcal{T}) \subseteq \text{tr}(\mathcal{T} \div x)$ corresponds to $\mathcal{T} \div x \subseteq \mathcal{T}$.
2. Not-entailment condition: $\text{tr}(\mathcal{T} \div x) \not\subseteq \text{tr}(x)$ corresponds to $x \notin Cn(\mathcal{T} \div x)$.
3. Maximality condition: $\text{tr}(\mathcal{T} \div x) = \text{tr}(\mathcal{T}) \cup \text{ca}(\neg x, \text{tr}(\mathcal{T}), W)$ corresponds to $\mathcal{T} \div x \in \mathcal{T} \bot x$ (where $\mathcal{T} \subseteq \mathcal{L}$ and W is the set of all valuation points for $\mathcal{L}$).

Example 6 Let $\mathcal{A} = \{p, q\}$ be the base set of propositional letters. Then $\text{tr}(\{p, q\} \div p) = \text{tr}(\{p, q\}) \cup \text{ca}(\neg p, \text{tr}(\{p, q\}), W) = \{w_{pq}\} \cup \{w_q\} = \{w_{pq}, w_q\}$.

Example 7 Some vacuous contractions: $\text{tr}(\{p \vee q\} \div p) = \text{tr}(\{p \vee q\} \div \neg p) = \text{tr}(\{p \vee q\})$.

The family of contraction operations in this semantic version is reduced to a single case, and thus underdetermination is gone. This is not to say that this image of an informational contraction is the correct one. Rather, the semantic interpretation of AGM notion of syntactic contraction unexpectedly forces upon us one instead of many candidate operations. The semantically defined operation gives preference to the most informative truth set. The semantic operation differs from Yamada's approach[3] in which contraction of truth set generated by a sequence of sentences $\varphi_1; \ldots; \varphi_n$ with a sentence x would be equated with the truth set generated by a sequence $\varphi_1/x; \ldots; \varphi_n/x$ (where $\varphi_i/x = \top$ if $\varphi_i = x$, and $\varphi_i/x = \varphi_i$ otherwise) in which all occurrences of x have been erased. The operation of adding "closest antipodes" may explicate the cancelation of the sentence that has only been implied although never actually uttered.

Definition 7 If φ is a sentence of a propositional language $\mathcal{L}$, then φ^+, φ^- and $\varphi^?$ are sentences of $\mathcal{L}_{act}$.

Definition 8 Function $\cdot[\cdot] : \wp W \times \mathcal{L}_{act} \to \wp W$ takes a state $\sigma \subseteq W$ and a sentence $\varphi \in \mathcal{L}_{act}$ and delivers a state σ':

$$\sigma[\varphi^+] = \sigma \cap \text{tr}(\varphi) \qquad \text{(update)}$$

$$\sigma[\varphi^?] = \begin{cases} \sigma & \text{if } \sigma[\varphi^+] \neq \emptyset, \\ \emptyset & \text{otherwise.} \end{cases} \qquad \text{(test)}$$

$$\sigma[\varphi^-] = \begin{cases} \sigma \cup \text{ca}(\varphi, \sigma, W) & \text{if } \sigma[\varphi^+] = \sigma, \\ \sigma & \text{otherwise.} \end{cases} \qquad \text{(downdate)}$$

The intended interpretation for functional expressions $\sigma[\varphi^\circ]$ ($\circ = +, -, ?$) is as follows: Speaker utters a sentence φ° thereby changing Hearer's mental state σ into $\sigma[\varphi^\circ]$. In this perspective, semantics cannot be divorced from pragmatics: the function $\cdot[\cdot]$ can be thought of as a "speech act function" or as "pragmatic interpretation function." The natural language counterparts for speech act function presumably can

---

[3] See Yamada, Chapter 10, this volume.

be found among constatives: *update* and *test* correspond to reporting—typically performed by uttering "It is the case that φ" and "It might be the case that φ", respectively; *downdate* corresponds to an act of withdrawing a report that has been previously stated or implied—there does not seem to be a typical sentence that can be used to perform withdrawal, albeit perhaps "It is not the case that φ" understood in the non-derivative sense. It is possible to conceptualize a speech act type that uses sentence φ° as one place function $\cdot[\varphi^\circ]$ thus assigning its pragmatic function to each sentence. The output of pragmatic sentence function depends on the *context* and is a *fixed* point (see Proposition 1 below).[4]

Proposition 1 *For* $\circ = +, -, ?,$

$$\text{If } \nvdash \varphi, \text{ then } \exists \sigma \exists \sigma' \sigma[\varphi^\circ] \neq \sigma'[\varphi^\circ]. \qquad (context)$$
$$\sigma[\varphi^\circ] = (\sigma[\varphi^\circ])[\varphi^\circ] \qquad (fixed)$$

Proof Routine.

Downdate gains *success* by enabling update by contradictory sentence in a way that makes *recovery* possible. In this way the notion of non-derivative denial as a speech act of "the commitment to the failure to obtain of the conditions that would have to obtain" [24, p. 282] for φ to be true has been captured. Proposition 2 shows that upon Speaker's non-derivative denial the Hearer's state σ changes into state $\sigma[\varphi^-]$ in which φ^+ is not accepted (*cancelation*), but in which both $\neg\varphi^+$ (*success*) and φ^+ are acceptable (*recovery*).[5]

Proposition 2

$$\sigma[\varphi^-] \neq (\sigma[\varphi^-])[\varphi^+] \qquad (cancelation)$$
$$\sigma[\varphi^-] = (\sigma[\varphi^-])[\neg\varphi^?] \qquad (success)$$
$$\sigma = (\sigma[\varphi^-])[\neg\varphi^+] \qquad (recovery)$$

Proof Routine.

11.3 Imperatives, Commands and Permissions

Compared to the language of indicative sentences, imperative language shows in a more transparent way the distinction between directive speech act with positive content, directive speech act with negated content and negated directive speech act. While the first two create obligations, the third gives permission. In order to examine the possibility of dynamic modeling of the distinction, we will follow the tradition

---

[4] The unbound variables are assumed to be universally quantified in all the formulas.
[5] Proposition on *recovery* is stronger than acceptability claim: it shows that what has been "undone" can also be "redone."

11 Is Unsaying Polite?

that connects the imperative semantics with action semantics. In particular, we will rely on the following ideas:

- the "propositional content" of an imperative should be syntactically represented by change expression, Lemmon [15][6];
- the content of imperative is a prescribed action, Belnap [2], Segerberg [21];
- the semantics of action requires existence of negative condition (counter-state, "null-point," avoidability), Kanger [14], Belnap [2], Von Wright [29].

According to Von Wright [29], a minimal semantics of action should capture the following three elements:

1. initial state, which the agent changes or which would have changed if the agent had not been active,
2. end-state, which results from the action, and
3. counter-state, which would have resulted from agent's passivity.

On these grounds Von Wright developed the fourfold classification of action types: producing $(\neg\varphi/\varphi)$, destroying $(\varphi/\neg\varphi)$, sustaining (φ/φ) and suppressing $(\neg\varphi/\neg\varphi)$ state of affairs φ. The classification of actions can be used as the basis of the twofold classification of imperatives: 1. complementary imperative, which is used for requesting production or destruction of the state of affairs: $!(\neg\varphi/\varphi)$, $!(\varphi/\neg\varphi)$, 2. symmetric imperative, which is used for requesting maintenance or suppression of the state of affairs: $!(\varphi/\varphi)$, $!(\neg\varphi/\neg\varphi)$. To those two, a third type of imperative should be added: "one-sided" imperative $!(\top/\varphi)$, $!(\top/\neg\varphi)$, which has drawn much attention in the literature, e.g. [7].

Example 8 Let C stand for "The door is closed". (i) "Close the door!" and (ii) "Don't close the door!" are complementary $!(\neg C/C)$ and symmetric imperatives $!(\neg C/\neg C)$, respectively. Pre-theoretically speaking, they are used for the same kind of speech act, for directives or requests. Their contents differ, and the aforementioned imperatives may be understood as having negated content with respect to the other. On the other hand, permission expressed by (iii) "You don't have to close the door" or "You may leave the door open" relate to imperative (i) as a negation of the speech act performed by uttering it.

Example 9 The meaning of complementary imperative "Close the door!" can be depicted by its implications: (initial state) "The door is open at the moment before;" (end-state) "The door shall (ought to) be closed at the moment after;" (negative condition) "It is possible that the door will not be closed at the moment after;" (positive condition) "It is possible that the door will be closed at the moment after."[7]

According to the proposed approach, the speech act φ^- negates φ^+. The former is conceived as a token of semantic relation $\text{con}_2(\varphi)$ which enables the acceptance

---

[6] Change expression syntax for imperatives was re-introduced in [31].
[7] The March Hare's suggestion in the motto violates positive condition.

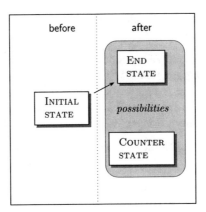

Fig. 11.1 Following Von Wright's action semantics, the semantics for imperatives as commanded actions should include: three valuation points—initial, end, and counter state; two moments—before and after; relation of commanded change (here represented by *arrow*); and set of *possible* after situations (here denoted by "*possibilities*").

of the speech act with the opposite content $(\sim \varphi)^+$. In other words, downdate with φ enables update with $\sim \varphi$. In order to apply this approach to the case of speech acts performed by uttering imperatives, one must define the relevant opposition for imperatives. As I have argued elsewhere [32],[8] a pair of imperative contraries consists of a complementary and a symmetric imperative; e.g. contrariety of $!(\neg C/C)$ is $!(\neg C/\neg C)$ and vice versa (see Example 8).

I will formalize imperatives as change expressions [15] having peculiar phenomenology concerning their "direction of fit with the world;" the left part should fit the world while it is the world that should fit the right part:

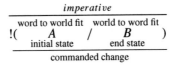

11.3.1 Language $\mathcal{L}_{imp}^{act}$

11.3.1.1 Syntax

Definition 9 Let language $\mathcal{L}_{PL}$ of classical propositional logic built over finite set $\mathcal{A}$ of propositional letters be given. If $\varphi \in \mathcal{L}_{PL}$, then $\cdot(\varphi/\top)$ is indicative **before**-sentence in $\mathcal{L}_{imp}$ and $\cdot(\top/\Box\varphi)$, $\cdot(\top/\Diamond\varphi)$ are indicative **after**-sentences in $\mathcal{L}_{imp}$. If $\varphi \in \mathcal{L}_{PL}$ and $\psi \in L_{PL}$, then $!(\varphi/\psi)$ and $!(\top/\varphi)$ are imperative sentences in $\mathcal{L}_{imp}$. If φ is indicative **before**-sentence in $\mathcal{L}_{imp}$ and if ψ is imperative sentence on $\mathcal{L}_{imp}$,

---

[8] In [32] contrariety of imperative is called "negative imperative."

then $(\varphi \to \psi)$ and $(\psi \to \varphi)$ are conditional imperative sentences in $\mathcal{L}_{imp}$. Nothing else is a sentence in $\mathcal{L}_{imp}$.

Definition 10 If $\varphi \in \mathcal{L}_{imp}$, then $\varphi^+, \varphi^-, \varphi^?$ are sentences in the language $\mathcal{L}_{imp}^{act}$.

11.3.1.2 Semantics

Definition 11 Set Σ of cognitive motivational states is the set constructed in the following way:

- $\mathcal{A}$ is a finite set of propositional letters,
- $W = \wp \mathcal{A}$ is the set of state descriptions (valuation points),
- Moments = {before, after} is the set of moments,
- $Init = W \times \{before\}$ is the set of initial situations,
- $Res = W \times \{after\}$ is the set of resulting situations,
- $Changes = Init \times Res$ is the set of changes,
- $\Sigma = \wp(Changes \times Res)$ is the set of cognitive-motivational states.

Definition 12 For $\varphi \in L_{PL}, X \subseteq W$ or $X \subseteq (W \times \text{Moments}), t \in \text{Moments}, |\varphi|_X^t$ is set of φ-state descriptions of X coupled with moment t:

$$|\varphi|_X^t = \begin{cases} \text{tr}_X(\{\varphi\}) \times \{t\} & \text{if } X \subseteq W, \\ X \cap (\text{tr}_W(\{\varphi\}) \times \{t\}) & \text{if } X \subseteq (W \times \text{Moments}). \end{cases}$$

Definition 13 Intension $[\![\varphi/\psi]\!]$ of a change expression (φ/ψ) is the set

$$[\![\varphi/\psi]\!] = |\varphi|_W^{\text{before}} \times |\psi|_W^{\text{after}}.$$

Definition 14 Set $\Phi \subseteq \Sigma$ of absurd states: $\Phi = \{\langle \rho, \pi \rangle \mid \rho = \emptyset \vee \neg mem_2(\rho) \subseteq \pi\}$. $\mathbf{1} = \langle \emptyset, \emptyset \rangle$ is a distinguished element in Φ.

Definition 15 For $\langle \rho_1, \pi_1 \rangle \in \Sigma$ and $\langle \rho_2, \pi_2 \rangle \in \Sigma$, operation $\uplus$ of merging structures is defined as: $\langle \rho_1, \pi_1 \rangle \uplus \langle \rho_2, \pi_2 \rangle = \langle \rho_1 \cup \rho_2, \pi_1 \cup \pi_2 \rangle$.

Interpretation function $\cdot [\cdot]$ for the language $\mathcal{L}_{imp}^{act}$ is function from $\Sigma \times \mathcal{L}_{imp}^{act}$ into Σ. Some of the interpretations turn out to be rather complex and not reducible to basic cases. Therefore, the definition of interpretation function will be split into several cases: text interpretation (Definition 16), interpretation of updates (Definition 17), interpretation of tests (Definition 18), interpretation of downdates (Definition 19). In the end definitions will be given for sentences definable in terms of others (Definition 20).

Definition 16

$$\langle \rho, \pi \rangle [\varphi_1] \ldots [\varphi_n] = \langle \rho, \pi \rangle [\varphi_1; \ldots; \varphi_n] = (((\langle \rho, \pi \rangle [\varphi_1]) \ldots)[\varphi_{n-1}])[\varphi_n], \quad (11.1)$$
$$\text{for } \varphi_1, \ldots, \varphi_{n-1}, \varphi_n \in \mathcal{L}_{imp}^{act}.$$

Definition 17

$$\langle \rho, \pi \rangle [!(\top/\varphi)^+] = \begin{cases} \langle \rho \cap [\![\top/\varphi]\!], \pi \rangle & \text{if } |\varphi|_\pi^{\text{after}} \neq \emptyset \text{ and } |\varphi|_\pi^{\text{after}} \subset \pi, \\ 1 & \text{otherwise.} \end{cases} \quad (11.2)$$

$$\langle \rho, \pi \rangle [\cdot(\varphi/\top)^+] = \langle \rho \cap [\![\varphi/\top]\!], \pi \rangle \quad (11.3)$$

$$\langle \rho, \pi \rangle [\cdot(\top/\Box\varphi)^+] = \langle \rho \cap [\![\top/\varphi]\!], \pi \cap |\varphi|_{\text{Res}}^{\text{after}} \rangle \quad (11.4)$$

$$\langle \rho, \pi \rangle [(\cdot(\varphi/\top) \to !(\top/\psi))^+] =$$
$$= \begin{cases} \langle \rho, \pi \rangle [!(\top/\psi)^+] & \text{if } \langle \rho, \pi \rangle [\cdot(\varphi/\top)^+] = \langle \rho, \pi \rangle, \\ \langle \rho, \pi \rangle [\cdot(\neg\varphi/\top)^+] \uplus \langle \rho, \pi \rangle [\cdot(\varphi/\top)^+][!(\top/\psi)^+] & \text{otherwise.} \end{cases} \quad (11.5)$$

The Intended Interpretation $\langle \rho, \pi \rangle$ is Hearer's cognitive-motivational state, $mem_1(\rho)$ is the truth set for her beliefs about the facts at moment before, $mem_2(\rho)$ is the truth set for her goals at moment after, π is the truth set for her beliefs about possible facts at moment after. Regarding imperative update in clause (11.2), Hearer's mental state may be receptive or not for the directive or the request $!(\top/\varphi)^+$. If the first is the case, she restricts her goals to φ situations, leaving her beliefs unchanged. Hearer is not receptive to directives or requests requiring either the impossible, $|\varphi|_\pi^{\text{after}} = \emptyset$, or the inevitable, $|\varphi|_\pi^{\text{after}} = \pi$. Receptiveness does not guarantee success since it might be the case that new goals cannot be consistently added, i.e. if $\rho \cap [\![\top/\varphi]\!] = \emptyset$. In the clause (11.3), constative $\cdot(\varphi/\top)^+$ changes beliefs about the facts at moment before; while in (11.4), constantive $\cdot(\top/\Box\varphi)^+$ changes beliefs about possible facts at moment after. Conditional imperative in the clause (11.5) shows that the desired semantics cannot be reduced to three sets: $mem_1(\rho)$, $mem_2(\rho)$, π. If the indicative antecedent is already accepted, the goals will change. But if not, the conditional may still have an effect on cognitive-motivational state. There are two possible cases. First, if antecedent is believed not to be the case, no goal change will occur. But, if the antecedent is neither believed nor disbelieved, the conditional imperative will be "memorized:" beliefs remain the same, but the relations between situations change. Among the relations starting with a φ-situation, i.e. those from $mem_1(\rho) \cap |\varphi|_W^{\text{before}}$, only the ones pointing to a ψ-situation, i.e. those from $mem_2(\rho) \cap |\psi|_W^{\text{after}}$, will persist. Therefore, if sometime later Hearer learns that φ is the case at moment before, then ψ will become her goal.

Von Wright's "three points of action semantics" can be built in the update semantics for complementary and symmetric imperatives. Information on initial state is encoded into the set $mem_1(\rho)$, information on end-state is encoded into the set $mem_2(\rho)$, information on counter-state (which would have or could have resulted if the agent had refrained from performing commanded action) is encoded in the set π, which also encodes information on the possibility of end-state (π represents both avoidability and possibility of end-state).

Definition 18 For $\varphi \in \mathcal{L}_{imp}$,

$$\sigma[\varphi^?] = \begin{cases} \sigma & \text{if } \sigma[(\varphi)^+] \notin \Phi, \\ 1 & \text{otherwise.} \end{cases} \quad (11.6)$$

11 Is Unsaying Polite?

Remark 2 The natural language expressions corresponding to test sentences, the clause (11.6), are those used for making suggestions: "It might be good that you see to it that φ will be the case" for $!(\mathsf{T}/\varphi)^?$; "It might be that φ is the case" for $\cdot(\varphi/\mathsf{T})^?$; "It might be that φ will be the case" for $\cdot(\mathsf{T}/\Box\varphi)^?$. In this approach, suggestions are seen as consistency or—using the terminology of update semantics—acceptability testing: is it so that $\varphi \in \mathcal{L}^{act}_{imp}$ can be "processed" without landing into absurd cognitive-motivational state $\sigma \in \Phi$? Extending the line of thought, the use of "therefore" belongs to the same type of operations on mental states; the difference being now that it is validity or acceptance that is being tested. Let us use the symbol $\therefore$ for this type of testing. Then, e.g. the speech act performed upon Hearer's mental state σ by Speaker uttering the sentence "Therefore, φ" would be formalized as:

$$\sigma[\varphi^{\therefore}] = \begin{cases} \sigma & \text{if } \sigma[\varphi] = \sigma, \\ \mathbf{1} & \text{otherwise}. \end{cases}$$

Notation The following equations hold:

$$|\varphi|^{\text{before}}_{\text{ca}(\varphi, mem_1(mem_1(\rho))), W} = \text{ca}(\varphi, mem_1(mem_1(\rho))), W) \times \{\text{before}\}$$
$$|\varphi|^{\text{after}}_{\text{ca}(\varphi, mem_1(mem_2(\rho))), W} = \text{ca}(\varphi, mem_1(mem_2(\rho))), W) \times \{\text{after}\}$$

For the ease of reading, the shorthand notation $[\![\varphi/\mathsf{T}]\!]^{\rho 1}_{ca}$ will be used for "intension of change expression restricted to time-designated closest antipodes of first members of ρ with respect to φ, and to second members of ρ," and $[\![\mathsf{T}/\varphi]\!]^{\rho 2}_{ca}$ will be used for "intension of change expression restricted first members of ρ, and to time-designated closest antipodes of second members of ρ with respect to φ:"

$$[\![\varphi/\mathsf{T}]\!]^{\rho 1}_{ca} = |\varphi|^{\text{before}}_{\text{ca}(\varphi, mem_1(mem_1(\rho))), W} \times mem_2(\rho)$$
$$[\![\mathsf{T}/\varphi]\!]^{\rho 2}_{ca} = mem_1(\rho) \times |\varphi|^{\text{after}}_{\text{ca}(\varphi, mem_1(mem_2(\rho))), W}.$$

Example 10 Let C stand for "The window is closed" and B for "The window is broken," and let

$$\sigma = \langle \underbrace{\{\langle\langle w_\emptyset, \text{before}\rangle, \langle w_C, \text{after}\rangle\rangle\}}_{\rho}, Res\rangle$$

be cognitive-motivational state built over the "two-letter" base, $\mathcal{A} = \{B, C\}$, $W = \wp\mathcal{A}$, etc. Agent i in the mental state σ intends to close the window without breaking it, or, in other words, i believes that the window is closed and unbroken at the moment before, wants it to be the case that the window is closed and unbroken at the moment after, and believes that the latter state of affairs is both possible, and avoidable in all respects. Now, the mental state

$$\langle \rho \cup [\![\mathsf{T}/\neg C]\!]^{\rho 2}_{ca}, Res\rangle = \langle\{\langle\langle w_\emptyset, \text{before}\rangle, \langle w_C, \text{after}\rangle\rangle, \langle\langle w_\emptyset, \text{before}\rangle, \langle w_\emptyset, \text{after}\rangle\rangle\}, Res\rangle$$

shows that i's mind has been minimally changed with respect to his wants regarding the window: no longer i wants to close the window, but i still wants to keep it unbroken.

Definition 19

$$\langle \rho, \pi \rangle [!(T/\varphi)^-] =$$
$$= \begin{cases} \langle \rho \cup [\![T/\neg\varphi]\!]_{ca}^{\rho 2}, \pi \rangle & \text{if } \langle \rho, \pi \rangle [!(T/\varphi)^+] = \langle \rho, \pi \rangle, \\ \sigma & \text{otherwise.} \end{cases} \quad (11.7)$$

$$\langle \rho, \pi \rangle [\cdot(\varphi/T)^-] = \begin{cases} \langle \rho \cup [\![\neg\varphi/T]\!]_{ca}^{\rho 1}, \pi \rangle & \text{if } \langle \rho, \pi \rangle [\cdot(\varphi/T)^+] = \langle \rho, \pi \rangle, \\ \sigma & \text{otherwise.} \end{cases}$$
$$(11.8)$$

$$\langle \rho, \pi \rangle [\cdot(T/\Box\varphi)^-] =$$
$$= \begin{cases} \langle \rho, \pi \cup mem_2([\![T/\neg\varphi]\!]_{ca}^{\rho 2}) \rangle & \text{if } \langle \rho, \pi \rangle [\cdot(T/\Box\varphi)^+] = \langle \rho, \pi \rangle, \\ \sigma & \text{otherwise.} \end{cases} \quad (11.9)$$

$$\sigma[(\cdot(\varphi/T) \to !(T/\psi))^-] =$$
$$= \begin{cases} \sigma[!(T/\psi)^-] & \text{if } \sigma[(\cdot(\varphi/T) \to !(T/\psi))^+][\cdot(\varphi/T)^+] = \sigma, \\ \sigma & \text{otherwise.} \end{cases} \quad (11.10)$$

Justification The acceptance test in downdate semantic clauses shows that "only what is done can be undone," i.e. for a speech act to be undone it must have been previously, either explicitly or implicitly effected. Semantic clauses determine the minimal modifications needed for enabling of update by a speech act having an opposite content with respect to the speech act that is downdated. The clause (11.7) is the most interesting one. Downdating by $!(T/\varphi)$ must make updating by $!(T/\neg\varphi)$ feasible. For that to happen: (i) there must be a $\neg\varphi$ situation in the goal set, which is therefore minimally expanded, (ii) the future possibility, and (iii) the existence of counter-point are already secured by the fact that $!(T/\varphi)^+$ is accepted in $\langle \rho, \pi \rangle$ since positive condition (possibility) for $!(T/\varphi)^+$ is negative condition (avoidability) for $!(T/\neg\varphi)^+$ and vice versa. In the clause (11.10) downdate of conditional presupposes pre-theoretical determination of the opposite sentence that is to be enabled. The act-conditional (i) $(\cdot(\varphi/T) \to !(T/\psi))^+$ blocks $\neg\psi$ goals for φ situations. So I take (ii) $(\cdot(\varphi/T) \to !(T/\neg\psi))^+$ as the opposite act-sentence. The acceptance test breaks in two subcases: if $\cdot(\neg\varphi/T)^+$ is accepted in $\sigma[(\cdot(\varphi/T) \to !(T/\psi))^+]$, then there is nothing to do since then (ii) is accepted as well (second line in (11.10)); otherwise, downdate with $!(T/\neg\psi)^-$ will suffice.

Finally, the "reducible" sentences will be defined, but, due to the limitations of space, their informal meaning or justification will be omitted.

Definition 20

$$\sigma[!(\varphi/\psi)^+] = \sigma[\cdot(\varphi/\mathsf{T})^+][!(\mathsf{T}/\psi)^+] \qquad (11.11)$$

$$\sigma[!(\varphi/\psi)^-] = \sigma[\cdot(\varphi/\mathsf{T})^-][!(\mathsf{T}/\psi)^-] \qquad (11.12)$$

$$\sigma[\cdot(\mathsf{T}/\Diamond\varphi)^+] = \sigma[\cdot(\mathsf{T}/\Box\varphi)^?] \qquad (11.13)$$

$$\sigma[\cdot(\mathsf{T}/\Diamond\varphi)^-] = \sigma[\cdot(\mathsf{T}/\Box\varphi)^-] \qquad (11.14)$$

$$\sigma[(!(\mathsf{T}/\varphi) \to \cdot(\psi/\mathsf{T}))^+] = \sigma[(\cdot(\neg\psi/\mathsf{T}) \to !(\mathsf{T}/\neg\varphi))^+] \qquad (11.15)$$

$$\sigma[(!(\mathsf{T}/\varphi) \to \cdot(\psi/\mathsf{T}))^-] = \sigma[(\cdot(\neg\psi/\mathsf{T}) \to !(\mathsf{T}/\neg\varphi))^-] \qquad (11.16)$$

Example 11 Implications listed in Example 9 hold[9]:

$$\sigma[!(\neg C/C)^+] = (\sigma[!(\neg C/C)^+])[\cdot(\neg C/\mathsf{T})^+; !(\mathsf{T}/C)^+; \cdot(\mathsf{T}/\Diamond C)^+; \cdot(\mathsf{T}/\Diamond\neg C)^+].$$

The language $\mathcal{L}_{imp}^{act}$ and interpretation function $\cdot[\cdot]$ provide an uncommon approach which drags the pragmatics into the syntax of the formal language and, consequently, it equates pragmatic effects with semantic actions. It is speech act that gets a formal translation, and not the sentence by whose utterance it is performed. If this approach is sound, then logic permeates all three branches of semiotics. Pragmatics might lie within the scope of logic.

Example 12 Command "Close the door!" is formalized as $!(\neg C/C)^+$; permission "You don't have to close the door" ("You may leave the door open") as $!(\neg C/C)^-$; suggestion "Maybe you should close the door" as $!(\neg C/C)^?$.

11.3.1.3 The Puzzle of Permission Distribution

According to Searle, permission "consists in removing antecedently existing restrictions [on] doing" [20, p. 22]. Command $!(\mathsf{T}/\varphi)^+$ restricts Hearer's action by making a change $\mathsf{T}/\neg\varphi$ forbidden for her. Downdate $!(\mathsf{T}/\varphi)^-$ enables update $!(\mathsf{T}/\neg\varphi)^+$ and, therefore, it may serve as a formal explication for "restrictions removing" notion of permission.

The puzzle of distribution of permission over disjunction has been much discussed in the literature: (i) "You may see to it that A or B" pre-theoretically implies (ii) "You may see to it that A," and (iii) "You may see to it that B." On the proposed approach (i) is translated as $!(\mathsf{T}/(\neg A \wedge \neg B))^-$ and interpreted as cancelation of (iv) "See to it that $\neg A$ and $\neg B$." Similarly, (ii) and (iii) are translated as $!(\mathsf{T}/\neg A)^-$ and $!(\mathsf{T}/\neg B)^-$, respectively. Proposition 3 shows that if there is a restriction to be removed, then by removing the whole of restriction, all of its "parts" will be removed.

---

[9] For discussion on varieties of relations of meaning inclusion that can be distinguished within dynamic semantics see [4].

Proposition 3 *Let* $\sigma[!(\top/(\neg A \wedge \neg B))^-] \neq \sigma$. *Then*

$$\sigma[!(\top/(\neg A \wedge \neg B))^-] = \sigma[!(\top/(\neg A \wedge \neg B))^-][!(\top/\neg A)^-]$$
$$= \sigma[!(\top/(\neg A \wedge \neg B))^-][!(\top/\neg B)^-]$$

Proof The proof relies on the fact that for any x such that $x \cap \text{tr}(\{\neg A \wedge \neg B\}) \neq \emptyset$, $\text{ca}(A \vee B, x, W) \cap \text{tr}(\{A\}) \neq \emptyset$ and $\text{ca}(A \vee B, x, W) \cap \text{tr}(\{B\}) \neq \emptyset$.

11.4 Expressive Completeness

There are several interesting questions that arise at the interface between natural language and its logical formalization. In the natural language there are three kinds of imperatives: complementary or produce imperative, symmetric or sustain imperative, and "right-side" or see-to-it-that imperative. Since the syntax of natural language restricts the range of change expressions to contradictory, identical and "truncated" pairs, the translation of natural language sentences will yield only a proper subset of imperative sentences in $\mathcal{L}_{imp}$. Namely, we find only $!(\neg\varphi/\varphi)$, $!(\varphi/\varphi)$ and $!(\top/\varphi)$ types of sentences in the subset.

1. Is the subset strong enough to generate each non-absurd cognitive-motivational state? If not, what are obstacles to communication that are inherent in the language itself?
2. Further, do negated speech acts add expressive power to the language?

Within the framework of language $\mathcal{L}_{imp}^{act}$ and its semantics, the answer to the first question is affirmative (Corollary 1) and, therefore, negative to the second. Theorem 1 shows that each non-absurd cognitive-motivational state $\sigma \in \Sigma - \Phi$ can be generated using a proper subset of language $\mathcal{L}_{imp}^{act}$ in which only "positive (i.e. non-negated) speech acts" occur.

Theorem 1 *For each* $\sigma \in \Sigma - \Phi$ *there are* $\varphi_1, \ldots, \varphi_n \in \mathcal{L}_{imp}$ *such that*

$$\langle Changes, Res \rangle [\varphi_1^+; \ldots; \varphi_n^+] = \sigma.$$

Proof Proof is given by construction of the required text.
Let $mem_1(mem_1(\rho)) = \{w_1, \ldots, w_n\}$. The construction takes three steps. First, the first members of ρ are cut out of $\langle Changes, Res \rangle$ using the sentence

$$\cdot(\text{nf}(mem_1(mem_1(\rho)))/\top)^+$$

and thus obtaining $\langle mem_1(\rho) \times Res, Res \rangle$ (see Proposition 5). Second, a sequence of sentences $s(w_1)^+; \ldots; s(w_n)^+$ is applied to $\langle mem_1(\rho) \times Res, Res \rangle$ (where each sentence $s(w_i)$ is either a conditional imperative or a tautology) yielding (Proposition 6):

$$\langle mem_1(\rho) \times Res, Res \rangle [s(w_1)^+] \ldots [s(w_n)^+] = \langle \rho, Res \rangle.$$

Third, application of $\cdot(\top/\square\mathrm{nf}(mem_1(\pi)))^+$ gives the desired result (Proposition 7):

$$\langle \rho, Res \rangle [\cdot(\top/\square\,\mathrm{nf}(mem_1(\pi)))^+] = \langle \rho, \pi \rangle.$$

The text

$$\cdot(\mathrm{nf}((mem_1(mem_1(\rho)))/\top)^+; s(w_1)^+; \ldots; s(w_n)^+; \cdot(\top/\square\,\mathrm{nf}(mem_1(\pi)))^+$$

is an instance that proves that each non-absurd state can be generated by a text of $\mathcal{L}^{act}_{imp}$. □

Corollary 1 *Let* $\mathcal{L}^{act}_{\to stit} \subset \mathcal{L}^{act}_{imp}$ *be a language comprising only sentences of the form:* $\cdot(\varphi/\top)^+$, $(\cdot(\varphi/\top) \to !(\top/\psi))^+$, $\cdot(\top/\square\varphi)^+$. *Language* $\mathcal{L}^{act}_{\to stit}$ *is expressively complete with respect to the set* $\Sigma - \Phi$ *of non-absurd states.*

Proof Note that text construction in the proof of Theorem 1 uses only the sentences from $\mathcal{L}^{act}_{\to stit}$.[10] □

Definition 21 (Literals λ) Given $l_1, \ldots, l_n$ list of all propositional letters in $\mathcal{A}$, $w_1, \ldots, w_m$ list of all valuation points in $X \subseteq W$, $\wp\mathcal{A} = W$, $1 \le i \le n$, $1 \le j \le m$, literals λ^i_j are defined by:

$$\lambda^{w_j}_{l_i} = \begin{cases} l_i & \text{if } l_i \in w_j, \\ \neg l_i & \text{if } l_i \notin w_j. \end{cases}$$

Definition 22 (Adequate description) Function nf delivers a disjunctive normal form for the set $X \subseteq W$ with respect to given lists of letters $l_1, \ldots, l_n$ and valuation points $w_1, \ldots, w_m$ in X[11]:

$$\mathrm{nf}(X) = ((\lambda^{w_1}_{l_1} \wedge \ldots \wedge \lambda^{w_1}_{l_n}) \vee \ldots \vee (\lambda^{w_m}_{l_1} \wedge \ldots \wedge \lambda^{w_m}_{l_n}))$$
$$= \mathrm{nf}(\{w_1\}) \vee \ldots \vee \mathrm{nf}(\{w_m\}).$$

Proposition 4 *For* $X \subseteq W$, $|\mathrm{nf}(X)|^t_W = X \times \{t\}$.

Proof The proof is straightforward and only right to left direction will be shown. Suppose for some arbitrary v that $\langle v, t \rangle \in X \times \{t\}$. Obviously, $h(\mathrm{nf}(\{v\}), v) = t$. By Definition 2, $h(\mathrm{nf}(X), v) = t$. By Definition 12, $\langle v, t \rangle \in |\mathrm{nf}(X)|^t_W$. □

---

[10] Note that a translation for the conditional imperative in dynamic modal language can be given by:

$$((\cdot(\varphi/\top))\,?;\,\mathrm{ex}\,(!(\top/\psi)))$$
$$\cup$$
$$((\mathrm{do}(\mathrm{ex}(\cdot(\neg\varphi/\top)) \vee \mathrm{do}(\mathrm{ex}(!(\top/\neg\psi)))))\,?;\,\mathrm{ex}\,(\mathrm{do}(!(\varphi/\psi)) \wedge \neg\mathrm{do}(!(\varphi/\neg\psi)))).$$

Therefore, the claim put forward in Section 11.1.1 has been proved as well.

[11] For this idea I am indebt to Vukičević, Damir. 2001. Digraph Representation of a Model of Dynamic Semantics. Unpublished manuscript.

Proposition 5

$$\langle Changes, Res \rangle [\cdot(\mathrm{nf}(mem_1(mem_1(\rho)))/\mathsf{T})^+] = \langle mem_1(\rho) \times Res, Res \rangle$$

Proof By Definition 13,

$$[\![\mathrm{nf}(mem_1(mem_1(\rho)))/\mathsf{T}]\!] = |\mathrm{nf}(mem_1(mem_1(\rho)))|_W^{\mathsf{before}} \times |\mathsf{T}|_W^{after}.$$

The fact that $|\mathsf{T}|_W^{after} = Res$ together with an application of Proposition 4, i.e. $|\mathrm{nf}(mem_1(mem_1(\rho)))|_W^{\mathsf{before}} = mem_1(\rho)$, gives the desired result.

Definition 23 Function $ex_\rho^{\langle w, \mathsf{before}\rangle}$ delivers set of resulting situations "visible" from situation $\langle w, \mathsf{before}\rangle$: $ex_\rho^{\langle w, \mathsf{before}\rangle} = mem_2((\{\langle w, \mathsf{before}\rangle\} \times Res) \cap \rho)$.

Definition 24 Let $mem_2(\rho) \subseteq \pi$. For each situation $\langle w, \mathsf{before}\rangle \in mem_1(\rho)$, function s delivers a sentence from $\mathcal{L}_{imp}$:

$$s(w) = \begin{cases} \cdot(\mathsf{T}/\mathsf{T}) & \text{if } ex_\rho^{\langle w, \mathsf{before}\rangle} = \pi, \\ (\cdot(\mathrm{nf}(\{w\})/\mathsf{T}) \to !(\mathsf{T}/\mathrm{nf}(mem_1(ex_\rho^{\langle w, \mathsf{before}\rangle})))) & \text{otherwise.} \end{cases}$$

Proposition 6 *Let* $\{w_1, \ldots, w_n\} = mem_1(\rho)$. *Then*

$$\langle Changes, Res \rangle [\cdot(\mathrm{nf}(mem_1(mem_1(\rho)))/\mathsf{T})^+; s(w_1)^+; \ldots; s(w_n)^+] = \langle \rho, Res \rangle.$$

Proof By Proposition 5,

$$\langle Changes, Res \rangle [\cdot(\mathrm{nf}(mem_1(mem_1(\rho)))/\mathsf{T})^+; s(w_1)^+; \ldots; s(w_n)^+] =$$
$$= \langle mem_1(\rho) \times Res, Res \rangle [s(w_1)^+; \ldots; s(w_n)^+].$$

There are two cases to examine concerning the number of situations in $mem_1(\rho)$.

1. First, for $|mem_1(\rho)| = 1$ let $mem_1(\rho) = \{\langle w, \mathsf{before}\rangle\}$. Therefore,

$$\rho = \{\langle w, \mathsf{before}\rangle\} \times mem_2(\rho).$$

There are two subcases.

a. If $ex_\rho^{\langle w, \mathsf{before}\rangle} = Res$, then $s(w_1) = \cdot(\mathsf{T}/\mathsf{T})$ and obviously

$$\langle mem_1(\rho) \times Res, Res \rangle [\cdot(\mathsf{T}/\mathsf{T})^+] = \langle \rho, Res \rangle.$$

b. In the second subcase, $ex_\rho^{\langle w, \mathsf{before}\rangle} \subset Res$. Then

$$s(w) = (\cdot(\mathrm{nf}(\{w\})/\mathsf{T}) \to !(\mathsf{T}/\mathrm{nf}(mem_1(ex_\rho^{\langle w, \mathsf{before}\rangle})))).$$

11 Is Unsaying Polite?

Since $|\text{nf}(\{w\})|_W^{\text{before}} = \{\langle w, \text{before}\rangle\} = mem_1(\rho)$, the conditional has the following impact:

$$\sigma[(\cdot(\text{nf}(\{w\})/\mathsf{T}) \to !(\mathsf{T}/\text{nf}(mem_1(ex_\rho^{\langle w,\text{before}\rangle}))))^+] =$$
$$= \sigma[!(\mathsf{T}/\text{nf}(mem_1(ex_\rho^{\langle w,\text{before}\rangle})))^+],$$

where $\sigma = \langle\{\langle w, \text{before}\rangle\} \times Res, Res\rangle$. Since

$$|\text{nf}(mem_1(ex_\rho^{\langle w,\text{before}\rangle}))|_W^{\text{after}} = mem_2(\rho),$$

we get the required result.

2. For the second case, when $|mem_1(\rho)| > 1$ we have to show that semantic impact (if any) of $s(w_i)$, $1 \leq i \leq n$ is localized to $\langle w_i, \text{before}\rangle$ generating

$$\{\langle w_i, \text{before}\rangle\} \times ex_\rho^{\langle w_i,\text{before}\rangle}$$

and leaving everything else as it is. In other words, we have to show that for each $w_i \in mem_1(\rho)$,

$$\langle mem_1(\rho) \times Res, Res\rangle[s(w_i)^+] =$$
$$= \langle((mem_1(\rho) - \{\langle w_i, \text{before}\rangle\}) \times Res) \cup (\{\langle w_i, \text{before}\rangle\} \times ex_\rho^{\langle w_i,\text{before}\rangle}), Res\rangle.$$

There are two subcases to examine. For typographic reasons symbol **b** will be used instead of **before**.

a. First, if $ex_\rho^{\langle w_i,\text{b}\rangle} = Res$, then $s(w_i) = \cdot(\mathsf{T}/\mathsf{T})$ and

$$\langle mem_1(\rho) \times Res, Res\rangle[\cdot(\mathsf{T}/\mathsf{T})^+] = \langle mem_1(\rho) \times Res, Res\rangle.$$

b. In the second subcase: $ex_\rho^{\langle w_i,\text{b}\rangle} \subset Res$. The assumption $|mem_1(\rho)| > 1$ guarantees that

$$\langle mem_1(\rho) \times Res, Res\rangle[\cdot(\text{nf}(\{w_i\})/\mathsf{T})^+] \neq \langle mem_1(\rho) \times Res, Res\rangle$$

since $|\text{nf}(\{w_i\})|_W^{\text{b}} \neq mem_1(\rho)$. Let σ stand for $\langle mem_1(\rho) \times Res, Res\rangle$. Then the update by conditional

$$s(w_i) = (\cdot(\text{nf}(\{w_i\})/\mathsf{T}) \to !(\mathsf{T}/\text{nf}(mem_1(ex_\rho^{\langle w_i,\text{b}\rangle}))))$$

has the following impact:

$$\sigma[\cdot(\mathrm{nf}(\{w_i\})/\top) \to !(\top/\mathrm{nf}(mem_1(ex_\rho^{\langle w_i, \mathsf{b}\rangle})))^+] =$$
$$= \sigma[\cdot(\neg\mathrm{nf}(\{w_i\})/\top)^+] \uplus \sigma[\cdot(\mathrm{nf}(\{w_i\})/\top)^+][!(\top/\mathrm{nf}(mem_1(ex_\rho^{\langle w_i, \mathsf{b}\rangle})))^+]$$
$$= \langle (mem_1(\rho) - \{\langle w_i, \mathsf{b}\rangle\}) \times Res, Res\rangle \uplus \langle \{\langle w_i, \mathsf{b}\rangle\} \times ex_\rho^{\langle w_i, \mathsf{b}\rangle}, Res\rangle$$
$$= \langle((mem_1(\rho) - \{\langle w_i, \mathsf{b}\rangle\}) \times Res) \cup (\{\langle w_i, \mathsf{b}\rangle\} \times ex_\rho^{\langle w_i, \mathsf{b}\rangle}), Res\rangle.$$

The sequence $s(w_1)^+; \ldots; s(w_n)^+$ of update functions generates the desired:

$$\langle \bigcap_{1 \leq i \leq n} (((mem_1(\rho) - \{\langle w_i, \mathsf{b}\rangle\}) \times Res) \cup (\{\langle w_i, \mathsf{b}\rangle\} \times ex_\rho^{\langle w_i, \mathsf{b}\rangle})), Res\rangle =$$
$$= \langle \rho, Res\rangle.$$
□

Proposition 7 $\langle \rho, Res\rangle[\cdot(\top/\boxdot \mathrm{nf}(mem_1(\pi)))^+] = \langle \rho, \pi\rangle.$

Proof Routine.

11.5 Concluding Remarks

AGM theory of contraction together with hereby proposed downdate semantics entails the fact that external denial, instead of reducing, increases the degree of uncertainty. After a sentence has been withdrawn (canceled, externally negated, unsaid, ...), Hearer's mental state not only becomes less determinate but also the path of change itself is under-determinate. It may turn out that the requirement of maximal preservation springs from the normative source of cooperative communication, but it might be just one among other admissible types of contraction. The negated speech acts do not make natural language more expressive, as Theorem 1 shows. Unsaying increases "communicative entropy" and is avoidable. Therefore, we should apologize if we negate a speech act. And not for the sake of cultural convention, but for the sake of logic.

Related Research Directive speech acts have been analyzed in terms of changing preferences [5] and obligation patterns [30] within the framework of "dynamic epistemic logic." The foundation for "shifting the logical perspective from valid argumentation to cooperative communication" has been laid down in [11]. A dynamic modal logic for imperatives is given in [9]; a variant of update semantics for imperatives has been developed in [16]. There is renewed interest in imperative logic in philosophy, e.g. [27] and linguistics, e.g. [19].

Acknowledgments The investigation presented in the paper is supported by the MZOŠ project "Logical structures and intentionality" (191-1911111-2730). Parts of the paper were presented at the 1st World Congress on Universal Logic 2005 (Montreux, Switzerland), the Analytic Philosophy and Logical Investigations 2006 conference (Rijeka, Croatia), and the Logical Foundations of Metaphysics 2007 course (Dubrovnik, Croatia). I wish to thank Srećko Kovač and Tomoyuki Yamada for discussion, and Mirjana Dedaić and Siniša Ninčević for language advice. All mistakes remain mine.

References

1. Alchourrón, Carlos, Peter Gärdenfors, and David Makinson. 1985. "On the Logic of Theory Change: Partial Meet Contraction and Revision Functions." *Journal of Symbolic Logic* 50:510–30.
2. Belnap, Nuel and Michael Perloff. 1988. "Seeing to It That: A Canonical Form of Agentives." *Theoria* 54:175–99.
3. Benthem, Johan van. 1989. *Modal Logic as a Theory of Information*. Technical Report LP-89-05. ILLC, University of Amsterdam.
4. Benthem, Johan van. 1993. *Exploring Logical Dynamics*. Stanford, CA: CSLI Publications.
5. Benthem, Johan van, and Fenrong Liu. 2007. "Dynamic Logic of Preference Upgrade." *Journal of Applied Non-classical Logics*. 17:157–82.
6. Carroll, Lewis. 2007. *Alice's Adventures in Wonderland: A Facsimile Reprint of the 1866 Edition*. Rockville, MD: Wildside Press.
7. Chellas, Brian. 1971. "Imperatives." *Theoria* 37:114–29.
8. Does, Jaap van der, Willem Groeneveld, and Frank Veltman. 1997. "An Update on "Might"." *Journal of Logic, Language, and Information* 6:361–80.
9. Eijck, Jan van. 2000. "Making Things Happen." *Studia Logica* 66:41–58.
10. Grice, Paul. 1989. *Studies in the Way of Words*. Cambridge, MA: Harvard University Press.
11. Groenendijk, Jeroen. 2007. "The Logic of Interrogation." In *Questions in Dynamic Semantics*, edited by Maria Aloni, Alastair Butler and Paul Dekker, 43–62. Amsterdam: Elsevier.
12. Hansson, Sven Ove. 1999. *A Textbook of Belief Dynamics : Theory Change and Database Updating*. Dordrecht: Kluwer Academic Publishers.
13. Horn, Laurence. 1985. "Metalinguistic Negation and Pragmatic Ambiguity." *Language* 61:121–74.
14. Kanger, Stig. 1972. "Law and Logic." *Theoria* 38:105–29.
15. Lemmon, Edward. 1965. "Deontic Logic and the Logic of Imperatives." *Logique et Analyse* 8:39–71.
16. Mastop, Rosja. 2005. What can you do?: Imperative Mood in Semantic Theory. Amsterdam: Institute for Logic, Language, and Computation.
17. Rijke, Maarten de. 1998. "A System of Dynamic Modal Logic." *Journal of Philosophical Logic* 27:109–42.
18. Ross, Alf. 1941. "Imperatives and Logic." *Theoria* 7:53–71.
19. Schwager, Magdalena. 2006. "Conditionalized Imperatives." In *Proceedings of Semantics and Linguistic Theory XVI*, edited by Masayuki Gibson and Jonathan Howell, 241–58. Ithaca, NY: Cornell University.
20. Searle, John. 1999. *Expression and Meaning: Studies in the Theory of Speech Acts*. Cambridge: Cambridge University Press.
21. Segerberg, Krister. 1990. "Validity and Satisfaction in Imperative Logic." *Notre Dame Journal of Formal Logic* 31:203–21.
22. Segerberg, Krister. 2001. "The Basic Dynamic Doxastic Logic of AGM." In *Frontiers in Belief Revision*, edited by Mary-Anne Williamson and Hans Rott, 57–84. Dordrecht: Kluwer Academic Publishers.
23. Stenius, Erik. 1967. "Mood and Language Game." *Synthese* 19:27–52.
24. Tappenden, Jamie. 1999. "Negation, Denial and Language Change in Philosophical Logic." In *What Is Negation?*, edited by Dov Gabbay and Heinrich Wansing, 261–98. Dordrecht: Kluwer.
25. Veltman, Frank. 1996. "Defaults in Update Semantics." *Journal of Philosophical Logic* 25:221–61.
26. Veltman, Frank. 2005. "Making Counterfactual Assumptions." *Journal of Semantics* 22:159–80.
27. Vranas, Peter. 2008. "New Foundations for Imperative Logic I: Logical Connectives, Consistency, and Quantifiers." *Noûs* 42:529–72.
28. Wittgenstein, Ludwig. 1986. *Philosophical Investigations*. Oxford: Basil Blackwell Ltd.

29. Wright, Georg Henrik von. 1963. *Norm and Action: A Logical Inquiry*. London: Routledge & Kegan Paul.
30. Yamada, Tomoyuki. 2008. Logical Dynamics of Some Speech Acts that Affect Obligations and Preferences. *Synthese* 165:295–315.
31. Žarnić, Berislav. 2003. "Imperative Change and Obligation to Do." In *Logic, Law, Morality: Thirteen Essays in Practical Philosophy in Honour of Lennart Åqvist*, edited by Krister Segerberg and Rysiek Sliwinski, 79–95. Uppsala: University of Uppsala.
32. Žarnić, Berislav. 2003. "Imperative Negation and Dynamic Semantics." In *Meaning: The Dynamic Turn*, edited by Jaroslav Peregrin, 201–11. Amsterdam: Elsevier.

Part IV
Logical Methods in Ontological and Linguistic Analyses

Chapter 12
Towards a Formal Account of Identity Criteria

Massimiliano Carrara and Silvia Gaio

12.1 Introduction

Consider the following thesis characterizing a strong ontological realism (for an overview on this topic see Devitt [5]):

> (SOR) There is a mind-independent world and it is structured: there are distinct objects, properties, etc.

If an ontological realist adopts (SOR), there is a problem of selecting, from among the many entities such as objects, properties, events, facts, etc., the real entities i.e. those entities existing independently of our mental states. Hence, with respect to objects of a specific kind, one can be a realist, if one takes them to be real entities, or an antirealist, if one takes them to be mere projections of one's thoughts.

Adopting a different jargon, we can say that the problem for ontological realists is selecting those objects that have ontological respectability. One standard (Quinian) solution in analytic philosophy is to argue that identity criteria are required for ontological respectability: only entities that have clearly determined identity criteria are ontologically respectable, i.e. acceptable. Think, for example, of the case of properties: following Quine [12], properties would not be ontologically acceptable because they do not have any no suitable identity criterion.

Question: are there general constraints to identity criteria for the individuation of real substances?

We distinguish between two kinds of constraints: *formal constraints* and *metaphysical constraints*. *Metaphysical constraints* normally derive from the theses of the general framework adopted, for example absolute identity vs. relative identity or four-dimensionalism vs. three-dimensionalism. Conversely, *formal constraints* are specified on the basis of the logical form of the identity criteria and some properties induced by it.

M. Carrara (✉)
Department of Philosophy, University of Padua, Padua, Italy
e-mail: massimiliano.carrara@unipd.it

In the present work we focus only on formal constraints, or requirements on identity criteria; more specifically, we focus on a specific formal constraint: equivalence. The main goal in our paper is to make some steps towards a formal characterization of identity criteria.

The paper is divided into four sections. In the first section we present the problem at issue, that is, the logical requirements that identity criteria are supposed to meet and some, commonly used identity criteria which fail to meet one of those requirements. In the second section, we will present Williamson's and De Clerq and Horsten's treatment (in [4, 13]) of logically inadequate identity criteria. In the third section, we will try to embody De Clercq and Horsten's proposal in an enlarged framework that takes into account contexts and levels of granularity too. In the fourth section we then conclude with some general remarks.

12.2 Logical Adequacy of Identity Criteria

The credit for introducing the notion of an identity criterion (from now on, IC) is usually attributed to Frege. In his *Foundations of Arithmetic* Frege introduces the idea of IC in a context where he wonders how we can grasp or formulate the concept of numbers (see [6, §62]):

> If we are to use the symbol a to signify an object, we must have a criterion for deciding in all cases whether b is the same as a, even if it is not always in our power to apply this criterion.

Even if it is not completely clear whether or not Frege thought of ICs as related only to abstract entities, his considerations about ICs seem to adapt both for concrete and abstract objects. He suggests that an IC has the function of providing a general way of answering the following question, with a and b objects in a given domain:

> *Fregean Question*: How can we know whether a is identical to b?

Consider two famous examples of ICs provided by Frege in [6]:

- *IC for directions*: if a and b are lines, then the direction of line a is identical to the direction of line b if and only if a is parallel to b;
- *Hume's principle*: for any concepts F and G, the number of F-things is equal to the number of G-things if and only if there is a one-to-one correspondence between the F-things and the G-things.

In the philosophical literature, the Fregean question has been reformulated in the following ways:

> *Ontological Question* (OQ): If a and b are Ks, what is it for the object a to be identical to b?
> *Epistemic Question* (EQ): If a and b are Ks, how can we know that a is the same as b?
> *Semantic Question* (SQ): If a and b are Ks, when do "a" and "b" refer to the same object?

12 Towards a Formal Account of Identity Criteria

The difference between an answer to (EQ) and an answer to (OQ) is not purely formal. When answering (EQ), you think of conditions associated with a procedure for deciding the identity questions concerning objects of some kind K. In answering (OQ), you think of conditions which are meant to provide an ontological analysis of the identity between objects of kind K. Finally, an answer to (SQ) concerns sameness and difference of reference of simple or complex names.

It is worthwhile considering what the logical form of ICs looks like even if different ways of conceiving the form have been proposed. The reason is that there are some requirements that ICs must satisfy to provide acceptable identity conditions, and part of those requirements are formal, i.e. given by their logical form. Among various formulations of IC, we consider the following ones:

$$\forall x \forall y((x \in K \wedge y \in K) \rightarrow (f(x) = f(y) \leftrightarrow R(x, y))), \qquad (\text{IC*})$$

and:

$$\forall x \forall y((x \in K \wedge y \in K) \rightarrow (x = y \leftrightarrow R(x, y))), \qquad (\text{IC})$$

where R constitutes the identity condition for $f(x)$s or for xs and is a relation holding between objects belonging to some kind K, and, in the (IC*) case, f is a function whose domain is K itself and the range is a set of elements which constitutes a different set, $f(K)$. The intuitive reading of (IC*) is the following: if x and y are K, then x is the same f as y if and only if R holds between x and y.[1] Sometime, (IC*) is formulated in the following way (without any reference to K):

$$\forall x \forall y (x' = y' \leftrightarrow R(x, y)), \qquad (\text{IC**})$$

where "x'" and "y'" are terms representing entities of the kind K suitably connected with x and y.

For Williamson (IC*), or (IC**), is the logical form of a *two-level identity criterion* (see [14, pp. 145–46]). Frege's criterion of identity for directions is an example of a two-level identity criterion:

$$\forall x \forall y (o(x) = o(y) \leftrightarrow P(x, y)) \qquad (\text{O})$$

where x and y range over lines, o is a letter for "the direction of" and P for "is parallel to". In (O) the identity sign is flanked by terms constructed with a functional letter, and the right-hand side of the biconditional introduces a relation among entities different from the entities for which the criterion is formulated. On the contrary, the *Axiom of extensionality* for sets:

$$\forall x \forall y (x = y \leftrightarrow \forall z (z \in x \leftrightarrow z \in y)) \qquad (\text{A})$$

---

[1] Brand [1] has given a different characterization for the *logical form* of ICs in terms of second order modal logic: $\exists F \forall x \forall y (\text{if } x \text{ and } y \text{ are } \phi\text{s then } \Box(x = y \leftrightarrow F(x, y)))$

is an example of *one-level identity criterion*. In (A) the identity sign is flanked by terms for sets, and the right-hand side states a relation equivalent to identity between sets. In the case of *two-level* ICs the conditions of identity concern objects which are not of the same kind of objects for which the IC is provided. On the contrary, in the case of *one-level* ICs the conditions of identity concern objects which are of the same kind of objects for which the identity criterion is provided.

Williamson ([14, p. 147]) points out that

> The idea of a two-level criterion of identity has an obvious advantage. No formula could be more basic (in any relevant sense) than "$x = y$", but some might be more basic than "$ox = oy$", by removing the symbol "o" and inserting something more basic than it.

In such cases one can speak of a reductivist conception of identity criteria because identity among objects of a certain kind depends on relations among more basic objects.[2]

In the next section of our paper we limit our analysis to the formal constraints on the relation R in (IC).

12.2.1 Requirements for R

In this section, some constraints for the relation R are listed and discussed. The relation R is what the identity condition consists of or, put otherwise, given an identity statement $a = b$, R is a relation that holds between a and b, is other than identity and analyzes what it is for the referents of a and b to be identical (See Linnebo in [8, p. 206]). How should R look to be a good candidate for being the identity condition of objects of some kind K? To answer this question, we take into account three contributions: Carrara and Giaretta [2], Brand [1] and Lombard [9].

Non-vacuousness The identity condition cannot have parts that are vacuously satisfiable. Consider the following example (see [9, pp. 32–33]). Let PO be the set of physical objects, S the set of sets, $R(x, y)$ the identity condition for PO and $R'(x, y)$ the identity condition for S:

$$\forall x \forall y(((x \in PO \vee x \in S) \wedge (y \in PO \vee y \in S)) \to (x = y \leftrightarrow (R(x, y) \vee R'(x, y)))).$$

The condition given above for the identity of x and y is not associated with a kind of entities in a metaphysically interesting sense, since the members of the alleged kind do not share an essence. The identity condition must specify a relation that holds between elements of a certain kind such that all of them are alike with respect to

---

[2] It is debatable if there is a real distinction between *two-level* and *one-level* ICs. J. Lowe has suggested that a *two-level* IC can be recast as *one-level*. For example (O) can be so reformulated:

$$\forall x \forall y((Direction(x) \wedge Direction(y)) \to (x = y \leftrightarrow \exists w \exists z(L(w) \wedge L(z) \wedge Of(x, w) \wedge Of(y, z) \wedge P(w, z))))$$

where "Direction" is "to be a direction", "L" "to be a line", and "Of" "to be of" (Lowe discusses *one-level* and *two-level* identity criteria in [10, 11]).

the properties associated to that kind. In such a perspective, the identity condition supplies a property of properties. Lombard calls this property *determinable* since it determines a class of properties, called *determinates*, having that property.

Informativeness R should contribute to specify the nature of the kind K of objects for which R acts as an identity condition. If the role of an IC is to specify some non-trivial essential properties for objects of kind K the form of the relation cannot be tautological, for instance, it cannot have the following form:

$$R(x, y) \vee \neg R(x, y)$$

Unfortunately, the identity condition does not completely characterize the nature of instances of K: to decide about identity questions concerning a K we need the concept of K, that is not provided by the ICs. The above observation is due to Frege. He argues that in:

> "the direction of line a is identical to the direction of line b" the direction of a plays the part of an object, and our definition affords us a means of recognising this object as the same again, in case it should happen to crop up in some other guise, say as the direction of b. But this means does not provide for all cases... That says nothing as to whether the proposition: the direction of line a is identical to q should be affirmed or denied, except for the one case where q is given in the form of the direction of b. (see [6, §66])

According to Frege, the nature of certain objects is entirely clarified only if one can find a way to refer to them such that it would determine the truth-value of any identity sentence concerning the given objects, without any restriction. What do we need to obtain the universal definiteness of identity questions concerning a K? Frege is absolutely clear about this: we need the concept of K ("What we lack is the concept of direction"(Frege [6, §66])).

Partial Exclusivity An identity condition for a kind K of objects cannot be so general that it can be applied to other kinds of objects. The example provided by Lombard is the following:

> If x and y are both non-physical objects, x and y are identical iff they have the same individual essence ([9, p. 36]).

Now, the properties falling under the "large" property "having an individual essence" do not apply only to non-physical objects and can be part of the identity conditions for many kinds of objects.

Minimality The identity condition for K-objects is required to specify the smallest number of determinables such that the determinates falling under them turn out to be necessary and sufficient to ensure identity between two objects of kind K. The determinables specified in the identity condition cannot be superfluous.

Non-circularity The identity condition for K-objects cannot make use of the concept of K itself, otherwise it is circular. There has been a long debate about the circularity of the IC for events proposed by Davidson (see [3]):

If x and y are events, $x = y$ iff x and y have the same causes and effects.

Since some causes and effects are events, the identity condition for events involves identity between events: in fact, to determine whether two events are the same we are required to determine, first, the identity of events taken as their causes or effects.

Non-tautologicity R cannot be a property that every two objects of kind K share. Formally:

$$R \subset K \times K$$

The formula says that the relation R is a *proper* subset of the set $K \times K$, that is, there is some pair of objects that are K such that the objects of the pair are not in the extension of R.

K-Maximality R must be maximal with respect to K. In other words, R is required to be the widest dyadic property that makes an identity condition true. A dyadic property G is wider than a property G' iff for any x and y, if $G'(x, y)$, then $G(x, y)$, but not vice versa. That means that the ordered pairs of G' are a subset of the set of ordered pairs of G. Formally, for all the relations R' that are possible candidates for the identity condition Φ:

$$R' \subseteq R$$

Uniqueness R is unique with respect to K. That means, if there are $R_1, R_2, \ldots, R_n$, such that (i) each R_i satisfies IC and (ii) each R_k is independent of each R_j (that is, every R_k is neither narrower nor wider than each R_j), then at most one of $R_1, R_2, \ldots, R_n$ provides a correct identity criterion for K-objects.

Equivalence R must be an equivalence relation. In the left side of the biconditional in (IC), there is an identity relation, which is an equivalence relation. Consequently, the relation R on the right side of the biconditional must be an equivalence relation, too. In order to be logically adequate, then, an identity criterion is required to exhibit an equivalence relation as identity condition.

In this paper we want to focus on identity criteria which fail to meet the equivalence constraint and show how this problem can be overcome by logical means.

12.2.2 Failure of Transitivity

As has been observed in the philosophical debate about identity criteria, some relations considered as intuitively good candidates for R often fail to be transitive. Consider some examples offered by Williamson [13]:

Example 1 Let $x, y, z, \ldots$ range over color samples and f be the function that maps color samples to perceived colors. A plausible candidate for R might be the relation of indistinguishability. It is easy to verify, though, that such an R is not necessarily transitive: it might happen that x is indistinguishable from y and y from z, but x and z can be perceived different in color.

Example 2 If $f(x)$ is a physical magnitude, to determine $f(x) = f(y)$ you measure x and y. If x and y differed by little, the measurement operation could give the identity of the physical magnitudes as a result. If R were defined on the basis of the measurement operations, it would turn out to be not transitive, since the sum of many little differences is not itself little.

The examples above show how some relations that are intuitively plausible candidates to be identity conditions do not meet the logical constraint of *Equivalence* that IC demands. However, instead of refusing this kind of plausible but inadequate identity criteria, it has been suggested to approximate the relation R whenever it is not transitive. That means that, given a non-transitive R, we can obtain equivalence relations that approximate R by some operations. Some approaches have been suggested: two of them are due to (Williamson [13, 14]), while a third approach is due to (De Clercq and Horsten [4]).

12.3 Approximations of Identity Conditions

12.3.1 Williamson's Approaches

Williamson's suggestion about the best approximation to a non transitive relation consists in giving up the requirement for the identity condition to be both necessary and sufficient. Consider R a non transitive relation that we take to be the best candidate for being the identity condition, for some kind of objects $f(x)$s. Consider such an R a constant. Consider then variables on relations R', R'', ... as possible approximations to R. To determine the best approximation R' to R Williamson suggests two constraints that R' must meet:

Weak constraint: no candidate relation R'' should approximate R better than R'.
Strong constraint: R' should approximate R better than any other candidate R''.

Williamson proposes two ways to find an adequate equivalence relation to substitute a non transitive R: an *approach form above* and an *approach from below*.

The approach from above seeks the smallest equivalence relation R^+ such that $R \subseteq R^+$. That means, some $f(x)$ and $f(y)$ that are not identical under R turn out to be identical under R^+ or, equivalently, R^+ is a super-relation of R. The equivalence classes given by R^+ are numerically more than the equivalence classes given by R. R^+ always exists and is unique. The identity criterion of this form

$$\forall x \forall y (f(x) = f(y) \leftrightarrow R^+(x, y)) \qquad (\text{IC}^+)$$

provides a sufficient, but not necessary, condition for the identity of $f(x)$s.

The approach from below seeks the largest equivalence relation R^- such that $R^- \subseteq R$. That means, R^- is a sub-relation of R since not all the ordered pairs in R are ordered pairs in R^-. R^- always exists on the assumption of the Axiom of Choice but it is not unique. To decide which relation can be preferable over others, some constraints can be put. One of it is what Williamson calls *Minimality Constraint*. According to it the relation R^- to be preferred is the one with the minimum number of equivalence classes. The identity criterion of this form

$$\forall x \forall y (f(x) = f(y) \leftrightarrow R^-(x, y)) \qquad \text{(IC}^-\text{)}$$

provides a necessary, but not sufficient, condition for the identity of $f(x)$s.

There are cases where a proposed identity condition is necessary for some kind of entities. For instance, the condition of being perceptually indistinguishable is a plausible identity condition for colors. On the contrary, there are other kinds of entities for which a good identity criterion is sufficient: certain forms of mental continuity can be considered as a sufficient condition for personal identity. But this is not so obviously sufficient. There are not always good reasons to consider a condition as obviously necessary or sufficient for the identity of some kinds of entities. There is a third option that is worthy to be considered: to regard the condition as neither necessary nor sufficient for the identity of the $f(x)$s.

12.3.2 De Clercq and Horsten's Approach

De Clercq and Horsten [4] suggest an approach to find approximating relations that is alternative to the one proposed by Williamson and is called *overlapping approach*: the equivalence relation that is sought partially overlaps R, instead of being a sub- or a super-relation with respect to R.

The advantages of such an approach are: (i) it can be used for cases where the most plausible identity condition is neither sufficient not necessary and (ii) it can generate closer approximations than Williamson's approach.

The proposal is based on the assumption that R is not indeterminate: any two objects either stand in the relation R or they do not. This assumption serves the scope to avoid difficulties that are not necessary to face, but it can be given up in case of a refinement of the approach.

The authors propose to define an equivalence relation $R^\pm$ that closely approximates R and achieves that task better that R^+ or R^-. For the sake of clarity, consider an example.

Example 3 Given a function f, let the domain of objects for f be the following:

$$\mathcal{D} = \{a, b, c, d, e\}$$

Assume there is a candidate relation R, reflexive and symmetric, for the identity condition for $f(x)$s. When R holds between two objects x and y we denote this as $\overline{xy}$ (as De Clercq and Horsten do). Put otherwise, $\overline{xy}$ means $R(x, y)$ and $R(y, x)$.

Let R on $\mathcal{D}$ be the following:

$$R = \{\overline{ac}, \overline{ad}, \overline{bc}, \overline{bd}, \overline{cd}, \overline{de}\}$$

R is not an equivalence relation. In fact, it fails to be transitive. For instance, R holds between a and d and between d and e, but it does not hold between a and e.

Consider now how R^+ looks like in this case. It is unique and it is the smallest equivalence relation that is a superset of R, that is:

$$R = \{\overline{ab}, \overline{ac}, \overline{ad}, \overline{ae}, \overline{bc}, \overline{bd}, \overline{be}, \overline{cd}, \overline{ce}, \overline{de}\}$$

On the contrary, R^- is not unique. For instance, one of the largest equivalence relations included in R is the following:

$$R^- = \{\overline{bc}, \overline{bd}, \overline{cd}\}$$

To determine whether R^+ or R^- is the best approximation to R, first you measure the degree of unfaithfulness of R^+ and R^- with respect to R. Such a degree is the number of revisions you make to get R^+, R^- from R. A revision is any adding or removing of an ordered pair to or from R. In the example considered above, R^+ is obtained by adding four ordered pairs to R and R^- by removing three ordered pairs. The degree of unfaithfulness of R^+ is 4 and the degree of R^- is 3. Thus, R^- is closer to R than R^+. That means, with R^- you stay closer to your intuitive identity condition R because R^- modifies R less than R^+ does.

Consider now the following equivalence relation:

$$R^\pm = \{\overline{ab}, \overline{ac}, \overline{ad}, \overline{bc}, \overline{bd}, \overline{cd}\}$$

With respect to R, $R^\pm$ adds one ordered pair and takes off another one. So the degree of unfaithfulness of $R^\pm$ is 2, that is, less than both R^+ and R^-. Formally, the *degree of unfaithfulness* (DOU) is given by the symmetric difference $\triangle$:

$$(R^\pm, R) = |R \triangle R^\pm| \tag{DOU}$$

How does $R^\pm$ look like? It is an overlapping relation with respect to R and it is a kind of hybrid relation between R^+ and R^-, since it both adds and removes one ordered pair. An overlapping relation can be closer to R than the relations obtained with the approach from below and from above.

12.4 Contexts and Levels of Granularity

Let us consider and revise the example about phenomenal colors given by Williamson. The case of colors is a well-known example of failure of transitivity and it has been discussed also in other places in the philosophical literature. Some observations by Hardin [7] on this issue are remarkable.

Hardin observes that many philosophers endorse a view according to which the following principle (that we will call **NT** from now on) holds:

> There exist triples of phenomenal colors x, y and z, such that x is indiscriminable from y and y is indiscriminable from z, but x is discriminable from z.

By "indiscriminability between colors" Hardin means "perceptual indistinguishability". By **NT** the relation of perceptual indistinguishability fails to be transitive; therefore, the IC for colors based on the relation of indistinguishability is incoherent: on the left side of the biconditional there is a necessarily equivalent relation (identity), on the right side a not necessarily equivalent relation. This problem seems to affect any semantic account of color terms relying on everyday uses of color predicates. Hardin argues that phenomenal colors are themselves indeterminate, that is, there is no sharp color-discrimination threshold; since the truth of **NT** is based on the assumption that there is a discrimination threshold, refusing this assumption implies refusing **NT** too.

In non problematic cases, that is, when we have to make judgments on very different colors, we report our observations using coarse-grained predicates because we do not need to express shade differences. When we have to deal with borderline cases of colors, we tend to be more precise in using color predicates. More fine-grained color predicates are used in color science and technology, but in everyday life people do not use them; that is not just because there are limits of hue discriminability, but because of "something like the limit of useful naming of phenomenal hues for the purposes of communicating between people" ([7, p. 221]). Put otherwise, the number of possible color discriminations is much higher than the number of color terms normally used. Why? First of all, there is a variability in discrimination between observers; second, people observe colors under normal conditions such as changing light, contrast, shadows, and not under standard conditions, and normal conditions make color comparisons problematic; third, it is more difficult to compare a color with a mental standard (like the standard of "red" that one could have seen in the Munsell Chart) than with another color perceived at the same time.

So, color perception is influenced by many factors and the use of color predicates is somewhat sloppy. Hardin suggests that to answer a question like "What are the boundaries of red?" we must first

> specify, explicitly or tacitly, a context and a level of precision and [...] realize the margin of error or indeterminacy which that context and level carry with them ([7, p. 230]).

In the following analysis, we wish to show that De Clercq and Horsten's framework can be improved if you consider the use of ICs in a *context* and in a *level of precision*. Moreover, we agree with Hardin's belief that the nature of our purposes imposes limits on the precision of our utterances: a too large set of color predicates would make our judgments more precise, but would also hinder a profitable communication among agents.

The IC for phenomenal colors is an example of an IC that has mostly an epistemic function: we do not know precisely whether two colors are identical. We only rely on our perception which is fallible. So, we express an IC for colors in a logically

12 Towards a Formal Account of Identity Criteria

inadequate way. Williamson and De Clercq and Horsten believe that there are logically adequate ICs and try to capture them by approximating our intuitively good, but logically inadequate ICs.

Consider now the following variations of the example of IC for perceived colors:

Example 4 You see two monochromatic spots, A and B, and you do not detect any difference with respect to their color. Following Williamson, you claim that they have the same color, because they are perceptually indistinguishable. Now, suppose you add two further monochromatic spots, C and D, such that they are perceptually distinguishable. However, A is indistinguishable from C and B from D. In such a scenario, you can accept to revise your previous judgement and say that A and B are distinct.

Example 5 You see two color samples A and B from a distant point of view such that you are not able to distinguish A-color from B-color. You say that A and B have the same color. Now, you get closer to them and detect a difference between them. So, you revise your previous judgement and say that A and B are distinct.

Example 6 You see two monochromatic spots again, A and B. You perceive them as equally, say, orange. Nevertheless a friend of yours, who is a painter, tells you that she perceives them actually different: B is more yellowish than A. According to her color perception, which is more refined than yours, there are more differences among color samples than you detect.

Example 4 shows how our perception of colors can be different, depending on the range of colors we see at the same moment. Better said, comparing a color sample with one or more color samples makes our judgements about colors differ. Thus, a relation R expressed by a criterion of identity can vary across contexts of judgment. For instance, consider a domain $\mathcal{D} = \{a, b, c, d, e\}$ and a context o, that is a subset of $\mathcal{D}$: $o = \{a, b\}$. Suppose $R = \{\overline{ab}\}$ in the context o. Consider now an enlarged context, o' containing a and b plus other elements, c and d: $o' = \{a, b, c, d\}$. In o' you may have the following R-pairs: $\overline{ac}$, $\overline{ad}$, but not $\overline{ab}$.

Example 5 and 6 present a different issue than 4. Given the same context, R varies along different granular levels of observation. When you are distant from the objects for which you have to make an identity statement, you are looking at them from a coarse point of view. Anyway, you make an identity statement. Getting closer to the elements of the context, you reach a more fine-grained observational level and so you can make a different identity statement. The point of view of the painter can be seen as well as a fine-grained observational level. In short, you can look at the elements of a context under different standards of precision, each of them corresponding to a granular level of observation. The finer the level is, the more differences between the individuals are detected.

In the following paragraph we try to formalise the notions of contexts and granular levels and integrate them with De Clercq and Horsten's formal treatment of approximate relations.

12.4.1 Granular Models

Let $\mathcal{L}$ be a formal language through which we can represent English expressions. $\mathcal{L}$ consists of:

- individual constant symbols: $\overline{a}, \overline{b}, \ldots$ (there is a constant symbol for each element of the domain);
- individual variables: $x_0, x_1, x_2, \ldots$ (countably many);
- 2-arity predicate symbols $P_1, P_2, \ldots$;
- usual logical connectives with identity, quantifiers.

The set of terms consists of individual constant and individual variable symbols. Formulas are defined as follows:

1. If t_1, t_2 are terms, then $P_1(t_1, t_2), P_2(t_1, t_2), \ldots$ are formulas;
2. If t_1, t_2 are terms, then $t_1 = t_2$ is a formula;
3. If ϕ, ψ are formulas, then $\phi \Box \psi$ is a formula, where $\Box$ is one of the usual logical connectives;
4. If ϕ is a formula, then $\neg \phi$ is a formula;
5. If ϕ is a formula, then $\forall x_i \phi, \exists x_i \phi$ are formulas.

Let us give now an interpretation to $\mathcal{L}$. Let $\mathcal{D}$ be a fixed non empty domain of objects. We define a context o as a subset of domain $\mathcal{D}$. So, the set of all contexts O in $\mathcal{D}$ is the powerset of $\mathcal{D}$:

Definition 1 $O = \wp(\mathcal{D})$.

We interpret, then, R as a binary relation, which is reflexive and symmetric, but not necessarily transitive. Moreover, R is a primitive relation and pairs the elements that are indistinguishable according to the identity condition it represents. For instance, in the case of color samples R gives rise to a set of ordered pairs, each of them consisting of elements that are indistinguishable with regard to their (perceived) color. R is then the relation that makes identity statements about the elements of the domain possible, according to IC.

Let $\mathcal{M} = \langle \mathcal{D}, R \rangle$ be a granular structure. Put otherwise, $\mathcal{M}$ is a structure consisting of the domain $\mathcal{D}$, together with all the contexts in $\mathcal{D}$, and a binary relation R (a two-arity predicate).

To account for Example 1 formulated above, we postulate that R varies across contexts. Before providing a formal definition, let us consider a further example. Given a certain domain $\mathcal{D}$, let us isolate three subsets of it, i.e. three contexts:

- $o_1 = \{a, b\}$
- $o_2 = \{a, b, c\}$
- $o_3 = \{a, b, c, d\}$

Observe that some elements, namely a and b, are in all the contexts, while c is in two of them. Consider now a granular structure $\mathcal{M}_1 = \langle \mathcal{D}, R \rangle$ and assume it not be a very fine structure; suppose that R come out with the following sets—each of them corresponding to one context:

- $R_{o_1}^{\mathcal{M}_1} = \{\overline{ab}\}$
- $R_{o_2}^{\mathcal{M}_1} = \{\overline{ab}\}$
- $R_{o_3}^{\mathcal{M}_1} = \{\overline{ac}, \overline{bd}\}$

The relation R in the granular structure $\mathcal{M}_1$ holds between a and b in contexts o_1 and o_2, but not in context o_3. This means that, given a certain granular structure $\mathcal{M}_i$, R can vary across contexts. Formally:

Definition 2 Given a granular structure $\mathcal{M}_i$ and given two contexts o_l and o_k, R varies across o_l and o_k iff there is a non empty intersection $o^* = o_l \cap o_k \neq \emptyset$ such that $\exists x \in o^* \exists y \in o^* \left((\overline{xy} \in R_{o_l}^{\mathcal{M}_i} \wedge \overline{xy} \notin R_{o_k}^{\mathcal{M}_i}) \vee (\overline{xy} \in R_{o_k}^{\mathcal{M}_i} \wedge \overline{xy} \notin R_{o_l}^{\mathcal{M}_i}) \right)$.

If in a granular structure $\mathcal{M}_i$ the relation R fails to be transitive with respect to some (if not all) contexts $o \subseteq O$, then the formal framework given by De Clercq and Horsten is applied. That means, for each R in each context o an equivalence overlapping relation $R^{\pm}$ can be defined.[3] If a relation R is transitive in a context o, then in that case $R^{\pm}$ coincides with the given R. In contexts where R is not transitive, $R^{\pm}$ denote a relation that differs from R in the fact that it adds and/or remove some ordered pairs from R, as described by De Clercq and Horsten.

R does not vary only across contexts. As the Examples 2 and 3 above show, R also varies across *granular levels*. While the notion of context refers to the number of elements considered and can be extensionally characterized, as proposed, we characterize the *epistemic notion of granular level* in an indirect way. Each granular structure belongs to a certain granular level, which corresponds to the level of precision of R in ordinating elements in contexts. Put otherwise, given the same context $o \subseteq O$, different granular structures can give different sets of ordered pairs generated by R with respect to o. If the relation R of a certain granular structure holds among all the elements of the context considered, no difference is detected among them (with respect to some property), so all of them are considered indistinguishable and at the same level. The granular structure is then considered coarse-grained. On the contrary, a more fine-grained granular structure shall have a relation R holding between a less number of elements of o.

Consider a further example. Fix the context $o_2 = \{a, b, c\}$ as above. The relation R in the granular structure $\mathcal{M}_1$ only holds between a and b. Consider now another granular structure, $\mathcal{M}_2 = \{\mathcal{D}, R\}$.[4] The relation R in $\mathcal{M}_2$ does not hold between any elements in the context o_2, and so neither between a and b. This means that the granular structure $\mathcal{M}_2$ is more fine-grained, since it is able to detect more differences among elements in contexts.

To determine whether two or more granular structures belong to different granular levels you apply the following definition:

---

[3] If you prefer to maintain Williamson's approaches, instead of $R^{\pm}$ you can get R^+ or R^-.
[4] Note that the domain $\mathcal{D}$ remains fixed in all the granular structures, and so the set of contexts O. The relation R also is the same—for example, perceptual indiscriminability—but its interpretation can differ along the grain size of the structure, as we see in the example.

Definition 3 Given a context o_i and two granular structures $\mathcal{M}_l$ and $\mathcal{M}_k$, $\mathcal{M}_l$ and $\mathcal{M}_k$ belong to *different granular* levels iff $\exists x \in o_i \exists y \in o_i \left((\overline{xy} \in R_{o_i}^{\mathcal{M}_l} \land \overline{xy} \notin R_{o_i}^{\mathcal{M}_k}) \lor (\overline{xy} \in R_{o_i}^{\mathcal{M}_k} \land \overline{xy} \notin R_{o_i}^{\mathcal{M}_l}) \right)$.

Finally, let us define the relation *to be at least as fine as* between granular structures. First, we define the relation, formally: $\leq^c$, between cardinality of sets:

Definition 4 Given an $o \in O$, for all the pairs $\overline{xy}$ in M and $\overline{xy}$ in M', $|\{\overline{xy}^{M'}\}| \leq^c |\{\overline{xy}^M\}|$ iff the number of $\overline{xy}^{M'}$ is less than or equal to the number of $\overline{xy}^M$ in o.

Then, we define the relation between granular structures with respect to some context $o \in O$:

Definition 5 Given a context $o \in O$, M' is at least as fine as M iff the number of $\overline{xy}^{M'}$ is less than or equal to the number of $\overline{xy}^M$, that is:

$$M' \leq^* M \text{ iff } |\{\overline{xy}^{M'}\}| \leq^c |\{\overline{xy}^M\}|.$$

Example 7 Let $o = \{a, b, c, d, e\}$ a given context. Consider two granular structures, $\mathcal{M}_1 = \langle \mathcal{D}, R \rangle$, $\mathcal{M}_2 = \langle \mathcal{D}, R \rangle$. According to $\mathcal{M}_1$, we have: $R_o = \{\overline{ab}, \overline{bc}, \overline{de}\}$. It is not transitive ($a$ is indistinguishable from b and b from c, but a is not indistinguishable from c). The best overlapping approximations is the following: $R^\pm = \{\overline{ab}, \overline{bc}, \overline{ac}\}$. The pair $\overline{ac}$ has been added. The degree of unfaithfulness of $R^\pm$ is 1. According to $\mathcal{M}_2$, we have: $R_o = \{\overline{ab}, \overline{bc}, \overline{cd}, \overline{de}, \overline{ce}\}$. In this case R it is not transitive either. The best overlapping approximation removes the pairs $\overline{ab}, \overline{bc}$ and it is the following: $R^\pm = \{\overline{cd}, \overline{de}, \overline{ce}\}$. According to Definitions 4 and 5 and given the context o, $\mathcal{M}_1$ is finer than $\mathcal{M}_2$ because its relation R gives a less number of pairs than the relation R in $\mathcal{M}_2$.

12.4.2 Objections and Replies

Some objections can be raised against the proposed formal characterization of ICs, as well as some problems in the account are to be underlined. We try to outline here some objections and problems, and sketch a reply to them.

ICs are usually associated with sortal concepts, that is, with concepts that answer the question "What is x?". The examples of non-transitive ICs considered are associated to kinds of objects like colors and physical magnitudes. It is not clear, though, whether *colors* or *physical magnitudes* are to be considered sortal concepts. For instance, the adjective "red" does not correspond to a sortal concept: we do not individuate an object x saying "x is a red".

This first objection seems to attack the notion of IC itself or, better said, the thesis that ICs are necessarily associated with sortal concepts. We accepted the standard thesis according to which only concepts associated with ICs are sortals. Being associated with an IC is a necessary condition for concepts to be sortals, but not a sufficient one. The possibility for some concepts to be associated with ICs without being sortals is not excluded.

Moreover, what happens if we consider "red" as a substantive standing for the color red, e.g. "Red suits you"? In this case, "red" can be considered as a sortal noun and, therefore, it would be easy to accommodate the problem via a revision of the formulation of the IC. We can formulate a one-level IC for colors as follows: given two perceived colors x and y, x is identical to y iff x is indistinguishable from y.

A second objection runs as follows: what changes from context to context or from granular level to granular level is the extension of the relation. But you are also dealing with epistemic issues: In a certain context and granular level you make an identity judgment according to a certain relation R. When the context or the granular level changes you make a sort of revision of our previous identity judgment. So, if you want to be faithful to our intuitions and account for epistemic issues, an intensional treatment is more appropriate.

We decided to provide an extensional model following Williamson's and De Clercq and Horsten's approaches. However, this second objection is very important. An intensional treatment of ICs would be interesting to be provided especially if you consider not only the ontological function of ICs, but also the epistemic one. If the goal is to model how we know and use ICs, we should think of an intensional formal framework. That is a possible further development of the account.

The proposed model for accounting for ICs is not suitable for an infinite domain. The domain of objects must be finite. The applicability of the model is then reduced to some specific cases, while it should be generalized.

As has already mentioned, the model for approximating ICs has been developed to face logical problems arising from the intuitive use of ICs for everyday problems (color comparisons and the like). De Clercq and Horsten too are aware of the problem that their approach is applicable only to finite domains. However, they attempt to accommodate the problem and suggest reducing infinite graphs to finite graphs. In a nutshell, it is worthwhile considering infinite graphs because we deal with relations that are potentially infinite, for instance the relations underlying the Sorites paradox. However, the transitivity failure of some relations is here at concern. Such a problem is shown by finite graphs, so there is nothing bad to represent the problem and the solution only using finite graphs. Moreover, it is rare that people in ordinary life make inferences with a great (even infinite) number of steps. Since we are dealing with ICs as they are commonly used by people and not by logicians, the infinity issue does not play a relevant role in the treatment of ICs.

Consider the following problem: If ICs have the function of answering questions (EQ), (OQ), and (SQ), which of those questions is answered by an intuitive IC that contains a non-transitive relation R? Moreover, does an IC with an approximated relation like $R^{\pm}$ answer the same question or a different one?

It seems plausible to claim that an IC containing a non-transitive relation R answers (EQ). Consider the IC for phenomenal colors: as we have seen, we do not know precisely whether two perceived colors are identical. We only rely on our perception, which is fallible. Therefore, the IC for colors we express is not logically adequate, but is sufficient for our pragmatic or epistemic purposes of color comparison.

Which question does an IC containing an approximated relation such as $R^\pm$ answer? The relation $R^\pm$ is logically adequate; therefore, thank to it we can determine whether or not two items are actually identical in reality. So, it is plausible to think that an IC containing an approximating relation answers (OQ).

12.5 Conclusion

ICs are very often matter of philosophical discussion. However, the formal requirements that they must meet to be acceptable are rarely taken into account. In this paper we listed some formal requirements and focused on some ICs that fail to meet one of them: transitivity. Instead of giving up ICs failing to meet the transitivity requirement, we considered the approaches proposed by Williamson and De Clercq and Horsten, by means of which transitive approximations to non-transitive ICs are defined.

Our purpose has been to improve De Clercq and Horsten's formal framework. Given a non transitive relation R, standing for an identity condition for some objects, we suggest fixing a context and a granular level of observation (a granular structure). We allow R varying across *contexts* and *granular levels*. If in a context and according to some level R fails to be transitive, you can apply De Clercq and Horsten's approach and build the closest approximation to R for that context and that level.

By the framework developed in this paper, we wish to have been able to make a short step towards a formal account of identity criteria.

References

1. Brand, Myles. 1977. "Identity Conditions for Events." *American Philosophical Quarterly* 14:329–37.
2. Carrara, Massimiliano, and Pierdaniele Giaretta. 2001. "Identity Criteria and Sortal Concepts." *Proceedings of The International Conference on Formal Ontology in Information Systems (FOIS 01)*, 234–43. Amsterdam: IOS Press.
3. Davidson, Donald. 1980. *Essays on Action and Events*. Oxford: Clarendon Press.
4. De Clercq, Rafael, and Leon Horsten. 2005. "Closer." *Synthese* 146:371–93.
5. Devitt, Michael. 1991. *Realism and Truth*, 2nd edition. Oxford: Basil Blackwell.
6. Frege, Gottlob. 1884. *Die Grundlagen der Arithmetik: eine logisch-mathematische Untersuchung über den Begriff der Zahl*. Breslau: Köbner.
7. Hardin, Larry. 1988. "Phenomenal Colors and Sorites." *Nous* 22:213–34.
8. Linnebo, Øystein. 2005. "To Be Is to Be an F." *Dialectica* 59:201–22.
9. Lombard, Lawrence Brian. 1986. *Events: A metaphysical Study*. London: Routledge & Kegan Paul Books.
10. Lowe, Jonathan. 1991. "One-Level Versus Two-Level Identity Criteria." *Analysis* 51:192–94.
11. Lowe, Jonathan. 1997. "Objects and Identity Criteria." In *A Companion to the Philosophy of Language*, edited by Bob Hale and Crispin Wright, 613–33. Oxford: Basil Blackwell.
12. Quine, Willard Van Orman. 1953. *From a Logical Point of View*. Cambridge, MA: Harvard University Press.
13. Williamson, Timothy. 1986. "Criteria of Identity and the Axiom of Choice." *The Journal of Philosophy* 83:380–94.
14. Williamson, Timothy. 1990. *Identity and Discrimination*. Oxford: Basil Blackwell.

Chapter 13
A Mereology for the Change of Parts

Pierdaniele Giaretta and Giuseppe Spolaore

13.1 Introduction

Mereology is not logic, and neither is it a part of logic. However, mereology is endowed with such wide generality that it might be taken as a slight extension of logic. Its relevance for the description of reality is generally acknowledged, but also heavily debated.

Some people hold that mereology cannot represent the general features of the material world without conflicting with an intuitive pre-scientific view. A reaction to the conflict is to restrict the generality of some of its principles. Wiggins thought of restricting the validity of mereological extensionality, also called *Uniqueness of Composition*. Van Inwagen rejected the general existence of sums, that is, *Existence of Composition*. In both cases the restrictions can be seen as a way of solving some well known ontological puzzles without abandoning a three-dimensionalist ontology. Indeed, the solution of such puzzles was a major motivation for the introduction of restrictions. However, it may be questioned as to whether it is really necessary to restrict or to give up some mereological principles to solve those puzzles in a three-dimensionalist perspective.

There seems to be a way of solving ontological puzzles that allows keeping all mereological principles in their generality, without adopting a four-dimensionalist space-time ontology. This solution appears to be possible only if mereological sums are not taken as set-like, that is, as such that they never change parts. Van Inwagen [25] admits that sums can change their parts but does not accept the existence of arbitrary sums. In the present paper, we agree with van Inwagen in regarding sums as composite entities that can change their parts, but we accept the existence of arbitrary sums in the context of a temporal version of mereology. The temporal mereology we state here is shown to be consistent with the change of parts.

P. Giaretta (✉)
Department of Philosophy, University of Padua, Padua, Italy
e-mail: pierdaniele.giaretta@unipd.it

The solution of ontological puzzles is achieved by denying the persistence of some of the entities involved, as in [6, 18]. Although good reasons for this move are provided, some difficult aspects of the solution are also highlighted and tentatively answered.

13.2 Temporal Mereology

It is usually assumed that sums are set-like entities not only in the sense that if they have the same parts, they are the same but also in the sense that they cannot change their parts from time to time.[1] The two assumptions are not equivalent. Indeed, according to van Inwagen [25], sums are composite objects that can have different parts at different times. Van Inwagen's view may seem paradoxical to some mereology theorists, those who regard sums as entities that cannot lose or acquire parts. Van Inwagen argues for this thesis by emphasizing that a mereological sum is a sum *of* certain things already given and taking parthood as a temporally relativized relationship: a is a part of b at t. Therefore a mereological sum is composed of certain things at one time and of possibly different things at a different time. Furthermore, according to van Inwagen, to block certain arguments against the possibility that mereological sums change their parts we should give up the general existence of sums. However, this move, as van Inwagen acknowledges, is not the only possible one.

In what follows, we shall describe a theory of temporal mereology consistent both with the view that sums can change their parts and with the general existence of sums.

Let us adopt a mereological language based on the logical vocabulary of second order logic, identity, a binary predicate of temporally relativized existence, and a ternary predicate of temporally relativized parthood.[2]

There are two sorts of first order variables: $x, y, z, \ldots, x_1, x_2, \ldots$, intended to range over material entities and $t, t', t'', \ldots$, intended to range over temporal instants.

The second order variables $X, Y, \ldots$ are plural variables as indicated by Boolos [3], that is, variables ranging over all pluralities of entities of the domain, each one to be simply understood as *some* (one or more) entities of the domain.

A mereological theory can be stated in such a formal language, but here we shall use translations of the formal sentences into a suitable portion of natural language integrated with first and second order variables. The quantification of plural

---

[1] Sums may be taken to exist in time, even if they are conceived as set-like, while existence in time for (certain) sets is not so clear. It is clear instead that if sets do not exist in time, it does not make sense to speak of their change of elements.

[2] As in, for example, [22]. Relativization to time is not always a natural move. We do not claim that a temporal parameter should be introduced for all predicates.

variables might be expressed by the clauses: "There are certain Xs such that", "For any Ys", namely "For Ys whatever they are". However, as in [3], we shall omit the final "s"—grammatically indicating the plural form—in any later use of the plural variables.

Plural interpretation of second order variables allows to take the values of first and second order variables as belonging to the same domain. The values of temporal variables belong to a disjoint domain.

We shall also use sentential forms such as "x is one of the X", or "a is one of the X", which may be considered as a way of translating Xx and Xa respectively.[3] (Bearing this convention in mind should clarify what further expressions used in this paper are short for.)

Individuals, including sums of individuals among them, exist at some times and may not exist at other times. To express such facts, a predicate E of existence at t is employed without making any special assumption about its nature.

Identity, expressed by "$=$", is absolute. In this language, it is not even possible to say that individuals are identical or distinct at a given moment: they are just identical or distinct. Usual rules are adopted for "$=$".

Let us remark that being (existence in the domain, here called "logical existence") does not entail temporal existence: $E(a, t)$ (i.e., a exists at t) does not follow from $\exists x(x = a)$ (i.e., there is something identical to a).

The relationship between temporal existence and parthood satisfies the following constraints, taken as axioms:

Axiom 1 *If x exists at t, then x is a part of x at t.*

Axiom 2 *If x is a part of y at t, x exists at t and y exists at t.*

Furthermore, temporally relativized parthood is anti-symmetric and transitive, as specified by the following axioms:

Axiom 3 *If x is a part of y at t and y is a part of x at t, then x is identical to y.*[4]

---

[3] Alternatively, "x is one of the X"/"a is one of the X" can be taken as the result of applying the predicate "is one of" to an individual variable/individual constant and to a plural variable. In this case "is one of" expresses a multigrade relation between one entity and one or more entities. The introduction of the predicate "is one of" enables us to adopt the expressions "each one of the X" as an abbreviation for "each entity x that is one of the X", "some of the X" as an abbreviation of "some entity x that is one of the X", and "at least one of the X" as an abbreviation of "at least an entity x that is one of the X".

[4] Assuming the following form of the second order comprehension:

If there is an x such that $\Phi(x)$, there are X such that x is one of the X if and only if $\Phi(x)$.

where $\Phi(x)$ is a well formed formula and X does not occur in it, and taking the temporal parameter as fixed, anti-symmetry of parthood does not need to be explicitly stated. It follows from Axioms 1, 2 and Axiom 6 below.

Axiom 4 *If x is a part of y at t and y is a part of z at t, then x is a part of z at t.*

From Axioms 1 and 2 it follows that:

Theorem 1 *x exists at t if, and only if, x is a part of x at t.*

Theorem 1 says that, as far as material objects are concerned, temporally existing is tantamount to being a part of oneself.[5]

We shall remain neutral as to the logical and temporal existence of atoms, that is, of entities having no proper part. (Of course, this does not exclude that some models of the theory involve atoms.) Overlapping-at-t and being-a-sum-of-at-t are introduced and defined as follows:

Definition 1 *x overlaps y at t* $=_{df}$ There is a *z* that is part of *x* and of *y* at *t*.

Definition 2 *x is a sum of the Y at t* $=_{df}$ Each one of the *Y* is a part of *x* at *t* and every part of *x* at *t* overlaps at least one of the *Y* at *t*.

Then it is possible to define composition as a multigrade relationship between one or more entities and an entity in the following way:

Definition 3 *The X compose y at t* $=_{df}$ *y is a sum of the X at t.*[6]

The two usual basic axioms of mereology, that is, Existence of Composition and Uniqueness of Composition, can be respectively stated as:

Axiom 5 *If the X exist at t, then there is a y such that y exists at t and is a sum of the X at t.*

Axiom 6 *If the X compose y at t and the X compose z at t, then y is identical to z.*[7]

If some of the *X* do not exist at *t*, from Axiom 5 it does not follow either that there is a sum of the *X* at *t* or that there is no such sum. We shall remain neutral on this issue. On the other hand, Axiom 6 excludes that the same entities have two distinct sums at the same time.

---

[5] This is a common thesis in the framework of temporal mereology (see e.g., [22, p. 215]). It entails that Caesar (assuming that he does not exist anymore) is presently not a part of itself. This consequence might sound odd, but it immediately follows from the plausible view that no material object is *now* a part of a presently non-existing object.

[6] Van Inwagen requires that composing entities do not overlap. Such a constraint avoids what Lewis [11] and Varzi [26] would call "double counting", that is, counting a part more than once when overlapping among the composing entities is allowed.

[7] There are various versions of Uniqueness of Composition, or mereological extensionality. Their relations are highlighted by Varzi [27]. We state here the most standard version.

13.3 The Mereological Consistency of the Change of Parts

A set-theoretical model of classical second order mereology, as stated, by example, in [11], can be easily transformed into a model of temporal mereology.

Let us start from a very simple model, where the domain D of individuals is the set $\{a, b, c, m_1, m_2, m_3, n\}$ such that: a, b and c are atoms; a and b compose m_1; b and c compose m_2; a and c compose m_3; a, b and c compose n. The values of second order variables are subsets of D.[8] The predicate of identity has the standard extensional interpretation relative to D. Parthood is interpreted on D in accordance with the above constraints on the objects of D. This array of objects is sketched in Fig. 13.1, left side.

To get a model of temporal mereology take 1 as the only temporal instant. Add the pair $\langle 1, 1 \rangle$ to the extension of the identity predicate. The extension of existence-at-t is provided by all pairs $\langle e, 1 \rangle$ such that e belongs to D. The triples of the extension of ternary parthood are obtained as follows: every pair belonging to the extension of the binary parthood of the previous model is transformed into a triple by adding 1 as third element (see Fig. 13.1, left side). It is easy to see that all axioms of temporal mereology are true in the derived model.

If temporal mereology has to describe the actual world, it should be consistent to take as an axiom the existence of entities changing their parts in time[9]:

Axiom 7 *There are distinct times t and t' and entities x and y such that x and y exist both at t and t' and x is a part of y at t but not at t'.*

It is easy to modify the above model of temporal mereology in order to make Axiom 7 true. Let us proceed as follows. Another instant, say 2, is added. Extensions of identity and of binary existence are modified to (also) include, respectively, the

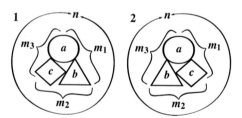

Fig. 13.1 Time 1: $a + b = m_1$, $b + c = m_2$, $a + c = m_3$. Time 2: $a + b = m_3$, $b + c = m_2$, $a + c = m_1$

---

[8] For the sake of simplicity, we take subsets of the domain, not pluralities of entities of the domain, as values of the second order variables. It would be possible, but much more complicated, to provide a full plural semantics for a second order language.
[9] It is an apparent empirical truth that some things change their parts. However, taking this truth as empirical does not imply that it cannot be contested. Here it will be assumed as an axiom, without dealing with the question of its justification.

pair $\langle 2, 2\rangle$ and all pairs $\langle e, 2\rangle$ such that e belongs to D. To get the extension of ternary parthood, add all the triples obtained by replacing 1 with 2, with two exceptions: $\langle b, m_1, 1\rangle$ is replaced with $\langle b, m_3, 2\rangle$ (instead of $\langle b, m_1, 2\rangle$), and $\langle c, m_3, 1\rangle$ with $\langle c, m_1, 2\rangle$ (instead of $\langle c, m_3, 2\rangle$). In the resulting model (see Fig. 13.1), two objects have different parts at distinct times: m_1 has a and b as parts at 1 and a and c at 2, while m_3 has a and c as parts at 1 and a and b at 2. No other object changes its parts.

It is easy to see that both Axiom 7 and the above theory of temporal mereology are satisfied by the envisaged model. So Axiom 7 is consistent with temporal mereology. Let us label as T the theory obtained by adding Axiom 7 to the above theory of temporal mereology.

Some theorems of T are interesting and easily proven. In the first place:

Theorem 2 *There are X, y, z, and distinct t, t' such that y is not identical to z and the X compose both y at t and z at t'.*

Theorem 2 can be proved in a very quick informal way by making an implicit appeal to the second order comprehension.

Proof Let us assume, by absurd:

(*) For every t and every t', if the X compose y at t and compose z at t', then $y = z$.

By Axiom 7 suppose that m and n exist both at t and t' ($t \neq t'$) and are such that

n is a part of m at t.
n is not a part of m at t'.

By Axiom 5 there is an x, say m', such that m' exists at t' and is a sum of m and n at t'. Thus

m and n compose m at t.
m and n compose m' at t'.

and $m \neq m'$, since n is a part of m' at t', and is not a part of m at t', but by (*) $m = m'$. Thus (*) is to be denied and its denial is equivalent to:

There are X, y, z, t and t' such that $y \neq z$ and the X compose both y at t and z at t'.

Identity of t and t' contradicts Axiom 6. Thus t and t' are distinct. □

The provability of Theorem 2 on the basis of very general principles may appear surprising, for, even if the change of parts is granted, whether or not some entities compose distinct objects at distinct times seems like a purely empirical and contingent issue.

From Theorem 2 it immediately follows that:

Theorem 3 *There are at least four material objects.*

Proof By Theorem 2, some X compose distinct objects y and z at distinct times, and obviously y and z cannot be atoms; thus at least two entities compose both y and z, and no one is identical either to y or to z. □

We shall neither derive other deductive consequences of the theory T, nor integrate T with an axiomatic specification of the relevant principles concerning the change of parts or structure. First, we need to have an idea of how to solve certain basic problems in accordance with the theory (and, of course, in a plausible way). Thus in what follows we shall focus on such basic problems and their solutions. We shall first consider puzzles whose main feature is the loss or acquisition of parts, and then turn to puzzles mainly involving the rearrangement of (certain) parts.

13.4 Puzzles of the Change of Parts

Mereological axioms seem to be intuitively involved in the derivation of ontological puzzles. In a number of puzzles, entities a and b are supposed to be such that:

(1) a is a proper part of b at t_1.
(2) a and b fully overlap at t_2.

where (2) amounts to saying that there are entities that compose both a and b at t_2. It follows from (1) that:

$a \neq b$.

Yet, from (2) it follows, by Uniqueness of Composition (Axiom 6), that:

$a = b$.

If besides a and b, taken as above, there is an entity c such that:

c is a proper part of b at t_1.
$b = a + c$ at t_1.
c is not a proper part of b at t_2.

where $+$ is the mereological operation of summation, it follows that

$b \neq a + c$ at t_2.

If it is taken for granted that $a + c$ at t_2 exists (at t_2) and is the same as $a + c$ at t_1, a contradiction arises. Existence of Composition is involved in the use of $+$, while Uniqueness of Composition is the basis on which the problematic identities are stated.

The famous story of the cat Tibbles[10] can be read in both the shorter and the longer version of the puzzle, by assuming that

> a is Tib, the body of Tibbles, i.e., Tibbles minus her tail.
> b is Tibbles.
> c is Tail, the tail of Tibbles.

Solutions for the two versions of the puzzle in the context of the outlined theory T are the following.

Concerning the first version, it can be claimed that a does not exist at t_2. So nothing is part of it at t_2 and Axiom 6 cannot be applied to derive that $a = b$.

Concerning the latter version, $a + c$, taken as the entity individuated with respect to t_1 by virtue of Axioms 5 and 6, is just b and does not have c as a part at t_2. So $a + c$, taken as the entity individuated with respect to t_2 by virtue of Axioms 5 and 6, is a "new" entity not existing at t_1. Shortly, "$a + c$"—with no explicit temporal specification—is ambiguous or context-dependent and no contradiction arises.

These solutions amount to denying the existence of certain entities at a certain time t, but it might appear arbitrary as to which ones are to be taken as non-existent at t. There should be a motivation for denying persistence (or pre-existence) and the motivation should be provided in a general way. An idea which appears to be worth pursuing ties the persistence of an entity after the change and its pre-existence before the change with the kind of structure the entity is endowed with.[11]

Usually, when we individuate an object through its components, we indirectly refer to a certain kind of organization of such components. This organization can be more or less cohesive and more or less intrinsically modifiable, depending on what sort of entities is at stake. In general we grasp an (ordinary) object as having the possibility of persisting through a range of changes. For instance, any animal, independent of the entities it is taken to be composed of, has an internal unity that allows it to persist through changes in composition and in spatial dislocation. Anyway, there are certain (more or less blurred) limits in the structural changes the object may undergo without passing out of existence, and knowing these limits is part of our common understanding of what such an object is.

If Axiom 5 is true, for any existing entities X, including arbitrarily chosen parts of (ordinary) objects, there exists a sum of the X.

Now it appears that many such composite entities are temporally very fragile, for it is reasonable to deny any kind of persistence when no kind of organization is

---

[10] The story is really an adaptation of a medieval puzzle, *Animal est pars animalis* (see [28]), but analogous puzzles have haunted philosophers at least since Plato. A cat, Tibbles, her tail, Tail, and the rest of her body, Tib, are considered at a certain time, say t_1. Later on, Tibbles's tail is cut. Soon after, say at t_2, it appears that Tibbles has the same parts, and so is the same, as Tib.

[11] For other approaches to this problem, see [5, 6, 18]. Here we shall not compare the view outlined below with these alternative proposals.

recognizable. If so, then strange, non-ordinary entities such as the sum of your index finger, the flower on the table, a match and the Moon—let us call it "Moof"[12]—have no significant internal unity such that they can survive change of parts or structure. Thus, an entity like Moof would not survive the loss or the displacement of parts, as it may happen, for instance, if the match is burned down or the flower is put on the chair. In these cases, we should say that Moof has been replaced, as it were, by a different albeit partially similar entity. Arguably, we may count among strange, non ordinary entities even Tib before Tail is cut, and the sum of Tibbles' tail and Tibbles after the cutting time. Accordingly, we may conclude that they are not so temporally robust as ordinary, paradigmatic material entities, for they lack a similar internal unity. (See below in this section for a tentative specification of this idea.)

A different way—more quantitative than qualitative—of accounting for the difference between the kind of unity Tibbles and Tib have might be provided by an analogy with geometrical entities. Tibbles can look like a segment and Tib like a segment minus a point, or minus a subsegment, which is itself a segment. Let us identify segments with closed intervals of real numbers. Then, according to this picture, Tib is not a closed interval since it lacks an endpoint or a subsegment, as it were.[13]

These considerations strongly suggest an ontological view that agrees with theory T in that:

(i) A composed entity is individuated by the composing entities.
(ii) Any statement of composition implies reference to time since composition can change in time.

and is characterized by the following further theses:

(iii) No composed entity is without unity of some kind; so reference to the composing entities at a time implies an indirect reference to the kind of unity of the composed entity.
(iv) The specific kind of unity of the composed entity grounds the (correct) judgement about the persistence (or the pre-existence) of such entity.

To further illustrate this point of view, let us apply it to the puzzle of the trunk and the tree (the so called *growing argument*). A tree b has some branches at a time t_1, so it is not identical to its trunk a. Let us assume, as can happen, that at a previous time t_2 the tree has no branches. Looking at the tree at t_2, we might be willing to say that the tree is identical to its trunk. If the trunk, taken at t_2, is identical to b, then we

---

[12] Thanks to an anonymous referee for this example.

[13] The analogy is partial because of the set-theoretical nature of geometrical entities. Moreover, the alleged vagueness of boundaries, which also affects fully integrated wholes, might make this analogy to appear too strong a simplification of the difference between Tibbles and Tib. However, it might be claimed that the degree of vagueness of entities that are not fully integrated wholes is higher in a quite intuitive sense, which could probably be further specified in some way.

have both $a \neq b$ and $a = b$. From the point of view we have outlined, the argument for identity can be blocked by claiming that there is no single (temporally) existing entity which "the trunk" picks out at t_2 and at t_1. The entity we may refer to as "the trunk" at t_1 (i.e., b) does not exist at t_2, and it is not the same as the entity we may refer to as "the trunk" at t_2 (i.e., a).

The kind of account provided here might be challenged by devising cases where the "whole" entity is compared with the entity minus a very small part. For example, let us suppose that Tib is identified at t as Tibbles minus a hair. Can we really say that the kind of unity displayed by Tib is different from that displayed by Tibbles? Tib appears to be like an open-structured entity, where the forces tying the lacking hair to the rest of it are still active. These forces cannot be active any longer, or should be active in a different way, when the hair is lost or separated. This remark might be enough to suggest, at an intuitive informal level, that Tib is an open unstable entity, which cannot become closed and stable without passing out of existence. To state this view in less intuitive terms, it could be useful to resort to the notion of wholeness proposed by Simons [20], according to which a whole satisfies the following condition:

> Every member of some division of the object stands in a certain relation to every other member, and no member bears the same relation to anything other than members of the division. (p. 327)[14]

According to this idea, Tib, taken as Tibbles minus a hair, is not a whole, while Tibbles and the hair Tib lacks are wholes. For, on one hand, the relation which grounds Tibbles's unity would link Tib with the lacking hair, external to Tib, and so cannot ground Tib's unity. On the other hand, it is difficult to think of a *similar* structuring relation tying only Tib's parts. There is surely a way in which Tib's parts, and only Tib's parts, are related to each other, but their natural links with the excluded hair do not appear to be essentially different from the natural links they have to each other. We might say that to conceive Tib as an (integral) entity, we have to think of it as endowed with a minor degree of integrity. However, speaking of degrees suggests a linear order and—it might be objected—that appears inadequate to represent the varieties of ways in which unity can be realised. It seems better to speak of kinds of unity, which might be taken to correspond to kinds of wholes. In this perspective one might, on the one hand, work out a general frame in which kinds of unity can be dealt with, and, on the other hand, look for examples having a paradigmatic value.[15]

---

[14] Other more or less formal ideas concerning unity and its ground are expressed in recent literature. See, for example, [8, 9, 13, 14, 21, 24]. In contrast to what was done in these writings, we pursue the idea that no entity is devoid of unity, while accepting the mereological axiom of Existence of Composition and avoiding to choose among the main ontological options.

[15] Simons [21] provides some case studies of natural wholes. However, he argues against the use of the notion of a kind of whole in the explication of what a whole is and prefers to raise the general question of what requirements a relation must satisfy in order to give rise to wholes. It should be said that Simons does not accept Existence of Composition in its full generality.

A more serious challenge to the above ontological view is the following puzzle proposed by Noonan [15] (and based on a similar case sketched in [6]). This time, Tib is the *brain* of Tibbles at t_1. Later on, so the story goes, Tibbles loses everything except his brain, but is kept alive by scientists. At t_2, Tibbles is still alive and alert. It appears that Tib is a proper part of Tibbles at t_1, while at t_2 Tibbles is the same as her brain, that is, Tib. Again, by Axiom 6, we obtain a contradiction.

If survival as a mere brain is accepted as possible,[16] there seems to be no direct and convincing answer to this puzzle in the theoretical framework outlined above. It is hard to deny that Tibbles's brain exists at t_2 and is the same at t_1 and at t_2. If a cat, identified with Tibbles's brain, exists at t_2, it also is difficult to deny that we have the same cat at t_1 and at t_2, since it is implicitly supposed that the previous "content" of Tibble's brain is preserved at t_2.

However this is a *special* difficulty, for it involves independent and obviously delicate issues concerning the relationships between minds, brains, and bodies. For instance, we are prone to say that Tibbles survives the loss of any part except its brain because we recognize both a physical and a psychological continuity between the cat and the brain. Yet, it might be objected that the physical continuity is too partial, and the view that psychological continuity alone is sufficient for identity across time is notoriously problematic (see, e.g., [16] for a survey). Furthermore, suppose that Tibbles's *body* is kept alive as well. What reasons are there, psychological continuity aside, to deny that Tibbles, qua organism, is the body rather than the brain at t_2? Or should we say that neither is? Hence, it might be objected, what the puzzle shows is that our common criteria of persistence for cats (dogs, persons, etc.)—rather than the metaphysical picture and the mereological theory outlined above—are ultimately problematic.

13.5 Puzzles of the Change of Structure

It should be clear that in our theoretical framework it is not possible that an entity a intuitively constitutes—and thus fully overlaps—an entity b at a time and a distinct entity c at another time, for full overlapping implies identity of composition and identity of composition implies identity by Uniqueness of Composition (Axiom 2). However, some cases seem to support the possibility of constitution without identity. Here we shall focus on a couple of such cases.[17]

---

[16] Survival as a mere brain appears to be physiologically impossible or, at least, highly unlikely, since to survive a brain needs a continuous exchange with the body at a chemical level (see e.g., [2]). But even if it were possible to simulate this exchange by employing a suitably designed device, it might be argued that, after the device is in function, the whole organism persists at least in part as (a certain portion of) such a device.

[17] The source of the former case is [7], but here we follow the formulation provided in [23]. The latter was stated in [19]. The literature concerning the notion of constitution is very wide. Let us mention, as some significant examples, [1, 10, 17, 20, 29, 30].

The most natural solution to this sort of puzzles in the above outlined ontological framework is denying that what constitutes distinct material entities at different times is itself a material entity.

1. A portion of clay (*LUMPL*) is bought at 9 am. A statue (*GOLIATH*) is made out of LUMPL and put on the table at 2 pm. Later on, the left hand of GOLIATH is replaced with a new one made out of a portion of clay different from LUMPL. At 3 pm GOLIATH has the new hand and the old hand is in the dustbin. It seems that (see e.g., [23]):

(I) LUMPL exists at 9 am, but GOLIATH does not.
(II) At 3 pm GOLIATH is wholly present on the table, but LUMPL is not wholly present on the table, since GOLIATH is a statue and a statue can undergo replacements of certain parts (not all parts of a statue are essential), but LUMPL is a portion of matter and no part of a portion of matter can be lost or changed.

It appears that at 2 pm, LUMPL shares all parts with the statue GOLIATH. According to Uniqueness of Composition, as expressed by Axiom 6, they are the same entity, against the reasons provided by (I)–(II) for taking them as distinct entities.

Assuming, as it is implicit in the above formulation, that portions of clay are sums of certain clay parts (at a certain time), this puzzle is to be solved along the same lines as the previous ones. Namely, if LUMPL is the object that, as a matter of fact, is the sum of certain clay parts C at 9 am, then it does not exist anymore at 2 pm. If, on the other hand, "LUMPL" is regarded as designating the sum of the C both at 9 am and at any following times, then there is no single material object "LUMPL" stands for. Either way, no contradiction arises.

However there is a problem here, for it may be argued that such entities as portions of stuff—regarded independently of time, shape, etc.—are convenient for many purposes, and are not to be dismissed so quickly. Consider for instance the following statement, which is (prima facie) true in the envisaged scenario:

(III) GOLIATH is made of a certain portion of clay at 2 pm, and that very portion of clay does not constitute GOLIATH at 3 pm.

Statement (III) strongly suggests that a single entity e, what was above called "LUMPL", fully overlaps GOLIATH at 2 pm and does not fully overlap GOLIATH at 3 pm. But by Axiom 6 this cannot be the case, at least insofar as e is taken to be a material object.

There are many possible answers to this objection, and we shall explore just one of them here, by claiming that when we speak of such objects as portions of stuff, qua entities that are identical across time if and only if they share certain composing parts across time, we are covertly making a plural reference to the composing parts, collectively taken. So, for instance, what would be meant by (III) is just that certain C compose GOLIATH at 2 pm, but not at 3 pm. The rationale behind this view is that

13 A Mereology for the Change of Parts

reference to what composes is reference to some appropriate composing entities. If what these entities compose at a time goes out of existence, they end up composing a different material object provided with a different kind of unity.[18]

In general, for any composed material entity existing at t, there is a way in which its component parts P are organized at t. Of course, we may abstract away from such an organization and speak accordingly, which is what happens when we use "LUMPL" to designate the entity that fully overlaps GOLIATH at 2 pm but not at 3 pm. However, in this way, we are just making one of many or reifying what is common to a class of material objects.[19]

For making this view more plausible, it may be observed that, pace Wiggins, it is not so wrong to say that a statue of clay is a portion of clay with some extra-features (a certain organization, shape, history, etc.). To the contrary, describing a statue as a portion (period) is offering an obviously under-informative characterization. What is left out are exactly those features—organization, shape, history, etc.—that are usually taken to ground the persistence of statues.

2.   A piece of yarn is knitted into a sweater at one time t_1, unravelled, and then knitted into a hat at t_2. It appears that the sweater is not the same as the hat. Yet, intuitively enough, the piece of yarn fully overlaps both the sweater (at t_1) and the hat (at t_2). Since fully overlapping at a time entails (absolute) identity by Axiom 6, we have a contradiction, that is, that the sweater is, and is not, identical with the hat.

It might appear that the kind of solution devised for the first case is quite unnatural for this one, in which we have a specific, well individuated piece of yarn first used to make a sweater and then a hat.

However, let us see how it is possible to apply here the same solution as above. We must deny that the piece of yarn knitted into a sweater is the same material object as the piece of yarn knitted into a hat. Again, when the same entity (the piece of yarn) seems to fully overlap two distinct objects at different times (the sweater at t_1 and the

---

[18] Alternatively, the portion of clay might be thought of as an entity obtained by means of an equivalence relation. The portion of clay just bought and the statue are both composed, respectively at 9 am and at 2 pm, by the same disjoint minimal parts of clay. The corresponding equivalence class could be identified with the portion of clay regarded as an amount without any qualification. From this point of view the portion of clay might be conceived as the materialization of an abstract entity.

[19] See note 18 above. It might be objected that, intuitively enough, portions of stuff may lose a minimal amount of matter without passing out of existence. And this entails—so the objection goes—that singular reference to portions, as ordinarily understood, is never eliminable in favor of plural reference to their components. We are not too impressed by this objection. Of course, we may speak of "the same portion" even if what we have is not, strictly speaking, the same portion. Like many empirical notions, our usual concept of a portion is vague. For instance, the view that portions survive the lost of a minimal part is obviously the first step of a soritical series. But in the same vein, we may also speak of the "same components" at different times even if the components have not, strictly speaking, remained the same. As far as ordinary understanding is concerned, it appears that vagueness affects both the singular reference to a portion and the plural reference to its components, contrary to what the objection assumes. Moreover, vagueness is a notoriously delicate issue, and not specifically involved in the puzzles we are discussing.

hat at t_2), no such entity exists and plural reference is made to certain appropriate parts of those objects. However, this time, the plural reference is to be qualified. Intuitively enough, a piece of yarn exists at time t only if certain composing parts W exists at t and are related one another in a certain ordered structure. So conceived, reference to a piece of yarn, qua object that remains the same even when knitted into a sweater (or a hat), would be reference to certain component parts under the constraint that they be organized in the manner of a thread. So, for instance, by:

The same piece of yarn constitute a sweater at t_1 and a hat at t_2.

what is meant is that certain entities, say the P, compose a sweater at t_1 and a hat at t_2, and the P are connected together as a piece of yarn, and in the same order, both at t_1 and t_2.[20]

It might be objected that even the sweater and the hat can be dispensed with in the same way, that is, by referring to the same components of the piece of yarn and considering different higher levels of their organization. What reason is there—so the objection goes—to regard the sweater (hat), and not the piece of yarn, as existing at t_1 (t_2)?

A possible reply is the following. Consider the view that, by suitably knitting a piece of yarn into a sweater (hat), we make a novel entity, distinct from the original piece of yarn, come into existence. Such a view is natural and commonsensical enough to be taken for granted, but it does not follow from the above outlined ontological perspective. If it is false, that is, if by knitting a piece of yarn into a sweater (hat) we do not obtain a novel entity, then no problem arises in our ontological framework. So, the objection makes sense only under the assumption that such a view is correct. And if it is, then there is no denial that the sweater (hat) exists at t_1 (t_2). Thus, if there is any problem here, it concerns the claim that the piece of yarn goes out of existence when knitted into a sweater (hat). Such a claim is usually deemed as counterintuitive. However, this is not so clear.

First observe that it is fully consistent both with common beliefs and practices and with the present ontological framework to say that the piece of yarn becomes *another* thing (a sweater, or a hat) through a certain change (being knitted).

To put this view in philosophically more respectable terms, we may say that, when we knit a piece of yarn into a sweater (hat), what we have is a change of entity, rather than a change affecting a single entity. And, whenever there is a change of entity, the original entity goes out of existence. So, the claim that the piece of yarn goes out of existence when knitted into a sweater (hat) is not inconsistent with

---

[20] Something similar to what was said above (note 18) of the portion of clay could be said of the piece of yarn, even though in a somewhat more complex manner. The piece of yarn might be thought of as an entity got by means of an equivalence relation. The unraveled piece of yarn, the sweater, and the hat are all composed, at the appropriate times, by the same disjoint connected parts linearly ordered. The corresponding equivalence class could be identified with the piece of yarn. From this point of view also the piece of yarn (without any qualification) might be conceived as the materialization of an abstract entity.

some intuitions (assuming that they are coherent). We suspect that, if it *appears* counterintuitive, this is because the notion of *going out of* (temporal) *existence* is conflated with that of *being destroyed* (or *disintegrated* etc.).

In the present framework, a thing may go out of existence without being *destroyed*, if being destroyed entails being unrecoverable, or at least extremely hard to recover.[21] Consider for instance a very simple, two-piece, Tinkertoy house. Most philosophers would agree that the house goes out of (temporal) existence when turned into a two-piece Tinkertoy car. Yet, in this scenario, we would not say that the Tinkertoy house has been *destroyed* (unless it is part of a make-believe game to so saying). And plausibly, the reason is that the house is easily recoverable: turn the car into a house, and you have it back.

There is another, more theoretical reply to the objection concerning the (temporal) co-existence of the piece of yarn and the sweater (hat). It could be claimed that an entity composed of certain other disjoint entities at a given time presents a maximal level of structuring at that time. That would distinguish the sweater (the hat) from what is regarded as the piece of yarn at a time in which the sweater (the hat) exists. A possible evidence for this perspective stems from the anti-symmetry of the intuitive relation of constitution. We may say that the piece of yarn constitutes the sweater at t_1, but not vice versa. A plausible explanation is that the sweater is structurally richer than what is regarded as the piece of yarn. The piece of yarn—qua object that remains the same no matter if knitted into a sweater, unravelled or knitted into a hat—may be seen as a lower level, non-maximally structured entity, and thus not as a single material entity at all.

Of course, to make this idea precise, and hence more acceptable, would not be an easy job, for it is difficult to specify which changes in the relations among the (relevant) parts affect the persistence of the entity. It is quite obvious, for instance, that the sweater worn and the sweater folded are the same entity, and this appears to entail that the preservation of the maximal level of structuring of the relevant existing parts is too strong a condition for persistence. In the cases we are discussing, where the entities in question are wholes (in Simon's sense) and all their composing parts are preserved, the level of structuring should be qualified as maximal up to certain mathematical transformations, including by example a limited variation of the distance among parts.

13.6 Conclusion

Clearly some work is still to be done to transform the outlined view into a fully developed theory. However, we think we have achieved some results. We proved that mereology is formally consistent with the statement that there are entities that

---

[21] Of course, this view presupposes that intermittent (temporal) existence is allowed. However, we know of no convincing objection to intermittent (temporal) existence, and of many reasons to endorse it. Anyway, see [4, 12] for a couple of contrasting views on this matter.

persist while changing some of their parts. We also indicated how puzzles can be accordingly solved and how two main kinds of change concerning parts might be accounted for, by providing a partially new analysis of some classical problems involving persistence through time.

References

1. Baker, Lynne Rudder. 2000. *Persons and Bodies: A Constitution View*. Cambridge, UK: Cambridge University Press.
2. Berlucchi, Giovanni. 2009. "Identità personale, corpo, mente e cervello." In *Filosofia della medicina. Modelli, metodo, cura ed errori*, edited by P. Giaretta, A. Moretto, G. Gensini, and M. Trabucchi, 613–29. Bologna: Il Mulino.
3. Boolos, George. 1984. "To Be Is to Be the Value of a Variable (or to Be Some Values of Some Variables)." *The Journal of Philosophy* 81:430–49.
4. Burke, Michael. 1980. "Cohabitation, Stuff and Intermittent Existence." *Mind* 89:391–405.
5. Burke, Michael. 1994. "Dion and Theon: An Essentialist Solution to an Ancient Puzzle." *The Journal of Philosophy* 91:129–39.
6. Burke, Michael. 1996. "Tibbles the Cat: A Modern Sophisma." *Philosophical Studies* 84:63–74.
7. Gibbard, Allan. 1975. "Contingent Identity." *Journal of Philosophical Logic* 4:187–221.
8. Guarino, Nicola and Christopher Welty. 2000. "Identity, Unity, and Individuation: Towards a Formal Toolkit for Ontological Analysis." In *Proceedings of ECAI-2000: The European Conference on Artificial intelligence*, edited by W. Horn, 219–23. Amsterdam: IOS Press.
9. Hawley, Katherine. 2001. *How Things Persist*. Oxford: Oxford University Press.
10. Johnston, Mark. 1992. "Constitution Is Not Identity." *Mind* 101:89–105.
11. Lewis, David. 1991. *Parts of Classes*. London: Blackwell.
12. Lowe, Edward Jonathan. 1998. "On the Identity of Artifacts." *The Journal of Philosophy* 80:220–32.
13. Lowe, Edward Jonathan. 1998. "Entity, Identity and Unity." *Erkenntnis* 48:191–208.
14. Lowe, Edward Jonathan. 2003. "Identity, Individuality, and Unity." *Philosophy* 78:321–36.
15. Noonan, Harold. 1999. "Tibbles the Cat—Reply to Burke." *Philosophical Studies* 95:215–18.
16. Olson, Eric. (Winter 2008). "Personal identity." In *The Stanford Encyclopedia of Philosophy*, edited by Edward N. Zalta. http://plato.stanford.edu/archives/win2008/entries/identity-personal.
17. Rea, Michael. 1995. "The Problem of Material Constitution." *The Philosophical Review* 104:525–52.
18. Rea, Michael. 2000. "Constitution and Kind Membership." *Philosophical Studies* 97:169–93.
19. Sidelle, Alan. 2002. "Is There a True Metaphysics of Material Objects?" *Philosophical Issues* 12:118–45.
20. Simons, Peter. 1987. *Parts: A Study in Ontology*. Oxford: Clarendon Press.
21. Simons, Peter. 2006. "Real Wholes, Real Parts: Mereology Without Algebra." *The Journal of Philosophy* 103:597–613.
22. Thomson, Judith Jarvis. 1983. "Parthood and Identity Across Time." *The Journal of Philosophy* 80:201–20.
23. Thomson, Judith Jarvis. 1998. "The Statue and the Clay." *Noûs* 32:149–73.
24. Van Inwagen, Peter. 1990. *Material Beings*. Ithaca, NY: Cornell University Press.
25. Van Inwagen, Peter. 2006. "Can Mereological Sums Change Their Parts?" *The Journal of Philosophy* 103:614–30.
26. Varzi, Achille. 2000. "Mereological Commitments." *Dialectica* 54:283–305.
27. Varzi, Achille. 2008. "The Extensionality of Parthood and Composition." *The Philosophical Quarterly* 58:108–33.

28. Wiggins, David. 1968. "On Being in the Same Place at the Same Time." *The Philosophical Review* 77:90–95.
29. Wiggins, David. 1980. *Sameness and Substance*. Oxford: Blackwell.
30. Wiggins, David. 2001. *Sameness and Substance Renewed*. Cambridge, UK: Cambridge University Press.

Chapter 14
Russell Versus Frege

Imre Rusza

Bertrand Russell's "On Denoting", published in 1905, has inspired lively debates, particularly among philosophers studying natural languages. The primary target of their criticism was Russell's proposal about the logical analysis of definite descriptions. At one point in the article, Russell explains that by distinguishing between meaning and denotation we are headed for confusion. Here, the basic target is Frege's "two-dimensional" semantics, the Fregean distinction between meaning (Sinn) and reference (Bedeutung). As far as I know, Russell's critics did not pick up on this particular line of reasoning, concentrating on others instead. The aim of the present article is to fill this gap and to take a close look at the Russellian argument in question.

An overview of Russell's overall line of thought in "On Denoting" will be helpful in clarifying how the parts fit together. According to him, the following types of expressions are *denoting phrases*:

(1) one man, some man, any man, every man, all men
(2) the present King of England, the present King of France, the center of mass of the Solar System at the first instant of the twentieth century, the revolution of the earth around the sun, the revolution of the sun around the earth.

Russell observes that there are three possibilities:

a. the denoting phrase does not denote anything, for example, "the present King of France";
b. the expression denotes a definite object, for example, "the present King of England";
c. the expression denotes ambiguously, for example, "a man" denotes an ambiguous man. (One might doubt whether this classification is exhaustive.)

Russell's thesis is as follows: denoting phrases do not have any meaning in isolation, but whenever they occur as parts of propositions, we can assign exact meanings to the propositions. He first focuses on assigning logical structures to sentences

---

Imre Rusza (1921–2008).

containing quantified expressions like those in (1) above (in effect, he demonstrates how universal and existential quantification works). He then goes on to consider the definite descriptions exemplified in (2). If $C(x)$ is an open sentence and "the F" is a definite description, then the logical structure of "C(the F)", according to Russell, is as follows:

$$\exists x(\forall y(F(y) \equiv y = x) \wedge C(x))$$

The Russellian reconstruction of "the King of France is bald" therefore becomes: "There is exactly one thing x that is King of France and this x is bald." This formulation no longer contains the expression "the King of France" (according to Russell, this shows that the expression by itself does not have a meaning of its own). And this sentence is bound to be false if France does not have a king (or if it has several kings).

According to Russell, if we were to assign meaning as well as denotation to definite descriptions, then the first complication would arise in those cases when the denotation is in fact missing (for example, if we state something now about the [present] King of France). Russell criticizes Meinong, who assumes that the denoting phrase still picks out an object, albeit one that is not included among the things that exist. Russell also rejects Frege's solution in the context of formalized languages: when there is no actual denotation, Frege posits an artificial one. We need not contest the validity of Russell's objections in order to criticize the solution he proposes. It is well to note, however, that—unlike for Russell—for Frege, atomic sentences containing non-denoting descriptions lack *truth value*, so they are not false (Frege [1, pp. 214–16, 221–23]). Admittedly, Frege did think that in a *logically perfect language* there is always a denotation (the trick of assigning an artificial denotation is related to this point), but in the context of natural languages, he conceded the possibility that denotation and truth value may go missing. (We might wonder whether Frege's opinion about a logically perfect language would remain standing in the light of what we know today. But that is a different issue that would lead us off track.)

Russell describes Frege's theory as follows:

> In this theory, we shall say that the denoting phrase *expresses* a meaning; and we shall say both of the phrase and of the meaning that they *denote* a denotation. In the other theory, which I advocate, there is no *meaning*, and only sometimes *a denotation*. (Russell [2, p. 483, fn. 10])

Frege has never claimed that the *meaning* denotes a denotation (only the sign does, the expression itself). Later on, we will see that Russell is attempting to identify linguistic expressions with their meaning.

We have now arrived at the part of "On Denoting" on which (as far as I am aware) hardly any attention was lavished by Russell's critics. This passage opens with the following:

14 Russell Versus Frege

> The relation of the meaning to the denotation involves certain rather curious difficulties, which seem in themselves sufficient to prove that the theory which leads to such difficulties must be wrong. (Russell [2, p. 485])

In order to demonstrate these difficulties, Russell introduces the following convention: if we want to talk about the *meaning* of a denoting expression, then we should put quotation marks around it.

This notational convention is objectionable because quotation marks are commonly used to *name* or *denote* the expression, to *talk about* the expression itself. The next example of Russell's immediately demonstrates the kind of confusion that ensues as a result:

(3) The center of mass of the Solar System is a point, not a denoting expression.
(4) "The center of mass of the Solar System" is a denoting expression, not a point.

The statement in (3) is unproblematic; but the only way to accept (4) without reservation is if the part enclosed in quotes serves to *denote* the expression. But if we were to use quotation to denote the meaning instead, then we would start having doubts: about the *meaning* of the expression appearing in quotes within (4), we would be reluctant to say that *it* was a denoting expression.

The Russellian notation therefore *identifies an expression with its meaning*. This is hardly consistent with Frege's conception, according to whom

> A proper name (word, sign, sign combination, expression) *expresses* its sense, *refers to* or *designates* its referent. By means of a sign we express its sense and designate its referent. (Frege ([1, p. 214])

In addition, Frege carefully distinguishes talk about words from talk about their meanings. He considers the possibility that...

> ...one wishes to talk about the words themselves or [about] their sense. This happens, for instance, when the words of another are quoted....In writing, the words are in this case enclosed in quotation marks....In order to speak of the sense of an expression "*A*" one may simply use the phrase "the sense of the expression '*A*'". In reported speech one talks about the sense, e.g., of another person's remarks. (Frege ([1, p. 211])

For the sake of exposition, let us introduce some useful notation. For any expression C, we use the schema

(5) MEAN(C)

to denote its meaning, and use the schema

(6) DEN(C)

to denote its denotation. Here, I use the letter "C" as a variable for linguistic expressions; in other words: the permissible values of this variable are linguistic expressions. In schemata that contain free variables, variables can be replaced by *names that denote* one of the permissible values of the variable. This way, for the variable "C" we may substitute *the name* of some expression. We may use a definite description as a name denoting a linguistic expression, or we may quote the expression. Let us agree to use single quotes to denote an expression whenever we do not know or do not want to denote it using a definite description. But this sort of quotation makes no attempt to denote the meaning, unlike the quotation Russell suggested. In accordance with this, we can give a concrete example of how the schemata in (5) and (6) can be used:

(7) MEAN ('the French President'), DEN ('the French President').

The quotes cannot be omitted; the substitution instances below are incorrect:

(8) MEAN (the French President), DEN (the French President).

Explanation: the French President is no linguistic expression and hence has neither meaning, nor denotation. By contrast, 'the French President' can have both.

Insisting on the quotation marks perhaps seems like unnecessary fussiness: we could just agree to omit them and use (8) instead of (7). But this would be a hasty move; for in the schemata in (5) and (6), for C we may also substitute a description that denotes an expression. Let us consider the following example from Russell:

(9) The first line of Gray's poem entitled *Elegy* = 'The curfew tolls the knell of parting day' (Russell [2, p. 486]).

The description on the left side of the identity denotes a linguistic expression (an English expression), whereas the right side quotes the same expression. We therefore have a true identity statement. Consequently:

(10) DEN (the first line of Gray's *Elegy*) = DEN ('The curfew tolls the knell of parting day'),[1]

but also

(11) DEN ('the first line of Gray's *Elegy*') = 'The curfew tolls the knell of parting day'.

The meaning of an expression is independent of how we denote that meaning. From the identity in (9) we therefore get:

(12) MEAN (the first line of Gray's *Elegy*) = MEAN ('The curfew tolls the knell of parting day').

By contrast:

(13) MEAN ('the first line of Gray's *Elegy*') ≠ MEAN (the first line of Gray's *Elegy*).

Let us keep in mind that based on the identity in (11), we can make a substitution on the right side of (12) to get the following:

(14) MEAN (the first line of Gray's *Elegy*) = MEAN [DEN ('the first line of Gray's *Elegy*')].

---

[1] The first line of the poem in question is a declarative sentence. Therefore the identity in (10) makes sense only if declarative sentences have denotations. (Frege thinks they do: declarative sentences denote their truth value.) But in this paper, we need not take a stand on this.

Russell says the following about the relation of (12) and (13):

> "The meaning of the first line of Gray's *Elegy*" is the same as "The meaning of 'The curfew tolls the knell of parting day'," and is not the same as "The meaning of 'the first line of Gray's Elegy'". (Russell [2, p. 486])

Russell finds it problematic that when we want to talk about the meaning of an expression *C* we end up with the meaning of *C*'s denotation, as shown in (14). But this way of putting the matter is inaccurate. In fact, the relation consists in the following.

Let *C* be a name denoting a linguistic expression *by means of a description*, and let *C** be the quoted version of this description. We then get:

(15) MEAN (*C*) = MEAN [DEN (*C**)].

In this schema, for a change, we substitute for *C* the description directly (without any quotation marks), and we can substitute for *C** the description in quotes. The identity in (14) is an instance of this relationship. Russell should have stressed the fact that this sort of case arises only when *C* itself is a linguistic expression denoted by means of a description. Instead, all he did was to warn us that the denotation of *C* might not have a meaning:

> But if we speak of "the meaning of C," that gives us the meaning (if any) of the denotation. (Russell [2, p. 486])

Indeed, if *C* denotes something other than a linguistic expression, then the denotation of *C* lacks meaning (as we have seen in the example about the French President).

The identity in (15) is meaningless if we fail to substitute *C* in accordance with our specifications. But with proper substitution, we do not get a paradox of any kind. The apparent paradox arises from Russell's failure to distinguish between the denotation of *C* and the denotation of *C in quotation marks*; and this difference is clearly marked in the identity statements in (10) and (11).

Russell continues:

> Similarly 'the denotation of C' does not mean the denotation we want, but means something which, if it denotes at all, denotes what is denoted by the denotation we want. (Russell [2, p. 486])

Again, this criterion is fulfilled only in those cases when *C* denotes a linguistic expression by means of a description. Russell gives the following example:

C = 'the first line of Gray's Elegy', and

(16) the denotation of C = The curfew tolls the knell of parting day.

> But what we *meant* to have as the denotation was 'the first line of Gray's Elegy'. (Russell [2, p. 486])[2]

---

[2] The unitalicized schematic letter "C" was Russell's choice. The numbering was added to the original.

The apparent trouble is again due to a mix-up between the expression and its quoted version. In the identity below, we can substitute for C any name with a denotation, and for C^*, the name in quotation.

DEN $(C^*) = C$.

For example:

DEN ('the French President') = the French President.

It is trivially true that the description 'the French President' denotes the French President (if it denotes anything at all). In the same way:

(17) DEN ('the first line of Gray's *Elegy*') = the first line of Gray's *Elegy* = 'The curfew tolls the knell of parting day'.

[See (11).] But the first line of Gray's *Elegy* denotes something different, as shown in (10): the denotation of the first sentence featured in the poem's first line (if sentences have a denotation at all).

In the identity statement in (16), Russell presumably intended to have for the left-side C the definite description enclosed in quotes [this is also suggested by the identity in the line preceding (16)]. But then the line of the poem appearing on the right side of the identity should have been enclosed in quotes, as demonstrated in (17). But this move provides us with the desired denotation, as shown, again, in (17). But if the role of C were played by an unquoted description, then the appropriate identity statement would be (10) (if the statement made any sense at all). We see then that the confusion has been due to the omission of one pair of parentheses. Accordingly, distinguishing meaning and reference in Russell's examples would cause no trouble, provided we play close attention to the parentheses.

In his subsequent reasoning, Russell explicitly says that he wants to identify an expression and its meaning:

> ...suppose C is our complex,[3] then we are to say that C *is* the meaning of the complex. Nevertheless, whenever C occurs without inverted commas, what is said is not true of the meaning, but only of the denotation, as when we say: The centre of mass of the Solar System is a point. Thus to speak of C itself, i.e. to make a proposition about the meaning, our subject must not be C, but something which denotes C. Thus "C," which is what we use when we want to speak of the meaning, must be not the meaning, but something which denotes the meaning. And C must not be a constituent of this complex (as it is of "the meaning of C"); for if C occurs in the complex, it will be its denotation, not its meaning, that will occur and there is no backward road from denotations to meanings, because every object can be denoted by an infinite number of different denoting phrases. (Russell [2, p. 487]) (emphasis in original)

---

[3] Complexes are complex linguistic expressions. Again, the unitalicized schematic letter "C" was Russell's choice.

Syntactic and semantic terms are tangled up throughout this passage, in just about every sentence. (For example, how could the *denotation* of a constituent expression occur within the whole expression, when a denotation is not a grammatical entity but a physical object, say?) But let us graciously set aside this aspect (similar confusion is common in the writings of Russell's contemporaries as well), in the hope that the reader can figure out the intended message. The genuinely interesting remark to make about this passage is that it does not fit with Frege's theory of meaning. Frege does not identify an expression with its meaning, and does not claim that "the meaning denotes the denotation" [Russell [2, p. 486]]. Let us consider the following passage from Frege:

> The regular connection between a sign, its sense, and its referent is of such a kind that to the sign there corresponds a definite sense and to that in turn a definite referent... The same sense has different expressions in different languages or even in the same language. (Frege [1, p. 211])

The second sentence of the passage makes clear that Frege does not identify the expression (the sign) with its meaning. The first sentence says (among other things) that a determinate reference *corresponds to* a determinate meaning. But to read this as claiming that the meaning *denotes* the denotation is possible only under the assumption that the sign is identical with its meaning.

Russell recognizes that there is a difference between the meaning of an expression and positing a name to denote that expression. But this much is trivially true: names that denote are grammatical entities; meanings, by contrast are not—even though according to Russell they are. Thus for Russell, the claim is not a trivial one but the basis for an argument to discredit the notion of meaning. Even though "*C*" denotes *C*, *C* cannot be a component of "*C*", making the relation between "*C*" and *C* seem mysterious.

Russell continues with this objection: if *C* is featured in a statement, then it is not just its denotation that matters; its meaning, too, will become relevant. Let us compare the following two statements:

(18) Scott is the author of *Waverley*.
(19) Scott is Scott.

(18) has a property that (19) lacks, namely that King George IV inquired about its truth [but did not ask about the truth of (19)]. Consequently, (18) and (19) do not express the same proposition, even though

(20) DEN ('the author of *Waverley*') = DEN('Scott') = Scott.

Consider the denoting expression 'the author of *Waverley*' within (18): in addition to its denotation, its meaning is also relevant. But Russell contends that according to advocates of a theory of meaning, the denotation remains the only relevant feature of a denoting expression until we enclose it in quotes (Russell [2, p. 488]).

Russell's solution to the "paradox" is familiar: just like descriptive phrases in general, descriptions featuring the definite article lack meaning in isolation, although meanings are assigned to each proposition in which the descriptions occur.

In the Russellian logical reconstruction of the sentence in (18), the definite description 'the author of *Waverley*' disappears, thus confirming the claim that there is no need to assign any meaning to the definite description.

The Fregean solution to the Scott-problem is also familiar; I will repeat it here for the sake of completeness. Based on the identity in (20), we have to admit that (18) and (19) have *the same truth value*.[4] By contrast:

MEAN ('the author of *Waverley*') $\neq$ MEAN ('Scott')

Therefore the *meanings* of (18) and (19) may be different (indeed they are). There is no need to give up the Fregean theory in order to reflect the difference in meaning between the two sentences.

To summarize: In the part of "On Denoting" discussed here, Russell attempts to discredit Frege's theory of meaning by first identifying denoting expressions with their meanings and then by deriving paradoxes involving definite descriptions that denote linguistic expressions (for example, 'the first line of Gray's *Elegy*'). These paradoxes disappear once we distinguish expressions from their meanings and handle our quotation marks with care.

Acknowledgments An earlier version of this article appeared in Hungarian in *Tertium non datur*, Vol. 3 (1986), 217–27. Published between 1984 and 1990, *Tertium non datur* was a yearbook series for the Department of Symbolic Logic and Scientific Methodology at the Humanities Faculty of the Eötvös Lóránd University, Budapest. Translated by Zsófia Zvolenszky.

References

1. Frege, Gottlob. 1948. "Sense and Reference." *The Philosophical Review* 57:207–30.
2. Russell, Bertrand. 1905. "On Denoting." *Mind* 14:479–93.

---

[4] The principle of substitutivity for identicals can be applied here because the term in question occurs in a purely extensional context (as Frege would put it, the term appears with its customary (not indirect) meaning).

Chapter 15
Goodman's Only World

Vladan Djordjević

Having realized that he was not able to finish his project, Goodman abandoned his theory of counterfactuals and left it in quite a mess. That left room for different interpretations. Goodman's paper is famous and has been cited, mentioned, or interpreted thousands of times (as can be seen on Google Scholar). Very often, these interpretations are imprecise, incorrect, or wrong, in a strange way—the incorrectness is obvious, or at least can be shown very easily. This also holds for what we can call "standard interpretations" of Goodman's theory, by which I mean similar interpretations written by some authors influential in the field of conditional logic, or written in some survey articles on conditionals. My goal in this paper is to investigate how this highly unlikely situation came about. Something went wrong, and I will argue that it is worthwhile to figure out what that is. First I will try to explain what Goodman did say, which of his claims are usually ignored, and what he did not say but is sometimes ascribed to him. I will emphasize one of the reasons why correcting the wrong interpretations is significant: because these interpretations give counterfactuals some formal properties that neither Goodman nor (usually) the interpreter would accept. At the end, I will give a brief comment on my motives to deal with Goodman's theory, since one might ask why bother with some old theory now that we have much more advanced theories? My answer will be that we need some intuitions from the old theory to test the new ones.

A counterfactual $A \rightarrow C$ (if it had been the case that A, it would have been the case that C) is true according to Goodman [8],[1] iff there is an argument of the form

(1)
$$\frac{A, B_1, B_2, \ldots, B_n}{C}$$

---

[1] Goodman 1947 [8], which is the subject of this paper, was reprinted in 1954 [9] and 1983 [11] and elsewhere. References here are to [11], where some changes have been made to the original 1947 paper.

V. Djordjević (✉)
Department of Philosophy, University of Belgrade, Belgrade, Serbia
e-mail: vladan@ualberta.ca

which is valid by the laws of logic and nature, and the B's are some true contingent propositions (usually called *background facts*) that satisfy certain conditions. Laws of nature played an important role in Goodman's paper, but will play none in mine. I will assume that natural laws could be among the B's. That way, a counterfactual is true iff there is a corresponding argument of the form (1) that is logically valid. This will make things simpler for us, and, having noticed the simplification, we will be in no further danger of misinterpreting Goodman because of that.

The main task and a difficult problem is to determine which propositions are allowed to be included among the B's. Since the antecedent is typically false, obviously not just any truths could come in. Otherwise, the negation of the antecedent would be among these truths, and (1) would be trivially valid, which would make too many counterfactuals true. After examining and rejecting many possible answers, Goodman came up with the following tentative definition:

> ...a counterfactual is true if and only if there is some set S of true sentences such that S is compatible with C and ¬C, and such that A ∧ S is self-compatible and leads by law to C; while there is no set S' compatible with C and C, and such that A ∧ S' is self-compatible and leads by law to ¬C. [11, p. 13]

The "law" mentioned is logical or natural, which I just commented on. Goodman never bothered to tell us what a conjunction of a proposition and a set is, and what it means that a set is compatible with a proposition, namely whether C has to be compatible with each member of S or with their conjunction; as we will see later, that might turn out to be important for the formal properties of "→". Let us for the time being formulate the tentative definition in the following way, emphasizing the positive and the negative requirement:

(TD)   A → C is true iff: (α) there is some set S of true sentences such that both S ∪ {C} and S ∪ {¬C} are consistent, and such that {A} ∪ S is consistent and entails C; while (β) there is no set S' such that both S' ∪ {C} and S' ∪ {¬C} are consistent, and such that {A} ∪ S' is consistent and entails ¬C.

Let A = the match m is struck, C = the match m lights, and let both A and C be false. Let the elements of the set S of true relevant propositions be: B_1 = m is dry, B_2 = m is well made, B_3 = oxygen enough is present. This is the example Goodman used to test TD. To make things simpler we can suppose that S contains the relevant law of nature, e.g. B_4 = All dry, well made matches light when struck in the presence of oxygen. Then S = {B_1, B_2, B_3, B_4}. That way the corresponding argument (1) is valid only in virtue of the laws of logic. We want (2) to come up true according to our definition:

(2) Had m been struck, it would have lit. (A → C)

At first sight, (2) seems to satisfy TD. However, Goodman points to the problem that A → ¬B_i, for some i, also seems to satisfy TD. For example

(3) Had m been struck, it would have been wet. (A → ¬B_1) [11, p. 14]

15 Goodman's Only World

The set of true relevant propositions for this conditional is $\{\neg C, B_2, B_3, B_4\}$ (call it S_1). S_1 and A together entail $\neg B_1$. Thus TD is wrong, because intuitively it is obvious that (2) is true and (3) false. We need a definition that would make the right choice between (2) and (3).

Although this is not part of Goodman's argumentation, it is worth noting here that the choice between (2) and (3) is related to another feature of counterfactuals, taken by many theorists to be essential, namely that counterfactuals should be distinguished from indicative conditionals. (2) is true and each of $A \to \neg B_i$ is false for any i, while for their corresponding indicative versions it should be the opposite—(2i) should be false and at least one of $A \to \neg B_i$ should be true:

(2i) If m was struck, it lighted.
(3i) If m was struck, then it was wet (or not well made, or there was not enough oxygen, or...).

We see a new match m that never lighted, so it did not light even if it was struck. Thus (2i) is false. And since it never lighted, then if it was struck, it must be that it didn't light either because it was wet or not well made or... etc., as (3i) says.

Therefore, beside the obvious reason that intuitively (2) is true and (3) false, there might be another theoretical reason to reject TD, since it does not distinguish indicative and counterfactual conditionals. However, Goodman's immediate reason to reject TD was not correct. It is not the case that both (2) and (3) come out true according to TD. In fact, TD makes them both false. Take $\{A \supset C\}$ to be the set of background propositions from the positive requirement (α) from TD and $\{A \supset \neg C\}$ to be the set from the negative requirement (β) for conditional (2), and take $\{A \supset \neg B_1\}$ and $\{A \supset B_1\}$ to be the sets from (α) and (β) respectively for conditional (3) ("$\supset$" is the material implication). Neither (2) nor (3) will be true according to TD. This problem was discovered by Parry [18]. Goodman admitted that Parry was right [10], and in later reprints of his 1947 essay we can see the footnote:

> Since this essay was first published, W.T. Parry has pointed out that no counterfactual satisfies this formula [TD]; for one could always take $\neg(A \wedge \neg C)$ as S, and take $\neg(A \wedge C)$ as S'. Thus we must add the requirement that neither S nor S' follows by law from $\neg A$. [11, footnote 7, p. 13]

(Note that $\neg(A \wedge \neg C)$ is equivalent to $A \supset C$ and $\neg(A \wedge C)$ to $A \supset \neg C$. Goodman apparently had in mind only the "real" counterfactuals, i.e. those with a false antecedent.)

Goodman never bothered to include this improvement in TD, probably because he was too worried about his main problem. That problem is related to the following observation: $\neg C$ *would not have been* true had A been true, which means that the set $S_1 = \{\neg C, B_2, B_3, B_4\}$ mentioned above would not have been a set of true propositions had A been true. In other words, $\neg C$ is not *cotenable* with A. It is implicit (but still very clear) in Goodman's paper that he would define cotenability thus: B is cotenable with A iff $\neg(A \to \neg B)$. To improve TD, Goodman suggested that $A \wedge S$ should not only be self-compatible, but S should be cotenable with A as well

[11, p. 15]. As I mentioned above, there was a dilemma how to interpret compatibility of a set with a proposition. Now we have the analogous problem to understand cotenability of a set with a proposition—is it the conjunction of the members of the set that is cotenable with the proposition, or each member separately?. Goodman never felt a need to be more precise on this point. This distinction should be made because it is possible that each member of a set is cotenable with a proposition, but their conjunction is not. Both propositions that it is and that it is not raining are cotenable with you reading my paper, but their conjunction is not. Or, to use an example from Goodman's paper [11, p. 11], each of the propositions (4)–(6)

(4) Jones is not in South Carolina
(5) Jones is not in North Carolina
(6) North Carolina plus South Carolina is identical with Carolina

is cotenable with the antecedent in a counterfactual beginning

    If Jones were in Carolina ...

but the conjunction of (4)–(6) is not.

What are the final truth conditions Goodman proposed? We cannot tell. Instead of putting them explicitly, Goodman said (square brackets are mine):

> Returning now to the proposed rule [TD], I shall neither offer further corrections of detail nor discuss whether the requirement that S be cotenable with A makes superfluous some other provisions of the criterion; for such matters become rather unimportant besides the really serious difficulty that now confronts us. [11, p. 16]

The difficulty is that he could not define counterfactuals without the notion of cotenability, while cotenability is defined in terms of counterfactuals. Being unable to avoid circularity or infinite regress, Goodman thought that his whole project was a failure, and wouldn't bother any more with technical details. Even more so since Goodman found the problem of defining the relevant background propositions only one of two major problems. The other problem that must be solved to define truth conditions for counterfactuals Goodman found in defining the notion of natural law, which is "even more serious" [11, p. 17]

Today we do not believe that Goodman's project was a total failure. He did fail to provide a *reductive* definition of counterfactuals, that is, a definition of truth conditions in terms of well-defined and precise logical notions that do not presuppose counterfactuals. However, even the most popular contemporary theories of counterfactuals fail to do that. Goodman's project was very ambitious, and the disappointment of not fulfilling the main ambition prevented him from looking for another useful thing he could have done with his theory. That useful thing could have been a logical system for counterfactuals. Stalnaker, who made the first such system, used the notions of possible worlds and a selection function which for any given antecedent picks up the closest world in which the antecedent is true [21, 23]. If the consequent as well is true in that world, the conditional is true. But Stalnaker never attempted a reductive definition of "closeness" of worlds. Nevertheless, that was not an obstacle to make a formal semantics that determined rules of inference, to find axioms and prove consistency and completeness. And, as shown by Loewer [15], the same can be done using Goodman's notion of cotenability as a primitive.

The facts that Goodman did not offer final formulation of the truth conditions, that TD is quite long, that it would be even longer with the addition of Parry's improvements and the notion of cotenability, that those additions might make parts of TD redundant, and that the background propositions might be considered cotenable either separately or as a conjunction, left room for different interpretations. Very often Goodman's theory is presented with most parts of his definition ignored, and the rest slightly changed. The reasons for that are often not given. Authors do that probably thinking that the ignored parts are redundant or even wrong, and that the changes they made either improve Goodman's definition, or express explicitly what they take was only implicit in Goodman's paper. Some of those interpretations are simply too inaccurate to be ascribed to Goodman. For example:

> Intuitively, S is to consist of sentences which (i) are true and (ii) would also have been true, if contrary to fact, ϕ [the antecedent] had been true. The second condition, ..., Goodman referred to as the cotenability of S with ϕ. [24, p. 453]

According to this definition, B being cotenable with A means $A \to B$, which is different from Goodman's definition $\neg(A \to \neg B)$. The difference is important because Goodman thought that in general $A \to B$ and $A \to \neg B$ are not contradictory but contrary propositions and could both be false [11, cf. footnote 2, p. 6, and footnote 9, p. 15]. $A \to B$ is therefore not equivalent to $\neg(A \to \neg B)$. What also follows from the claim that $A \to B$ and $A \to \neg B$ are only contraries is that Goodman rejects the so-called law of *conditional excluded middle*: $(A \to B) \vee (A \to \neg B)$, a controversial formula, which is a distinctive feature of Stalnaker's semantics. Despite Stalnaker's elaborated and very interesting defense of the law [22], it seems that philosophers more often reject it than accept it.

Today the usual interpretation of Goodman says that

(UI) $A \to C$ is true iff A, together with a set S of true premises, each of them cotenable with A, entail C.

Cotenability thus becomes sufficient instead of necessary condition for a truth to be among the B's. Cotenability/compatibility with C and $\neg C$ is dropped; no mention of Parry's requirement; the negative condition (β) disappears; the B's are cotenable with the antecedent separately, not as a conjunction. Obviously, (UI) cannot be ascribed to Goodman. Nevertheless, (UI) or a similar or equivalent formulation can easily be found in the literature. Talking of theories similar to Goodman's, Arlo-Costa [1] said:

> The basic idea of this view is that a conditional is assertable if its antecedent, together with suitable (co-tenable) premises, entails its consequent. ... In fact, one can also evaluate the *truth conditions* of conditionals under this point of view by saying that a conditional is true if an argument from the antecedent and suitable co-tenable premises to the conditional's conclusion exists. ... The type of analysis of conditionals a la Goodman, for example, provides truth conditions for conditionals in terms of the following test: $a \to b$ is true if b follows by law from a together with the set Γ of true sentences c such that it is not the case that $a \to \neg c$.

In a survey article on conditionals one might want to point to the main problem and omit what might look like technical details, as Arlo-Costa did here. The "technical details", however, deserve more attention, as I will try to show. Arlo-Costa, of course, did not ascribe (UI) to Goodman, since he speaks of the "basic idea" and the "type of analysis a la Goodman". But sometimes (UI) or something very similar is explicitly ascribed to Goodman, as we can see from Nute's explanation:

> So Goodman's ultimate position is that $\phi \rightarrow \psi$ is true just in case ψ is entailed by ϕ together with the set of all physical laws and the set of all true propositions cotenable with ϕ, i.e. with the set of all true propositions such that no member of that set counterfactually implies the negation of ϕ and the negation of no member of that set is counterfactually implied by ϕ. [17, p. 5]

Defining S as a set of cotenable truths means that S contains all such truths. Therefore S is an infinite set, of a cardinality as big as our supposed formal language permits it. This is one more point that Goodman is silent about. Do we include in S all the truths that do not make troubles? Or only the relevant ones? Or something in between? Goodman's subtitle "The problem of relevant conditions" suggests only the relevant B's. In the match example, S would then contain only the four propositions B_1-B_4. The fact that he speaks of a conjunction $A \wedge S$ suggests that S should be finite, since he relies on classical logic where formulae are finite by definition. On the other hand, at the beginning of his section on relevant background propositions Goodman said:

> It might seem natural to propose that the consequent follows by law from the antecedent and a description of the actual state-of-affairs of the world, that we need hardly define relevant conditions because it will do no harm to include irrelevant ones. But ...[11, p. 9]

...but then he goes on to reject this proposal, and never goes back to tell us clearly whether his ultimate goal was to define a set of good propositions, or a set that excludes bad propositions. The former might be finite. The latter is likely to be infinite. When Lewis mentions theories of Goodman's type, he talks about a finite number of auxiliary premises [13, sections 2.6, 3.1, 3.2]. However, Lewis is not primarily interested in presenting such theories, but rather in making a point about his own theory. The S according to (UI) and the above citations from Arlo-Costa and Nute is infinite. The interpretation from another survey paper, by Dorothy Edgington, is, like Goodman's paper, also not clear at this point, for the similar reasons—she gives a version of (UI) as an interpretation of Goodman and mentions cotenability as the condition for a truth to be among the B's (which suggests that there are infinitely many of them), but instead of a set S she mentions a conjunction of B's (which suggests a finite number).[2] Thus we have another reason to think of (UI) as an interpretation that adds things that cannot be found in Goodman—it requires an infinite number of B's, while he didn't say if it was finite or infinite.

---

[2] Edgington [6, p. 248]. The interpretation says: "A counterfactual conditional '$A \rightarrow C$' is true if and only if there is a conjunction of truths T which include a law of nature [and satisfy condition X] such that $A\&T$ entails C." And a bit later on the same page: "Then the square bracket reads 'and are cotenable with A'."

15 Goodman's Only World

Goodman didn't care about such details, probably because he was concentrated on his main project—providing a reductive analysis, and didn't think of the less ambitious project of making a formal system with the "useless" circular truth conditions. Otherwise, he might have noticed that the number of the B's is important for the formal properties of counterfactuals (to be shown later).

It has been noticed early that there is some tension between (UI) (with an infinity of B's) and the conditional excluded middle (CEM), which Goodman rejects as mentioned above. Pollock claimed that Goodman's theory validated CEM for conditionals with false antecedents, and used that as an argument against Goodman. He provided the following proof for the claim [19, p. 11] (text in the square brackets is mine; the funny brackets "⌈, ⌉" are apparently Quine's quotes [20, pp. 33–37]):

> Given this difference [between $\neg(P \to \neg Q)$ and $P \to Q$, which are not equivalent for Pollock because he rejects CEM] I think it is clear that Goodman's requirement of cotenability is too weak. This is demonstrated by seeing that it would lead right back to a special case of the principle that if ⌈$\neg(P \to \neg Q)$⌉ is true then ⌈$P \to Q$⌉ is true. More precisely, Goodman's proposal implies that whenever P is false and ⌈$\neg(P \to \neg Q)$⌉ is true, then ⌈$P \to Q$⌉ is true. This implication is established as follows. First, we need two obvious principles regarding subjunctive conditionals:
>
> (a) If ⌈$P \to Q$⌉ is true and Q entails R, then ⌈$P \to R$⌉ is true.
> (b) If ⌈$P \to (P \supset Q)$⌉ is true, then ⌈$P \to Q$⌉ is true.
>
> (a) is so obvious as to need no defence. (b) holds because if ⌈$P \supset Q$⌉ would be true if P were true, then both P and ⌈$P \supset Q$⌉ would be true if P were true, and hence Q would have to be true if P were true. Given these principles, let us suppose, with Goodman, that truth and cotenability are all that is required for inclusion in C [Pollock uses "C" for the set of background propositions that Goodman called S]. Suppose P is false and ⌈$\neg(P \to \neg Q)$⌉ is true. Then by (a) ⌈$\neg(P \to (P \wedge \neg Q))$⌉ is true and so ⌈$\neg(P \to \neg(P \supset Q))$⌉ is true. But as P is false, ⌈$P \supset Q$⌉ is true, and if follows from Goodman's proposal that ⌈$P \to (P \supset Q)$⌉ is true. Then from (b) it follows that ⌈$P \to Q$⌉ is true.

From the citation we can see that Pollock reads Goodman the same way as stated in (UI) ("truth and cotenability are all that is required for inclusion in C"), so Pollock's conclusion holds for (UI) and the similar versions we mentioned above, like Nute's, Edgington's and Arlo-Costa's. Note that the principles (a) and (b) are "safe", that is, they can easily be derived from (UI).

Bennett would agree with Pollock that a theory is to be rejected if it implies CEM [2, p. 308], but he came closer to a more general result about (UI). Bennett didn't explicitly ascribe (UI) to Goodman, but he did analyze it and claimed that "surprisingly" [2, p. 233] (UI) implies CEM without any restriction [2, p. 308]. Here is why: (UI) implies what Bennett called (PF*)[2, p. 233]:

(PF*) $C \wedge \neg(A \to \neg C)$ entails $A \to C$.

In yet another context Cross proved that (PF*) entails CEM [3]. This can be proven as follows.

Theorem 1 *If (PF*) is valid, so is CEM.*

Proof Suppose the negation of CEM:

$$\neg(A \to C) \land \neg(A \to \neg C).$$

Then suppose C. Together with the right conjunct $\neg(A \to \neg C)$, C implies $A \to C$ by (PF*). But this contradicts the left conjunct $\neg(A \to C)$. Now suppose $\neg C$. Given that $A \to C$ is equivalent to $A \to \neg\neg C$, $\neg C$ and the left conjunct $\neg(A \to C)$ by (PF*) imply $A \to \neg C$. But $A \to \neg C$ contradicts the right conjunct. Therefore CEM. □

Therefore, if PF* is valid, so is CEM. This proof shows that (UI) validates CEM, because PF* is obviously implied by (UI): PF* says that $A \to C$ is true whenever C is true and cotenable with A, and $A \to C$ is true according to (UI) iff A and all cotenable truths entail C. If C is true and cotenable with A, then it is already in S, so, trivially, it is entailed by $\{A\} \cup S$, and $A \to C$ follows.

It should be noted that two more people came to the same result that (UI) validates CEM. Barry Loewer mentioned it, but only as a by-the-way notice, without proof or a further comment. In that paper he was not interested in the background facts being cotenable with the antecedent separately (as it is assumed in (UI)), but as a conjunction.[3] The simplest proof I found is by Johan Mårtensson [16, section 2.8 "Cotenability", p. 125][4]:

> If the requirement of cotenability is understood to present not only necessary but also a sufficient condition on inclusion in the contracted set of true sentences S then it seems the resulting facts revision semantics will validate the principle CEM: If $A \to \neg C$ is not true and C is true then C is cotenable with A and so should be included in the contracted set S, but then obviously $S \cup \{A\} \models C$ and hence $A \to C$ is true. If on the other hand $\neg C$ is true then $\neg C$ is not cotenable with A since otherwise it would be included in S (and hence $A \to \neg C$ would be true after all) and hence $A \to \neg\neg C$ is true, so (by RCK) $A \to C$ is true in either case.

The mentioned arguments that show the connections between (UI) and CEM were not enough for broader audience to realize that (UI) is not a good interpretation of Goodman (even for Pollock who gave one of these arguments). Beside the fact that Goodman explicitly claimed that $A \to C$ and $A \to \neg C$ are not contradictory but contrary propositions, there is his famous Carolina-example that should cast some doubt that he would accept (UI). The example was Goodman's immediate reason to introduce the negative condition (β) in TD. Since each of (4), (5) and (6) might be cotenable with the antecedent "Jones is in Carolina", if we put them all in S, $\{A\} \cup S$ would be inconsistent. If we drop (β), it seems that we have to *assume* CEM in order to avoid inconsistency: CEM would not allow both (4) and (5) to

---

[3] Loewer [15, p. 106]: "It is interesting to note that had we construed Goodman's definition of cotenability as requiring that A be cotenable with each member of S rather than with the conjunction of the members of S we would have obtained a system in which CEM is valid."

[4] The rule RCK that allows the last step need not concerns us here. The book used to be available on-line at http://www.phil.gu.se/johan/johan.html and the page number refers to the version downloaded from that site.

be cotenable with the antecedent. Had Goodman ever assumed CEM, the Carolina-example would not have been enough for him to introduce (β). He would have needed a different argument.

Now, there is another way to prove that (UI) implies CEM, a way which is not simpler than Mårtensson's, but I prefer it for the following two reasons. First, it is a semantic proof that might offer also an intuitive explanation of what is going on. One may be aware of a technical result without having an intuitive grasp of why the result holds; it seems to me that this is the case with Bennett, who is aware of Theorem 1 above, but, as I will try to show a bit later, has a wrong opinion about the things that make the theorem right. Second, it is expressed in terms of possible worlds, and gives us an opportunity to make a point not only about Goodman's theory, but about the possible worlds semantics for counterfactuals as well. The letter reason will be more significant by the end of this paper, where I will give, as promised, an answer to the question why bother with such an old theory as Goodman's?

It is possible that (UI) has been formulated under the influence of the idea of minimal change. The idea is very popular, since the most popular theories of counterfactuals, like Stalnaker's and Lewis's, are minimal change theories.[5] However, the idea is not to be found in Goodman's paper. So it seems that (UI) smuggles the idea of minimal change. What has (UI) to do with minimal change? The set S, it seems, contains propositions that depict our world, minus *only* the propositions that do not go together with the antecedent. That is, the full description of our world is changed minimally, only to allow for the antecedent. Now, be my guess about the influence of the idea of minimal change right or not, once we add the antecedent to the background propositions, it seems that the hole is filled in and that we have again a full description of a world. That is, the antecedent A and the set S of background propositions as described by (UI) determine uniquely one world. That means that {A} ∪ S is a subset of only one maximal possible set. In that world where all the members from {A} ∪ S hold, either C is true or ¬C is. Thus either A → C or A → ¬C must be true, because {A} ∪ S entails either C or ¬C. So CEM follows from (UI).

Theorem 2 *The set* {A} ∪ S *determines uniquely one world.*

Proof Suppose there are two different worlds j and k such that every proposition from {A} ∪ S holds at both j and k. S is a set of truths from the actual world i that are cotenable with A. Since $j \neq k$ there is a proposition D true at the actual world such that $j \models D$ and $k \models \neg D$.

D is either cotenable with A or not. If not, then $i \models A \to \neg D$, which means that {A} ∪ S entails $\neg D$, and j is then an impossible world. If D is cotenable with A, then D is in S and then k is an impossible world. Therefore $j = k$. □

Why is (UI) persistently being offered as Goodman's theory? Beside the possible reasons mentioned so far, the main reason might be the following opinion, advocated and very nicely explained in details by Bennett, but wrong as I believe. It is essential

---

[5] See Nute's classification of minimal, small, and maximal change theories in Nute and Cross [17].

for this view that the classical logic is monotonic, and the validity of (1) is defined in classical logic. Bennett explains (italics and square brackets are mine; "Support" is Bennett's name for Goodman's set S):

> What constraints must a truth satisfy to qualify as a conjunct in a value of Support? Goodman (1947) approached this under the heading "The problem of *Relevant* Conditions", but this is a *misnomer*. If C can be law-derived from (A&Support) for a value of Support that contains irrelevant material, then it can also be law-derived from (A&Support∗) where this is what remains of Support after its irrelevant content has been removed. Irrelevant conjuncts are mere clutter: *they cannot lead to any conditional's being accorded a truth value that it does not deserve.* [Possible] Worlds analysis [of counterfactuals] take in vast amounts of irrelevant materials, and *clearly get away* with it. A Worlds theorist will say that the truth value of "If you had unplugged the computer, it would not have been damaged by lightning" depends upon what obtains at certain worlds that are just like [the actual world] α up to a certain moment...*Just* like α? Worlds resembling α in respect of the number of sardines in the Atlantic, the average colour of alpine lilies in Tibet, and the salinity of the smallest rock pool in Iceland? What have those to do with the conditional about the computer? Nothing, but Worlds theories bring them in because they are too much trouble to keep out, and—the main point—they do no harm. *Irrelevance is harmless*. [2, pp. 307–8]

If we put in S all the irrelevant truths we can, that would suffice to determine a single world and make CEM valid, which Bennett finds harmful enough. This is the first point where he is wrong, because *irrelevant background propositions have influence on the formal properties of* "→". A further point: these formal properties would eventually lead to a "conditional being accorded a truth value that it does not deserve", namely they force us to consider one of A → B and A → ¬B true even when we or Bennett think that both are false. Different restrictions on the irrelevant load may give us different logical systems. Say we let *some*, but *not all*, irrelevant propositions in the set S, for example all such propositions that hold throughout the closest antecedent worlds according to Lewis's system VC + limit assumption[6]; then {A} ∪ S would not determine one but lots of worlds, and the resulting system (which would be VC of course) is different from the system determined by (UI). Suppose now we allow *only* the relevant facts to be included in S. The conditional (2) from the match example would then require the set S = {B_1, B_2, B_3, B_4}. Which propositions are relevant in such cases depends both on the antecedent and the consequent. Another counterfactual with the same antecedent and a different consequent would require different background propositions, for example: "Had I struck m, you would have heard the typical sound of a match being struck". For this conditional, some of the Bs from S are irrelevant, and some others that are not in S become relevant, like those pertaining to your hearing abilities, laws of acoustics, etc. If we wanted to translate such truth conditions to a possible worlds semantics, we would need a selection function that is relative to both antecedents and consequents (or takes them both as arguments), and that leads us to the idea that Gabbay [7] wanted to capture in his system. Gabbay's system is the weakest proposed for counterfactuals. So, roughly speaking, the more irrelevance, the stronger the logic.

---

[6] This system is the same as Stalnaker's minus CEM. Cf. Lewis [13, chapter 6].

We might never be able to define a set S containing only relevant stuff. Still, when we go from case to case, in the situations where we have a satisfactory explanation of why a particular conditional is true, we can use that explanation to determine the relevant background facts without much trouble. This was the case with the match conditional (2). Why is it true? Because the match is dry and well made and all such matches light when struck in the presence of enough oxygen. That is, because the four B's from S hold. If I am right about that, we can use this point to answer the question posed at the beginning of this paper: why bother with the old theories like Goodman's and other of that type?[7] Because our intuitions about the background facts are useful for testing the adequacy of our possible worlds semantics. All such semantics have the basic task to somehow separate important from unimportant worlds. Obviously, when evaluating a conditional, we do not need all the possible worlds. When evaluating (2), we are not interested in worlds with different laws of nature, for example those where we light matches by putting them into water. Each such semantics is interested in what happens with the consequent in the important antecedent-worlds only. There are lots of answers to the question which worlds are important. Every different system for counterfactuals has a different answer. But for that answer to make sense, to be adequate, the following interpretation must be possible:

(*) All the relevant background propositions must hold in each important world.

Different theories of counterfactuals might include more propositions besides the relevant ones, i.e. some irrelevant propositions might hold in each relevant world (this is the "vast amount of irrelevant materials" that Bennett mentioned, that possible worlds theories "get away with"). But they mustn't *exclude* any of the relevant propositions if they are to be adequate.[8] If a theory says that (2) is true because the match lights in the important-according-to-the-theory worlds where it was struck, and at the same time we cannot know whether the match is dry in these worlds, we wouldn't call these worlds "important", and would not think that the theory is adequate.

Acknowledgments I would like to thank Miloš Arsenijević, Bernie Linsky, Adam Morton, Jelena Ostojić, and Jeff Pelletier for helpful discussions, and an anonymous referee for pointing to some mistakes.

---

[7] These theories are know in the literature under different names. Lewis [13] called them "metalinguistic", and later [14] thought that "premise semantics" was a better name. Bennett [2, p. 303] calls them "support" theories. Hansson [12] uses the term "derivability theory". Arlo-Costa [1] calls them "cotenability theories".

[8] It is often just assumed that such a simple requirement as (*) is obeyed by a possible world theory, but it is not a trivial matter. In [4, chapters 4 and 5], and [5] I have argued that the so called standard theories of counterfactuals (more precisely, any *total* ordering *minimal* or *small change* semantics for counterfactuals based on an *absolute* similarity relation or selection function) cannot fulfil that requirement, which makes them inadequate.

References

1. Arlo-Costa, Horacio. 2009. "The Logic of Conditionals." In *The Stanford Encyclopedia of Philosophy* (Spring 2009 Edition), edited by Edward N. Zalta. Accessed Mar 20, 2010. http://plato.stanford.edu/archives/spr2009/entries/logic-conditionals/
2. Bennett, Jonathan. 2003. *A Philosophical Guide to Conditionals*. New York, NY Oxford University Press.
3. Cross, Charles B. 1985. "Jonathan Bennett on 'even if'." *Linguistics and Philosophy* 8:353–57.
4. Djordjevic, Vladan. 2005. *Counterfactuals*. PhD Thesis. Alberta: University of Alberta.
5. Djordjevic, Vladan. Forthcoming. "Similarity and Cotenability." In *Between Logic and Intuition: David Lewis and the Future of Formal Methods in Philosophy*, edited by J. van Benthem, V. Hendricks, J. Symons, and S. A. Pedersen. Synthese Library.
6. Edgington, Dorothy. 1995. "On Conditionals." *Mind* 104:235–329.
7. Gabbay, Dov M. 1972. "A General Theory of the Conditional in Terms of a Ternary Operator." *Theoria* 38:97–104.
8. Goodman, Nelson. 1947. "The Problem of Counterfactual Conditionals." *Journal of Philosophy* 44:113–28.
9. Goodman, Nelson. 1954. *Fact, Fiction, and Forecast*. Cambridge, MA: Harvard University Press.
10. Goodman, Nelson. 1957. "Parry on Counterfactuals." *Journal of Philosophy* 54:442–45.
11. Goodman, Nelson. 1983. *Fact, Fiction, and Forecast*. Fourth edition. Cambridge, MA: Harvard University Press.
12. Hansson, Sven Ove. 1995. "The Emperor's New Clothes: Some Recurring Problems in the Formal Analysis of Counterfactuals." In *Conditionals: From Philosophy to Computer Science*, edited by G. Crocco, L. Farinas del Cerro, and A. Herzig, 13–31. Oxford, NY, Oxford University Press.
13. Lewis, David. 1973. *Counterfactuals*. Cambridge, MA: Harvard University Press.
14. Lewis, David. 1981. "Ordering Semantics and Premise Semantics for Counterfactuals." *Journal of Philosophical Logic* 10:217–34.
15. Loewer, Barry. 1979. "Cotenability and Counterfactual Logics." *Journal of Philosophical Logic* 8:99–115.
16. Mårtensson, Johan. 1999. *Subjunctive Conditionals and Time: A Defense of a Weak Classical Approach*. Accessed April 15, 2005. http://www.phil.gu.se/johan/johan.html
17. Nute, Donald and Charles B. Cross. 2002. "Conditional Logic." In *Handbook of Philosophical Logic 2nd edition Volume 4*, edited by D.M. Gabbay and F. Guenthner, 1–98. Dordrecht: Kluwer Academic Publishers.
18. Parry, W.T. 1957. "Reexamination of the Problem of Counterfactual Conditionals." *Journal of Philosophy* 54:85–94.
19. Pollock, John L. 1976. *Subjunctive Reasoning*. Dordrecht: D. Reidel Publishing Company.
20. Quine, W.V.O. 1981. *Mathematical Logic*. Cambridge, MA: Harvard University Press.
21. Stalnaker, Robert. 1968. "A Theory of Conditionals." In *Studies in Logical Theory, American Philosophical Quarterly Monograph Series, No. 2*, edited by Nisholas Rescher, 98–112. Oxford: Blackwell.
22. Stalnaker, Robert. 1981. "A Defense of Conditional Excluded Middle." In *Ifs*, edited by W. Harper, R. Stalnaker, and G. Pearce, 87–104. Dordrecht: Reidel.
23. Stalnaker, Robert, and Richmond Thomason. 1970. A Semantic Analysis of Conditional Logic." *Theoria* 36:23–42.
24. Turner, Raymond. 1981. "Counterfactuals Without Possible Worlds." *Journal of Philosophical Logic* 10:453–93.

Index

A
AGM
  approach, 184, 196
  postulate, 196
  theory, 6, 206, 222
ARG conditions, 3, 102, 110, 112–114, 118
Argumentation
  game, 184, 197–198
  theory, 104, 108, 184

B
Belief revision, 6, 184, 196

C
CEM sentence, 7, 275–278
Cogency, 102, 108–110, 112, 116
Commitment
  a-commitment, 185–190, 195, 197
  c-commitment, 185–190, 196–197
  commitment affecting act sequence, 194
  positive commitment act sequence, 194
  propositional, 184–190, 193, 195–198
Completeness, 184, 187, 192, 198
Consequence (logical), 3–4, 39, 101–102, 109–110, 112–113, 117, 121–131
  pre-theoretic notion of, 4, 121, 123–124, 128
Counterfactual conditional, 7, 269–272, 274, 278

D
Discourse, 193, 195–197
Dynamifying, 183–184, 188

E
Epistemology, 1–3, 18, 33–36, 46, 49–50, 86–88, 94–95, 104, 112, 138, 140, 208

Equivalence relation, 228, 232–235
  approximation of, 233–234
Expressive adequacy (completeness), 6, 204, 218–219

F
Formalism, 13, 16, 38–39, 42, 46, 51, 54–55, 64, 103
Function
  dig, 169, 171, 174–176, 178
  interpretation, 164, 167–168, 171, 174–175
  Skolem, 162–164, 167–171, 173–175, 177–181

G
Granularity, 237, 239, 242

H
Hume's principle, *see* Principle

I
Identity
  condition, 168, 229–230, 233–234, 238
  criterion of, 6, 90–91, 227–230, 234, 240, 242
Imperatives, theory of, 6, 201–202, 204–206, 211–214, 218, 222
Indispensability
  argument (Quine-Putnam), 2, 18, 24, 140, 147
  of logic, 135–137, 140–142, 145, 147, 152, 154–155
Intuition, 12, 15, 20, 35, 40, 85, 89, 95, 109, 114, 126, 138–140, 154, 241, 257, 269, 279
  Kantian, 12, 15
  logical, 13, 135, 138, 141
  mathematical, 2, 85, 94
Intuitionism, 12–15, 17, 40, 46, 63–64, 66

K

Knowledge
  logical, 2, 4, 101, 125
  mathematical, 2, 4, 33, 40, 50, 83–84, 86, 90, 92–94, 96

L

Logic
  deontic, 183
  doxastic, 185–186
  dynamic epistemic, 183
  dynamic deontic, 183
  dynamic modal, 204
  epistemic, 5, 164, 183, 185–186, 222
  informal, 3, 101–114, 117–118
  modal, 183–185
Logicism, 3, 13, 15, 17, 19, 21, 45, 64, 83–84, 88, 92–94, 97, 136–137
Löwenheim-Skolem theorem, 3, 59, 61–79

M

Meaning
  abstract, 169, 174–175
  eGTS, 162, 168–169, 171, 174–178
  Sinn (sense), 7, 60, 168, 176, 178, 261, 263, 267
  strategic, 161, 169, 173–175
Mereology, 6, 243, 246, 257
  temporal, 6, 244, 247–248
  second-order, 247

N

Nominalism, 23, 37–40, 50

O

Ontology, 1–2, 6, 18, 21, 24, 33–36, 46, 50, 71, 227, 243

P

Platonism, 36–38, 46, 64
Preference change, 183

Principle
  abstraction, 19–22, 92–93
  conservation, 41, 45
  context, 85
  direction, 95
  Hume's, 3, 20, 22, 83–86, 88–96, 228

R

Rationality, 4, 7, 113, 121, 126–127, 131, 141, 143, 184, 187
Reference (*Bedeutung*), 7, 60, 136, 261, 266–267

S

Semantics, 2, 33–36, 48, 55, 71, 103, 206, 209, 214, 272–273, 276–279
  action, 212, 214
  dynamic, 5–6, 204, 217
  extended game-theoretical (eGTS), 164–167, 179
  formal, 5
  game-theoretical (GTS), 5, 161–162, 164, 169
  Henkin's, 19
  imperative, 210
  possible-world, 171, 179
  two-dimensional, 176, 178, 261
  update/downdate, 183, 185, 189, 191–198, 206, 221–222
Skolemization, 163–165, 180–181
Social deontic score, 197
Social reality, 4, 198
Sortal concept, 240
Speech-act, 4–5, 118, 183–185, 190, 193–197, 202–206, 209–211, 215–216, 218, 222
  withdrawal of, 5, 184, 187, 192–198, 210
Stereotype, 171, 173
  eGTS, 162, 168, 171, 173–178
Structuralism, 18, 42–45
Structure
  logical, 1, 261
  mathematical, 2–3, 19, 21, 42, 53